CHILDREN CARING PARENTS WITH HIV AIDS

Global issues and policy responses

Ruth Evans and Saul Becker

This edition published in Great Britain in 2009 by

The Policy Press
University of Bristol
Fourth Floor
Beacon House
Queen's Road
Bristol BS8 1QU
UK

Tel +44 (0)117 331 4054
Fax +44 (0)117 331 4093
e-mail tpp-info@bristol.ac.uk
www.policypress.org.uk

North American office:
The Policy Press
c/o International Specialized Books Services (ISBS)
920 NE 58th Avenue, Suite 300
Portland, OR 97213-3786, USA
Tel +1 503 287 3093
Fax +1 503 280 8832
e-mail info@isbs.com

© The Policy Press 2009

British Library Cataloguing in Publication Data
A catalogue record for this book is available from the British Library.

Library of Congress Cataloging-in-Publication Data
A catalog record for this book has been requested.

ISBN 978 1 84742 021 3 paperback
ISBN 978 1 84742 022 0 hardcover

Cover design by InText design, Bristol
Front cover: drawing kindly supplied by John (aged 16, Tanzania): *"This is my mum
when I was caring for her. I used to feed her sometimes because she didn't used to feel like
eating and she used to get ill from time to time."*
Printed and bound in Great Britain by TJ International, Padstow

Ruth Evans
For my parents

Saul Becker
For my children, Jessica, Sophie and Zachary

Contents

List of figures, tables and boxes

Figures

Tables

Boxes

Preface

This book contributes to the growing academic literature on children's caring responsibilities in families affected by HIV and AIDS and offers a comparative perspective between the global North and South. The book is based on findings from a qualitative research study that involved fieldwork with children with caring responsibilities, parents and relatives living with HIV/AIDS and service providers in the UK and Tanzania. The research was funded by the Economic and Social Research Council (grant number RES-000-22-1732-A) from 2006–07, and the data produced by the study have been deposited with the UK Data Archive, Economic and Social Data Service, University of Essex. The research developed from shared research interests when Ruth Evans and Saul Becker were based at the Institute of Applied Social Studies, University of Birmingham. Saul and Ruth moved to the School of Sociology and Social Policy, University of Nottingham, during the course of the study, and the book was completed after Ruth's move to the Department of Geography, School of Human and Environmental Sciences, University of Reading. We would like to thank the ESRC for funding the study and our colleagues at the University of Birmingham, University of Nottingham and the University of Reading for institutional and informal support and encouragement throughout the research and writing process.

This research would not have been possible without the help of many individuals and organisations in Tanzania and the UK. We would like to express particular thanks to the Research Advisory Group who offered advice and guidance throughout the study. We are grateful to Magda Conway, Alex Fox, Jenny Frank, Yvonne Heath, Tracey Jones, Helen Leadbitter, Lois Robinson and Elsbeth Robson. We are also grateful to the Institute of Development Studies, University of Dar es Salaam, for hosting Ruth Evans as part of the Research Associate Scheme during the fieldwork in Tanzania and would particularly like to thank Dr Rose Shayo and Edson Nyingi for their assistance.

A number of individuals and organisations provided assistance and support with the research in various ways. In Tanzania, special thanks go to: the translators, Mathias Masesa and Dr Seleman Sewangi; and stakeholders and project workers from AWITA, Bagamoyo Most Vulnerable Children Committee, Department of Social Welfare, KIWAMWAKKU (Women against AIDS in Mwanga), KIWAKKUKI (Women Against AIDS in Kilimanjaro), the Most Vulnerable Children Implementing Partners Group, National AIDS Control Programme,

PACT Tanzania, PASADA, REPSSI, Social Welfare Department Muhimbili Hospital, Southern African AIDS Trust, Tanzania Youth Network of People living with HIV/AIDS, TANOPHA (Tanzania Network of People living with HIV and AIDS), UMWI, UNICEF Tanzania, WAMATA Arusha, Women's Research and Documentation Project, and World Vision Tanzania.

In the UK, we are especially grateful to: the translators and transcribers, Mbelwa Gabagambi, Hannah Gibson, Linda Poxon and Alison Taylor; and stakeholders and project workers from Africa Advocacy Foundation, Barnardo's, Birmingham Health and Social Care Directorate, Brighton Citizens Advice Bureau, Carers Lewisham, Centre for African Families Positive Health, National Children's Bureau Children and Young People HIV Network, Faith in People with HIV, Healthlink Worldwide, Heartlands Hospital HIV team, Jigsaw 4 U, Karibu Merton Welcare, Open Door, Panos London, Positive Parenting and Children, The Princess Royal Trust for Carers, The Children's Society and Waverley Care Solas.

We are particularly grateful to the project workers and volunteers for taking the time to help identify potential young people, parents and relatives to participate in the study and for agreeing to be interviewed themselves. Above all, we are indebted to the families for sharing their life stories with us and talking about sensitive and often difficult experiences.

Finally, our thanks go to Alison Shaw, Karen Bowler, Emily Watt, Leila Ebrahimi, Jo Morton and others at The Policy Press for all their support

ONE

Children's and young people's caring responsibilities within the family

Globally it is family members and communities that are usually relied upon – before state, charitable or other welfare agencies and sectors – to provide care, help, money and support to other family members who are ill, have physical impairments, mental health problems, chronic or life-limiting illnesses, or any other condition or need which requires personal intervention and assistance. The significance of the family as both an institution of welfare and for caregiving exists almost irrespective of the country's familial, social and sociopolitical structures (Jani-Le Bris, 1993), although what is *expected* of family members and what they must do as carers is related to the formal and informal resources available to families, as well as the sociocultural, economic and policy context that exists in that place and at that time (Millar and Warman, 1996). While there is a high degree of acceptance (and cultural legitimacy) when adults (usually women) take on unpaid caring roles, children's and young people's involvement in caring for parents and relatives in the global North[1] and, to some extent, in the global South challenges norms of childhood and youth.

Taking global constructions of childhood and youth as our starting point, this chapter reviews the literature on childhood responsibilities, informal care and young caregiving and introduces key theoretical perspectives, such as the social construction of childhood and youth, the ethic of care, and risk and resilience discourses, which we draw on in our analyses of children's and young people's caring responsibilities in families affected by HIV/AIDS. As we demonstrate in later chapters, our comparative research between two countries (the UK and Tanzania) with very different socioeconomic and cultural characteristics and welfare systems provides insight into the global and local processes and policies influencing children's and parents' experiences, needs and resilience in the context of HIV/AIDS.

Global constructions of childhood and youth

In Western constructions of childhood, children are not expected (or encouraged) to take on substantial or regular caregiving responsibilities. 'Childhood' is viewed as a 'special' or 'protected' phase, with adults, state agencies and social welfare professionals in the global North charged with safeguarding and protecting children and young people until they make the transition into 'adulthood' (Dearden and Becker, 2000; Frank et al, 1999). Such and Walker (2005: 43) argue, for example, that family policy in the UK is underpinned by idealised notions of childhood as a 'temporal oasis' of innocence, when children are free of 'pressures and cares', while responsibility is constructed as an 'attribute of adulthood'.

However, official statistics and research have demonstrated that many children and young people in the global South and North have significant caring responsibilities for family members with chronic illnesses and impairments within the home, as we will see later in the chapter (Becker et al, 1998; Robson, 2004; Becker, 2007). Furthermore, evidence from many countries suggests that children are regularly involved in household and domestic chores and that responsibilities form an everyday part of children's lives and social relationships with family members (Katz, 1993; Solberg, 1997; Punch, 2001; Katz, 2004; Such and Walker, 2004; Miller, 2005; Ridge, 2006). In many countries in the global North, boys and girls have a low average level of involvement in housework (Miller, 2005), but a minority make a substantial contribution to sustaining family life through their responsibilities for domestic chores, financial support, childcare, emotional care and self-care (Morrow, 1996; Solberg, 1997; Ridge, 2006). In her review of time-use studies, Miller (2005) argues that in all societies, girls spend significantly more time doing household work than boys. While girls often have substantial household responsibilities in the global South, this may be balanced to some extent by boys' greater involvement in income-generating work (Miller, 2005). Research reveals that in many different contexts, globally, children are actively engaged in negotiating and renegotiating their duties with parents and others within the household (Solberg, 1997; Punch, 2002; Ridge, 2006). Furthermore, children's roles and responsibilities are often differentiated according to norms of gender, age, intergenerational relations, household composition and sibling birth order (Solberg, 1997; Punch, 2001; Such and Walker, 2004).

Idealised Western constructions of childhood have become globalised through discourses of international development and human rights and national social welfare institutions and policies, resulting in the emergence of a global concept of a 'good childhood' (Edwards, 1996; Boyden, 1997). However, this notion of childhood, in which children's time is spent predominantly within the family home, in full-time education or recreation as part of their socialisation and preparation for a productive adult life, bears little resemblance to the lived realities of childhood for children and young people in the global South. Despite decreases in the overall proportion of children who are engaged in productive work globally, over a quarter (26%) of children aged 5-14 in Sub-Saharan Africa were estimated to be 'economically active'[2] in 2004, a far greater proportion than in any other continent (worldwide average of 16%) (ILO, 2006). However, the International Labour Organization's definition of 'economic activity' excludes children's unpaid reproductive work within the household (ILO, 2006).

The socioeconomic and political environment has a significant impact on family life and children's economic and social well-being. Since the 1980s, global processes of economic restructuring have led to reductions in government expenditure on health and education in many low-income countries, undermining state mechanisms for redistribution (Mohan et al, 2000). Levels of national poverty, inadequate governmental welfare support and very limited basic services in many countries in the global South call into question universal notions of children's economic and social rights. The fulfilment of children's rights to an adequate standard of living, for example, is clearly problematic in low income countries of the global South, where state welfare assistance is virtually non-existent.

In addition, Western individualistic notions of children's rights, as enshrined in the UN Convention on the Rights of the Child, can be problematic in many African societies where notions of 'rights' are founded on interdependence and reciprocity, and children have responsibilities and duties towards their families and communities as much (if not more so) than they have 'rights' and entitlements (Laird, 2005: 460; Becker, 2007: 44). Indeed, disenchantment with the Western bias of UN Human Rights discourse led to the drawing up of the African Charter on Human and People's Rights (1986) and the African Charter on the Rights and Welfare of the Child (1990), which reflect the communal values system and reciprocal responsibilities of children, families and communities (UNICEF, 1999).

African constructions of childhood view children not as the exclusive property or responsibility of their biological parents, but as integral to extended families and the communities in which they live (UNICEF, 1999). According to Stephens (1995: 37), the Convention on the Rights of the Child not only 'relies on a naturalized and individualized notion of the child', but also 'implies that biologically based relations between parents and children are more fundamental than other sorts of family relations', constructing as 'deviant' the many other non-nuclear family forms. The Western concept of the nuclear family underlying the principles of the Convention is inappropriate in many countries in the global South. African societies, in particular, are characterised by a rich diversity of household structures, kinship responsibilities and traditional child fosterage within the extended family (Creighton and Omari, 1995; Panter-Brick, 2000). For example, 10% of married women in Tanzania reported being in a polygamous union in 2003, which has important implications for decision-making within the household (TACAIDS et al, 2005). Furthermore, in many African countries, the tradition of child fosterage, where families send one or more children to live with relatives for various reasons, including schooling and coping with economic crisis, for extended periods, challenges the Western view that children need one stable set of parental figures throughout childhood (Omari, 1995; Koda, 2000; Panter-Brick, 2000). Indeed, according to the Tanzanian Demographic and Health Survey, approximately 10% of children aged under 18 do not live with their biological parents, even though both are alive, with urban children more likely to live with other relatives than rural children (NBS/ORC Macro, 2005).

Comparative and cross-cultural studies have thus revealed a diversity of global childhoods, rather than 'a single and universal phenomenon', with childhood and age intersecting with other social identities including class, gender, disability, race and ethnicity (James and Prout, 1997: 8). Children across different societies, cultures and regions engage in a wide range of household tasks and care work for their families and communities (Foster et al, 1997; Robson, 2000; 2004; Miller, 2005; Bauman et al, 2006; Robson et al, 2006), challenging conventional notions of 'childhood', 'youth' and 'adulthood' and the boundaries between these life phases. Proponents of the 'new social studies of childhood' argue that the concept of 'childhood' that underlies discourses of children's rights, social welfare and development policies is a historically and geographically contingent, sociocultural construct (Boyden, 1997). 'Childhood' varies according to historical and sociocultural perceptions of 'the child', as well as according to the socioeconomic and political context in which children's lives are situated. Rather than viewing children as passive objects of social structures and processes, this theoretical perspective acknowledges children's agency as social actors, who are actively engaged in shaping their social worlds within the structural constraints and possibilities that influence these (James and Prout, 1997; James et al, 1998).

The notion of 'youth' has also been recognised as a social construction that varies across and within different cultures, historical periods and socioeconomic and political environments. The term 'youth' usually denotes young people aged 15-24 (UN, 2007) and is often seen as a Western concept that describes the in-between, transitional phase of 'adolescence' between childhood and adulthood (Ansell, 2005; Valentine, 2003). Dominant representations of 'youth-as-trouble' in the global North reveal adult concerns about young people's transitions during the increasingly extended period between childhood and adulthood, which are focused on young people's educational outcomes, leaving home and entry into the labour market (Ansell, 2005). Recent perspectives on 'youth', including cross-cultural studies, emphasise that the concept of youth is dynamic and fluid and call for attention to be paid to the ways that young people position themselves as well as how they are positioned within generational categories in different times and places (Jeffrey and McDowell, 2004; Honwana and De Boeck, 2005; Christiansen et al, 2006).

Gender, social reproduction and informal care

Since the 1970s feminists have argued that the notion of 'care' is socially constructed as a gendered activity and have drawn attention to the unequal division of labour within the household (Rich, 1980; Graham, 1983; Lewis and Meredith, 1988). The household represents a fundamental form of social organisation in most regions of the world and has been recognised as 'the primary site for the structuring of gender relations and women's specific experience' (Brydon and Chant, 1989: 8). In Western societies, in particular, the heterosexual nuclear family is constructed as the 'natural' site of caregiving (Bowlby et al, 1997; Cancian and Oliker, 2000).

Despite women's increased participation in paid employment in the global North in recent decades, gender inequalities in both paid and unpaid work persist and there have been only small increases in men's contributions to unpaid care work and domestic duties (Lewis, 2006). Numerous studies have shown that despite their paid work commitments, women remain primarily responsible for unpaid reproductive work within the family, including caring for children and male partners as well as disabled, sick or elderly family members (Lewis and Meredith, 1988; Bowlby et al, 1997; Gershuny, 2000; Lewis, 2006). Furthermore, research has revealed the ways that gendered notions of care intersect with other social identities such as class, race and ethnicity. Many carers from black and minority ethnic communities have similar experiences to white carers, for example, but their 'experiences are made more difficult by racism and inappropriate assumptions about the nature of family relationships within different ethnic communities' (Barnes, 2006: 5; see also Atkin and Rollings, 1992). Lewis (2006) argues that while care is now much more evident in political agendas in the UK, policies are linked to concerns about women's labour market participation and childcare provision rather than being 'care-centred'. Within the context of welfare state restructuring and greater emphasis on the home and community as the preferred locations for care provision of elderly and disabled people, commentators suggest that demand for unpaid care work within the family seems likely to expand further in future (Milligan, 2000; Lewis, 2006).

In the context of the global South, gender and development commentators have called for recognition of women's unequal work burden and identified women's triple roles of *productive work*, including income-generation activities in the informal sector and agricultural work on the family farm; social reproductive work, comprising care and maintenance of the household, food preparation, caring for ill or disabled family members and responsibilities for the health, education and socialisation of children, as well as subsistence agriculture; and *community managing*, which includes maintaining kinship ties and social networks with neighbours and fulfilling religious, ceremonial and social obligations in the community (Moser, 1989; Momsen, 1991). Gender and development analysts have deconstructed the 'black box' of the household, revealing the limitations of the conventional unified concept of the household that has shaped development policy and planning. The unified household model is implicitly based on Western notions of the nuclear family, which assume that household preferences and interests are the same and incomes are pooled (Fapohunda, cited in Dwyer and Bruce, 1988). Commentators have argued that intrahousehold relations and decision-making processes are instead characterised by unequal power relations and conflicting interests, rather than by cooperation and harmony (Sen, 1995; 1999; Kandiyoti, 1998).

Sen's concept (1995) of 'co-operative conflict' highlights the conflicting interests and complex intergenerational and gendered negotiations about domestic and caring duties that children, parents and other family members engage in. Research has shown that in the context of the global South, the tasks performed by girls and younger boys tend to be the low-status activities usually undertaken by women, such as household chores, load bearing and subsistence agriculture

(Bradley, 1993; Kielland and Tovo, 2006). Furthermore, girls and boys are often socialised to perform different household tasks according to a traditional gendered division of labour, which has differential impacts on boys' and girls' spatial mobility and time. In Tanzania, for example, girls are assigned many reproductive activities within the home to assist their mother, leaving little time for recreation and leisure, while boys are usually assigned outdoor agricultural tasks, such as grazing cattle, which give them more freedom, both in terms of time and space, to 'play' and explore the outside environment, as well as to study and complete their school work (Omari and Mbilinyi, 1997; Koda, 2000). Despite making significant contributions to their households, however, boys and girls generally occupy a weak bargaining position and are often marginalised within household decision-making processes (Koda, 2000).

Many commentators have suggested that caring comprises both emotional and physical elements, which are often distinguished by the terms 'caring about' and 'caring for' respectively (Ungerson, 1983). Owing to the association of the emotional labour of caring with femininity, caregiving is perceived as part of women's and girls' 'natural' roles as nurturers. Furthermore, domestic and care work within the home is 'never done', constantly having to be remade, thereby sustaining the material and emotional needs of the 'family' as well as reproducing the ideological concept of the 'family' (Bowlby et al, 1997). As Graham notes (1983: 26), caring is experienced as 'an unspecific and unspecifiable kind of labour, the contours of which shift constantly'. Furthermore, the association of caring with femininity and its location within the private space of the 'home' mean that care work is 'a labour, which, although essential for survival, is invisible, devalued and privatised' (Graham, 1983: 27).

Family members undertaking caring tasks, who are often women, are sometimes referred to as 'informal' or 'family carers/caregivers' although in most countries in both the global North and South there is no formal 'title' or specific recognition given to this group. Caring activities are usually seen as part of 'normal' familial and kinship responsibilities and duties, and thus the people providing this care are not identified as a distinct group requiring interventions or support in their own right. Indeed, research suggests that many carers do not recognise themselves as a distinct 'group' or identify with the label of 'carer' (Jones et al, 2002; Barnes, 2006). Rather, they see themselves as daughters, sons, wives, husbands, partners, mothers, fathers, grandmothers, grandfathers, aunts, uncles, sisters, brothers, friends or others who help to look after another family member. Many do not view their caring responsibilities as extensions of their family, personal or kinship relations or as a distinct type of inter- or intra-familial responsibility.

In the global South, especially, unpaid family caregiving is rarely perceived as anything unusual. Customary practice and cultural expectations mean that immediate and extended families routinely look after and support each other in many ways, within a long-established framework of cultural and community values, kinship responsibilities and obligations, and as part of an 'inter-generational contract' (Foster et al, 1997; Omari and Mbilinyi, 1997; Foster and Williamson, 2000; Howard et al, 2006; Van Blerk and Ansell, 2007). The reliance on the extended family and the community as a 'social safety net' is reinforced by the policies of governments and the state that conceptualise informal caregiving as part of familial and kinship obligations and community responsibilities. The experiences of most of those who provide care in the North and South are therefore 'largely taken for granted, undocumented and unaccounted for' (Ogden et al, 2004: 21).

To some extent, however, some unpaid caring can be seen as something that extends beyond routine family responsibilities, especially where family members have very substantial and regular caring responsibilities – for example where they are caring for more than 20 or even 50 hours each week – and where the outcomes of caring can significantly restrict their independence, health, well-being and social participation. In some countries in the global North, including the UK, US, Canada and Western Europe, informal caregivers are becoming increasingly recognised as a distinct social group (Becker, 2007). In the UK this recognition extends to clear legal rights and entitlements secured over decades (Becker, 2008). An implication of this recognition, to some extent, is that informal caregiving is perceived and responded to as an *extension* of family responsibilities – informal caring goes beyond routine familial and cultural values and expectations and informal carers are taking on tasks and responsibilities which are either somehow 'extra' or the responsibilities of others (for example, the state). As we shall see later in this chapter, this is particularly the case with children who have caring responsibilities ('young carers') – where, in some Northern countries at least, these responsibilities are seen to go beyond what is 'normal' or 'acceptable'.

A UK official definition of informal carers is 'people who look after a relative or friend who needs support because of age, physical or learning disability or illness, including mental illness' (DH, 2005). Informal care in the global North and South, unlike the 'formal' care provided by social workers, health workers and other 'professionals', is founded on an unpaid, non-professionalised 'caring relationship' between a family carer and the person(s) for whom they care. This informal care is personally directed and is usually given free of charge by virtue of an established relationship based on love, attachment, family obligation, duty, friendship and, additionally in many countries in the global South, within a context of reciprocal kinship responsibilities and communal values. It is the unpaid, familial and personal nature of 'caring relationships', based on prior social relations and emotional connections between the 'carer' and the person requiring assistance that primarily distinguish informal care and informal carers from other forms of caregiving or from other care providers (for example, the state, private or community/non-governmental sectors).

To some extent caring can be viewed as 'labour' and 'care work' (Brown and Stetz, 1999). Certainly, recognising informal caring activities as care work is to politicise and to make public the services, roles, value and outcomes that characterise unpaid caregiving, and to identify these issues as concerns for social and public policy (Becker, 2000b; 2007). In the UK, for example, it has been calculated that the annual cost of the 'hidden' contribution by the UK's six million adult family carers is £87 billion if their care was to be provided by paid care workers, greater than the annual budget for the National Health Service itself (£82 billion in 2006/07) (Yeandle and Buckner, 2007). In the US, in 2004, family carers contributed an estimated US$306 billion worth of unpaid caregiving. This dwarfs the costs of US formal home healthcare ($43 billion) and nursing home care ($115 billion) (Arno et al, 1999; Arno, 2006).

The 'welfare mix': families, carers and the state

In most countries of the North there is no firm consensus on where the contribution of the family should end and where the responsibility of the state should begin or vice versa. The balance between the state, family and other sectors of care provision varies considerably between different countries, changing over time as well as place (Becker et al, 1998: 78-103). In the UK, there is a 'mixed economy of care' (Powell, 2007), with the state, family, voluntary/community organisations and private (for profit) agencies currently providing a 'patch-work quilt' of services to people with care needs (such as older people and those with physical impairments) and, more recently, to support informal family carers. In the UK it has been suggested that there is a need for increased clarity in overall policy on the role and responsibilities of the state, family and individuals (Wanless, 2006: 150).

Millar and Warman (1996) have examined how the balance between state provision and informal family support is defined in law and policy across 15 European nations, including the UK. Their analysis of the structures and policies within these countries enabled them to divide nations into four groups, in which common approaches to defining the extent and range of family obligations towards older or disabled relatives can be identified. These groups ranged from those with legally defined family obligations (i.e. laws and rules which place the responsibility on extended or nuclear family members to care for, or pay for, dependent relatives), to those countries with individual entitlements and clearly defined state responsibilities, with far less reliance on family members to provide or pay for care. The UK is characteristic of those countries where there is 'No clear state responsibility'. In this group of countries family members have no formal, legal obligations to provide or pay for the care of older people or disabled relatives, but the responsibilities of the state are also not clearly or consistently defined.

While Millar and Warman's analysis relates only to European countries it is of relevance to our discussion here. Drawing on their classification it is possible to suggest that Tanzania, alongside other Sub-Saharan African countries, has many of the characteristics of the 'Extended family' classification. In 'Extended family' countries there are customary obligations between extended family members to provide financial support for each other and the state has little responsibility for supporting individuals. Anyone needing assistance with care tasks, or long-term care would have to pay for it. Those without the means turn to family members who are in effect obliged to pay for the care or provide the support themselves. As we have seen, across Sub-Saharan Africa it is the responsibility of extended families and communities to provide care for each other. In Zimbabwe, for example, the National Plan of Action for Orphans and Vulnerable Children, developed by the government, identifies five tiers of support for the care of children in these circumstances, with the three top tiers being the immediate and extended family, then community, followed by foster care that is highly sensitive to the parents' cultural values, and, finally, institutional care as a temporary measure to enable a later placement in a family environment (Child Protection Society, 2004; Madziva, 2008).

Across Sub-Saharan Africa, impoverished state provision in health and social care, constrained by structural adjustment policies, has led to public hospitals and healthcare becoming increasingly inaccessible for the majority of the population. There is little social protection available through existing social security systems and those in poverty can least afford to pay for healthcare or domestic help (Dhemba et al,

2002; Kaseke, 2003; Ogden et al, 2006). Increasingly, with the spread of the HIV/AIDS epidemic, many hospitals have become hospices for the terminally ill, with over half of all hospital beds in some countries being occupied by people with HIV-related illnesses (UNDP, 2005). While there is a growing private (for profit) sector in health, social care and education, most families are not able to afford these services. Thus, the majority of the population requiring care, for HIV-related illnesses or other chronic illness or impairments, remain in their homes in the community, looked after by immediate or extended family members, with little access to formal healthcare, social security or other external support (Ogden et al, 2004). Home-based care provided by non-governmental, community or faith-based organisations is the only available support offered to most families. In this context the family is endorsed as the dominant provider of caregiving, reinforced and maintained by government policies that prioritise home-based care and offer no adequate or affordable alternatives. Not surprisingly, the role of non-governmental and community-based organisations has become crucial in filling some of the care gaps between the family, state and the private sector.

Reciprocity and an ethic of care

Some of the literature on informal care (and on young carers – see later) might imply that caregiving is a 'one-way' process and that ill and disabled family members are dependent on family carers. In the UK and some other countries, however, this has been challenged by, among others, disability theorists and proponents of the 'Social Model of Disability'. The social model rejects medical models of illness and disability that portray disabled people as passive 'victims' of individual misfortune and emphasises the social structural, environmental and attitudinal barriers that exclude disabled people from full participation in society (Oliver, 1990; Morris, 1991). Furthermore, the social model challenges the language and ideology of 'care', arguing that notions of 'dependency' and 'caregiving' misrepresent both the needs of ill and disabled people and their relationships with 'carers', social workers and service providers (Morris, 1991; Morris, 1993; Keith and Morris, 1995). This model of disability suggests that the distinction between 'carer' and 'cared-for person' (and the assumptions of dependency that may accompany these labels) is difficult to sustain in theory and in practice when so many people both give and receive help (from different sources, informal and formal) simultaneously. Caring relationships are rarely 'one-sided' (with one person 'giving' and the other 'receiving') but rather are characterised by reciprocity and interdependence, whereby all parties both 'give and take', including helping each other with household tasks, household finances, personal care, supervision of children, emotional support, advice and looking out for each other (Becker and Silburn, 1999; Becker, 2008).

Within the context of young caregiving, proponents of the social model of disability have argued that the identification and labelling of 'young carers' as a focus for support and interventions, without reference to the experiences of their parents, obscures the social structural inequalities and support needs of disabled parents. Keith and Morris (1995), Stables and Smith (1999) and others have highlighted the fact that a child caring for a parent challenges normative notions of parenting – in particular motherhood – that define children as being dependent on their mothers (and fathers) for nurturing, care and socialisation. Furthermore, the label of 'young carers' can reinforce stigmatising attitudes that construct disabled people as 'inadequate parents' (Keith and Morris, 1995; Stables and Smith, 1999). Proponents of the social model of disability have challenged assumptions about disabled parents' inadequacy and rejected the notion that children have become their 'parent's parent' or that ill parents have become their children's dependants (Keith and Morris, 1995; Olsen, 1996; Olsen and Parker, 1997; Newman, 2002a; Wates, 2002). Instead, they have called for greater recognition of the social structural and attitudinal barriers that undermine disabled parents and for greater support and assistance to enable disabled people to perform their parenting role (Keith and Morris, 1995; Olsen, 1996; Newman, 2002a).

Debates between proponents of the social model of disability and researchers and practitioners in the field of young carers have led to greater recognition of the need for interventions and approaches that focus on the 'whole family', rather than just young carers and the acknowledgement that despite their illness (in this case mental illness), 'children [with caring responsibilities] continue to perceive their parents as mainly fulfilling loving parental and disciplinary roles' (Aldridge and Becker, 2003: 87). Indeed, the study by Jones et al (2002: 4) of black families in which young people have caring responsibilities concluded that, 'categorising children and young people as "young carers" ignores the complexity of caring roles within family life and may simply mask or perpetuate the social inequality experienced by the whole family'. The authors felt that use of the term 'young carer' obscured 'the important links between children's work and parenting support needs' (Jones et al, 2002: 4). Confirming the findings of Tisdall et al (2004) and Evans (2005), the research evidence we present shows that parents with HIV/AIDS in the global North and South continue to retain their parental authority and strive to fulfil their parenting role, despite the constraints of poverty and ill health. Indeed, this parenting role represents an important protective factor in developing children's resilience (see Chapters 6 and 9). Children who care for siblings, and those who live with grandparents or others following their parents' death, also engage in reciprocal caring relationships. In many families the identity of 'carer' is often not recognised and may be contested, while in some families it forms an important part of that person's sense of worth.

The theoretical concept of the ethic of care draws attention to these interdependent relationships and acknowledges that there is no absolute or fixed division of roles between 'caregivers' and 'care-receivers' (Tronto, 1993; Sevenhuijsen, 1998).

Tronto defines care as:

> a species activity that includes everything that we do to maintain, continue and repair our 'world' so that we can live in it as well as possible. That world includes our bodies, our selves, and our environment, all of which we seek to interweave in a complex, life-sustaining web. (Tronto and Fisher, cited in Tronto, 1993: 103)

From this perspective, care is an ongoing process, 'both a practice and a disposition', that involves 'taking the concerns and needs of the other as the basis for action' (Tronto, 1993: 105). Care is culturally defined, varying according to different cultures at different times and in different places (Tronto, 1993: 103). Four key phases of the process of caring are identified: *caring about*, which involves 'the recognition in the first place that care is necessary'; *taking care of*, that is 'assuming some responsibility for the identified need and determining how to respond to it'; *caregiving*, which 'involves the direct meeting of needs for care'; and *care-receiving*, 'recognising that the object [sic] of care will respond to the care it receives […] which provides the only way to know that caring needs have actually been met' (Tronto, 1993: 106-8). Linked to these four phases, four core values of an ethic of care emerge: attentiveness, responsibility, competence and responsiveness (Tronto, 1993). This approach emphasises that the perspective of the person receiving care is an integral part of the caring process and that caring relationships are characterised by interdependence and reciprocity, since we are all involved in caregiving and care-receiving at different times in our lives. The ethic of care thus provides a useful framework for conceptualising the identities and practices of caregiving relationships in households affected by HIV/AIDS. It also helps us understand how interdependence and reciprocity can mitigate some of the negative outcomes associated with caring and promote protective factors and resilience among children and parents.

The evidence from the research we present in this book shows that reciprocity and intergenerational interdependence are common features of families where children are 'caring' for parents with HIV/AIDS in the UK and Tanzania, and that meanings and experiences of care 'giving' and care 'receiving' are complex and blurred, sometimes embraced and sometimes contested. We use the experiences of young people with caring responsibilities in these two countries as a window on the global and local processes and policies that influence caring relationships within families, and as a lens through which to make some comparisons and observations about policy responses to young caregiving and HIV/AIDS in the global North and South.

Children and young people with caring responsibilities

Context and definition

In the UK, the Netherlands, Germany, Australia, New Zealand, the US, Canada and some other high-income countries, researchers, policy makers, social welfare agencies and professionals in health, social care and education have taken a growing interest during the 1990s in the extent, nature and outcomes of children's informal caregiving within the family. A research interest is now also emerging in other regions, particularly Sub-Saharan Africa, where the HIV/AIDS epidemic has led to millions of children being drawn into unpaid caring that seems to go beyond their traditionally and culturally defined responsibilities within the household (Robson, 2000; Robson and Ansell, 2000; Robson et al, 2006; Becker, 2007).

No financial estimates have yet been made in any country of the hidden economic or social costs of children's unpaid care work. Significantly, for our purposes, children's care work is excluded from the International Labour Organization definition of 'children at work in economic activity', which the ILO is trying to eliminate (Robson et al, 2006: 97). As noted earlier, children's reproductive work within the family is not recognised as 'child labour' and, as a consequence, is rarely identified in UNICEF or governmental and intergovernmental publications as a specific issue to be addressed or confronted through collective actions and social policies.

While some level of attachment and 'caring about' and 'caring for' by children would be viewed across most societies and cultures today as beneficial or necessary for children's socialisation and development, research suggests that children who undertake substantial or regular caregiving can experience significant restrictions in their education, social participation and opportunities, even when there may be some 'positives' associated with caring – such as enhanced coping strategies; the development of life, social and other skills; maturity; a sense of purpose and closer relationships within the family (Dearden and Becker, 2000; Aldridge and Becker, 2003; Becker and Becker, 2008). Becker suggests that the term 'young carer' (or 'young caregiver' in US diction) needs to be employed precisely and deliberately to refer to a specific group of children who take on a quantity or quality of caring roles that are substantial and/or significant to families themselves, and which are different to, and go beyond, not only what we (as adults) would normally expect of children but also what many children would expect routinely to do within the home:

> Young carers can be defined as children and young persons under 18 who provide or intend to provide care, assistance or support to another family member. They carry out, often on a regular basis, significant or substantial caring tasks and assume a level of responsibility that would usually be associated with an adult. The person receiving care is often a parent but can be a sibling, grandparent or other relative who is disabled, has some chronic illness, mental health problem or other condition connected with a need for care, support or supervision. (Becker, 2000a: 378)

While there are variations in the operational definition of young carers across the UK, Australia and the US, and within countries (see, for example, Frank, 2002: 6-8 for UK definitions and Oreb, 2001: 27 for Australian definitions), the basic components of Becker's definition are in common currency and have informed conceptualisations in the global North (Moore, 2005b: 65). In the global South, the term is not commonly used, although some research has suggested that young people with caring responsibilities in Africa could also be included within this definition (Robson et al, 2006: 96). The definition allows a distinction to be made between those children who are involved in 'significant, substantial or regular care', many of whom may take on these responsibilities at an early age, and those children who, as part of their routine family lives and roles, may be involved in some elements of caring but at a level which is neither substantial or regular, and, importantly, nor are the outcomes for children negative or restrictive.

Levine et al (2005) have argued that young adult caregivers aged 18-24 have largely been ignored in research both in the US and globally. As a group, however, they are an important sub-population of family carers to consider because, as young adults, they are at a critical 'developmental' stage, with many – especially in the global North – having not yet solidified their life plans and choices about higher education, work, marriage and child bearing (Shifren, 2009). While there is a growing body of research evidence on young carers aged under 18, there is far less research evidence on young adult carers aged 18-24. This lack of attention to, and recognition of, young adult carers in research is mirrored in the policy world by a paucity of *specific* policies, services and interventions for carers aged 18-24 in the UK, Tanzania and globally (Becker and Becker, 2008).

While there are a few existing UK studies specifically of young adult carers aged up to 24 (Frank et al, 1999; Dearden and Becker, 2000; Harrison and O'Rooke, 2003; Action for Young Carers, 2005; Barnardo's, 2007; Becker and Becker, 2008), most are small-scale and based on a local population. We are not aware of any specific studies of Tanzanian carers in this age group. Becker and Becker (2008) suggest that existing research on young adult carers is limited in its ability to provide answers to a series of critical questions about this group's experiences and needs, including: what are the factors that affect the extent and nature of caring among this group? How do educational experiences and outcomes affect young adult carers' choices and decisions about further and higher education? How are aspirations affected by caring roles and responsibilities? What specific support and services do young adult carers need and receive in practice? Information is therefore sparse about the issues and challenges that young adult carers face on account of their caring responsibilities, as well as about appropriate support and the best methods and routes to reach them in the UK and Tanzania.

As recently acknowledged in a report by the Social Exclusion Unit in the UK (2006: 7):

> The transition from childhood to adulthood is becoming increasingly complex, difficult and risky.... The transition to adulthood is more difficult if you also have to deal with one or more of the following issues: poor housing; homelessness;

substance misuse; mental health issues; poor education or long-term employment.

The decisions made at this age can be some of the most important and far-reaching decisions taken at any time of life. The opportunities and choices of disadvantaged young adults, including young adult carers, are likely to be constrained by their caring responsibilities, low income, educational disadvantage and inequalities based on class, gender, race, disability among others. Young adult carers in the UK and Tanzania, especially those caring for a parent with a life-limiting illness, may not have access to advice or guidance from parents or other family members at the right time to help them navigate through this period of change in their lives, to help them deal with and respond to their parent's illness or disability, while at the same time continuing with their caring roles and responsibilities.

Dearden and Becker (2000: 43) identify three important aspects of the effects of caring on young adults in the UK and the implications for transitions to 'adulthood' and so-called independence. First, '[c]aring can be stressful, particularly for young people living with parents who experience pain, mental distress, or who have a terminal or life threatening illness. In a few cases stress and depression were severe enough to lead to physical and psychological ill health.' Second, even where young adult carers had left home they often continue to worry about the 'cared for' person. Some resumed their caring responsibilities when they returned home or made arrangements to visit the family home on a daily basis in order to provide care. Finally, young adult carers may gain skills and competencies through young caring but these were often gained at a cost of them missing school and not getting qualifications – such that caring cannot be regarded as an *acceptable* way for young people to acquire these skills. More recently, research on young adult carers in the UK has shown that caregiving is associated with many positive aspects among young people themselves (Becker and Becker, 2008), although the transition to adulthood, and to adult services in the UK context, is problematic for many of these young people, who may need additional support and services to assist them.

Risk, resilience and protective factors

Recent developments in the literature on young carers have recognised that not all children with caring responsibilities experience physical, emotional, relationship or other psychosocial problems, and many may not experience difficulties in school or elsewhere. While just under a quarter of young carers in a UK-wide survey in 2003 had educational problems, the majority appeared not to have such difficulties (Dearden and Becker, 2004). Research to date has not explored the reasons why some young people experience significant difficulties at school or elsewhere in their lives, while others do not, nor is there any certainty that it is children's caregiving responsibilities that account solely for any problems encountered. For example, low income and poverty (and chronic poverty in the South) have been identified as a common characteristic of many families where children have significant caring responsibilities. While research to date has helped to chart and describe the broad landscape of young carers' experiences and outcomes, the research evidence is still under-developed in terms of critical analysis of the differential impacts on children of caregiving and whether it is caring per se or other factors such as poverty that lead to particular outcomes (for example, low educational attainment).

The evidence to date suggests that a combination of caregiving and other factors are likely to account for differential outcomes for children. In the UK only 30,000 children with caring responsibilities (out of at least 175,000) are in contact with dedicated young carers projects. We know very little about the characteristics of the majority of children with caring responsibilities who are 'invisible' to specialist services. Do these children demonstrate resilience in particular spheres of their lives, such as school, thus experiencing less negative outcomes, and so do not need or use targeted services? Do these children with caring responsibilities constitute the majority of children who are involved in low levels of caring (providing under 20 hours of caring per week – see Table 1.2 on page 29)? Do these children receive help from other support agencies? In the UK context this could include both universal children's services such as schools, or support targeted towards children or parents on the basis of the family's other characteristics, such as low income or the risk of social exclusion, poor educational attendance or performance, ethnicity or immigration status (Evans et al, 2006; Evans and Pinnock, 2007). Or could these children with caring responsibilities be particularly isolated and in greater need, but have remained invisible for other reasons, such as the stigma surrounding HIV?

Some researchers suggest that the concept of 'resilience' may help to explain individual differences in coping with stress and adversity (Newman, 2002a; 2002b). The concept of resilience has been heavily debated and contested in the literature, but is generally defined as 'a dynamic process whereby individuals show adaptive functioning in the face of significant adversity' (Schoon, 2006: 6; see also Rutter, 1990; Luthar and Cicchetti, 2000). Risk or adversity is composed of 'genetic, biological, psychological, environmental or socio-economic factors that are associated with an increased probability of maladjustment' (Schoon, 2006: 9). Much of the resilience literature is based on quantitative psychopathological studies of individuals' adaptive functioning in the face of 'risk' factors. Sociological accounts, however, have critiqued the reliance on biological and psychosocial constructs of 'risk', which focus on individual behaviour and outcomes (Howard et al, 1999; Evans and Pinnock, 2007). The identification of risk factors is considered by some to stigmatise individuals (Howard et al, 1999) and underplay the influence of social structural inequalities (Evans, 2005). Individuals perceived to be 'at risk' are often treated as homogenous groups (Schoon, 2006) and children labelled as 'vulnerable' or 'at risk' are often those whose particular characteristics or behaviour are perceived as different from the dominant culture (Howard et al, 1999). The identification and management of risk is thus often based on a deficit model of children and families that overlooks the importance of the interaction of risk with social inequalities and environmental factors (Howard et al, 1999). Furthermore, individuals identified as 'at risk' may not consider this label appropriate to describe themselves (Howard and Johnson, 2000; Schoon, 2006).

The concept of resilience is seen by some as providing a useful counterpart to a focus on risk, as it attempts to provide a more contextualised understanding of the processes by which children and families negotiate risk situations (Rutter, 1990; Schoon, 2006). Instead of focusing on risk, the concept of resilience emphasises people's strengths in coping with adversity and their agency in engaging with protective factors that may help to reduce their vulnerability (Rutter, 1990). Protective factors may be associated with individual attributes, such as problem-solving skills, high aspirations, faith and religious beliefs, positive peer relationships; family characteristics, such as caring and supportive family relationships, a secure base and sense of belonging; or aspects of the wider community, such as the availability of external support or resources, a positive school environment, opportunities for participation (Newman, 2002b; Schoon and Bynner, 2003; Schoon, 2006; Evans and Pinnock, 2007). However, these factors are likely to be context-specific and may vary cross-culturally (Howard et al, 1999; Schoon and Parsons, 2002; Evans, 2005).

Many of the criticisms of the risk discourse could, however, be equally applied to the concept of resilience. Researchers have highlighted the danger of perceiving resilience as an individual attribute and labelling children as 'resilient' as this can lead to perspectives that blame the individual for failing to succeed or adapt well to adversity (Luthar and Cicchetti, 2000; Schoon, 2006). Indeed, Ungar (2004) argues that definitions of resilience are socially constructed, and normative values about what constitute universal positive outcomes for children reflect hegemonic cultural values of Western societies, where the majority of studies on resilience have been conducted. Furthermore, Howard and Johnson (2000) suggest that children's understandings of risk and resilience are likely to differ from adult interpretations, which may undermine the success of adult-designed interventions aiming to promote resilience.

Child development researchers have argued that resilience should not be seen as a personal attribute or a static state, but is rather a dynamic process that depends on the interaction between the sociohistorical context and the developing individual (Howard et al, 1999). A growing number of more sociological studies have emphasised the importance of the domains of the family and community in promoting children's resilience (Wolkow and Ferguson, 2001; Mackay, 2003; Seaman et al, 2005; Evans and Pinnock, 2007). Children's social networks have been identified as potential sources of informal social support that can help to protect children from adversity (Gilligan, 1999). Several researchers have developed the notion of children's different pathways or 'trajectories' in which children may demonstrate resilience at particular times or in particular domains or spheres of their lives (Luthar and Cicchetti, 2000; Ungar, 2004; Schoon, 2006). Gilligan (2000) discusses the notion of 'turning points' in children's lives, whereby a favourable experience may represent a turning point in a child's trajectory. However, trajectories should not be seen as unilinear, but fluid, recursive and varying between multiple spheres and domains (Schoon, 2006).

Recent research in the UK and Sub-Saharan Africa suggests that there are some positive outcomes associated with caring which may help to promote children's resilience. Dearden and Becker (2000), for example, found that caring developed children's knowledge, understanding, sense of responsibility, maturity and a range of life, social and care-related skills. Caring also helped to bring many children closer to their parents in terms of a loving, caring, relationship – a critical protective factor found in our study reported here of children caring for parents with HIV/AIDS (see also Chapters 6 and 9). Similarly, Aldridge and Becker's (2003) research with 40 families where a child was caring for a parent with severe mental illness found that children's caregiving helped to allay some of the fears, concerns and anxieties that they had about their parent's condition because it gave children control and direct involvement in the provision and management of care work. The authors suggested that in some instances caring helped to enhance parent–child relationships and helped children to feel included when often, outside the domain of the family, they were ignored and not recognised by health, social care and other professionals. Robson et al's (2006) research in Zimbabwe identified a number of educational, personal and emotional benefits for young carers, such as learning new skills, gaining experience and taking on responsibilities, developing stronger emotional bonds between the 'carer' and 'care recipient', and developing emotional maturity and pride in caring. The authors suggest, however, that these positive benefits that young people identified as part of their caregiving could represent survival strategies for dealing with distressing experiences of caring for a sick and dying relative.

By exploring children's and parents' own perspectives of their 'culturally embedded pathways to resilience' (Ungar, 2004: 358) in the qualitative findings we present in this book, we aim to provide insight into the dynamic interactions between individual, relational and structural risk and protective processes that influence outcomes of young caregiving for children and parents within different spheres of their lives (see Chapters 6-9). We focus in particular on the caring relationships, social networks, formal and informal support that children and parents draw on within the domains of the family, school and neighbourhood that help to mitigate children's and parents' vulnerability within households affected by HIV/AIDS.

A continuum of children's and young people's caring responsibilities

Children's caring responsibilities in the global North

Despite assertions by some UK commentators that there are no scientifically 'proven' differences between what young carers do within the family compared with other children (Parker and Olsen, 1995; Olsen, 1996; Olsen and Parker, 1997; Newman, 2002a), there is now reliable research evidence from the North and South which shows that young people with caring responsibilities do differ from other (randomly selected) children across countries and cultures. The differences relate to the extent of young people's caregiving, its nature, the time involved and the outcomes for children's development and their social and economic participation.

Research evidence from three countries, the UK, US and Australia (Becker, 2007) has shown that when children are involved in caring for many hours each week from an early age, they are vulnerable to a cluster of negative outcomes. These can include: restricted opportunities for social networking and for developing peer friendships; limited opportunities to engage in leisure and other activities; poverty and social exclusion; physical and mental health problems or emotional difficulties; educational problems; limited horizons and aspirations for the future; a sense of 'stigma by association' (particularly where parents have mental health problems, misuse alcohol or drugs, or have HIV/AIDS); a fear of what professionals might do to the family if their circumstances are known; the keeping of 'silence' and secrets (again because of the fear of public hostility or punitive professional responses); and significant difficulties in making a successful transition from 'childhood' to 'adulthood' (Becker et al, 1998; Becker, 2005).

In the context of the study presented here on HIV/AIDS, research on children caring for parents with mental health problems shows the sense of stigma that many young people can experience because of the nature of their parent's condition and how this is viewed by neighbours, communities and society in general (Aldridge and Becker, 2003). This 'stigma by association' can manifest itself in many ways, including young people and their families trying to keep secret their caring circumstances and families experiencing isolation from potential sources of help and support and local communities.

Statistical and other profiles of the characteristics and experiences of young carers have been conducted in some Northern countries, drawn from large samples of children in contact with dedicated young carers support projects and from in-depth qualitative studies. In the UK, for example, three national surveys (Dearden and Becker, 1995; 1998; 2004) show that children's caring roles are very similar to those of adult carers and that children's caregiving tasks range along a continuum from basic domestic duties to personal care. Most children (68%) in a survey of over 6,000 young carers did some level of domestic work within the home; 48% of young carers were involved in general and nursing care, which included organising and administering medication, injections, and lifting and moving parents; and 82% of children provided emotional support and supervision, particularly to parents with severe and enduring mental health problems (Dearden and Becker, 2004; see also Aldridge and Becker, 2003). One in five provided personal and intimate care including assistance with the toilet and bathing tasks. A small proportion (11%), also took on childcare responsibilities in addition to their caring roles for other family members. Around 7% were involved in other household responsibilities, including translating (where English was not the first language), dealing with professionals and managing the family's money (Dearden and Becker, 2004). Research from a few other Northern countries, particularly from

Australia, confirms this picture of the caring tasks and responsibilities of children (Becker, 2007).

Morrow (2005) suggests that a way of differentiating what young carers do from other children is to distinguish between household tasks that are seen as 'Instrumental Activities of Daily Living' (such as taking out the rubbish or cleaning), and between tasks seen as 'Activities of Daily Living', such as assisting relatives with mobility and providing personal care including assisting to shower, use the toilet, dress, get in and out of bed. Morrow argues that 'non-carers will not bath, shower and toilet [sic] a sibling or parent' (p 58). Research from Australia (Carers Australia, 2001: 9) shows that young carers spend most of their time either providing care or thinking about the person with care needs, unlike non-caring peers. Gays (2000) suggests that Australian young carers take on caring tasks and levels of responsibility not found among other children, and young carers report more injuries, start housework from a younger age and perform a wider range of jobs around the house more often and on a regular basis. Moore's study of 50 Australian young carers found that their caring responsibilities 'are more intense than their non-caring peers and are most often provided without supervision or support' (Moore, 2005a: 5).

In the UK, Warren (2005; 2007) compares the caring tasks of 'known' young carers with a group of almost 400 children selected at random. She found that 'what sets young carers apart from their peers is the nature, frequency and time spent each week on domestic and caring tasks' (Warren, 2005: 6). Young carers performed a wider range of domestic, emotional, general nursing-type care, and intimate care tasks and they spent longer on these activities than other children. Warren's study also found that young carers were more likely than other children to have restricted opportunities for social, recreational and extracurricular participation and to identify a range of barriers that might prevent them from fulfilling their future ambitions. These included a lack of money, a need to look after a family member and a lack of qualifications. In contrast, children who were not young carers reported that their future ambitions could be restricted primarily by a lack of money (Warren, 2007).

The only US research to date that examines specifically the differences between young caregivers and other children compared the experiences of 213 young caregivers with 250 other children as part of a national prevalence study (National Alliance for Caregiving/United Hospital Fund, 2005). The researchers suggest that 'child caregivers who provide significant amounts of care have life experiences different from those of their non caregiving peers' (p 2). They found that 'young caregivers' in the US were more likely than other children to spend more time doing a wide range of household and caring tasks, including shopping, doing laundry, making dinner, looking after siblings and were more likely to show anxious, depressed or antisocial behaviour.

Children's caring responsibilities in the global South

This pattern of findings from a few countries is reinforced by recent research with young people with caring responsibilities in Sub-Saharan Africa. As Laird has observed, in the absence of public utilities, welfare services or social security, households in Africa are dependent on children to perform many time-consuming and strenuous household labours and productive activity to enable the household to meet its survival needs (2005: 462). This form of social organisation, as we argued earlier, 'is underpinned by a value system which emphasises the obligations owed by children to their parents in terms of contributing to the household and providing care during sickness or old age'. Laird suggests that '[f]ailure to fulfill these responsibilities will attract censure and probably penalty both from kin and the wider community' (2005: 462).

The HIV/AIDS epidemic in Sub-Saharan Africa has affected millions of children in diverse ways, as will be discussed in detail in Chapter 2. Children affected by HIV/AIDS are often referred to as 'vulnerable' or 'orphaned' children, rather than as 'young carers'. Within the extensive literature on the impacts of the HIV and AIDS epidemic in Africa, most of the emphasis to date has been on the impacts of orphanhood (Foster et al, 2005), rather than on the outcomes of children's caring roles during their parents' and relatives' illness. The term 'young carer' does not adequately convey the multiple meanings and experiences of these children – where caregiving may be only one dimension of their experience of living in a household affected by HIV/AIDS. At the same time, however, the lack of recognition of young people's caring responsibilities hides young people's particular contributions, roles and responsibilities in families affected by HIV/AIDS. Foster and Williamson (2000: S278) have argued that 'research is needed into the impacts, both negative and positive, that caring has on children, the needs of children as caregivers and the ways in which disruptions to schooling can be minimised'. There is little recognition of the distinct role of children with caring responsibilities in Sub-Saharan Africa, particularly the extent, nature and outcomes of their caring tasks, and there are few services specifically designed to support them.

According to UNAIDS, anecdotal evidence from various African countries suggests that children who care in Africa are often young – between 8 and 11 years old, as older siblings tend to leave home to find work or seek survival on the streets as family poverty deepens (UNAIDS, 2000). However, international governmental organisations such as UNICEF and international non-governmental organisations such as Save the Children have not focused explicitly on the caregiving roles of children affected by AIDS, or the impacts of these roles on children's health and welfare and, significantly, their access to education. This latter area is particularly important in light of the Millennium Development Goals and international commitments to achieve Universal Primary Education. There is evidence from some African countries, for example, that school enrolment has fallen dramatically, sometimes by a third, as children drop out of school to provide care for sick family members (Steinberg et al, 2002).

The growing research evidence from a number of Sub-Saharan African countries suggests that there are some important differences between what many African young carers do and other children, including those children who regularly perform household and caring tasks as part of their everyday responsibilities to their families: 'Even within an African sociological and anthropological context, what young people like Doris [young carer] do, can be considered more than a child's "normal" range of tasks and burdens of responsibility' (Robson et al, 2006: 96). Robson et al go on: 'It is the intimate care…that most clearly distinguishes the labour of young caregivers from the usual work young people do in Africa with respect to household chores' (p 100). Additionally, '[a]s caregivers, young people do more domestic work and have greater responsibility for tasks like cooking, fetching water and wood than other young people, because they live in a household with a sick grandmother, parent or sibling' (p 100).

A continuum of young caregiving

The existing research evidence from both the North and South indicates that many young carers perform more tasks that are Instrumental Activities of Daily Living (such as shopping and housework), and spend longer on them, *in addition* to the more care-related Activities of Daily Living (such as intimate and personal care). All of these activities can start at a young age and continue for many years. In the UK, for example, one fifth of young carers in a survey of more than 6,000 children had been caring for more than six years, even when the average age of the group was just 12 years old (Dearden and Becker, 2004). In

Australia, research suggested that some children had been caring for 14 years (Morrow, 2005).

Becker (2007) has suggested that it is possible to conceptualise children's informal caring in the North and South as a continuum along which all children's caregiving activity can be located (Figure 1.1). Young carers would be placed at the 'high' (substantial and regular caregiving) end of the continuum, and many would also be involved in a significant amount of tasks associated with Instrumental Activities of Daily Living. Warren's (2005; 2007) research in the UK also found, unexpectedly, that around a tenth of her randomly selected group of children also had considerable caring responsibilities, sometimes as substantial and significant as the known 'young carers' in her study. This suggests that there is a 'hidden' group of children with caring responsibilities within the general population of UK children, and this group too can be located at the 'high' end of the continuum. This group

Figure 1.1: A continuum of young caregiving

Low levels of caregiving and responsibility	➔➔➔ ➔➔➔ ➔➔➔ ➔➔➔	High levels of caregiving and responsibility
Most children and young people		Few children and young people
'Routine' levels and types of caregiving including some help with Instrumental Activities of Daily Living	➔➔➔ **Caregiving tasks and responsibilities increase in amount, regularity, complexity, time involved (hours per week), intimacy and duration (months and years)**	'Substantial, regular and significant' caregiving including considerable help with Instrumental Activities of Daily Living
Household tasks and caregiving tasks can be considered age and culturally appropriate		Household tasks and caregiving tasks can be considered age and culturally inappropriate
Children and young people providing a few hours of care and support each week with no evidence of negative outcomes	➔➔➔	Young carers providing 'full-time' caregiving each week with evidence of significant negative outcomes
	Many 'hidden' young carers (unknown to service providers/receiving no support)	

appears not to be recognised or identified as young carers as they were not in receipt of any dedicated support services or interventions. As this book will show, the experience of most Tanzanian and UK children caring for parents with HIV/AIDS has some similarity with this hidden group, in that they too are often invisible and rarely receive formal support in relation to their caring roles – irrespective of the welfare regime that characterises the country in which they live.

The extent of children's involvement in care work

There are few reliable and comparative indicators of the extent of children's caregiving, largely because young carers represent a 'hidden' group globally, and their tasks and responsibilities have only recently been conceptualised as problematic in a few countries of the North. In this section we synthesise and review the most reliable data that are currently available.

In the UK there are almost 3 million children under the age of 16 (equivalent to 23% of all children) who live in households where one family member requires assistance with daily activities because of a physical impairment, chronic illness or mental health problem (Becker et al, 1998). However, only a small proportion of these children and young people will become involved in caregiving to the extent or nature captured in the definition of a young carer given earlier (Becker, 2000a: 378). Most children do not become young carers because there are other family members available to provide care, or because families receive social care or health-related support or services, thus reducing the need for children to take on caring roles and reducing in some cases the negative outcomes that can be associated with substantial and regular caregiving.

The UK 2001 Census shows that 175,000 children provide some level of unpaid care to other family members. This is approximately 6% of children who live in families with illness and disability. Table 1.1 shows the number and proportion of children who provide unpaid care in the four countries that constitute the UK. There are small variations between the four UK nations, with the highest concentration of children who are carers to be found in Northern Ireland, with 2.5% of all children aged 5-17 years being involved in caring. Overall, across the UK, 2.1% of all children are young carers and 29,142 of these are providing more than 20 hours of care per week, and 13,029 of these provide more than 50 hours of unpaid care work per week. These figures and proportions are *minimums* rather than maximums because of limitations inherent within the Census questions and methodology.

Table 1.1: Number and proportion of children under the age of 18 who have caring responsibilities in the UK, by country and hours caring per week

Country in UK	Number caring for 1–19 hours	Number caring for 20–49 hours	Number caring for 50+ hours	Total number caring	Proportion of children providing informal care
England	116,823	12,284	10,092	139,199	1.7%
Wales	8,854	1,029	861	10,744	2.2%
Scotland	13,511	1,826	1,364	16,701	2.1%
N Ireland	6,666	974	712	8,352	2.5%
Total number of young carers in UK	145,854	16,113	13,029	174,996	2.1% (UK average)
Total number as % of all young carers in UK	83%	9%	8%	100%	

Source: Becker (2008)

The Census figures rely on parents' self reporting their children's caring roles, and thus the data are not likely to adequately identify or count children in some caring situations, for example those who may be caring for parents who misuse alcohol or drugs or where there is enduring parental mental ill health or HIV/AIDS.

Table 1.2 shows the number of young carers in the UK by age and hours per week caring, based on 2001 UK Census data. There are 6,563 young carers in the UK aged between 5 and 7 years, and 940 of these provide at least 50 hours of care per week. Another 9,524 children are aged 8 or 9 years, and 1,055 of these are providing 50 hours of care or more each week. In total, around 35,000 children with caring responsibilities are of primary school age and nearly 4,000 of these are caring for more than 50 hours per week. These figures indicate that some children are drawn into a caring role from a very young age and that some care for very long hours each week, with one in six children caring for more than 20 hours per week and almost one in ten caring for more than 50 hours each week. These figures are likely to be minimums rather than maximums, however, and the full extent of young caregiving is likely to be higher.

There are few reliable figures on the number of children involved in caregiving in other countries. However, data from Australia and the

Table 1.2: Number and proportion of children under the age of 18 who are involved in care work in the UK, by age and hours caring per week

Age (years)	1–19 hours	20–49 hours	50+ hours	Total number	Total %
0–4	0	0	0	0	0
5–7	5,015	608	940	6,563	4%
8–9	7,717	752	1,055	9,524	5%
10–11	16,120	1,433	1,615	19,168	11%
12–14	46,267	4,103	3,519	53,889	31%
15	21,024	2,282	1,494	24,800	14%
16–17	49,711	6,935	4,406	61,052	35%
All	145,854	16,113	13,029	174,996	100%
All as %	83%	9%	8%	100%	

Source: Becker (2008)

US help to generate a picture of the possible extent of children's care work across the global North. Australian Bureau of Statistics data (ABS, 2003) show that there were 169,900 young carers aged under 18 in Australia, that is 3.6% of all people of that age group. This proportion is approximately double that of children of the same age identified in the UK Census as carers, although the variation is likely to be related to the survey design rather than evidence of a significant difference in the extent of young caring between the two countries (Becker, 2007). The first (and, to date, only) US survey of young caregivers, drawing on a random sample of 2,000 households funded by the US Administration on Aging, asked whether any child between 8 and 18 years of age in the household provided unpaid help or care to any other person in 2003. Approximately 1.3 to 1.4 million young caregivers aged between 8 and 18 were reported to have caring responsibilities, that is 3.2% of all US households (National Alliance for Caregiving/United Hospital Fund, 2005). A limitation of this research, however, is that the age band for inclusion starts at 8 years. The UK Census data, in contrast, show that 4% of all young carers in the UK are aged between 5 and 7 years (see Table 1.2).

Despite the differences in survey methodologies and age bands included in the UK, Australian and US data sets, the statistical evidence shows a degree of uniformity in the proportion of children in these three countries who are involved in caregiving. While the data from all countries are likely to underestimate the extent of young caregiving because of definitional and methodological limitations, these official or quasi-official sets of statistics (all undertaken or funded by government) suggest that between 2% and 4% of all children will take on informal caring roles in the UK, Australia and the US. Across the North, this would constitute millions of children. There are no official or reliable figures for the number of children involved in caregiving in Sub-Saharan Africa (Ogden et al, 2004; Robson et al, 2006: 97). Robson et al identify a large survey in Tanzania in the early 1990s that found that about 4% of children aged between 7 and 14 years were reported to have engaged in caring for sick relatives in the previous seven days (Ainsworth et al, 2000: 22, cited in Robson et al, 2006: 97). However, since this study an increasing number of African children have become affected by the HIV/AIDS epidemic, suggesting that a higher proportion of children are now likely to be involved in caring for sick parents and relatives.

While these data might indicate broadly that between 2% and 4% of children in the North could be considered to have significant caring responsibilities, it is clear that more accurate and reliable data are required globally. Moreover, these figures provide no information about the number and proportion of people who require assistance in each country. In view of the scale of the HIV/AIDS epidemic in Sub-Saharan Africa, significant proportions of the population in severely affected communities will require care assistance, especially in the context of restricted access to, and availability of, affordable formal health and social care support. Two per cent of the world's population and over two thirds of all people living with HIV/AIDS live in Sub-Saharan Africa (UNAIDS, 2006). Furthermore, women and girls are disproportionately affected by the impacts of the epidemic, in terms of providing care for people living with HIV/AIDS (Mutangadura, 2001; Foster, 2004; Evans, 2005). Children (aged up to 14 years) constitute on average 43% of the population in Sub-Saharan Africa (Robson et al, 2006: 95, Table 1). In this context, it is not surprising that millions of children are drawn into unpaid caregiving roles, particularly for mothers living with HIV.

The extent of young adults' (aged 18–24) involvement in care work

As we noted earlier, research on the experiences of 'young adult caregivers' is very limited, both in the global North and South. The lack of research on young adult carers in the UK is perhaps more surprising given the numbers involved. Census 2001 data show that while there are at least 175,000 young carers under the age of 18 in the UK, there are an additional 230,000 aged 18-24, which is 5.3% of all people in that age group (Becker and Becker, 2008). However, as shown in Table 1.3, this proportion varies among the four UK nations, with the highest levels of young adult caring being in Wales (where someone in the 18–24 age group has a 5.7% probability of being a carer, compared with a probability of 4.8% in England). This regional variation may reflect different levels of illness, disability, geography and need across countries, and also differences in the availability of health and social care services and support for ill and disabled people, and for carers.

Identifying the number and characteristics of young adults who have the most substantial caring responsibilities (caring over 20 hours per week, and particularly those who are caring for more than 50 hours each week) is important for policy and service planning purposes. This is a reliable indicator of 'need' in that research on young carers (aged under 18), and Office for National Statistics and other research on 'adult carers', shows that carers who provide the longest hours of caring each week are those most likely to experience impaired physical and mental health, stress and relationship difficulties and to experience restrictions in their social participation and access to education, recreational and leisure opportunities, and are those most likely to need services and

Table 1.3: Number and proportion of young adults aged 18–24 who are involved in care work in the UK, by country and hours caring per week

Country in UK	Number caring for 1–19 hours	Number caring for 20–49 hours	Number caring for 50+ hours	Total number caring	Proportion of this age group who provide informal care
England	140,903	22,547	21,571	185,021	4.8%
Wales	9,675	1,697	1,690	13,062	5.7%
Scotland	15,417	3,203	2,495	21,115	5.0%
N Ireland	7,254	1,681	1,185	10,120	5.5%
Total number of young adult carers in UK	173,249	29,128	26,941	229,318	5.25% (UK average)
Total as % of all young adult carers in UK	75%	13%	12%	100%	

Source: Becker and Becker (2008)

support in their caring roles and to meet their own needs (Becker, 2008). Demographic and other changes (for example, the growing number of people with life-limiting illness who live in their own homes in the UK and Tanzania on an appropriate medication regime) will exert a strong demand for informal family care, some of which (in the UK) and much of which (in Tanzania) will be placed on young people. Thus, over time, it is likely that more young adults will be drawn into caring roles in the UK and Tanzania.

Explanations for why children and young people become involved in caregiving

The reasons why a particular child or young person becomes involved in caregiving within any family in the North or South will be multifaceted and complex. Becker and colleagues (Becker et al, 1998; Becker, 2005) have suggested an analytical framework for understanding the 'pushes and pulls' into caring, grounded in their own and others' research findings and emphasising individual, relational and structural dynamics. Factors such as the nature of the illness/condition, love and attachment, co-residence, family structure, gender, age, socialisation, low income, a lack of choice and alternatives, have all been shown in quantitative and qualitative studies in high-income countries to draw children into caregiving (Becker et al, 1998: 21-6; see also Becker, 2005; 2007). Researchers investigating young carers in Zimbabwe have also confirmed that these same factors partly explain why some children take on caring responsibilities in the South (Robson and Ansell, 2000: 187).

However, as yet, the research evidence does not allow a more sophisticated understanding of the relative strengths of these factors and how they combine and interact to draw some children into caregiving. Studies have not been able to analyse the influence of one variable over another. For example, in some families, gender plays a critical role in determining who will take on caring responsibilities and what tasks they do. A national survey in the UK of over 6,000 young carers (Dearden and Becker, 2004) shows that the involvement of girls is higher than that of boys in all aspects of care, and that this also increases with age, particularly for domestic and intimate or personal care. The amount of time spent caring and the perceived 'age appropriateness' of tasks also varies across the age groups. A consequence of this is that older girls (and older boys) are likely to have more significant caring responsibilities than younger children, who are perceived as less physically and intellectually competent to perform particular tasks and responsibilities (see also Becker and Becker, 2008).

Existing research suggests that the interactions between gender, age, co-residence and other relational aspects, and structural factors (such as poverty, a family's financial resources and the availability of external support systems), are especially important. In most families in the North and South, young people are drawn into caring because of a combination of these factors, as well as a lack of alternatives. Their caregiving is an outcome of the interplay between the demands for, and availability of, informal care within any family, community or society; a lack of available or affordable health and social care provision (particularly home-based care); and the lack of recognition and support available to meet the parenting, health and social needs of ill or disabled parents and other family members needing care.

In an Australian context, it has been argued that '[i]t is largely in the absence of other support that young people become carers of an adult with a disability' (Price, 1996: 26), while Dearden and Becker have suggested that in the UK '[t]he receipt, quality and timing of professional services and support, and the level and adequacy of family income, are critical' (2000: 46). In the African context, Robson et al (2006: 107) have argued that the existence of young carers may be seen in part as an outcome of reduced state healthcare provision and the promotion of policies advocating home care for people with HIV/AIDS. User fees and cost-sharing measures for healthcare and education, introduced as part of structural adjustment programmes (Mohan et al, 2000; Laird, 2005), reduce families' disposable income and access to basic services and as a result many parents and relatives requiring assistance are forced to rely on their children.

In the UK, Australian and African research there is often explicit reference to the fact that low income distinguishes most of the families where children are known to be caregivers. A major US study also confirms that children with caring responsibilities live in low-income households (National Alliance for Caregiving/United Hospital Fund, 2005: 15). Globally, these families lack the financial and other resources to be able to afford good-quality care alternatives, which could prevent children from having to undertake caregiving in the first place and which could reduce the amount of caring that they have to perform currently. In particular, higher disposable income could help to reduce or limit the quantity and intimacy of caregiving – the type of caring that can cause most unease or distress for children and for the person requiring assistance (Aldridge and Becker, 1994; Becker et al, 1998; Newman, 2002a; Wates, 2002; Aldridge and Becker, 2003). For many young people in the North and South, participation in informal care is therefore not a 'positive choice' but is rather a necessity that results from a lack of alternative support, and reinforced by familial, cultural and community values and intergenerational expectations. Taking on these levels and types of caregiving, including other household tasks, can move many children in the North and South along a continuum of children's caregiving, where they are subsequently involved in substantial, regular and significant care that distinguishes the extent, nature and outcomes of their caring from that of other children (see also Figure 1.1).

The relationship between disability, illness, caring and low income is also a recurring and dominant theme in research on young adult carers in the UK (Dearden and Becker, 2000; Becker and Becker, 2008). Dearden and Becker found that, '[v]irtually all the families were in receipt of welfare benefits and were outside the paid labour market. Experience of poverty and social exclusion were common' (2000: 32). The authors argued that increasing the school leaving age and reducing eligibility to social security benefits in the UK has extended the period of transition during which young adults are financially dependent on their parents. In their study, none of the parents with illness or disability was engaged in paid employment, and when they had partners few were working. In relation to ill or disabled people, an adequate income enables them to pay for appropriate care and support, reducing the need to rely on family members: 'However, illness, disability and poverty tend to go hand in hand and conversely those families most likely to require social care and support are those least able to afford it' (Dearden and Becker, 2000: 28). Furthermore, the authors suggest, '[y]oung people who have ill or disabled parents who require their support may be less available for work and more likely to have fewer and lower educational qualifications' (Dearden and Becker, 2000: 25).

Becker and Becker's (2008) research confirms these findings and highlights the centrality of poverty in understanding young adult carers' experiences and roles in the UK (and globally; see also Becker, 2007). In common with other research on adult 'carers' (Carers UK, 2007; Yeandle et al, 2007) many young adult carers aged 18-24 experience significant financial hardship as a direct consequence of caring. Professionals in contact with young adult carers in the UK reported that most young people had complained of financial difficulties, which restricted their ability to go out socially, take a holiday or buy personal items like clothing, or pay for alternative sources of caregiving. Four fifths of Becker and Becker's (2008) sample were living in families reliant on state benefits for their income – which was causing hardship for the *whole* family, and restricted carers' and the 'cared for' person's opportunities for inclusion and participation in everyday life.

Families often have additional costs (because of illness and caring) that also put a strain on already limited finances, such as expenditure on mobile phones (which are seen as a critical 'lifeline' for young people and their family, enabling them to be on constant call if required), and public transport to take the 'cared for' person to medical and other appointments and to go shopping. Despite the limited amount of money available from the UK social security 'safety net' (Silburn and Becker, 2009), many of the experiences and needs of disabled parents and young adult carers were linked closely with their material and financial circumstances. In Tanzania, where there is very limited state income maintenance provision, these problems are exacerbated as families face severe poverty, and in some cases destitution, unless young people are able to combine caring responsibilities with bringing in an income from casual agricultural labour or work in the informal sector. Indeed, as we highlight in Chapter 5, the need for many Tanzanian young people to replace or provide a family income to support the household is one of the main differences between young people with caring responsibilities in the UK and Tanzania.

In the UK context, research has shown that the receipt of appropriate services and support for parents has a significant influence on the level of young people's involvement in caregiving. Dearden and Becker (2000) found that about a third of their sample of parents being cared for by their children had received helpful and valued services, a third received nothing at all, a fifth had their homes adapted, and some had cancelled services that they viewed as intrusive, unnecessary, poor quality or too expensive. The authors concluded that where families received good-quality and reliable support and services, this reduced young people's caring roles:

> Services that are affordable, adaptable and acceptable can greatly improve the lives of all family members and reduce the caring responsibilities adopted by children and young people. These services should support disabled adults as parents as well as supporting their personal care needs. Perhaps the way forward is early assessment of the needs of whole families…. Family-focused assessment should acknowledge and recognise the needs and rights of all family members and should lead to the provision of services which meet these needs and promote these rights. (Dearden and Becker 2000: 32)

The Social Exclusion Unit's report highlights the fact that, in the UK at least, services are often age-related, provided either for adults *or* children and that: '...there are relatively few examples of public services that address the specific needs of 16-25 year olds in the round or can ensure effective transition from youth services to adult services' (2006: 8). There is evidence in the UK (Becker and Becker, 2008) that few carers in this age group take advantage of the services and groups offered by young or adult carers' services, suggesting that many young adult carers, at present, disengage from young carers services from around the age of 16 or 17, and are unsupported and do not relate to the 'adult' services that are available from voluntary sector carers centres (such as those offered by the Princess Royal Trust for Carers in the UK), or adult social care services provided, administered or commissioned through UK local authorities.

Conclusion

This chapter has revealed that young caregiving is a complex and contested issue globally. Our discussion has raised a number of salient issues and theoretical perspectives that we draw on throughout the book, in relation to the social construction of childhood and youth, the gendering of care, reciprocity and the ethic of care, outcomes of caring and children's and families' resilience, and explanations for children's and young people's involvement in care work within the family. Despite the growing literature on young people's caring responsibilities in the UK and some other countries in the global North, there is little research on the specific experiences of children caring for parents and relatives with HIV/AIDS, although research on young caring in Sub-Saharan Africa is gradually becoming a focus of attention. To situate the empirical findings from children and families affected by HIV/AIDS in Tanzania and the UK that we discuss in later chapters, the following chapter draws out important themes from the literature on HIV and the family in the global North and South.

Notes
[1] The terms 'global North' and 'global South' are used with an awareness of their problematic nature, as they are geographically imprecise and establish a simplistic binary opposition between rich and poor countries that does not adequately account for diversity within each region.

[2] The International Labour Organization's definition of 'economic activity' encompasses 'most productive activities undertaken by children,

whether for the market or not, paid or unpaid, for a few hours or full time, on a casual or regular basis, legal or illegal'. However, 'it excludes chores undertaken in the child's own household and schooling. To be counted as economically active, a child must have worked for at least one hour on any day during a seven-day reference period' (ILO, 2006: 6).

TWO

HIV and the family

The global HIV/AIDS epidemic

Since the first cases emerged in the early 1980s, HIV (human immunodeficiency virus) and AIDS (acquired immunodeficiency syndrome) have been recognised not only as a *health* issue, but as a social issue that can have profound effects on people's sense of self, emotional well-being, relationships with partners, family members and friends and their requirements for care and support. During the early years of the epidemic in the US, Western Europe and other high-income countries, HIV was associated with particular 'risk groups', notably gay men and intravenous drug users (Bor et al, 1993). Since the late 1990s, however, there has been a rapid increase in the number of new HIV diagnoses associated with heterosexual transmission in Western Europe, including in the UK, but a relatively stable number of new HIV infections each year in North America (UNAIDS/WHO, 2007). An estimated 2.1 million people were living with HIV in North America, Western and Central Europe in 2007 (UNAIDS/WHO, 2007).

Enormous gains have been made in the life expectancy of people living with HIV, since the introduction of highly active antiretroviral therapy (HAART) in high-income countries in the 1990s, resulting in a comparatively low number of AIDS-related deaths in these countries (UNAIDS/WHO, 2007). In the UK and other countries in Western Europe, African migrant populations are disproportionately affected by HIV (UK Collaborative Group for HIV and STI Surveillance, 2006). Medical advances, migration and increases in heterosexual transmission have to some extent changed the dynamics of the epidemic in countries such as the UK, with a growing number of children and young people affected by parental HIV. Despite medical advances, however, HIV and AIDS remain highly stigmatised conditions that reinforce inequalities based on race, gender, sexuality and class in many countries in the global North. HIV has been shown to lead to and exacerbate poverty, social exclusion and marginalisation, affecting children's and parents' access to and experiences of family or community support, health and social care, education, employment, housing, and immigration processes.

While HIV affects individuals from different cultures in different ways, Miller and Murray (1999:285) suggest that, based on their experiences as HIV counsellors in London, there are many similarities in the ways that HIV affects parents and children that 'transcend race, religion, culture and migration'.

As the scale of the HIV/AIDS epidemic in Sub-Saharan Africa became evident in the late 1980s and 1990s, AIDS was increasingly recognised as constituting a major threat to social and economic development. According to UNAIDS/WHO (2007), over two thirds (68%) of the global population of people with HIV live in Sub-Saharan Africa (22.5 million), where more than three quarters (76%) of all AIDS-related deaths globally occurred in 2007. Southern Africa is the most severely affected region – national adult HIV prevalence exceeded 15% in eight Southern African countries in 2005, with a Sub-Saharan average of 5% of all adults living with HIV in 2007 (UNAIDS/WHO, 2007). As a result of high mortality rates and a lack of access to HIV treatment and care, an estimated 20 million children globally will have lost at least one parent to AIDS by 2010, the majority of whom live in Sub-Saharan Africa (UNICEF, 2006). However, only 10% of orphans and children made vulnerable by HIV and AIDS who are in need of support are able to access any support (UNICEF, 2006). While the UNAIDS/WHO (2007) report suggests that adult HIV prevalence is either stable or has started to decline in most countries in Southern, East and West Africa, HIV and AIDS will continue to have major socioeconomic impacts on children and families as the epidemic matures. As Bicego et al (2003) note, because of the time period between infection of parents and subsequent death, countries with a mature epidemic, such as Uganda and Tanzania, will produce greater numbers of orphans than a newer epidemic in another country, even if the incidence of HIV is much higher in that country.

In many Sub-Saharan African countries, the loss of millions of skilled professionals in the healthcare and education sectors has had a devastating impact on already impoverished public sectors, constrained by structural adjustment programmes that restrict government spending on basic services. Only a minority of those living with HIV who are in need of care and support are able to access any care at all. In some countries, such as Uganda and Côte d'Ivoire, over half of all beds in many hospitals across the country are occupied by people with HIV-related illnesses (UNDP, 2005). High levels of absenteeism and deaths among healthcare professionals have placed further pressure on already weak formal healthcare services (Ogden et al, 2006). In the education sector, the epidemic has significantly increased absenteeism, as teachers become ill, are required to care for family members, or are transferred to other sectors to replace personnel lost to AIDS (Robson and Kanyanta, 2007a).

More women than men are living with HIV in Sub-Saharan Africa (61% of adults living with HIV), a trend unseen on other continents (UNAIDS/WHO, 2007). Globally, young women are 1.6 times more likely to be living with HIV than young men (UNAIDS et al, 2004). In some Southern African countries, young women (aged 15-24) are estimated to be up to three times more likely to be infected than young men of the same age (UNAIDS, 2006). Studies have linked young women's greater vulnerability to HIV to biological, economic, social and cultural factors (Baylies, 2000; Akeroyd, 2004; UNAIDS et al, 2004; Hargreaves and Boler, 2006). The UN Secretary-General's Task Force on Women, Girls and HIV/AIDS in Southern Africa identified key factors in young women's vulnerability as: 'the culture of silence surrounding sexuality; exploitative transactional and intergenerational sex; and violence against women within relationships' (UNAIDS et al, 2004: 2). In the context of poverty and inequalities in Sub-Saharan Africa, young women's low socioeconomic status means that they may seek or be coerced into transactional sexual relationships with older men who support them financially. However, their low social and economic status places them in a weak bargaining position to negotiate safer sex, particularly in the context of strong cultural taboos about the discussion of sexual matters between genders and generations. Young women's greater biological susceptibility (due to greater probability of male to female transmission than vice versa) and widespread gender related violence further increase their vulnerability to HIV.

Differential access to effective prevention of mother-to-child transmission in the global North and South means that the majority of children with HIV live in Sub-Saharan Africa (90% of the 2.1 million children (aged under 15) globally living with HIV) (UNAIDS/WHO, 2007). However, services to prevent vertical transmission of HIV have increased rapidly in recent years. According to the World Health Organization (WHO, 2008), 33% of pregnant women living with HIV in low- and middle-income countries received antiretroviral drugs to prevent transmission to their children in 2007 compared with just 10% in 2004. Similarly, more children living with HIV are able to access antiretroviral therapy (ART) than in previous years, although early diagnosis of HIV among young children remains a challenge in resource-limited settings (WHO, 2008).

Efforts to halt and begin to reverse the spread of HIV/AIDS and to achieve universal access to treatment for HIV/AIDS for all those who need it by 2010 constitute one of the eight major UN Millennium Development Goals (UN, 2008). Global health initiatives and funding streams such as the Global Fund to Fight AIDS, Tuberculosis and Malaria and the United States President's Emergency Programme for AIDS Relief (PEPFAR) among others are helping to build health infrastructure and provide access to affordable HIV treatment for people in the global South. Access to ART has the potential to transform the lives of millions of people with HIV in the global North and in the South, if treatment is significantly scaled up and barriers to accessing treatment are reduced. Almost 3 million people living with HIV in low- and middle-income countries were receiving ART by the end of 2007 (WHO, 2008). The largest increase in the numbers of people receiving treatment in 2007 was in Sub-Saharan Africa, where 30% of those requiring treatment received ART (WHO, 2008). Overall, however, only 31% of the global population of people living with HIV who require treatment are currently accessing ART (WHO, 2008). The WHO estimates that the annual gap between the required and available financial resources necessary to achieve universal access goals is US$ 8.1 billion and the 2007 level of resources needs to be quadrupled to meet targets for 2010 (WHO, 2008).

Within this global context, we examine the social dimensions of the HIV/AIDS epidemic and the multiple ways that these affect the lives of children and families. After a brief summary of the dynamics of the epidemic in our two case study countries, Tanzania and the UK, we discuss key themes emerging from the literature on the impacts of HIV and AIDS on children and families globally. Our focus is on the diverse ways that children and families are affected by HIV and AIDS at the household level; the embodied experiences of people living with HIV and AIDS and the particular dynamics of parenting in this context are explored in more detail in Chapter 4.

The dynamics of HIV/AIDS in Tanzania and the UK

Tanzania, along with its East African neighbours, was one of the first countries in Sub-Saharan Africa to be affected by the HIV/AIDS epidemic in the early 1980s. Initially, the epidemic was seen as largely a health issue and efforts to combat it involved only the health sector under the control of the National AIDS Control Programme (TACAIDS et al, 2005). However, HIV/AIDS has been declared a national disaster and, since 2000, a multisectoral strategy and national policy on AIDS have been developed, with considerably more government funds allocated to fight the epidemic (TACAIDS et al, 2005). Over 1 million adults (aged 15-59) were estimated to be living with HIV in 2005, with an overall prevalence rate of 7% among adults (TACAIDS et al, 2005; RAWG, 2005). The country average masks considerable diversity within the country, with the highest HIV prevalence in Mbeya (14%), Iringa (13%) and Dar es Salaam (11%) (the latter was one of our research locations) (TACAIDS et al, 2005). The other regions where our research was conducted have HIV prevalence rates of: 7% in Kilimanjaro, 5% in Arusha and 2% in Manyara (TACAIDS et al, 2005). According to WHO (2008), Tanzania is one of 27 countries where 31-50% of those who require treatment receive ART, with a rapid increase in the number of people receiving treatment in 2007 compared with 2006 (over 100% increase).

Overall, 11% of children aged under 18 are estimated to have lost one or both parents (TACAIDS et al, 2005). Following Mbeya (17%) and Iringa (16%), three of the regions where our study was conducted have among the highest rates of 'orphanhood' in Tanzania: 14% in Kilimanjaro; 13% in Dar es Salaam; 12% in Arusha region (TACAIDS et al, 2005). It should be noted, however, that these figures include children living with a surviving parent. Of particular relevance to our study is the fact that the research locations have some of the highest rates of 'paternal orphans' in the country: 8% of children in the Kilimanjaro region, 7% in Arusha and 4% in Dar es Salaam were living with their mother and their father had died (TACAIDS et al, 2005). As we discuss in Chapter 3, the majority of young people with caring responsibilities involved in the research in Tanzania had lost their father to AIDS and were living in lone-parent households with their mother with HIV. Over 1.1 million children were estimated to be 'most vulnerable' in 2007, that is, over 5% of the population of children under 18 years (MHSW, 2006). However, only 4%-6% of orphans and vulnerable children in Tanzania receive any external support (MHSW, 2006) and only 12%-16% of chronically ill adults receive external medical, emotional, material or practical support (TACAIDS et al, 2005).

While the HIV/AIDS epidemic in the UK does not match the scale of Tanzania's, HIV prevalence has increased rapidly since the late 1990s (Terence Higgins Trust, 2003). An estimated 63,500 people (aged 15-59) were living with HIV in 2005, two thirds of whom are diagnosed and accessing treatment and care (UK Collaborative Group for HIV and STI Surveillance, 2006). Since the 1990s, the UK and other countries in Western Europe have seen large increases in new diagnoses of HIV acquired in high prevalence regions such as Sub-Saharan Africa, the majority of which were heterosexually acquired (Sinka et al, 2003). Despite reductions in the late 1980s and early 1990s in HIV diagnoses among men who have sex with men, new diagnoses have increased dramatically in recent years (UK Collaborative Group for HIV and STI Surveillance, 2006).

The number of new diagnoses and prevalence of HIV in England remains highest in London (where the majority of families interviewed lived), although the North West of England, East of England, East Midlands and West Midlands (the latter was another area where some respondents lived) saw large increases in new HIV diagnoses between 1996 and 2005 (UK Collaborative Group for HIV and STI Surveillance, 2006). In Scotland, HIV infection has historically been associated with needle contamination among injecting drug users (SCIEH, 2000, cited in Tisdall et al, 2004). The annual number of new diagnoses among men who have sex with men has increased dramatically in Scotland since 2003 and the number of people diagnosed with heterosexually acquired HIV remains high (UK Collaborative Group for HIV and STI Surveillance, 2006).

The number of HIV-affected children (those living in families where one or more members is HIV infected) in the UK is unknown but has been estimated as between 15,000 to 20,000 (Conway, 2006a). Since the introduction of HAART and the resulting increased longevity and lower risk of vertical transmission, more people living with HIV are deciding to have children (Green and Smith, 2004). As Green and Smith (2004) note, motherhood is an important part of women's identity in most cultures. In the UK, effective treatment to prevent vertical transmission from pregnant women to their baby means that few children born to women with HIV are likely to be HIV-infected (UK Collaborative Group for HIV and STI Surveillance, 2006). Similarly, access to effective combination therapies and specialist paediatric HIV treatment in recent years has improved the health and life expectancy of young people living with HIV in the UK, resulting in a cohort of adolescents and young adults who have grown up with HIV (UK Collaborative Group for HIV and STI Surveillance, 2006). Doyal and Anderson's (2005) study in London found that African women living with HIV saw motherhood as an important source of legitimacy and identity and the failure to have children could have significant economic and social consequences. Studies have shown that the poverty, poor housing, immigration restrictions (such as dispersal policies) and racism that pregnant migrant women with HIV experience place their babies at higher risk of infection (McLeish, 2002; Green and Smith, 2004).

Orphanhood and care

While early studies of children affected by HIV were concentrated in the global North, since the 1990s an extensive literature has emerged that examines the impacts of the HIV/AIDS epidemic on children and families in Sub-Saharan Africa, largely in response to growing concern about the 'orphanhood' phenomenon (Bray, 2003; Meintjes and Giese, 2006). Several studies suggest that traditional patterns of care for orphans are changing in response to the epidemic in severely affected communities (Urassa et al, 1997; Nyambedha et al, 2003; Van Blerk and Ansell, 2007). While the extended family continues to be the main safety net and source of care and support for the majority of orphans, maternal relatives have become the main carers of orphaned children rather than paternal extended family members. This signifies a change in the familial obligations of paternal relatives in patrilineal societies, who were traditionally responsible for providing for children in the event of a parent's death (Urassa et al, 1997). As discussed in Chapter 1, reciprocal familial obligations and the 'intergenerational contract' (Van Blerk and Ansell, 2007) between family members in many countries in the global South means that elderly grandparents would normally expect to be cared for by their adult children in old age. However, due to the fact that AIDS disproportionately affects the most productive and reproductive age group of the population, grandparents find themselves in the role of caregiver, providing care for orphaned children. Indeed, Barnett (1998) suggests that the socioeconomic consequences of the epidemic impact most on the survivors of AIDS-affected households, that is, children and elderly people.

Many studies have recognised that the majority of orphaned children in Sub-Saharan Africa are being cared for by female relatives, particularly grandmothers, who are often already experiencing extreme poverty and may be unable to meet the material and emotional needs of orphaned children (Nyambedha et al, 2003; Van Blerk and Ansell, 2007). The inversion of the tradition of grandparents being cared for by younger members of the family puts a severe strain on the household economy as well as family relationships (Grainger et al, 2001; Evans, 2005). Research in Uganda found that children being cared for by grandparents were particularly vulnerable to malnutrition and infectious diseases, since food production was low and medical care was unaffordable (Barnett and Blaikie, 1992). However, orphaned children and young people often make considerable contributions to the household in terms of agricultural work and income-generation activities, performing household chores and caring for their elderly grandparents and siblings

(Evans, 2005; Robson et al, 2006; Van Blerk et al, 2008), despite the widespread portrayal of orphaned children in the literature as passive dependents of grandparent caregivers.

As discussed in Chapter 1, gendered constructions of care mean that women and girls are disproportionately affected by the epidemic and often bear the greatest 'opportunity costs' (Godwin, 1998: 3) of ill health and death because of gendered norms and expectations of their roles as carers and nurturers of family members who are ill or dying or as carers of orphaned children. Urassa et al's (1997) study in Tanzania found that women were heads of 37% of orphan households, compared with 15% of non-orphan households. Female-headed households are often poorer than male-headed households, especially in rural areas (NBS/ORC Macro, 2005). However, Bicego et al (2003) suggest that although 'double orphans' (who have lost both parents) do more commonly live in woman-headed households than non-orphans, there is considerable variation among African countries and that in Zimbabwe, for example, non-orphan households were nearly as likely as orphan households to be woman-headed.

Women's caring responsibilities mean that they may be forced to neglect subsistence crop production and income-generation activities, which can lead to food insecurity (Baylies, 2002; Donahue, 2005). Furthermore, following a husband's death, the widow and children are particularly vulnerable to the loss of household assets, property and inheritance rights as a result of 'property grabbing' by the husband's relatives (Donahue, 2005; Evans, 2005). Evans' (2005) research with families affected by HIV/AIDS in Tanzania suggested that while different generations of women were affected by the 'burden of care', children and mothers demonstrated resilience through developing survival strategies to mitigate the impacts of the epidemic, such as migration and seeking support from informal social networks, which were crucial to the survival of female- and child-headed households.

The migration of household members is often used as a coping strategy for the survival of the family, and orphaned children may engage in migration to receive care and support from relatives or to earn a livelihood (Young and Ansell, 2003; Evans, 2005). Urassa et al's (1997) study found that orphans and foster children were more mobile than other children; 30% of orphans and 32% of foster children had moved to another household during a two-year period compared with only 16% of other children. Studies have highlighted the fluidity of household structures in many African countries, as children, parents and relatives affected by HIV and AIDS migrate between rural and urban areas to access or provide care and support (Young and Ansell,

2003). Our research in Tanzania confirms the findings of Young and Ansell's (2003) and Robson et al's (2006) studies in Zimbabwe and Lesotho that some young people migrate to a sick relative's household or move with their sick mother to a close relative's household in order to provide care, sometimes for temporary periods during the final months of AIDS-related illness. Orphaned children may also move to live with relatives in households that are already affected by HIV and AIDS, thereby increasing the economic pressures and care burden on family members within these households.

While the care of orphans has received much less attention in the literature on children affected by HIV/AIDS in the global North, some studies have suggested that African parents affected by HIV may be less likely than other groups to plan for their eventual death or to make future care arrangements for their children. Thorne et al's (2000) study in Western Europe found that while half of the parents surveyed had made plans for their children's future care, European parents with HIV were almost twice as likely to have made long-term plans for their children's care than those whose country of origin was elsewhere (the majority of whom were from Africa). Parents who had known about their HIV status for several years were also more likely to have made long-term plans for their children's care. As the previous discussion has shown, the extended family plays a crucial role in providing care and support in Sub-Saharan Africa and relatives are expected to care for children in the event of parental death. However, many African migrant and refugee families are geographically separated or isolated from their extended families and thus are unable to rely on extended family support (Imrie and Coombes, 1995; Thorne et al, 2000). Imrie and Coombes (1995: 46) suggest that the lack of availability of extended family networks in the UK increases the likelihood of children's involvement in caring for a parent with HIV, placing the 'burden of care' on children and voluntary sector providers. Furthermore, cultural taboos about the discussion of death in many African communities, particularly for heavily stigmatised AIDS-related deaths that are often considered a 'bad' death, can make preparation for dying and planning for children's future care very difficult (Liddell et al, 2005; Wood et al, 2006).

Children's emotional well-being and bereavement

Many studies argue that parental chronic or life-limiting illness represents a significant psychological risk factor for children, with older children and girls identified as more vulnerable than young children and boys (Mok and Cooper, 1997; Bauman with Germann, 2005). Bauman with Germann (2005) suggest that children's worry about the health of ill parents can lead to anxiety, fear of abandonment and chronic insecurity. Many parents with HIV/AIDS experience depression, which in turn often affects children's psychosocial well-being (Bauman with Germann, 2005). Reyland et al (2002: 286) suggest that young people affected by parental HIV are likely to experience 'anxiety about the future, fears that other members of the family may also die of AIDS, concern that no one will be left to care for them, and fear that they may also die of AIDS themselves'. Bauman with Germann (2005) suggest that parental HIV illness and death are more likely to be associated with psychosocial problems in children when combined with other stress factors such as poverty, exposure to violence, or previous loss. Research in the US has shown that most children affected by maternal HIV/AIDS live in low-income households that are disproportionately affected by violence and many come from households in which one or both parents used intravenous drugs (Ciambrone, 2001; Bauman with Germann, 2005).

Ribbens McCarthy with Jessop (2005) suggest that very little research has explored young people's perceptions and understandings of bereavement and highlight the need for greater attention to be paid to the significance of wider social, historical and cultural contexts in which young people experience bereavement. For young people caring for a parent with a life-limiting illness, the emotional impact of providing care in the final stages of their parent's illness is likely to further complicate their responses to the loss of their parent and their bereavement experiences. Indeed, young people may engage in a process of 'anticipatory grief' before their parent's eventual death (Fulton and Gottesman, 1980). As we discuss in Chapter 8, some non-governmental organisations in Tanzania aimed to support young people with chronically ill parents to engage in memory work and 'anticipatory grief' processes. However, as more parents are able to access ART and people with HIV are able to live for longer in Sub-Saharan Africa, interventions appear to be shifting away from 'classical' memory work approaches focused on succession planning for children and grieving, towards assisting people with HIV and their children to live positively and celebrate life (Morgan, 2008). In particular, *Hero Books*, rather than the original *Memory Books*,[1] are seen as a way of addressing young people's psychosocial support needs and building resilience to cope with the present and the future (Morgan, 2008).

Very few studies have investigated childhood bereavement caused by parental AIDS death. Despite the scale of orphanhood associated with

AIDS globally, research on the psychological consequences of AIDS on children is very limited (Bauman with Germann, 2005; Cluver et al, 2007). The few studies of the psychological effects of HIV/AIDS and parental death on children in Sub-Saharan Africa suggest that children may be at increased risk of depression, post-traumatic stress, guilt and fear, and possible long-term mental health problems (Foster, 2006; Cluver et al, 2007). Cluver et al's (2007) study of a large sample of children from deprived urban areas in South Africa suggests that orphanhood by AIDS (but not orphanhood by non-AIDS causes) was associated with depression, post-traumatic stress, peer relationship problems and suicidal ideation. The authors note that these findings correspond with other studies of 'parentally bereaved children', which identified 'emotional and behavioural symptoms but little evidence of anxiety disorders' (Cluver et al, 2007: 760). The authors suggest that the causes of these psychological problems may be related to poverty, stigma or children's responsibilities for caring for a parent with AIDS.

Siegel and Gorey (1998) suggest that there are a number of factors that may complicate the grief process for those who lose a family member to AIDS, especially for children, including the likelihood that children may lose more than one family member to AIDS and the stigma of AIDS, which may make it difficult to talk about illness and death within and outside the family. As Wood et al (2006: 1925) note:

> With respect to parental AIDS-related loss in Africa, the cultural difficulty of preparing for death, manifested in the social unacceptability of writing wills – considered in many settings to risk bringing on misfortune in the form of premature death – means that children may be unprepared when bereavement occurs, despite the often long period of illness characterising AIDS.

Important factors which affect children's adjustment to parental loss from AIDS have been identified as: the quality of care and support children receive after the death; open family communication about the illness and death; external social support from the extended family and community, and the stability of their environment and relationship with new guardians (Siegel and Gorey, 1998: 265; Bauman with Germann, 2005).

The household economy and children's education in the global South

While much of the literature on the impacts of HIV/AIDS focuses on the care and support of the growing number of orphaned children across Africa, there has been increasing attention paid to the effects of HIV-related illness on the household economy and the socioeconomic well-being of children and other family members (Donahue, 2005; Hosegood et al, 2007). According to Donahue (2005), household surveys in Côte d'Ivoire, Tanzania and Thailand have shown that HIV/AIDS can reduce income by 40-60%. As the health of parents with HIV deteriorates, households struggle to pay for increased expenditure on healthcare, while simultaneously having to deal with reduced productivity and loss of income of parents and other relatives who are ill or involved in caregiving. Households experiencing extreme poverty in many countries rely on the informal safety net of the extended family and community and adopt a range of strategies to meet their survival needs. These include diversifying household, crop or income earning activities; reducing household consumption; withdrawing children from school (because of an inability to pay school expenses) to work in the fields, to engage in income-generation activities or to care for sick family members; borrowing money; and often, as a last resort, selling assets (Donahue, 2005; Kelly, 2005).

Some studies suggest that children whose parents are ill can be as vulnerable, if not more so, than orphaned children, because of the financial stress on households during parental illness (Kelly, 2005; MHSW, 2006). Indeed, the Tanzanian Action Plan for Most Vulnerable Children recognises that financial pressures may be greatest on households experiencing parental illness, which negatively affects children's schooling, nutrition and household responsibilities. The Plan suggests that the circumstances of children may improve following their parent's death if households are able to, 'with or without external support, stabilize and improve their economic situation' (MHSW, 2006: 78).

In households facing extreme financial pressure, children may never enrol in school or drop out of school because of the family's inability to meet schooling expenses (Kelly, 2005; Robson and Kanyanta, 2007b). While primary school fees have been abolished in Tanzania and other African countries as the result of the Heavily Indebted Poor Countries (HIPC) poverty alleviation initiative and international commitments to achieve Universal Primary Education, many parents still struggle to meet educational expenses for school uniforms, educational supplies (books, paper, pens), examination fees and parental contributions, for example for the maintenance of school buildings. Kelly (2005: 72) suggests that the cash costs associated with primary school attendance in many countries in the global South range from US$15-60 a year, which is beyond the reach of many parents surviving on less than US$1 a day. In addition to economic constraints, schooling is associated with significant opportunity costs of children's (especially girls') contributions to the household's reproductive and care work.

Even when families are able to meet schooling costs and children combine schooling with their domestic and caring responsibilities, HIV-related illness or death within the family are likely to affect children's school attendance and academic performance. Children may miss school because of their caring responsibilities for a sick family member, because of their own illness, or because of a death in the family or local community followed by a period of mourning (Kelly, 2005; Robson and Kanyanta, 2007b). Children's capacity to learn may also be impaired by poor nutrition, hunger, tiredness due to long hours of household labour or emotional distress caused by parental illness or death (Kelly, 2005; Robson and Kanyanta, 2007b). As Robson and Kanyanta (2007b: 427) conclude in their study of basic education for orphans and vulnerable children in Zambia, 'Many students carry responsibilities within the family that prevent them from attending school regularly and create stress and anxiety which impact on their capacity to learn effectively'. When these factors are combined with large class sizes and the poor quality of education available in many schools in Sub-Saharan Africa (Kelly, 2005; Robson and Kanyanta, 2007b), children's chances of achieving good educational outcomes are considerably constrained and few are able to meet the costs of secondary education or vocational training.

Poverty, social exclusion and immigration in the global North

While few studies specifically address the impacts of HIV on poverty and the socioeconomic position of the household in the global North, several studies acknowledge that HIV often has serious economic consequences on families, as the health of the main income earner deteriorates (Imrie and Coombes, 1995; Bor et al, 1993). As Bor et al (1993) observe, illness tends to place a financial burden on families because of the costs of care and treatment and disruption caused by a loss of productivity of family members relied upon as the principal income earner. Imrie and Coombes' (1995) UK study found that although 'many families cope very well with HIV infection and ...are not affected by additional social, economic or psychological problems' (Imrie and Coombes, 1995: 11), HIV-affected children were: more likely to live in sub-standard housing or be homeless and were more likely to be poor; were more likely to experience educational disadvantage, as many children's first language was not English; and they were more likely to be responsible for caring for sick parents and siblings. The authors highlighted the fact that immigrant families could be reluctant to engage with mainstream services and support, thereby increasing informal care work within the family:

> the burden of domestic care, particularly in recent immigrant communities, falls heavily on children and extended families. The greatest need is thus most likely to exist in the families that may be most reluctant, and least well equipped, to seek help. (Imrie and Coombes, 1995: 7)

Even when welfare support is available, as in the UK, it has been found to be often inadequate in meeting the special requirements of parents with HIV (such as special diets, extra household expenses, transport to hospital, additional childcare requirements etc) and the basic needs of families (Imrie and Coombes, 1995).

The lack of research on the experiences of Africans living with HIV in the UK has only recently started to be addressed (Green and Smith, 2004). However, recent studies have highlighted the impacts of poverty, immigration and asylum policies, racial and gendered inequalities and wider processes of social exclusion on African migrant families affected by HIV (Anderson and Doyal, 2004; Doyal and Anderson, 2005; Prost, 2005; Conway, 2006b). In their review, Green and Smith (2004) suggest that treatment issues are a lower priority for Africans living with HIV than practical concerns related to immigration, housing, employment and income. Studies have noted the intersection of issues of gender, race and immigration status, as well as HIV in shaping the experiences of African migrants (Anderson and Doyal, 2004; Doyal and Anderson, 2005; Doyal et al, 2005; Prost, 2005). Large surveys of Africans with HIV in London found that while many African migrants were well qualified, often with college or university education, only a minority (less than 20%) were in employment and thus had very limited economic resources available to them (Green and Smith, 2004). Research has also shown that many African women '[are] raising their children in considerable poverty without the support of an extended family and often as single parents' (Doyal and Anderson, 2005: 1731).

Indeed, Imrie and Coombes (1995) suggest that a significant proportion of families affected by HIV in the UK are headed by lone parents, most often mothers.

Pressures linked to insecure immigration status exacerbate the social exclusion faced by migrant families affected by HIV in the global North. Asylum seekers and refugees who have been forced to leave their country of origin are particularly vulnerable to poverty and destitution and often have differential access to health, social care and welfare benefits compared with those with full citizenship rights. Increasingly punitive asylum and immigration policies introduced by the UK and other European governments in recent years (Bloch and Schuster, 2005) mean that refugees and asylum seekers with HIV may experience a range of difficulties accessing healthcare. New regulations introduced in the UK in 2003 mean that individuals who do not apply for asylum 'as soon as is practicably possible' are vulnerable to destitution, which could have particularly negative impacts for people living with HIV (Green and Smith, 2004). Asylum seekers sent to detention centres while their claims are processed may be prevented from adhering to ART treatment regimes because of a lack of coordination of meal times and drug administration (Green and Smith, 2004). Furthermore, Green and Smith (2004: 13) note that the Home Office policy of dispersal (introduced in 2000) from London and the South East to parts of the UK which may have 'low prevalence of HIV, little experience of managing HIV infection, a lack of infrastructure and no appropriate community-based support services' creates further barriers to receiving appropriate healthcare for asylum seekers with HIV, particularly for HIV-positive pregnant women (Terence Higgins Trust, 2001; National Aids Trust, 2006).

New charging arrangements for overseas visitors seeking National Health Service treatment in the UK came into force in 2004. These restrict access to ART for 'failed asylum seekers' who have exhausted all rights of appeal and to undocumented migrants and visa overstayers (Conway, 2006b). Migrant parents whose asylum claims are rejected or who have overstayed their visas may face potential charges for ART and other healthcare, withdrawal of housing and National Asylum Support Service (NASS) welfare support, detention and disruptions to ART regimes, their children may be taken into care of the local authority and the family may be deported (Conway, 2006b). For African migrant women, fear of deportation is linked to the potential loss of access to life-prolonging HIV treatment that is unlikely to be available in their country of origin. As Doyal and Anderson (2005: 1729) note, this results in a paradoxical situation in which 'women have access to treatment that would be unavailable in their own countries but their survival depends on them remaining in a country few regard as "home"'. Studies have also noted significant fear among asylum seekers that disclosure of their HIV status would be detrimental to their asylum application, leading to difficulties for NASS and medical professionals in providing appropriate support (Terence Higgins Trust, 2001; Conway, 2006b).

Secrets and disclosure within families

A major theme in studies of people living with HIV in the global North concerns disclosure of an HIV diagnosis and communication within the family. Reluctance to tell partners and adult family members may be related to fear of stigma, rejection, abandonment and the potential loss of relationships, as well as a desire to protect family members from the emotional effects of living with HIV (Bor et al, 1993; Imrie and Coombes, 1995). However, as Leask et al (1997: 60) note, not telling close family or friends about one's HIV status may 'decrease opportunities for social support, which in turn buffers the anxiety and stress associated with ill-health'. Indeed, many studies suggest that social support helps to reduce stress and other emotional impacts of living with HIV and other chronic and life-threatening illnesses (Lie and Biswalo, 1998). Furthermore, disclosure of HIV status may be associated with positive benefits, in terms of closer relationships with family and friends and greater access to informal care and social support (Leask et al, 1997; Bor et al, 1993).

However, many people living with HIV and their relatives may not discover their HIV status until a late stage in the illness, reducing their access to potential sources of support. According to the UK Collaborative Group for HIV and STI Surveillance (2006), a third of people estimated to be living with HIV in the UK in 2006 were unaware of their status, resulting in late diagnosis and low uptake of social support interventions, particularly among Africans (Sinka et al, 2003). In Sub-Saharan Africa, the majority of people living with HIV are unaware of their status and hence are not diagnosed until a late stage of the disease (Lie and Biswalo, 1998). However, Lie and Biswalo's study of an HIV/AIDS counselling programme in northern Tanzania found that when the patients surveyed did discover their status, the majority identified a close family member (most frequently cited were brothers, sisters and mothers) of the same gender as themselves, as the person they trusted to support them in the process of coping with HIV, rather than their sexual partner or spouse. Traditional taboos about talking about sexual matters between members of the opposite sex, even within marriage, were shown to inhibit communication about HIV between heterosexual couples. The 'significant other' identified by most patients was also of the same generation as themselves, reflecting cultural norms about the 'near prohibition' of discussion of sexuality with elders (Lie and Biswalo, 1998).

Most studies about disclosure of HIV within families have been conducted in the US and suggest that the sharing of HIV status with their children can cause high levels of stress for parents (Imrie and Coombes, 1995; Lee and Rotheram-Borus, 2002). Thorne et al's (2000) study in seven countries in Western Europe found that disclosure of both the child's and the parent's HIV status to children was rare and usually associated with the child's age. Chinouya's (2006) qualitative study of disclosure among 60 African migrant parents with HIV whose children were also living with HIV in England found that only one third of children and young adults had been informed of their parent's diagnosis. As in studies undertaken by Thorne et al (2000) and Lee and Rotheram-Borus (2002) age was a key factor in parents' decisions about telling their children about HIV. Parents' perceptions about their children's potential reactions to the news and the benefit of the information to the life of their children, including making plans for the future and ensuring children were aware of their inheritance rights in their country of origin, were also important factors influencing parents' decisions (Chinouya, 2006).

Within the context of Sub-Saharan Africa, few studies have investigated communication about HIV/AIDS between children and parents. As noted earlier, African cultural taboos about the discussion of sexuality and death between generations inhibit communication about HIV within families (Liddell et al, 2005; Wood et al, 2006). A study of orphaned teenagers in Zimbabwe, however, confirms the findings of Lewis' (2001) study in the UK that 'many children, who are not directly told, have partial knowledge (or at least strong suspicions) about the nature of their parent's illness' (Wood et al, 2006: 1930). Wood et al's (2006) study suggests that parental disclosure within households, including to older teenagers, was rare, despite young people's own knowledge and awareness about AIDS-related symptoms. As our research also found, 'where young people suspected the nature of their parent's illness, but were not told openly, this caused them pain' (Wood et al, 2006: 1929) and frustration (see Chapter 4).

Stigma and discrimination

Issues of disclosure and decisions about 'who to tell' are closely related to fear of HIV-related stigma and discrimination. A growing number of studies have highlighted the different dimensions of HIV/AIDS-related stigma and the discrimination that people living with HIV and their families may experience. These studies suggest that there are many similarities in the key causes, the forms that HIV/AIDS-related stigma takes and the consequences of stigma across a wide range of sociocultural contexts (Ogden and Nyblade, 2005).

Goffman's (1963) classic work identified three types of stigma: 'abominations of the body' or stigma related to disfiguring physical transformations and ultimately death; 'blemishes of character' or stigma that is related to immoral or foolish behaviour; 'tribal stigma' or stigma that is related to race, religion or membership of a despised social group (Cree et al, 2004; Ogden and Nyblade, 2005). All members of the family may be affected by 'tribal stigma' through their association and kinship with the 'discredited' or stigmatised person; this is also referred to as 'stigma by association', 'secondary' or 'courtesy stigma' (Aldridge and Becker, 2003; Ogden and Nyblade, 2005). Research suggests that HIV and AIDS are especially stigmatising, since HIV reflects all three types of stigma identified by Goffman (Cree et al, 2004; Ogden and Nyblade, 2005). Goffman (1963: 100) also highlighted the ways that people try to conceal their 'differentness' and 'pass' as 'normals', as well as the issue of self-stigma, when those who are 'discredited' internalise dominant social values and attitudes. As Cree et al (2004: 4) point out, this leads to self-hatred and shame which can 'spoil' people's social identity and interactions with others.

Commentators have argued that rather than being understood purely in terms of individual experiences of a 'discredited identity', stigmatisation and discrimination are social processes that are based on and reproduce social inequalities and difference (Parker and Aggleton with Attawell et al, 2002). Ogden and Nyblade (2005) identify four main forms of stigma from research in Vietnam, Ethiopia, Tanzania and Zambia: *physical*, including isolation, separation and violence; *social*, such as exclusion from family and community events, loss of social networks and loss of identity/role; *verbal*, such as gossip, taunting, expressions of blame and shame; and *institutional*, including loss of livelihood, housing, differential treatment in school, healthcare settings or public spaces, and in media and public health messages. They suggest that HIV-related stigma often reinforces unequal gender relations, as women tend to be both more heavily stigmatised than men because of the association of

HIV with judgements about sexual morality, as well as blamed more often for 'bringing' HIV into a family or marriage (Ogden and Nyblade, 2005). In the context of limited formal safety nets and the reliance on family members to provide care and support to people living with HIV in many countries in the global South, HIV-related stigma can result in the refusal of family members to provide care, which may mean that children are more likely to be drawn into caring roles.

In the UK, recent changes to disability discrimination legislation (introduced by the 2005 Disability Discrimination Act) mean that people with HIV (and those with cancer or MS) are now protected against unfair treatment in the workplace, education, housing or in accessing services, *from the point of diagnosis*, rather than (as previously) from the moment their condition leads to an impairment that has some effect on ability to carry out normal day-to-day activities (Disability Rights Commission, 2005). Significantly, these changes recognise that stigma is often associated with the diagnosis and disclosure of these conditions to others. However, despite medical advances and anti-discrimination policies, research suggests that HIV-related stigma and discrimination continues to have significant impacts on the lives of people living with HIV and their families in the UK and other European countries (Terence Higgins Trust, 2001; Anderson and Doyal, 2004; Prost, 2005).

Doyal and Anderson's (2005) study of African women with HIV in London found that fear of stigma was pervasive and a third of the women reported direct experiences of discrimination as a result of disclosure of their status. These included rejection by husbands or partners, eviction from their home, marking or special washing of kitchen utensils and refusal to allow contact with children, all of which had profound impacts on the women's mental health (Doyal and Anderson, 2005). Cree et al's (2004) study found that stigma was a common experience for white Scottish children affected by parental HIV and was articulated by young people predominantly through feelings of 'differentness' from their peers. Young people adopted a range of strategies for managing stigma, such as 'passing' as 'normal', which was seen as necessary at school; selective disclosure to trusted individuals; and being open about parental HIV, often following opportunities for peer support and collective action with other young people in similar situations.

Caring relationships in households affected by HIV/ AIDS

Most early studies of caregiving for people with HIV/AIDS were conducted in the US and focused on caregivers of gay men and intravenous drug users, as these were the main groups affected by HIV (see, for example, Wrubel and Folkman, 1997). Pakenham et al (1998) suggest that there is a high degree of correlation between patients' and carers' level of adjustment to HIV and that carers engage in a difficult process of adjustment, as they come to terms with the fact that their loved one has a stigmatised life-threatening illness and they are required to provide emotional support. The study by Brown and Stetz of caregivers of people with AIDS or cancer suggested four phases to family caregiving for people with life-threatening illnesses: 'becoming a caregiver', 'taking care', 'midwifing the death' and 'taking the next step' (1999: 182). The authors highlight the importance of the existing relationship between the caregiver and care recipient in the decision to become a caregiver and their commitment to care (Brown and Stetz, 1999). The authors note that the 'taking care' phase is characterised by providing physical care and managing the illness, such as monitoring illness progression and the amount of food the ill person was eating, as well as the emotional work involved in caring for a very ill or dying person, which can cause 'stress, exhaustion, loss and anticipatory grief' for caregivers (Brown and Stetz, 1999: 190). Few studies have investigated the role of carers of people with HIV in the contemporary context of ART in the global North.

A growing body of research has investigated the experiences of relatives and neighbours who care for people with HIV/AIDS in Sub-Saharan Africa. As discussed earlier, research from many countries in Sub-Saharan Africa has highlighted the gendered nature of caring responsibilities and revealed that caregivers are predominantly female relatives of the person with HIV (Seeley et al, 1993; Ndaba-Mbata and Seloilwe, 2000; Chimwaza and Watkins, 2004; Thomas, 2006; Opiyo et al, 2008). Several studies suggest that there is considerable fluidity of household structures and movement between rural and urban areas for the purpose of receiving or providing care, particularly in Southern Africa where there is a long history of labour migration (Ansell and Van Blerk, 2004; Chimwaza and Watkins, 2004; IOM, 2005). Many women with HIV, particularly widows, return from a city or other district to their own relatives in rural areas, often to be cared for by their mothers, who may have limited financial and labour resources (Chimwaza and Watkins, 2004; IOM, 2005; Thomas, 2006).

Carers in Sub-Saharan Africa report providing both physical and emotional support to people living with HIV. Levels of poverty, lack of running water and electricity in many AIDS-affected households mean that care tasks are time-consuming and place considerable physical strain on carers (Chimwaza and Watkins, 2004). Tasks include preparing food and traditional medicines for the ill person, assisting them to eat and take medicine, heating water and bathing them, cleaning sores, massaging or exercising their limbs, carrying those who are immobile to the pit latrine or to sit outside, washing soiled sheets and clothes (Chimwaza and Watkins, 2004; Thomas, 2006). In addition to performing substantial domestic and personal care tasks, carers in Malawi also reported providing emotional and moral support and 'being available' to sick relatives, as they were considered too ill to be left alone (Chimwaza and Watkins, 2004).

Chimwaza and Watkins' (2004) study in rural Malawi found that carers received practical assistance with their care work from other female relatives living in the same house or living nearby (such as preparing food, helping with bathing the ill person or sitting with them to enable the carer to go out), while male relatives and husbands of the carers sometimes provided financial support, such as money for transport to hospital, for buying food or medicines. Furthermore, most carers did not consider caregiving a problem, primarily because the 'patients' were close relatives. A study by Thomas (2006) in Namibia revealed, however, that while informal support from other household members and people outside the household was available in the early stages of illness, if the ill person did not recover, help was less forthcoming and the main carer became increasingly isolated. This was often linked to stigma and relatives' suspicions about the nature of the person's illness. Indeed, the material and emotional resources of extended families are being overstretched in many severely affected communities across Africa. As Seely et al (1993: 122) comment, 'blanket statements about the role of the extended family in Africa as a safety net need to be questioned and assumptions that the extended family will be ready and able to assist sick members, treated with caution'. They suggest that the extended family should rather be seen as a 'safety net with holes'.

Donahue (2005) suggests that the most severe financial pressures on caregiving households occur when the family member with AIDS becomes 'bedridden', since caregivers are likely to have used all their economic resources, particularly if the relative is in hospital. Caregivers are unable to work because of their full-time caring responsibilities and households often sell their remaining assets to pay for medical bills and other daily expenses (Donahue, 2005). A Tanzanian survey found that 29% of household labour was spent on AIDS-related care work in households where one person was ill with AIDS (Kelly, 2005). Furthermore, when two family members were devoted to nursing care, the average household loss from agricultural activities was 43% (Kelly, 2005). However, Chimwaza and Watkins (2004: 796) suggest that studies in Uganda and Zimbabwe found that the loss of income for caregivers in households affected by AIDS was modest 'since only a fraction of those at home receive remittances from relatives working elsewhere and when they do, the amount is usually small'.

As noted in Chapter 1, few studies have investigated the experiences of children and young people in caring for parents and relatives with HIV and the focus of much of the literature on the socioeconomic impacts of the HIV/AIDS epidemic in Africa has centred on children living with HIV and those who have been orphaned by AIDS, rather than those affected by their parents' and relatives' chronic, life-limiting illness. However, an emerging body of research has started to explore the caring responsibilities of children and young people in families affected by HIV/AIDS in Southern and East Africa (Robson, 2000; Robson and Ansell, 2000; Robson, 2004; Bauman et al, 2006; Robson et al, 2006; Evans and Becker, 2007; Cluver and Operario, 2008). Other studies, while not explicitly focused on young people's caring responsibilities, have demonstrated that children and young people, particularly girls and young women, are involved in caring for sick and elderly relatives in Africa (Steinberg et al, 2002; Young and Ansell, 2003; Chimwaza and Watkins, 2004; Evans, 2005). A survey of 771 AIDS-affected households in South Africa, for example, found that children under the age of 18, the majority of whom were girls, were responsible for caring for a family member with AIDS-related illness in approximately 8% of households (Steinberg et al, 2002). Evans' (2005) qualitative research in Tanzania revealed that while children, particularly girls, may express resilience by caring for parents with HIV/AIDS and for surviving members of AIDS-affected households, such as elderly grandparents and younger siblings, they remain vulnerable to chronic poverty and social exclusion that stem from structural inequalities and hegemonic gender norms.

Robson's (2000; 2004) qualitative research with young people (aged 15-17) caring for ill family members in Zimbabwe suggested that the 'push and pull' factors for young caregiving identified in the young carers literature in the UK (Becker et al, 1998) were relevant in a Southern context (see also Chapters 1 and 9). Robson (2000; 2004) notes that children are often the 'invisible carers' of people with HIV/AIDS in home-based healthcare in Sub-Saharan Africa and their involvement in care work is growing partly as a result of processes of global economic restructuring and the HIV/AIDS epidemic. Robson et al (2006) highlight the range of caring tasks that young people engage in and the positive and negative impacts of their care work on their physical and emotional well-being, education and income from three studies in Lesotho, Tanzania and Zimbabwe. The authors conclude that:

> more research is needed to attempt to place the caregiving of young people into the broader context of families/households and how they deal with the problems posed by HIV/AIDS. Such research would necessarily involve data collection from other family members, as well as young carers themselves. (Robson et al, 2006: 107)

In the UK context, we are not aware of any previous studies that focused specifically on the experiences of children caring for parents with HIV. However, studies with children affected by parental HIV have revealed that some children take on additional caring responsibilities when their parents are ill (Imrie and Coombes, 1995; Chinouya-Mudari and O'Brien, 1999; Lewis, 2001; Tisdall et al, 2004). Tisdall et al's study in Scotland, for example, found that while most young people said that they did no more for their parents than their friends did, the responsibilities of a few young people increased significantly during periods of parental illness. Their responsibilities included 'housework and cooking, helping the parent with bathing, helping the parent in and out of bed, cleaning the bed, and caring for younger siblings' (Tisdall et al, 2004: 1104). The authors note that there was very little evidence that children resented their caring responsibilities and all of the children had contact with extended family and most received considerable support from them.

In contrast, Chinouya-Mudari and O'Brien's (1999: 27) research with African refugee children affected by HIV suggested that many families had limited family networks and support in the UK, with the result that children were increasingly involved in care work within the home. The study found that children had a range of caring responsibilities and children experienced a number of negative impacts of their caring responsibilities including: reduced time for play and peer interaction, irregular school attendance and the emotional effects of exclusion and isolation, separation from close family members and multiple family losses. Chinouya-Mudari and O'Brien highlight the contested nature of children's caring roles and suggest that African children may find it particularly difficult to express their feelings or seek external support because of cultural norms about sharing information about family circumstances with 'strangers', such as professionals and others outside the family, which may be exacerbated by traumatic life experiences. Furthermore, Lewis' (2001) study with children and parents affected by HIV in London, the majority of whom were of Black African ethnicity, suggested that the lack of social care support was a key factor in whether young people became involved in caring roles within the family.

Bauman et al's (2006; 2009) study of children caring for ill parents with HIV/AIDS in New York (US) and Mutare (Zimbabwe) represents the only previous comparative study that we are aware of that investigates the experiences of children caring for parents with HIV in the global North and South. The survey of 50 mothers with HIV and one of their children (aged 8–16) in each country found that 'the amount of care children provide is directly related to need as defined by the extent of the parent's illness and disability and does not appear to be related to the child's age or gender or the presence of other adults or older siblings' (Bauman et al, 2006: 12), which contrasts with the findings of Becker et al (1998) and Robson (2000; 2004). Bauman et al found that children in Mutare had more substantial caring duties than children in New York, were more likely to experience 'interference with normal activities' such as schooling and spending time with friends, and almost two thirds of Mutare children had depression scores in the clinically significant range (Bauman et al, 2006: 12). The research concludes that young caregiving in itself is not necessarily harmful to children and the parent–child relationship is the most important predictor of child mental health, recognising that 'children may in fact benefit from helping to make a parent feel better, and their importance to the family may be a source of pride' (Bauman et al, 2006: 13).

Policy responses to the global HIV/AIDS epidemic

As we have discussed, the HIV/AIDS epidemic affects children's lives in many diverse ways. Since 2000, UNICEF, UNAIDS and other international and national policy and advocacy agencies have moved away from referring only to 'AIDS orphans' or 'children orphaned by AIDS' and instead recognised the multiple ways that children are affected by the HIV/AIDS epidemic with the use of the term 'Orphans and Vulnerable Children' (OVC) (Meintjes and Giese, 2006). The category 'OVC' denotes a wider group of children who may be directly and indirectly affected by the socioeconomic impacts of the epidemic. However, Meintjes and Giese (2006: 410) argue that although the term OVC has been widely accepted by international development agencies, government and non-governmental organisations, responses to the epidemic remain 'orphan-centred'. The authors argue that the conflation of children who have lost one parent to AIDS, but have a surviving parent ('maternal' or 'paternal' orphans), with those who have lost both parents ('double orphans') is based on a deficit model that obscures the presence of a parent in a child's life. As we discuss in later chapters, loving, supportive relationships between children and their surviving parent (often their mother) represent a crucial protective factor for children affected by HIV/AIDS, as well as a motivation for the survival of mothers with HIV (see Chapters 4, 6 and 9).

Richter and Rama (2006) critique the term OVC for focusing attention on the child as 'the cause of vulnerability' and the 'site for intervention', rather than recognising that the vulnerability and resilience of children are dependent on the social and material conditions in which they live. The authors argue that 'interventions to support children are often best directed at caregivers, families, communities and services' rather than just targeted towards children (Richter and Rama, 2006: 37). They suggest that the term 'children living in communities affected by HIV/AIDS' best encompasses the many different categories of children affected by HIV/AIDS, including children living with HIV-positive parents and sick adults, who may be affected by 'loss of income, compromised parenting, childcare practices associated with maternal HIV infection and the physical and psychological burden on children living with and caring for sick and dying parents' (Richter and Rama, 2006: 18).

A growing number of studies have highlighted the resilience of the family and community in adapting to the HIV/AIDS epidemic in Africa and have called for community-based support and interventions that build on people's coping mechanisms and strengths at the household and community levels (Donahue, 2005; Phiri and Tolfree, 2005; Richter and Rama, 2006). Campbell et al (2008) note that the language of 'community mobilisation' and 'partnerships' has become a dominant feature of international HIV/AIDS discourse and several authors highlight the importance of strengthening local community networks to support carers and challenge stigma (Robson, 2000; Thomas, 2006; Campbell et al, 2008). The UNAIDS et al (2004) Framework for the Protection, Care and Support of Orphans and Vulnerable Children Living in a World with HIV and AIDS emphasises the importance of strengthening the capacity of families to protect and care for orphans and vulnerable children and supporting community-based responses. The five key strategies of the framework are to:

1 Strengthen the capacity of families to protect and care for orphans and vulnerable children by prolonging the lives of parents and providing economic, psychosocial, and other support.

2 Mobilize and support community-based responses to provide both immediate and long-term support to vulnerable households.

3 Ensure access for orphans and vulnerable children to essential services, including education, healthcare, birth registration, and others.

4 Ensure that governments protect the most vulnerable children through improved policy and legislation and by channeling resources to communities.

5 Raise awareness at all levels through advocacy and social mobilization to create a supportive environment for children affected by HIV/AIDS. (UNAIDS et al, 2004: 24-5)

While the framework has generally been welcomed, Baylies (2002) argues that there is a danger that the emphasis of government and external agencies on 'coping' and increasing the 'capacity' of households is used to justify the presumption that care of the sick is a 'private misfortune' and individual household responsibility. Those most afflicted by the epidemic may be placed under pressure to 'maintain the semblance of household integrity' while struggling to survive and sustain family members (Baylies, 2002: 618). Indeed, Ogden et al (2006: 333) argue that care provides 'fundamental public goods' and international development and national government strategies of 'downloading' the responsibility for care of people with HIV/AIDS onto women, families and communities, 'can no longer be a viable, appropriate or sustainable response'. As Seeley et al (1993), Baylies (2002) and others have noted, the informal safety nets of the family and community are 'fragile' and 'unreliable', as even when they are available, they can 'systematically discriminate among potential beneficiaries', reflecting existing power relations and unequal entitlements within communities (Baylies, 2002: 622). Baylies (2002) advocates a 'multi-pronged approach' that adopts both universal as well as targeted approaches to entitlements to ensure those made vulnerable by unequal power relations and those without support or livelihood security are given particular attention.

Commentators have highlighted the crucial need to expand home care services to meet the growing requirements for care of people living with HIV/AIDS in Africa (Nsutebu et al, 2001). Nsutebu et al (2001) suggest that the limited involvement of government in home-based care has resulted in a low level of coverage of home-based care services in Zambia and other African countries. While Ogden et al (2006) welcome the WHO's (2000) 'care continuum' (which includes 'home care' and 'community care') in helping to develop an international care agenda, they suggest that the focus remains largely on formal health sector interventions, does not take adequate account of factors affecting access to services such as poverty and unequal gender relations, and obscures the needs of individuals and families affected by HIV and AIDS. WHO (2000: 6) defines Community Home-Based Care (CHBC) as 'any form of care given to ill people in their homes. Such care includes physical, psychosocial, palliative and spiritual activities.' Ogden et al (2006: 338) suggest that while the WHO (2000) framework for Community Home-Based Care in Resource-Limited Settings recognises the family as a key partner, 'the carer as beneficiary remains largely implicit'. They argue for greater recognition of the specific needs of unpaid carers of people living with HIV within international development policy and CHBC interventions. As we show in the following chapters, the narratives of young people and parents reveal the need for greater recognition of young people's active roles in caring for parents and relatives with HIV within wider policy debates and interventions aiming to address the support needs both of carers of people with HIV and of children living in communities affected by HIV/AIDS.

Conclusion

This chapter has revealed the many diverse ways that the global HIV/AIDS epidemic shapes the lives of children and families in the North and South. Key dimensions include the socioeconomic and emotional impacts for children and parents of living with a chronic life-limiting illness and adapting to the loss of parents and relatives, managing secrets and disclosure of HIV status within the family, experiences of stigma and discrimination, the nature and effects of women's and children's caring responsibilities and relationships within households and communities and the framing of policy responses to the global epidemic. The research evidence from previous studies suggests that HIV intersects in complex ways with social inequalities and differences of gender, age, race, sexuality, disability and religion that often result in the marginalisation and social exclusion of those living in communities affected by HIV/AIDS. Our research seeks to provide greater insight into the ways these processes affect the experiences, needs and resilience of children and parents in the context of the global North and South.

Before discussing our findings in relation to the themes we have highlighted, the following chapter outlines the scope of our study and reflects on the research process.

Notes

[1] The Memory Book is the central tool used in memory work with parents with HIV and their children which was first developed by the National Community of Women living with HIV/AIDS in Uganda (Healthlink Worldwide, 2006).

THREE

Reflexivity, methodology and ethics: the research process

This book draws on qualitative research conducted for a comparative study[1] that aimed to explore the similarities and differences in the experiences, needs and resilience of children and young people who cared for parents/relatives with HIV/AIDS in Tanzania and the UK. The key objectives of the study were to, firstly, compare and contrast the structural and relational factors which influence whether and why children become carers in Tanzania and the UK; second, to develop an understanding of the experiences, needs and resilience of children caring for parents/relatives with HIV/AIDS in Tanzania and the UK; and third, to begin to identify the policy and practice implications of young carers' experiences, resilience and needs for health, social care, education, voluntary and community sectors in Tanzania and the UK. This chapter provides a reflexive account of the research process. It discusses the research methodology and reflects on the stance of the authors and their approach to the research topic. The chapter describes the process of gaining access to families and negotiating informed consent to participate in the study as well as researcher/ researched relations. The chapter then highlights some of the ethical issues raised by cross-cultural research and interviewing respondents about sensitive topics, including the importance of confidentiality and anonymity and the need to manage respondents' expectations. Finally, the chapter describes the main characteristics of interviewees and the locations for the research, as well as the approach to data analysis and dissemination.

Research with children and the 'new social studies of childhood'

The empirical study of children in Europe and North America over the last 150 years has largely been regarded as the domain of psychology, which positioned children as passive objects of study to be 'scrutinized, tested and measured' (Alldred, 1998: 150). As Quortrup comments, this constructs children as more like 'human becomings' than human beings (Quortrup, 1987, cited in Alldred, 1998: 150) and denies children's agency. In contrast, the 'new social studies of childhood', which developed from the 1970s onwards, acknowledges that children are not just passive recipients of social structures and processes (James and Prout, 1997), but rather are social actors who actively shape their environments and social worlds. Childhood researchers recognise that children occupy a subordinate and marginal position in relation to adults, in terms of discourses of childhood, power relations, organisational structures and social inequalities, and therefore researchers, both ethically and practically, have a responsibility to take this into account during the research process (Christensen and James, 2000: 6). Alderson proposes that a key question in research about children is: 'how can adults get beyond the power constraints and expose the intricacies of power in relations between adults and children?' (Alderson, 2000: 254). Christensen and James conclude:

> Only through listening and hearing what children say and paying attention to the ways in which they communicate with us will progress be made towards conducting research with, rather than simply on, children. (Christensen and James, 2000: 7)

Proponents of the new social studies of childhood have suggested that ethnography and participatory research methodologies may be particularly suitable to gain insight into children's lifeworlds, but also acknowledge that an adult/child distinction should not be taken for granted (Christensen and James, 2000). As in all research, it is recognised that the particular methods chosen for a piece of research should be appropriate for the people involved in the study, its social and cultural context and the kinds of research questions posed (Christensen and James, 2000).

A child- and youth-focused methodology, which paid attention to differentials of age, gender, race and ethnicity, was therefore considered most appropriate for our study into the experiences, needs and resilience of children caring for parents with HIV/AIDS in Tanzania and the UK. Informed by the perspective of the 'new social studies of childhood', the methodology both acknowledges children's agency in the construction of their social lives and the social constraints and possibilities that influence these (James and Prout, 1997). Children and young people are thus seen as social actors who actively negotiate their caring roles and responsibilities within the constraints and possibilities of individual, relational and structural factors.

Reflexivity, power and ethics

Feminist social researchers since the 1970s have been largely credited with 'debunking the myth of value-free scientific inquiry', calling instead for researchers to 'acknowledge their interests and sympathies' (Ellis et al, 1997: 123). Indeed, feminist and ethnographic research has long recognised the need for researchers to clearly situate their identity and the roles adopted in field relations, and the influence of this on their interactions with participants. As Alldred sums up, reflexivity involves being explicit about the operation of power within actual processes of researching and representing people (Alldred, 1998: 162). According to feminist methodologies, the researcher is seen as a, '"situated actor" (that is, an active participant in the process of meaning creation)' (Hertz, 1997: viii). Since researchers are acknowledged as active participants in the research process, Hertz comments that, 'it is essential to understand the researcher's location of self (for example, within power hierarchies and within a constellation of gender, race, class and citizenship)' (Hertz, 1997: viii);

> Through personal accounting, researchers must become more aware of how their own positions and interests are imposed at all stages of the research process – from the questions they ask to those they ignore, from who they study to who they ignore, from problem formation to analysis, representation and writing, in order to produce less distorted accounts of the social world. (Hertz, 1997: viii)

Feminist debates over power relations between researcher and the researched, which traditionally positioned women as 'other' and denied them agency, have been paralleled in cross-cultural research. Scheyvens and Leslie (2000) note that since the 1990s a crisis of legitimacy has affected both male and female Western researchers who have been forced to reconsider their role in the research process in Third World [sic] contexts. Unease over the dominance of Westerners as researchers of 'other' people's cultures, has emerged, leading researchers to question whether we can 'incorporate the voices of "others" without colonizing them in a manner that reinforces patterns of domination' (England, 1994, cited in Scheyvens and Leslie, 2000: 120). However, responses that abandon cross-cultural research completely or that romanticise or privilege 'Third World knowledge' both fail to consider the potential value of cross-cultural and cross-gendered research (England, 1994, cited in Scheyvens and Leslie, 2000: 122). As Kobayashi argues:

> … the question of 'who speaks for whom?' cannot be answered upon the slippery slope of what personal attributes – what color, what gender, what sexuality – legitimise our existence, but on the basis of our history of involvement, and on the basis of understanding how difference is constructed and used as a political tool. (Kobayashi, 1994, in Scheyvens and Leslie, 2000: 126)

Thus, as Scheyvens and Leslie comment, issues such as how well informed, how politically aware and how sensitive the researcher is to the topic in question and to the local context, seem 'a more pertinent means of judging suitability to conduct research with women of the Third World [sic] than an essentialising characteristic, such as sex or nationality' (Scheyvens and Leslie, 2000: 126). Furthermore, social researchers recognise that personal, social and emotional factors affect each stage of the fieldwork process and these should be acknowledged in written accounts (Holmes, 1998; Widdowfield, 2000).

The research process

In view of the importance of reflexivity and recognising the power dynamics inherent within researcher/researched relationships, the following sections offer a reflexive account of the research process, the methods used and ethical issues that emerged in the course of the study.

Choice of research topic

The focus of the research developed from Ruth Evans' and Saul Becker's research interests and experience. As noted in Chapter 1, despite a growing body of research on children who have caring responsibilities, very few studies focus specifically on children caring for parents/relatives with HIV/AIDS. There are also few comparative studies of young carers in 'mixed economy of welfare' (Powell, 2007) systems in the global North and those with limited state welfare systems in the South. Children caring for parents/relatives with HIV in the UK represent a hidden group (Becker, 2005), while in Tanzania and other Sub-Saharan African countries, it is a much more frequent occurrence (Ogden et al, 2004). We felt that by investigating children's experiences of caring in Tanzania, using the analytic lens developed by Becker et al (1998) in their UK studies, this would expand our understanding of the relationship between resilience and structural and relational aspects of society and the family. We felt that this understanding would in turn inform analyses of young carers in the UK and the comparison between advanced and limited state welfare systems.

Ruth Evans' previous research experience with children and families affected by HIV/AIDS and her personal experience working as a volunteer at a local centre for street children in northern Tanzania largely determined the choice of Tanzania as one of the countries for the study. Tanzania, as a Sub-Saharan African country where many children were likely to be caring for parents with HIV because of the scale of the HIV/AIDS epidemic and the limited welfare support, provided a useful contrast to the situation of young people in the UK, where legislation, social policy and services for young carers are relatively 'advanced' (Becker, 2007). Despite this, children caring for parents with HIV in the UK appeared to be a group that service providers found particularly 'hard to reach' and when contacted about recruiting respondents for the study, most young carers projects reported that they were not supporting or in contact with this group of children.

Saul Becker has been involved in research on young carers since the early 1990s, when he established and directed (until 2004) the Young Carers Research Group at Loughborough University. He worked closely with Jo Aldridge and Chris Dearden at Loughborough on a wide range of research projects during this period and, since moving to the University of Birmingham (in 2005) and then the University of Nottingham (in 2006), he has worked with Ruth Evans and others on a number of interrelated studies of young carers and young adult carers (aged 18-24). During this 15-year period Saul has been concerned not only to 'research' young carers, but to inform and influence the development and implementation of policy in the UK and internationally. He has taken an active engagement with policy makers and practitioners across the UK, and also overseas (especially in Australia and the US), in order to utilise research evidence to inform policy and practice *for* young carers and their families. He maintains a close working collaboration with professional bodies working in this field, particularly The Princess Royal Trust for Carers and the Children's Society in the UK, and Carers Australia.

Saul's research interests in young carers (and adult carers) are related to his own experiences during his childhood and more recently. As a child he helped to care for his grandmother, who had Parkinson's disease. In his teens Saul was involved more heavily in his grandmother's care as, at that time, there was little formal recognition or professional support for family carers. More recently, Saul's mother has required informal and now residential care. Saul has never doubted that these intergenerational 'caring' life experiences, particularly those from his childhood, and the values and ethics associated with these experiences, have influenced his choice of career (social work, doctorate, welfare rights, social policy academic) and his commitment to conduct 'real life' research which tries to promote the well-being and rights of vulnerable groups.

Ruth's interest in the topic developed from her doctoral research into the gendered experiences of street children and families affected by HIV/AIDS in Tanzania. While building on Saul's previous research experience and expertise in the field of young carers, her experiences inevitably influenced her approach to the research topic, the questions she asked, the interactions with respondents, the interpretation of the data and written accounts of the findings. Ruth's continuing friendship with a former research participant, a mother living with HIV in Tanzania, who had lost her husband and two children to AIDS, influenced her commitment to research that highlighted the experiences of families affected by HIV living in poverty.

Ruth's own experiences of caring for her mother (although her father is her mother's main carer) and her mother's everyday experiences of living with a progressive chronic illness also have a significant influence on Ruth's perspective on disability, impairment and caring relationships within the family. As a young person, Ruth gained an understanding of the social model of disability and the need for appropriate support for disabled parents, as a result of her mother's personal experiences of disabling social and attitudinal barriers, particularly assumptions about her sexuality and parenting ability, as a disabled person. Ruth also learned about service user involvement, peer support and independent living through her mother's work with disabled people. Throughout the research, we have tried to be sensitive to the critiques from the disability movement of the emphasis on young carers and concerned to understand caring relationships and the perspectives of parents with HIV as much as those of 'young carers' (see Chapter 1). Indeed, we have chosen not to use the term 'young carers' when referring to the young people involved in this study, because this label is contested and problematic in the context of HIV/AIDS, as was highlighted by many of the respondents (discussed in more detail in Chapter 10).

Qualitative methods

Given the hidden situation of young people caring for family members with HIV, the importance of confidentiality and the need to minimise the risk of disclosure of respondents' HIV status within the community, qualitative methods were considered most appropriate for the study. Tape-recorded semi-structured interviews were used to gain an in-depth understanding of the perspectives and experiences of this group of children, their families and key professionals in contact with them. A small number of focus groups were also conducted in Tanzania with two groups of young adults living with HIV and members of a Most Vulnerable Children village committee. Ruth Evans conducted almost all the interviews in Tanzania in Kiswahili, and in English in the UK, except in two instances where respondents from East Africa requested some questions or the full interview to be conducted in Kiswahili. Translators were employed to transcribe and translate the anonymised tape-recorded interviews and summary of the research findings.

Participatory methods

Participatory methodologies are seen to offer a way of addressing some of the ethical concerns over unequal power relations raised in both feminist and cross-cultural research discussed earlier. Some researchers suggest that participation in the research process can actually be an empowering experience for research participants, especially those who face significant social disadvantage (Scheyvens and Leslie, 2000: 127). Participatory rural appraisal (PRA) and participatory poverty assessment (PPA) approaches used within the development field are considered to offer 'new ways in which those who are poor and marginalised can present their realities to those in power and be believed, influence policy, and make a difference' (Chambers, 1998: xvii). Similarly, Opie suggests that feminist research can empower through seeking the opinions of the socially marginalised, because this assumes they can contribute to the description and analysis of a social issue (Opie, cited in Scheyvens and Leslie, 2000: 127). However, the 'empowering' nature of participatory research has been debated and critiqued in recent years in terms of masking continuing inequalities and power relations between researcher and participants (Cooke and Kothari, 2001).

Participatory methods which focus on 'task-centred activities' are often advocated by childhood researchers as effective in engaging children in research and enabling them to express their ideas and opinions (Hill, 1997; Christensen and James, 2000). Thus, in addition to semi-structured interviews with children, parents/relatives and professionals, a range of other participatory methods were used to engage children and young people, depending on age and levels of literacy including: drawings, map-making, diaries and sentence completion exercises. The use of participatory visual and written methods aimed to give the children more control over the representation of their lived realities, thereby addressing some of the ethical concerns about hierarchical power relations between the researcher and researched raised both in cross-cultural research and research with children (Pink, 2001).

The use of photography has increasingly been recognised as particularly suitable ethnographic media to develop successful collaborative or participatory projects (Pink, 2001). Because of the sensitive nature of the research, the stigma surrounding HIV and the importance of reassuring respondents about confidentiality and anonymity, the participation of children and parents was limited to involvement in data collection activities. However, through the use of participatory visual and written methods of data collection, we aimed to offer children and young people a range of media to express their views and perspectives.

A life story book, loosely based on the idea of 'memory books',[2] was designed for the project (in English and Kiswahili) for young people to complete in their own time. The book included sentence completion exercises, a diary of a typical day and spaces for drawing or collage (see Figure 3.1). The main themes of the 'My Story' book were focused on:

- family and caring relationships
- important memories and significant life events
- every day caring responsibilities and daily routine
- sources of social support and strategies for dealing with adversity within the family, school, wider community
- aspirations and priorities for the future.

Young people were given colouring pens, folders and stickers showing a range of emotions to use in their life story book. We also included space for children and young people to tell the researcher anything else about themselves or their caring responsibilities in their own words, which many young people in Tanzania used to express their feelings about their circumstances.

Digital photographs of completed pages were taken as a record of the data so that children could keep their books. Young people were also given disposable cameras to take photographs of people and places that were important to them and to show their everyday experiences of care work. As part of the interview, young people were asked to explain their photographs and were given a copy to keep. More than one visit to children and their families was often necessary, because of the need to build a degree of trust in the research relationship and to enable

Figure 3.1: 'A typical day' diary page completed by a young person as part of the life story book

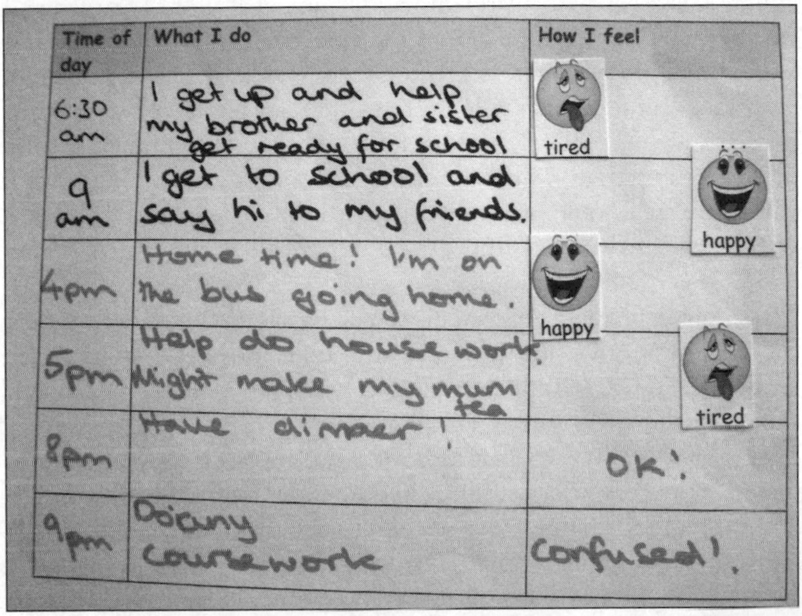

young people to complete the life story book and photographic diaries in their own time before a more in-depth interview was conducted.

The use of participatory methods with children and young people enabled us to gain a more complex, multi-dimensional understanding of different domains of their lives They also helped to make interviews more fun and interactive. Young people in Tanzania seemed to particularly enjoy the opportunity to write about and draw pictures of their experiences and took photographs of their everyday care work and caring relationships, while some young people in the UK preferred to 'just talk', perceiving the life story book and camera as extra 'homework' and a demand on their time.

Gaining access to children and parents

We aimed to identify a sample of children in each country aged under 18 who cared for parents/relatives with HIV/AIDS at the time or those who had been orphaned but previously cared for parents with AIDS. Owing to potential difficulties in accessing this group because of the stigma and their invisibility, as well as the gap in research on the experiences of young adult carers, we also aimed to include young adults aged 18-24 who continue to care for parents/relatives with HIV/AIDS or who cared for them when they were younger. This approach to selection has been used in several young carers studies where accessing children has been particularly difficult (Frank et al, 1999; Dearden and Becker, 2000). We also aimed to interview parents/relatives with HIV being cared for by their children or, in the case of orphaned children, their guardian or siblings. Children and parents were only selected to participate where HIV or AIDS had been recognised, either medically or by organisations working with family members. Children and parents/relatives themselves identified the project worker who had worked most closely with them to be interviewed, following Aldridge and Becker's (2003) approach.

To identify children and parents to participate in the study, we drew on our links with voluntary and community organisations working with young carers and children affected by HIV/AIDS in Tanzania and the UK. Arusha, Manyara, Kilimanjaro and Dar es Salaam regions were selected as the main research locations in Tanzania largely because of pragmatic reasons of limited time and previous familiarity of working in these locations. However, these regions also provided a range of both rural and urban settings and had relatively high levels of HIV prevalence within Tanzania (see Chapter 2 for an overview of the dynamics of the epidemic in Tanzania).

Owing to the smaller population of HIV-affected families in the UK, the stigma and concerns about confidentiality, negotiating access to children and parents in the UK was a more complicated and time-consuming process. This resulted in a smaller sample of families in comparison with those interviewed in Tanzania. Despite contacting many young carers projects (of which there are over 350 across the UK), few providers reported that they were in contact with children caring for a parent with HIV or explained that because of confidentiality workers were not necessarily aware of the nature of parents' illness or disability. Furthermore, while several specialist HIV organisations working with families were in contact with children with caring responsibilities through family support or peer support groups, many children were not aware of their parent's illness. Some organisations also expressed concerns about confidentiality and doubts about whether children and parents would be ready to talk to an outsider about their experiences. This highlights the key role that professionals can play as gatekeepers to particularly marginalised groups, as Cree et al (2002) found in their research with children with a parent with HIV in Scotland. Indeed, trusting relationships between potential respondents and project workers were key to gaining access to this hidden group. Project workers also helped to clarify and reassure respondents about confidentiality and anonymity and could offer follow-up support if necessary.

The Research Advisory Group[3] helped to facilitate access to some potential respondents. Identifying the UK sample also involved networking at relevant voluntary sector conferences and seminars, posting information on relevant websites and in email newsletters, as well as arranging meetings with HIV organisations and statutory stakeholders in different cities across England. A small number of young people who originally agreed to participate in the study decided to withdraw before Ruth met them. As Cree et al (2002) found, parents' and young people's reasons for not wanting to participate were related to not wishing to talk about sensitive issues that they may prefer not to think about, as well as concerns about confidentiality and anonymity. In addition, one parent with HIV who originally agreed to participate was unwell during the fieldwork period and it was not possible to reschedule the interview at a later date. While fully respecting the right of parents and young people to withdraw from the research at any time without an explanation, these experiences highlight the importance of allowing adequate time for fieldwork in the research design for a study of this nature. A more flexible timescale would have provided greater opportunities for potential respondents to get to know the researcher and find out more about the research before committing themselves to participating, as well as enabling parents with intermittent health problems to opt in or opt out of the study over a longer period.

Negotiating informed consent and the interview process

Because of the stigma surrounding HIV, respect for privacy, confidentiality and rights to anonymity were considered paramount at every stage of the research, as was the safety and security of the researcher and respondents (Becker and Bryman, 2004). Accessible information leaflets (in Kiswahili and English) were designed to introduce the research to children and parents prior to meeting the researcher. The leaflet stated that the study was about children caring for parents and relatives, but did not specify that the study was concerned with those affected by HIV/AIDS. Similarly, written consent forms, the feedback for young people and parents, and any other written information for respondents about the project did not mention HIV or AIDS, in order to minimise the risk of disclosure of the respondent's HIV status through participation in the study.

Following introductions to potential respondents by project workers, informed consent to participate in the study was negotiated with parents and young people. To ensure that consent to participate was as informed as possible, children and young people were only selected if they were aware of their parents'/relatives' illness and were willing to speak to the researcher about their caring responsibilities. Consent was renegotiated at each session and the right of participants to withdraw at any time without giving a reason was emphasised. Parents in the UK were particularly concerned about confidentiality and anonymity, both of the tape-recorded interviews and written outputs of the research. They emphasised the need for potentially identifying characteristics such as their family circumstances, country of origin and place of residence in the UK to be anonymised when presenting their stories or using direct quotations. Efforts were made to ensure that interviews took place at convenient times and locations, including at evenings or weekends. The majority of interviews took place in respondents' homes and sometimes at the offices of non-governmental organisations (NGOs), depending on respondents' preferences.

Following interviews, a financial payment was offered to young people, parents/relatives and, in Tanzania, also to NGO workers/volunteers participating in the study, to compensate for their time and potential loss of earnings when speaking to the researcher. We recognise that giving cash payments or vouchers to respondents is contentious, as it could be seen as an inducement to agree to participate in the study (Cree et al, 2002). Researchers in Africa have also been concerned that providing financial payments to research participants could set precedents and raise people's expectations, which future local researchers might find difficult to meet. However, the gender and development literature has revealed the need to fit in with women's routines and pay participants in community development projects a subsistence wage as compensation for time lost in earnings, in respect of women's 'time constraints' (Brydon and Chant, 1989; Ostergaard, 1992). Many children and young people caring for parents with HIV in Tanzania also face considerable time pressures, some combining income-generation activities with their caring responsibilities and other domestic duties within the household as well as schooling (as discussed in Chapter 4). The majority of respondents came from low-income families and, in Tanzania, were often living in very difficult circumstances. Thus, following consultation with NGO workers in Tanzania, it was decided that a small financial payment would be offered to acknowledge respondents' contribution to the research and help to compensate for any potential loss of earnings. In the UK context, some ethical research guidelines advocate cash payments or vouchers as an acknowledgement of participants' time and contribution (National

Children's Bureau, 1993; Ward, 1997), and since the 1990s it has become common social research practice. We considered a financial payment more appropriate than offering vouchers to young people, in line with our methodological stance of recognising children and young people's agency and competence. Following the final session, information was offered to young people and families about accessing support services from local organisations where these were available.

Researcher/researched relationship

Feminist approaches to social research advocate the development of rapport with the people involved in the study and therefore treating them in a non-exploitative way (Reinharz, 1992). However, the possibility of this has been questioned in recent years by social scientists, who have suggested that the researcher's relationships with his/her participants 'necessarily involve some degree of cultivation, exploitation and manipulation' (Fielding, 1993: 158; Cooke and Kothari, 2001). Ruth was acutely aware of unequal power differentials in the researcher/researched relationship, in terms of age, race, education and relative wealth, particularly in interviews with Tanzanian children and parents living in chronic poverty. Her position as a white, middle class *mzungu* [European] woman from a high-income country inevitably influenced how respondents related to her, despite attempts to manage respondents' expectations about the research project. The legacy of colonialism and global inequalities between the North and South mean that white people who travel or live in Tanzania are much more wealthy than the average Tanzanian. We emphasised through the information leaflet and when negotiating informed consent that although we hoped that the research would help to raise awareness and improve the situation of families in similar situations in future, we were not able to offer ongoing support to families and that respondents should contact local project workers for advice or assistance.

Despite these efforts to manage expectations, some parents and children inevitably saw Ruth as a potential source of financial support or as a means to secure a foreign sponsor for their children's education in future. Project workers in Tanzania also often asked what we were planning to do to help the families who had been involved in the study and Ruth found these questions one of the most difficult ethical issues raised by the research. Long-term academic goals of building knowledge about previously hidden, marginalised groups, which may help to improve the circumstances of others in future, are difficult to reconcile with the immediate practical needs for support that families involved in the study identified. Participatory, collaborative approaches and research conducted alongside interventions may go some way towards addressing these concerns. While the involvement of respondents was limited in our study, because of the sensitive, confidential nature of the research, measures that we adopted, including providing feedback to respondents about the findings of the study and a financial payment, attempted at the very least to compensate people's time and involvement in the research and to provide them with information about what we found out.

Conducting interviews on sensitive topics

We were concerned to minimise the potential distress that could be caused by interviewing respondents about sensitive topics, such as their feelings about living with HIV, young people's caring responsibilities and how they saw the future. The life story book and photographs helped young people to talk about their caring responsibilities and difficult life experiences if they wished, such as their memories of their father's death, as well as sometimes providing a distraction if a young person became upset during the interview. In the research design, we recognised that revisits could be necessary if a child became distressed or did not wish to continue with the interview in one session (Robson, 2001). Similarly, if the young person or their parent was ill, interviews were rearranged at a more convenient time where possible (this occurred once in the UK). We tried to ensure that interviews were conducted in private; in Tanzania Ruth often had to ask other children, family members and project workers to sit outside the house while the interview was in progress, in order to ensure privacy and confidentiality. However, securing a private space for sensitive interviews was sometimes difficult at respondents' homes. In a few instances when parents were unwell in bed in the only room in the house (which occurred twice in Tanzania and once in the UK), Ruth offered to interview the young person at another time. The parents and young people, however, preferred to continue with the interview, although it was sometimes difficult for children to talk openly about their feelings in this context.

We sought to put respondents at as much ease as possible and to minimise distress by designing the interview schedule and life story book from a resilience perspective that aimed to help respondents identify informal and formal sources of support they were able to access. In interview settings, Ruth tried to remain sensitive to signs of distress, verbal and non-verbal communication and judged the appropriateness of particular questions in context, according to each interviewee's responses. As Cree et al (2002: 51) acknowledge, it is the responsibility of researchers to make ethical judgements about 'what is (and is not) a necessary line of investigation in a given research study'. In particular, researchers need to judge when to encourage the respondent to share a confidence, and when to move on when they feel that young people or parents were not ready or willing to talk about a sensitive issue (Cree et al, 2002: 51).

Despite efforts to minimise distress, in Tanzania, several girls and young women and a few mothers shed tears when talking about their lives in the interview setting. Ruth asked them if they wanted to stop the interview or continue another day, but they all wished to continue telling their life story, expressing their feelings of sadness, grief or despair. Some young women felt overwhelmed by their responsibilities of caring for their family and appeared to value the opportunity to talk about their feelings and experiences, explaining that no one had ever asked them about their caring experiences before. Conducting interviews on sensitive topics such as HIV can also cause respondents to reflect on issues they may not have talked about before and bring new questions or concerns to the surface. This highlights the need to be clear about the limits of a researcher's role and expertise. During some interviews, parents in both countries asked Ruth's advice about issues related to HIV transmission, medication or about seeking financial or welfare support. Where appropriate, she responded to these queries as best she could, but emphasised that she was not an expert and referred them to the organisation they were in contact with for specialist advice and support.

The importance of acknowledging personal and emotional aspects of the research process has increasingly been acknowledged by feminists and other social researchers (Holmes, 1998; Widdowfield, 2000). Ruth found the fieldwork, particularly in Tanzania, quite an emotionally draining experience and it was difficult for Ruth to share what people had told her with project workers or friends because of the need for confidentiality. Owing to practical reasons, several interviews with different families were often set up over a few days in each location in Tanzania, which made the fieldwork an intensive experience. This highlights the need for researchers working on sensitive and difficult topics such as life-limiting illness and bereavement to have opportunities to share their experiences and emotions of the research process through both informal and formal support mechanisms within the research/ university context.

Characteristics of interviewees

Semi-structured interviews were conducted with a total of 93 participants in Tanzania and the UK (see Table 3.1). Life story books were completed by a further four orphaned children and focus group discussions were conducted with young adults with HIV (aged 24-30) and with members of a Most Vulnerable Children village committee in Tanzania.

The majority of young people interviewed were children (aged 9-17) who were caring for their mother with HIV and sometimes also siblings with HIV and living in one-parent households at the time of interview. In Tanzania, a third of the young people interviewed were young adults (aged 18-24) with caring responsibilities. A few children in Tanzania used to care for their mother until she died and were caring for their younger siblings at the time of interview. The majority of the

Table 3.1: Number of interviewees

Number of interviewees			
	Tanzania	UK	Total
Children with caring responsibilities (aged 9–17)	**15**	**9**	**24**
• Girls	8	7	15
• Boys	7	2	9
• Presently caring for parent/relative with HIV	14	9	23
• Used to care for parent/relative with HIV and presently caring for siblings	1	0	1
Young adults with caring responsibilities (aged 18–24)	**7**	**2**	**9**
• Young women	6	2	8
• Young men	1	0	1
• Presently caring for parent/relative with HIV	5	2	7
• Used to care for parent/relative with HIV and presently caring for siblings	2	0	2
Parents/relatives	**21**	**12**	**33**
• Mothers living with HIV	18	12	30
• Female relatives living with HIV	2	0	2
• Guardian	1	0	1
NGO project workers and volunteers	**13**	**14**	**27**
Total respondents	**56**	**37**	**93**

young people started caring for their parent/relative when they were 10 years old or older (range: from 6 to 16 years), with a mean age (based on children's accounts) of 12 and 11 years old in Tanzania and the UK respectively. The majority of young people were girls, particularly in the UK. In both countries, most of the parents interviewed were mothers with HIV. In Tanzania, two women with HIV were cared for by their grandson and niece respectively and one female guardian of a former young carer whose mother had died of AIDS was interviewed. In the UK, all of the parents interviewed were mothers with HIV.

The qualitative sample cannot be seen as representative of young people with caring responsibilities in families affected by HIV and AIDS across Tanzania and the UK and the aim of the study was not to generalise about this group of young people and their families. Rather, we aimed to explore the complexities of young caregiving in the context of HIV and gain insight into the hitherto hidden experiences of this group of children. While the purposive sample of children and parents illustrates a diverse range of perspectives, there are limitations to the study. As discussed earlier, it was considerably more difficult to gain access to children and parents who met our criteria in the UK, which resulted in a smaller sample compared with those interviewed in Tanzania. As a result of our method of recruitment via NGOs, we were only able to interview children and parents who were in contact with organisations and receiving services and willing to talk openly about their experiences, and so we are unlikely to have identified some of the most marginalised or isolated families.

In both countries, mothers/female relatives constituted the entire sample of parents/relatives, and project workers identified very few young people caring for fathers with HIV (discussed in more detail in Chapter 9). Providers in Tanzania suggested that the lack of visibility of children caring for fathers with HIV could be linked to a lack of openness about men's HIV status, as well as cultural and gender norms that mean that men were more likely to be cared for by their wives or other female relatives, rather than their children. The difficulty in recruiting fathers with HIV to participate in the study is also likely to be linked to the widely reported reluctance of men to be involved in research studies more generally, particularly those focusing on health issues, children and families. In particular, African men in the UK are often considered isolated and less willing to talk about their experiences of HIV than African women (Doyal et al, 2005; Ridge et al, 2008).

Residence, ethnicity and household composition

Interviews were conducted in rural and urban locations in four regions of Tanzania (Dar es Salaam, Arusha, Manyara, Kilimanjaro) and in cities/ towns in five regions of England (London, the South East, Eastern, West Midlands and East Midlands) (see Table 3.2 for breakdown). Most UK families were African migrants, some with insecure immigration status. As discussed in Chapter 2, this reflects the dynamics of the HIV epidemic in England, where recent African migrant families are disproportionately affected by HIV (UK Collaborative Group for HIV and STI Surveillance, 2006). The majority of parents had fled violence and conflict or migrated from East and Southern Africa, including Uganda, Tanzania, Somalia, Malawi, South Africa and Zimbabwe, and had been living in the UK for between three and eight years. The majority of families were thus of Black African ethnicity, with two of White British and one of Asian British ethnicity.[4]

The majority of families in both countries were comprised of one-parent households (see Table 3.3). Almost all the women with HIV interviewed in Tanzania had been widowed or had lost their male partner due to AIDS-related illness. In the UK, half of the women

Table 3.2: Residence and ethnicity of interviewees

Residence and ethnicity of interviewees		Number of households
Tanzania		**24**
Rural/urban households	• City – Dar es Salaam • Small town • Rural/ village	5 7 12
Ethnicity	Black African (Tanzanian) from a range of ethnic groups, depending on region of origin in Tanzania	24
UK		**14**
Rural/urban households	• Capital city – London • City/ large town • Small town	6 7 1
Ethnicity	• Black African • White British • Asian British	11 2 1
Immigration status	Refugee granted indefinite leave to remain or British citizenship Long-standing British citizen Seeking asylum or insecure immigration status	7 4 3

with HIV were separated or divorced from their husband/partner and a third had been widowed or lost their partner to AIDS. A fifth of households in the UK and only one in Tanzania were two-parent families; a few women in the UK lived with their husband or male partner; two women lived with an uninfected husband/partner ('sero-discordant couples') and one woman lived with her husband who was also HIV positive. Over a third of households in Tanzania were extended families, comprised of young people caring for their mother and living with adult relatives; young people caring for a female relative; or young people caring for their siblings and living with relatives or a guardian. There was also one youth-headed household, comprised of a young woman who cared for her mother until she died and continued to care for her younger siblings at the time of interview.

Over half of the families in Tanzania and a quarter of those in the UK were large families with three or more children living in the household. Almost half of the women in Tanzania had older sons (most were aged over 18) living elsewhere, either independently or with relatives or friends. A small number of households in Tanzania and the UK included children who had lost both parents to AIDS and were nieces, nephews or grandchildren of the women with HIV interviewed.

In Tanzania, a third of the households included one or more children (aged 2 to 13 years old) who were identified either by the parent or an NGO worker as living with HIV. In the UK, 3 of the 14 households included young people identified as living with HIV (aged 13 to 18 years old) and in 2 households, the young person with HIV was caring for their mother. Almost all of the young people and their siblings from refugee and migrant families had been reunited with their parent in the UK within a few years of their parent's migration. However, over a quarter of the households in the UK can be characterised as transnational families, comprised of a parent and their younger children living in the UK, while their older children, and sometimes their partner, remained in their country of origin or a neighbouring country in Africa.

Data analysis

All the interviews and focus groups were transcribed and the Tanzanian interviews were translated into English by Tanzanian translators. Interview transcripts, life story books and photographs were then reviewed to identify key themes and analytic summaries were written for each interview. Theoretical concepts such as resilience, the new social studies of childhood, gender analysis, sociology of health and

Table 3.3: Household composition of interviewees

Household composition of interviewees		Number of households
Tanzania		**24**
One-parent families	• Young person caring for mother with HIV and siblings; father died or parents separated	13 (54%)
Two-parent families	• Young person living with mother and step-father who both have HIV, caring for mother with HIV	1 (4%)
Extended families	• Young person caring for mother with HIV, living with adult relatives	5 (21%)
	• Young person caring for female relative with HIV	2 (8%)
	• Young person who has lost both parents to AIDS, used to care for mother with HIV, presently caring for siblings and living with relatives/ guardian	2 (8%)
Youth-headed household	• Young adult who has lost both parents to AIDS, used to care for mother with HIV, presently caring for siblings	1 (4%)
Number of large families (three or more children aged 0–17)		13 (54%)
Number of households where one or more children are living with HIV		8 (33%)
UK		**14**
One-parent families	• Young person caring for mother with HIV and siblings; father died or parents separated	10 (71%)
	• Young person caring for father with HIV, separated from rest of family	1 (4%)
Two-parent families	• Young person living with both parents with HIV and caring for mother	1 (4%)
	• Young person living with mother and her partner, caring for mother with HIV	2 (8%)
Number of large families (three or more children aged 0–17)		6 (25%)
Number of households where one or more children are living with HIV		3 (13%)
Number of transnational families (defined as where parents and/or siblings are separated through international migration)		4 (29%)

illness, embodiment and the ethic of care informed the analysis and interpretation of the data. The transcripts and digital photographs of the life story books were coded, anonymised and stored according to ethical protocols for future research use.[5]

Dissemination

A report summarising the key findings was prepared in English and Kiswahili and disseminated through seminars, conferences and policy and practice networks in Tanzania and the UK. An accessible summary of the key findings was prepared in English and Kiswahili for the parents and young people who participated in the research. Written outputs ensure respondents' anonymity, including when direct quotations or descriptions of family circumstances are provided. Young people chose pseudonyms for themselves to be used in written outputs and written consent was sought for the use of specific photographs.

As part of the dissemination activities, feedback from parents and young people on the research summary and updates about their lives were sought a year after the initial research had been conducted. In the UK, where it was possible to write to respondents, parents and young people were invited to contact the researcher if they wished to give any feedback or share any changes in their lives. One parent contacted Ruth about her news. On a return visit to Tanzania to present the findings to NGO workers and policy makers, Ruth re-visited a small number of young people and parents to seek their written consent to use anonymised photographs for the book. This also provided an opportunity for informal interviews with the families. We were pleased to hear from the families we were in contact with and from project workers in Tanzania and the UK that the young people were doing well both in school/college and other social activities they were involved in, with support from the NGOs. Most parents were also living well with antiretroviral therapy, although we were very sad to learn at the time of writing that two mothers in Tanzania had died.

Conclusion

This chapter has provided a reflexive account of the research process, methodology and ethical issues raised by cross-cultural research with families affected by HIV/AIDS in Tanzania and the UK. The process of fieldwork with a hidden and marginalised group, in the context of both the global South and North, highlights several important issues about methodologies, power relations and ethics in cross-cultural research. The overarching concern lies in balancing the risk of possible harm to respondents with the importance of eliciting the perspectives of hidden populations. In particular, the research demonstrated the paramount importance of confidentiality and anonymity at every stage of the research process, as well as the need for informed consent to be an ongoing process that is continually negotiated with respondents. The research highlighted the need to allocate sufficient time to build trust within researcher/researched relations, including negotiating the involvement of key gatekeepers, and to develop a range of strategies to gain access to hidden groups. The study highlighted the need to minimise distress when interviewing respondents about sensitive topics and for researchers to be responsive to verbal and non-verbal communication, judging the appropriateness of interview questions in context.

The research also suggests the need to manage expectations and consider what respondents will gain through their involvement in research, particularly in low-income countries. Researchers also need to ensure that the findings are disseminated in both the global North and South, including providing accessible feedback for respondents. This chapter has also provided an overview of the characteristics of the young people and parents involved in the study in Tanzania and the UK, to contextualise the findings of the research. The following chapters discuss key themes from our research with families affected by HIV/AIDS in Tanzania and the UK, interpreted in the light of the theoretical concepts discussed in Chapters 1 and 2.

Notes

[1] This research was funded by the Economic and Social Research Council, UK from 2006 to 2007, grant number RES-000-22-1732-A. Ethical approval for the study was granted by the Social Sciences Research Ethics Committee, University of Birmingham and the National Institute for Medical Research, Tanzania. Authorisation for the research was granted by the Tanzania Commission for Science and Technology and the University of Dar es Salaam. The research was informed by the British Sociological Association's and Social Research Association's codes of ethics.

[2] The Memory Book is the central tool used in memory work with parents with HIV and their children which was first developed by the National Community of Women living with HIV/AIDS in Uganda (Healthlink Worldwide, 2006).

[3] The Research Advisory Group was established to provide ongoing advice and ethical scrutiny for the project and included academics and statutory and voluntary sector professionals working with young carers and young people affected by HIV in the UK.

[4] Ethnic groups are based on UK 2001 Census classifications (Office for National Statistics, www.statistics.gov.uk, accessed 10 January 2009).

[5] Anonymised interview transcripts and life story book pictures are stored with UK Data Archive, University of Essex, service provider for the Economic and Social Data Service and can be accessed via the UK Data Archive, www.data-archive.ac.uk.

FOUR

Living with HIV and the effects on family life: parents' narratives

This chapter draws on a range of theoretical concepts to interpret the everyday lived experiences of women living with HIV. Based on in-depth interviews with mothers and female relatives living with HIV in Tanzania and the UK, this chapter focuses on the effects of HIV on family life. We explore women's changing health identities over time, from discovery of their status, their embodied everyday experiences of HIV and AIDS, to secrets and disclosure within the family. We discuss changes in family relationships and the wider socioeconomic factors that intersect with HIV/AIDS at the household and community levels, including poverty and welfare support, migration, stigma and discrimination.

Embodiment, illness and disability

Social constructionist perspectives, dominant in much contemporary theorising about the body, health and disability in the social sciences, challenge the objectivity of medical knowledge about the body (Longhurst, 1997; Parr and Butler, 1999) These perspectives have been influenced by critiques of the medical model of knowledge about the body, illness and disability by feminists and disability activists (Oliver, 1990; Barnes, 1991; Morris, 1991; Longhurst, 1997). In Western societies, disability and impairments have been seen as 'individual medical tragedies' (Shakespeare, 1993), in which the body is conceptualised as 'failing to meet normal standards of form, ability and mobility' (Parr and Butler, 1999: 3). The social model of disability developed by disability theorists distinguished between impairment and disability, defining impairment as 'the medically defined condition of a person's body/mind' and disability as 'the socially constructed disadvantage based upon impairment' (Wendell, 2001: 22).

While this distinction has been crucial to the disability movement and campaigns for the civil rights of disabled people, feminists have highlighted a tendency within social model approaches to equate illness with impairment and deny the materiality of the body (Morris, 1991; Wendell, 2001). Similarly, medical sociologists and geographers have been criticised for tending to treat the body as 'Other' in their studies and focusing only on negative consequences and meanings associated with illness and impairment (Barnes and Mercer, 1996; Longhurst, 1997; Parr and Butler, 1999). Feminist disability theorists advocate a focus on the phenomenology of impairment that views impairments as forms of difference: 'Knowing more about how people experience, live with and think about their own impairments could contribute to an appreciation of disability as a valuable difference from the medical norms of body and mind' (Wendell, 2001: 23).

Poststructuralist accounts of the body have also been influential in social constructionist approaches. Cultural/discursive approaches suggest that discourses structure institutional practices and shape the bodies and subjectivities of women and men, producing and reproducing power relations (Weedon, 1999). Scholars have drawn on Foucault's analysis of power as decentralised and diffuse, working 'from below', to gain insight into the ways that local social contexts produce particular 'health identities' (James and Hockey, 2007). In common with critiques of the social model of disability, however, poststructuralist approaches to the body have been criticised for rendering the body 'incorporeal, fleshless, fluidless, little more than a linguistic territory' (Longhurst, 2001: 23) and reinforcing masculinist, abstract notions of the body. Such approaches have also been critiqued for under-theorising individuals' agency and resistance to hegemonic discourses (Nelson, 1999; Alsop et al, 2002).

Despite these critiques, social constructionist perspectives have highlighted the way that concepts of health and illness take on different meanings within different sets of social relations and in different everyday social and cultural contexts (James and Hockey, 2007). Furthermore, approaches that emphasise individuals' agency have revealed the everyday interactions and social processes that are involved in the construction of health and illness and the ways people 'take on, reject or negotiate different kinds of health identities' (James and Hockey, 2007: 37).

While often broadly informed by social constructionist perspectives, recent approaches to the body, health and illness have emphasised the need to take account of the changing materiality of the body and embodied experiences of health and illness in the construction of health identities (Moss and Dyck, 1999; Parr and Butler, 1999; Teather, 1999; Hall, 2000; James and Hockey, 2007). This approach has been shown to be particularly relevant in understanding the lived, embodied experiences of people with fluctuating and unpredictable chronic illnesses, such as multiple sclerosis, arthritis and HIV among others (Dyck, 1995; Parr and Butler, 1999; Wendell, 2001).

Drawing on anthropological concepts of ritual, James and Hockey develop the notion of the 'ritual drama of illness' to understand embodied experiences of sickness and the agency of individuals in negotiating illness and changing identities (James and Hockey, 2007). These authors suggest that:

> As a drama which unfolds in an individual's life, sickness is, at one and the same time, a common and shared social experience, but one which is also highly personal in that it has, potentially, profound implications for a changed identity. (James and Hockey, 2007: 19)

This concept is useful in theorising the process of identification and adaptation to living with a chronic, life-limiting illness that women with HIV are confronted with following their diagnosis. The narratives of women with HIV in Tanzania and the UK suggest that they were engaged in a process of coming to terms with their status and negotiating a changed health identity. This process was often characterised by initial shock, disbelief, possible self-stigma or depression, to gradual acceptance and adjustment to living with a life-limiting illness, including sharing their status with family members and others in the community. However, this did not appear to be a linear process; some women who had known that they were living with HIV for many years had not shared their status with anyone in their family or community. Rather, women's negotiations of their health identities were shaped by a complex range of social interactions and processes, which will be explored in this chapter. These include the ways that they discovered their status, their embodied experiences, sociocultural and biomedical understandings of HIV-related illness, socioeconomic impacts of HIV/AIDS on the household, access to medical care and social support, family and intimate relationships and experiences of stigma and discrimination within the family and community.

Discovering their HIV status

The majority of parents/relatives interviewed in Tanzania had been diagnosed with HIV relatively recently (within the previous three years); a few had been diagnosed nine or ten years previously. As discussed in Chapter 2, heterosexual transmission between partners and mother-to-child transmission means that HIV clusters in families, often affecting more than one family member. This was reflected in the ways women discovered their status. While many women were diagnosed when they became ill themselves and sought medical care, several women in Tanzania decided or were advised to go for an HIV test following their husband's or partner's death and a few discovered their status when their child became ill and was diagnosed with HIV. Although many women had only recently tested positive, many thought they had been living with HIV for up to 13 years, associating the time of infection with the period when they first became ill, the birth of their child later discovered to be HIV positive or their husband's or partner's illness or death.

In the UK, over half of the women interviewed (mainly those who were recent refugees and migrants) had been diagnosed in the previous three to seven years. However, just under half of the women had discovered their status between 11 and 19 years previously (those with long-standing British citizenship as well as African migrants who had been diagnosed in their country of origin). Most women in the UK were diagnosed with HIV when they became ill, while a few discovered their status through antenatal testing during pregnancy or when their child became ill and was diagnosed.

Women's narratives of discovering their HIV status illustrate the notion of the 'ritual drama of illness' (James and Hockey, 2007). As Wilton (1999: 258) suggests, diagnosis represents 'the moment at which HIV/AIDS is officially "named"', which can produce a range of contradictory reactions. Many women described the discovery of their HIV status as a traumatic experience that had a major impact on their emotional well-being and sense of identity. In both countries, many women experienced shock and disbelief on discovering their status. They saw diagnosis as a death sentence and were worried about whether their children were also infected. For example, one woman from East Africa who was diagnosed soon after her arrival in the UK, described her sense of shock and disbelief:

> When they told me that I was HIV positive, it was a moment when I feel like maybe I'm going to die tomorrow, I couldn't believe it, I thought the world was against me or something. Because that is the last thing I was thinking about.

Some women's narratives of discovering their status suggest that medical professionals in Africa were reluctant to officially name HIV. The experience of Yvonne (living in the UK at the time of interview) in East Africa in the late 1990s suggests that the stigma surrounding

HIV at that time was such that even doctors feared telling people about their HIV status.

Many women in Tanzania were not told that their husband or partner had died of an AIDS-related illness and it was only when they became ill and tried to find out the cause of their husband's death that they discovered their status. Furthermore, mistrust of medical professionals, combined with initial feelings of shock and disbelief meant that some women had gone for tests several times at different hospitals before they could acknowledge the diagnosis.

Some women in both countries described a sense of confusion and did not understand how they had become infected, leading them to question, 'why me?' As Pierret (2000), James and Hockey (2007) and others note, lay understandings of illness are often characterised by questioning 'why me?' By drawing on different relational, sociocultural, religious and biomedical accounts to make sense of 'the ritual drama of illness', HIV can take on different meanings and significance in people's lives. Many women in Tanzania and some African women in the UK drew on their faith as a source of hope and support, which helped them to accept their changed health identity. Husna and her daughter had been diagnosed with HIV soon after they had fled to the UK as refugees from the Horn of Africa. Husna drew on a biomedical discourse of infected medical supplies to try to make sense of their status:

> – *How was it when your daughter found out about her illness?*
> – *She was so sad. I think in your country, I don't know how they get it, from needle or syringe. I don't know how we got it. Syringes I think are not clean in our country. We don't have tests for blood, as something to be avoided. I still don't know how we got it.*

For several women, exposure to risk through unequal power relations within heterosexual relationships formed part of their narratives of discovering their HIV status. Several women were unknowingly exposed to HIV through unsafe sex with a husband or partner who was either aware of his status or who refused to have an HIV test despite engaging in risky behaviour, such as having multiple sexual partners or using intravenous drugs (the latter only reported in the UK). One woman in Tanzania, for example, did not know that her husband's illness was AIDS-related until after his death. Her husband forced her to engage in sexual intercourse, despite being aware of his status (see Box 4.1). In the UK, one woman's partner did not disclose his HIV status to her until she became pregnant. After initial tests had proved negative, she was diagnosed with HIV when she was eight

Box 4.1: Unequal gender relations: women's exposure to risk in intimate heterosexual relationships in Tanzania

Hosiana only discovered that her husband was suffering from an AIDS-related illness after his death. She experienced physical and sexual violence from her husband during his illness:

> *When his health got worse he seemed as if he was mad. I didn't know about the real cause. He used to come back drunk and call for me. The neighbours used to wonder and some said he was crazy. He used to beat us all, including the children. He used to demand sex by force. I had been advised not to indulge in too much sex, as there were a lot of sexually transmitted diseases around. They had told me to tell him to go for testing. I told him to go for testing, he refused. He said that if there was a disease, we would all die from it. 'You are my legally wedded wife. I am not testing.' He already knew he was HIV positive but he was not telling me the truth. 'You are my legally wedded wife, if you want to get tested, you go alone', he used to say. Whenever he came back from his drinking sprees he would force me to have sex. If he found the children were fast asleep, he would beat them and chase them out of the room, threatening to kill them if they did not leave fast enough. The children put up with all that he threw at them. I just kept quiet or sometimes jumped through the window and ran away from him. He would then go on mumbling to himself. When I saw that he had quietened down and gone to sleep, I would creep in and go to sleep. I suffered a lot. [...] I didn't know my husband was having TB injections at the time, we even have his TB notebook but I didn't know it was connected to HIV. I just thought it was just the normal TB and that he would get better later on.*

months pregnant. The relationship broke down and she described feeling *'suicidal for months'* following the discovery of her status. Such accounts of discovering their status were often linked to feelings of anger and blame directed against their former partner, which could be difficult for women to deal with, particularly when talking to their children about their illness.

Negotiating changed family and intimate relationships

Sexual and reproductive identities

Women's narratives revealed that living with HIV could lead to changed sexual and reproductive identities. While the majority of women in

Tanzania had been widowed or had lost their male partner due to AIDS-related illness, a few women were separated from their male partner. They felt that discovery of their HIV status had led to the break up of their relationships. In the UK, half of the women were separated or divorced from their husband/partner and a third had been widowed or had lost their partner to AIDS. A few women lived with their husband or male partner; two women had formed new relationships with an uninfected husband/partner ('sero-discordant couples') and one woman lived with her husband who was also HIV positive. Several women in the UK who were not in a relationship at the time of interview expressed feelings of apprehension about forming a new sexual partnership, perceiving this as a complex and fraught process. For example, Sandra and Anna (see Box 4.2) felt that it would be difficult for them to find a new partner who would accept and understand the implications of living with HIV, as well as get on with, and be accepted by, their children. Furthermore, Rachel's narrative suggests that apprehension about forming a new relationship may also be linked to a parent's acceptance of their own status and a changed sense of self (see Box 4.2). This reinforces the idea that discovery of HIV status may be experienced as a threat to women's sense of self and sexual identity, as they take on a different health identity.

HIV can also threaten women's reproductive identities, as Sandra and Anna's embodied experiences of HIV demonstrate (see Box 4.2). For many women, motherhood can represent a defining element of their identity (Doyal and Anderson, 2005). The inability to have any more children due to HIV-related illness may be experienced in terms of a profound sense of loss or grief for the children they were not able to have. Women's loss of childbearing capacity could also be difficult for a new partner, or for children who want another sibling, to accept. Furthermore, while medical advances have dramatically reduced the risk of mother-to-child transmission of HIV in the UK and other high-income countries, women with HIV who decide to have a baby may face judgemental attitudes about their decision. Women may encounter stigmatising attitudes for risking mother-to-child or heterosexual transmission of HIV in order to conceive, as well as judgements about women's entitlements to motherhood and their ability to care for their children due to the life-limiting nature of AIDS (Wilson, 2007). This is linked to discriminatory attitudes towards disabled women who may be portrayed as asexual or considered 'inadequate parents' (Stables and Smith, 1999). Indeed, Sandra's decision to have another child with her husband was questioned by her peers in an HIV support group at the time: *'People said, well, why did I have another one when I had already got*

Box 4.2: Negotiating changing sexual and reproductive identities: experiences of women with HIV in the UK

Rachel felt that she was still coming to terms with her own status and was not ready to deal with the complexities of sharing her status with a new sexual partner:

> *I don't think I'll have a partner now. I'm just getting used to my life myself, it's, so to have someone and complicate their life with your life, it's another thing.*

Anna commented on the difficulty of finding a new partner who understood about HIV and thought that HIV organisations could help people living with HIV to meet new partners:

> *You see being HIV as well is like a death penalty in indirect ways because you can't go out and get a relationship, you can't socialise with people. It would be easier, I think I would be less stressful, if I could get a relationship, but the only way for me to get a relationship is for people like [voluntary organisation] and stuff to have a dating agency for people with HIV or something possible to get together, because the things they do organise is mainly for the kids, not for the adults, and my kids are dying for me to have a relationship.*

Anna and her children had found it difficult to accept that she would not be able to have any more children:

> *That was another blow when I had to have a hysterectomy. But I took it ok, my kids today still want a little brother or sister, they're always asking me for that, but they've learned to understand it. I can't give them any of that just yet, any more. And I've learned to accept it. Now and again I go into depression, and my kids see a lot of that.*

Sandra expressed her regret that she only had two children and was not able to have children with her new partner:

> *I met somebody else four years ago who's not HIV positive so it was a big thing to get together because he wanted children, it's very difficult. Anyway he decided he wanted to be with me more, so he counts mine as his children and we've been together ever since.[…] I get down sometimes just because I didn't have more children, you know I would have liked more children. I had a miscarriage last year and I'd just have liked more children but I'm also happy with the ones I've got you know, it's a mixed thing, a mixed bag.*

one that was fine, why did I risk having another one?' These experiences highlight the complexity of issues women may face in negotiating their sexual and reproductive identities with HIV.

Performing motherhood

Studies conducted in the UK and US found that caring for children can be stressful as well as being important as a 'normalising' activity for mothers with HIV (Ciambrone, 2003: 110, cited in Doyal and Anderson, 2005). While mothers in both countries expressed their anxiety about providing for their children and meeting their physical and emotional needs, children were clearly profoundly important to women's sense of self and emotional well-being, providing a reason to live positively with HIV for as long as possible. For example, a White British woman who was diagnosed with HIV in the late 1980s felt that her decision to start combination therapy in 2000 was linked to a desire to prolong her life for her children's sake:

> *Basically, if I didn't take them when I did I wouldn't have lived more than two years they reckoned. But I took them because of my children I felt, I know they'd be alright if I died, you know, that's life, but I felt they'd do better if I was around [laughs].*

This suggests that children can represent an important motivation for struggling with the life-limiting nature of HIV, confirming the findings of studies made by Doyal and Anderson (2005), Ciambrone (2003) and others with HIV-positive women in a range of contexts. Indeed, as we discuss in Chapter 5, children play a key role in providing emotional support to their parents with HIV through simply 'being there', whether or not children were aware of this. Mothers commented on how loving, close relationships with their children enhanced their emotional well-being. For example, Laura felt that her own mother was undermining her role as a mother and was worried that her parents wanted to take custody of her daughter and raise her in their country of origin. She highlighted the significance of her daughter's presence to her emotional well-being: *'My mum still she wants to take her [daughter] with her but I need her to keep me company, otherwise I'd go mad, you know what I mean?'* Furthermore, the evidence from children and parents suggests that relationships between mothers and children are characterised by reciprocal relationships of love and emotional support (see Chapter 6). Despite their illness, parents with HIV maintain their parental roles in providing informal teaching, advice and moral guidance to their children. Indeed, as we discuss in Chapters 6 and 9, loving relationships between children and parents can have a strong protective effect for children affected by HIV.

However, mothers' experiences in both countries suggest that HIV illness, poverty and lack of alternative care and support can sometimes undermine women's attempts to perform 'motherhood' and support their children. Doyal and Anderson found that the pressures women faced as mothers living with HIV were reinforced by 'moral anxieties associated with the social construction of motherhood' (2005: 1732). Many parents in both Tanzania and the UK expressed feelings of frustration, sadness and guilt that they had to rely on their children to care for them when they were ill. While most thought that caring enabled children to gain useful life skills and helped to prepare them for the future, they also felt that it was 'unfair' that children had to take on these responsibilities at a young age. Parents felt guilty that they were not able to provide for their children and perform the tasks and responsibilities usually expected of mothers, according to cultural norms (see Box 4.3). In Tanzania, this was linked to concerns about future care arrangements for children following their mother's death.

Some women expressed self-doubts about whether they were performing their role as a mother adequately and were worried about others' perceptions of their ability to parent. For example, one African woman living in the UK described feelings of shame and felt that HIV challenged her role and identity as a mother. However, her faith appeared to help her accept her illness:

> *Sometimes I feel like that, if I'm feeling bad, what do people think, this illness, that I'm really bad mother, you know sometimes you think about it, like why, why me, why me, but God is great.*

Despite their unease at having to rely on their children to care for them, parents felt that they had no choice, as they lacked alternative sources of care and support. The ambivalence and tensions caused by caring relationships within the family are discussed in more detail in Chapter 6.

Having explored the ways that women adapted to changed health identities and the effects of HIV on their sense of self, intimate and family relationships, the following section discusses parents' embodied experiences of living with a life-limiting chronic illness.

Box 4.3: Performing motherhood: concerns of mothers with HIV in the UK and Tanzania

Rachel expressed her frustration and anger that she was not able to ensure that there was enough food in the house when she was ill and regretted having to rely on her son to care for her instead of playing with his peers:

> *I can't even go and do shopping for my kids, like stuff like food, drink, you know, it's just a bad day. Like this week my house it's just empty because I couldn't go anywhere. [...] It does hurt me, it's painful. I can get furious, I get angry but I can't change. If there's a way of changing my body I would, or there's a way of changing my bladder or immune system or whatever I would do for the sake of my child to have time to play with the other kids, to be a child himself. (UK)*

Husna expressed her regrets about her daughter's caring responsibilities and felt strongly that education would help her daughters to ensure their rights to inheritance were not violated.

> *I am sad but I have no choice. I feel sorry for her because I feel she is carrying the burden of someone else's responsibility, but that someone else isn't there. [...] It will be better if they have enough education, so that in case something happens to violate their rights, they will be able to defend themselves. They will be able to say that this is ours.... (Tanzania)*

Embodied experiences of living with HIV

The women interviewed in Tanzania and the UK described a range of embodied, lay and biomedical understandings of HIV-related illness that affected their physical and emotional well-being. Women's narratives suggest that it is difficult to talk in general terms about people's embodied experiences of HIV/AIDS, since they are characterised by considerable diversity. As Wilton (1999: 258) found, quality of life at a given point in time is dependent on many different factors and 'a number of dimensions of daily life must be continually (re)negotiated'.

During interviews, the women were asked to describe their experiences of living with HIV on a day-to-day basis and during periods of illness. While half of the women in the UK and a few women in Tanzania said that they were in good health at the time of interview as the result of effective combination therapy, half of the women in both countries reported frequent colds, coughing, fevers and chest pains, as well as serious episodes of influenza, tonsillitis and bronchitis (see Table 4.1). A large proportion of women also experienced chronic fatigue and a lack of energy. Many women cited a number of physical symptoms that affected their appetite, weight and general health. Many also reported pain and swelling in their limbs and other physical impairments that reduced their mobility, either on a temporary or more permanent basis. A significant proportion of women in Tanzania experienced skin rashes, sores and fungal infections.

Many women in both countries found the chronic fatigue and unpredictable, episodic nature of HIV-related illness very difficult to deal with. They perceived the unpredictability of illness episodes as the main aspect of HIV that prevented them from being able to work (see Box 4.4). As Wendell (2001) notes, fluctuating and severely limited energy is a common impairment of people with chronic illnesses. Furthermore, fatigue is 'unpredictable and resists control' (Wendell, 2001). In Tanzania, many women had few options to earn money except in physically demanding agricultural labour or casual work in the informal sector. As the main income-earner in female-headed households, the loss of women's ability to earn a livelihood had devastating impacts on the household economy, increasing children's involvement in income-generation activities (discussed more fully

Table 4.1: Women's embodied experiences of living with HIV-related illness

Women's embodied experiences of living with HIV-related illness	Number of women in Tanzania (n=21)	Number of women in the UK (n=12)
Colds, coughing, fevers, chest pains, influenza, tonsillitis, bronchitis	11	6
Fatigue and lack of energy	8	5
Depression, loneliness, stress	4	9
Diarrhoea, nausea, vomiting, loss of appetite, weight loss, headaches, dizziness	7	5
Swelling, pain, numbness and weakness in the limbs and other physical impairments	7	4
Period of critical illness and hospitalisation, for example for pneumonia, tuberculosis, cancer, fits and memory loss	4	7
Skin rashes, sores, fungal infections, shingles	6	1

Box 4.4: Dealing with unpredictable periods of poor health and chronic fatigue: embodied experiences of living with HIV in the UK and Tanzania

Lucy described a day when she was feeling ill:

> *In the morning you don't feel like getting up, you feel cold. You feel the whole body is aching, aches all over my body. You don't feel any energy, there's nothing in your body to make you wake up, so you just feel like sleeping all the time, more and more throughout the whole day, and sometimes there is no appetite, don't feel like eating anything. Every day is different. Then there is times when you feel itching, itches all over the body, and as I've already said I've got this chronic back problem that is always there, but these other [symptoms] come and make life more harder.... (UK)*

Flomina described how exhaustion and fatigue affected her ability to work at the market:

> *I started selling fruit, later I started selling second-hand clothes. While I was working doing this, I used to constantly get tired, maybe this illness was wearing me down without my knowledge. As I used to go from street to street selling these clothes, I could no longer continue because of this tiredness. That was in 2004. Then I started selling carrots at [...] market. That was my last job before I tested positive and started being poorly.*

She commented on how her poor health impacted on her emotional well-being:

> *I feel very lonely. Sometimes I am filled with a lot of thoughts. You suffer one illness after another, not one week goes by without some illness. It's a vicious circle. (Tanzania)*

later in the chapter). In the UK, the episodic nature of HIV illness can mean that women with HIV may not meet the thresholds for welfare assistance and/or social care, thereby increasing children's caring roles and the financial pressures on households.

Three quarters of the women in the UK and several women in Tanzania reported suffering from depression, loneliness or stress as a result of living with a life-limiting illness. Many women were worried about their death and how their children would manage in the future. For African women with insecure immigration status in the UK, the emotional impacts of HIV were also linked to stress and uncertainty about their asylum claim (discussed in more detail later in the chapter). Several African women linked their feelings of loneliness and depression to a lack of opportunities to work or to *'go out and meet people'* and a sense of isolation living far away from their extended family in a different culture in the UK.

Some women in both countries thought that working or studying would help to keep them 'busy' and prevent them from thinking too much about their illness (see Box 4.5). However, African women who were seeking asylum and who were well were not allowed to work because of Home Office regulations, which reinforced their sense of social exclusion and isolation. Furthermore, sickness, combined with the social exclusion, harassment and discriminatory practices often faced by black and immigrant communities in the UK (Anderson and Doyal, 2004; Doyal et al, 2005; Salway et al, 2007) made it difficult for African women who had been granted refugee status to obtain employment.

The smaller proportion of women with HIV reporting depression and mental illness in Tanzania than in the UK sample is likely to be linked to the fact that diagnosis and treatment of depression and mental illness is much less common in resource-limited settings in the global South compared with the global North. While only a few women in Tanzania articulated emotional impacts of living with HIV in terms of feeling down or depressed, many women expressed their worry, stress and fears about not being able to meet the basic needs of their family and living with an unpredictable chronic illness that would lead to their eventual death. As one mother being cared for by her sons commented: *'I feel fine when I am not thinking too much about things, but when I am worried, I feel bad. If I could get everything I need I would feel much happier.'* A few women expressed their sense of hopelessness and despair about their situation through their tears during the interview.

Opportunities for disabled people and other marginalised groups to develop peer support are often perceived as empowering, as commonalities in their lived experiences can enable new collective identities to be constituted (Oliver, 1990; Alsop et al, 2002; Evans and Evans, 2004). Many parents in both Tanzania and the UK regularly attended peer support groups of people living with HIV, which they felt helped them to live more positively with HIV and reduced their social isolation and loneliness. Women also gained from informal advice from their peers about HIV-related issues, including adherence to treatment, side-effects of particular drugs, nutrition and gaining access to informal material support, confirming the findings of previous studies (Doyal and Anderson, 2005). Peer support groups thus appear to have

Box 4.5: Emotional impacts of living with a life-limiting illness in a different culture: experiences of African mothers with HIV in the UK

Angela was very worried about her death and the future for her daughters. She was afraid that she would not be able to afford a Muslim burial in the UK:

> *I'm worried about I'm sick and I'm dying [...] I'm worried about dying, I'm Muslim and I don't know how I will be buried, because Muslim culture if you die, you have to be buried in the ground, not be burned and you have to be washed and dressed. I hear that here in England they don't bury, if you want to be buried, you have to buy a plot to be buried, and I don't have the money to pay for that.*

Before her daughters joined her in the UK, Yvonne was very ill and depressed:

> *That was a terrible time. I was hospitalised for a while. I didn't know many people at that time. I was lonely, a bit depressed, I wanted to give up really, I wanted to just go home and then die. But the support and encouragement and the supporting agencies did help a lot.*

She felt lonely and isolated, living in a different culture to her country of origin, but felt that studying would help to keep her busy:

> *I'm really on my own, their father passed away. I'm not, at the moment I don't have a partner, I've tried to keep myself, that's why I've gone back to college to see if I can get myself more busy. Most people in this country mind their own business really, it's not like our culture where you've got people around.*

an important protective role for mothers with HIV in helping them to deal with the emotional impacts of living with HIV in both low- and high-income countries (see also Chapters 7 and 8). For example, one mother in Tanzania commented on the emotional support she gained from meeting her peers and realising that she is not the only one living with HIV: *'I go and talk to other people like me who are infected; I see there are many of us. We talk about this and that and I'm comforted.'*

The majority of women in the UK and some in Tanzania had experienced episodes of serious illness, sometimes staying in hospital for periods of several months. When parents returned home from hospital, they often experienced reduced mobility, which, in the absence of alternative support, resulted in an increase in the intensity of children's caring responsibilities. For example, when one mother returned from hospital, she had to rely on her children to care for her, despite her attempts to access temporary home care support:

> *I went into hospital with pneumonia so I was in hospital for a month and then when I came home […] I've just started to walk again because all my ability to do anything completely went so I was only just able to get around the house and that was just by holding onto things. But I couldn't carry or lift anything, pull, stand so you know the children were literally expected to do everything, they were completely, they were doing the housework, the cooking, the cleaning, the shopping, you know, virtually everything they were doing.*

Recent medical advances in HIV treatment have significantly improved the quality of life and life expectancy of people with HIV/AIDS in the global North since the late 1990s. All the women with HIV interviewed in the UK accessed antiretroviral therapy (ART) at the time of interview; the majority had started their treatment between three and seven years previously. A few women who had been diagnosed with HIV in the early 1990s delayed the start of medication, suggesting that their decisions about starting combination therapy were influenced by medical advances, the advice of healthcare practitioners and their own perceptions of mortality and the future. For example, an East African woman who had been diagnosed with HIV in her country of origin in 1991 waited as long as she could until she started treatment, so that she would be able to benefit from the medical advances in combination therapy that developed in the late 1990s:

> *I was trying to hang on, you know, the drugs were just coming, were in their trial stage I think. Then in 2000 I decided I have to start, after I'd been hospitalised.*

Although gross inequalities in access to HIV treatment between the global North and South continue (Doyal and Anderson, 2005), some people with HIV/AIDS in Sub-Saharan Africa are starting to see the benefits of international commitments and resources from funding streams such as the Global Fund and the US President's Emergency Plan for AIDS Relief (PEPFAR) spent on scaling up HIV treatment in resource-limited settings. As we discussed in Chapter 2, almost 3 million people living with HIV in low- and middle-income countries were receiving ART by the end of 2007 (WHO, 2008). ART became available free of charge to people with HIV in Tanzania in 2005 (Chipfakacha, 2006). Two thirds of the women with HIV interviewed in Tanzania had started ART within the previous two years. Most women felt that the antiretroviral drugs (ARVs) helped to alleviate the symptoms of HIV-related illness they had previously experienced, although some mentioned negative side-effects of the drugs. A few women had been advised by doctors that their level of immunity was still high and they did not need to start ART unless their CD4 count decreased significantly.[1]

The narratives of mothers with HIV in the UK and Tanzania highlight the difference that access to effective HIV treatment can make to people's lives, both in terms of a reduction in stigma and discrimination, as well as improvements in their physical and emotional health. For example, one mother, who discovered her status in 1996 before HIV treatment was available in Tanzania, became very depressed and felt as if she was *'waiting for her turn to die'* for several years. However, when she heard that treatment was available free of charge, she went for another test and was able to access ARVs through an NGO. Since starting the treatment in 2005, her physical and emotional health had improved dramatically and she was able to cultivate enough food for herself and her family (see Box 4.6).

Women who were diagnosed in the UK in the late 1980s or early 1990s before HIV treatment was widely available highlighted the lack of counselling or support available at the time. Indeed, in the light of recent advances in the effectiveness of HIV treatment, some women commented on the need to re-evaluate their own sense of mortality, which could be difficult to adjust to after many years of believing they were unlikely to see their children grow up (see Box 4.6). The psychological (and material) adjustment for people with HIV to carrying on living due to advances in medical treatment has also been noted in studies conducted in the US and other high-income countries (see Wilton, 1999).

While all the women accessing ART felt that the medication helped to prolong their lives, many women in the UK and Tanzania also commented on the difficulty of dealing with the side-effects of the drugs and adhering to the strict regimes required for their success. For example, Lucy, from East Africa and living in the UK, commented on the difficulty of ensuring that she took four tablets after a full meal in both the morning and evening, as otherwise she felt dizzy. At the time of interview, Lucy had recently changed to a drug regime of two tablets a day following her evening meal, which she found much easier to follow. Other parents also highlighted the ways they sought informal support and encouragement from their children to help them adhere to the drug regime. For example, Sandra suggested that she sometimes struggled within herself about conforming to the drug regime:

I have to remember my tablets all the time, I remember [my daughter] panicking about that, about my tablets when I was very forgetful, she felt responsible to tell me that.[…] I always did manage but I needed help and sometimes I don't want to take them, I just feel, oh God I don't want them today, I just don't want to take them but I've got to and I know that so I take them.

Box 4.6: Access to treatment: mothers' narratives in Tanzania and the UK

Tanzania

I started being sick in 1996. It was then that I discovered that I was HIV positive. It was after I came back from hospital where I had asked them what my husband had died of. They didn't tell me anything. I was then obliged to go to his former place of work to ask about the illness that had caused his death. They told me it was AIDS. So I came back home and started waiting for my turn to die. I never told anybody anything, not even the children. I just stopped and waited. At that time there were no medicines for AIDS. So I lived in these difficult circumstances waiting to die, my health deteriorated, I lost weight and was very depressed. We had no food, the children had no one to pay for their education.

In 1999 I went back to the hospital for a test and they confirmed that I was HIV positive. So I came back home and continued waiting for death to come. Whenever the children asked about what was wrong I used to tell them that I was suffering from stomach ulcers and low blood pressure. I would stay for a month without getting up from bed. Last year I again went for a test telling myself that this was the last test I was going to have. They confirmed my illness. I didn't tell them that I had had a test before. So I asked them where I could get help from, as I had heard on the radio and on TV that medicines were now available. They told me to get in touch with [NGO], so that is how I came to be registered with [NGO] last year…. [Since I started using ARVs] there are great changes. When I started using them my weight was very low, I am now around 97 pounds in weight. My strength is back and I don't feel like sleeping all the time. I can even cultivate enough food to eat as these medicines require a good diet.

UK

I get confused because I still think, oh I shouldn't be here now. Like I was never, I never expected to see my children go to senior school […] you live for so many years thinking that you are, you know, in a certain year you know you're not going to be around or you're going to become ill and sick [...] I'm still alive yet I was told I wouldn't be and it's very hard to come to terms with.

While the women interviewed in the UK all used medication, some combined mainstream medical treatment with complementary therapies, such as acupuncture and massage, where these were available, which they highly valued as a way of relieving stress.

When asked about their everyday experiences of living with HIV, many women accessing ART in Tanzania said that the main problem was hunger and ensuring that they had sufficient nutritious food for their medication to be effective. Indeed, the 'critical connection' between hunger and poor health in relation to HIV/AIDS in low-income countries has only recently been recognised by the UN World Food Programme (WFP) and other policy makers (WFP, 2007). A mother who had physical impairments and was cared for in bed said that she felt hungry every two hours because of the HIV treatment and so her children had a routine of cooking for her every three hours. Another mother commented on how difficult it was to ensure that there was enough food for her and her four children:

> *When I feel sick my real problem is food because I've already started taking these medicines, and the little food I get I have to share between the children, everyone gets their share, so the food is not enough for all of us. I need a really proper diet. The food is not enough, that is why I get constantly ill.*

After the interview, she revealed that her youngest son, who was also living with HIV, did not want to start ART because he knew that there was not enough food for himself and his mother to both eat well. Indeed, surveys in Rwanda and Tanzania suggest that lack of food is a major reason for people *not* to seek treatment for HIV/AIDS, for fear that when they access treatment, their appetite will grow and they will lack sufficient food to meet their increased needs (WFP, 2007).

In addition to lacking sufficient food, many women accessing free ART in Tanzania struggled to afford basic medication to treat minor infections, sores and pains that they experienced on a day-to-day basis or lacked the money to pay for transport to the hospital or clinic. This meant that many women delayed seeking medical treatment until their health deteriorated significantly and they presented at hospital at a late stage of illness. For example, one mother commented: *'So next time I am seriously ill, I don't say a word, I just bear the pain as much as I can for fear of inconveniencing others, because I have no money. This hurts me more and more.'*

Having discussed women's embodied experiences of living with HIV, the next section focuses on the socioeconomic impacts of HIV at the household level.

Poverty and impacts on the household economy

Research in low-income countries has consistently demonstrated the links between HIV/AIDS-related illness and death and financial crisis and deepening poverty at the household level, as we discussed in Chapter 2 (Barnett et al, 2001; Hosegood et al, 2007). In Sub-Saharan Africa, increased expenditure as a result of multiple episodes of illness and death often leads to food insecurity, withdrawal of children from school because of parents' inability to meet their educational expenses and a need for children's labour, as well as the loss of assets (Foster and Williamson, 2000; Yamano and Jayne, 2004; Hosegood et al, 2007). In low-income, female-headed households in the global South, chronic, life-limiting illnesses such as HIV can have a profound impact on the household economy, as women's ability to perform their usual productive and reproductive tasks is gradually reduced through increasing periods of sickness, physical impairment and eventual death.

Many women interviewed in Tanzania perceived the main impacts of living with HIV in terms of the loss of their capacity to support their family as the result of increasing episodes of ill health and/or their husband's death. The majority of women in rural areas were subsistence farmers or used to engage in casual agricultural work, while those living in urban areas used to engage in small business activities in the informal sector. Many women had seen a dramatic decline in the household economy following their husband's death and their increasing ill health. They expressed their frustration and sadness that they were no longer able to work to support their children (see Box 4.7). Some mothers reported that their children engaged in casual work and income-generation activities to try to compensate to some extent for the loss of income to the household (see example of Rose in Box 4.7). Indeed, half of the young people interviewed in Tanzania reported engaging in income-generation activities to help pay for food, medical expenses and other basic needs for their families (see Chapter 5).

Many women were forced to rely on material support and financial assistance from relatives, neighbours and home-based care workers from NGOs, community-based organisations, or faith-based organisations to meet their basic needs for food, medicine, housing, clothing, children's school uniform and other educational expenses, hospital bills and transport to hospital. Several women living in urban areas struggled to pay the rent every month and feared eviction; others also highlighted the problem of overcrowding. Several women commented on the poor quality of housing they had to endure, because of a lack of money for repairs or because they could not afford better quality rented accommodation. Many of the interviewees' homes were draughty and in a poor state of repair, which clearly had detrimental effects on their own and their children's health (see Box 4.7).

The growing body of research on young carers in the global North suggests that the majority of children caring for parents with a range of physical and mental illnesses and impairments come from low-income households (Becker et al, 1998; Becker, 2007; Becker and Becker, 2008). Few studies have explicitly focused on the socioeconomic impacts

---

Box 4.7: Impacts of HIV/AIDS on the household economy in Tanzania: mothers' experiences of chronic poverty, food insecurity and poor housing

Rose commented on the impacts of her ill health on her business and her daughter's caring responsibilities, as she relied on her to support the family (including seven children, four of whom had been orphaned):

> I used to carry the burden when I was in good health. I used to do business, which was enough to meet the family needs. Since I contracted this illness, the business has stopped and the investment money was used up, so I had nothing to depend on. That is when [my eldest daughter] started taking on these responsibilities. [...] I couldn't work and she was still at school. Our problems at home were worse because of this. Her school fees, rent, electricity and water bills, all were a problem. So she was forced to join a drama group to make ends meet. Whatever little she brought in helped with paying the house rent, water and electricity bills, and buying food. Time has gone by and here we are still struggling.

Angelina used to hawk second-hand clothes, but had to stop because of severe chest pains. She relied on support from neighbours and friends for food for herself and her three children:

> I go hungry. When we have maize flour like we did the other day, I ask for a hundred shillings from someone to buy fuel and I then make porridge for the children, so that they have something to eat when they come home from school. Sometimes the neighbours give us food so the children can eat. [...] You can see the house is not built properly. It is cold, but I can't afford to move because I cannot afford to pay for a better house and I live here on charity. It is tough.

of HIV/AIDS on households in the global North. However, as we discussed in Chapter 2, research with African migrants in the UK highlights the ways that living with HIV is exacerbated by pressures linked to immigration and asylum policies, racial and gendered inequalities and wider processes of social exclusion facing recently arrived African migrants (Lewis, 2001; Anderson and Doyal, 2004; Doyal and Anderson, 2005).

The majority of the women interviewed in the UK as part of our study can be characterised as low-income, lone-parent households. Entitlements to state benefits, health and social care and access to employment were dependent on the parent's immigration status, resulting in wide disparities in access to state support within the group of women interviewed. Half of the women reported that they were unable to work due to ill health. As British citizens or refugees who had been granted indefinite leave to remain in the UK they were entitled to state benefits for low-income families (housing benefit, income support, child benefit, child tax credit) and in two instances received disability living allowance. Two African women who were seeking asylum were not permitted to work because of their immigration status and relied on the minimal support provided by the National Asylum Support Service (NASS).[2] Two African women were registered as full-time students and two women (of White British and Black African ethnicity, who were both British citizens) were employed full time.

Although British citizens or those who have been granted refugee status are entitled to state benefits and health and social care provision, they may find it difficult to access the social care support they require. Several women reported difficulties in accessing disability living allowance or home care support following periods of hospitalisation. The national policy context of cut-backs in social services, the changing perception of HIV as a chronic, rather than a terminal illness because of medical advances in treatment, combined with the fluctuating nature of HIV illness and impairment meant that many women's support needs were not deemed to meet the thresholds for entitlements to social care provision (see also Chapters 8 and 10). Most of the women who relied on state benefits or financial support from the NASS commented on how they struggled to pay their bills with the limited support they received. Many associated their stress and depression with the financial pressures they faced in meeting the needs of their family (see Box 4.8).

As well as financial pressures, several women with HIV commented on the extreme stress, fear and insecurity they experienced while they were waiting for a decision on their asylum claim. The emotional impact on families of living with insecure immigration status has been documented in other studies (Lewis, 2001; Anderson and Doyal, 2004; Doyal and Anderson, 2005; Doyal et al, 2005; Conway, 2006b). Indeed, pressures related to immigration and asylum procedures, securing access to legal advice, housing, welfare support, a school place for children and so on may demand much more immediate attention than issues related to HIV.

As the experiences of Lina and Yvonne show (see Box 4.9), the stress and anxiety of insecure immigration status for parents with HIV was linked to very real fears about the threat of deportation as well as

---

Box 4.8: Immigration and access to welfare support in the UK: the experiences of African mothers with HIV

Lucy, from East Africa, who was seeking asylum in the UK, found it difficult to pay the bills for herself and her two children with the welfare support she received from the NASS. She also faced financial pressure to send money back to her country of origin to pay for her older daughter's school fees and found it difficult to afford the transport costs of attending the HIV clinic and hospital appointments for herself and her son:

> *It's so difficult because I'm getting some allowance, £47 for myself, £30 for my children, but I've got to pay my electricity, I've got to pay the gas bill, and then buy food, and, you know, things for the house, so I find life so difficult, I can't make it, even the children having no clothes right now, they don't have any winter clothes, because I can't afford. [...] Whenever he's sick I've got to take him to the clinic, plus myself, I have to go to walk-in clinic all the time, and I find it so difficult to meet transport costs. I feel I can't make it any more, moving up and down, the money is not enough for us.*

Anna, from Southern Africa, who had been granted refugee status, felt frustrated that she could not afford to heat the house for when her sons got back from school in the winter. She struggled to eat well and pay all the bills with the state benefits she received:

> *I can't afford to eat well, I've got bills to pay, and I can't get no income. So maybe one week in a whole month, one week we'll have fruit, the next we won't have no fruit. And eating well, all the money is spent, £60. I get £150 a week, £60 goes on food, £50 goes on gas and electric, in a week, and then I've got my TV licence, and bus fares. So I think also that all just comes down into my depression and builds up depression and that's how it gets to my kids, I think.*

the loss of access to welfare support and medical treatment. Insecure immigration status meant that parents and children were at risk of detention or dispersal in the UK, which could result in disrupted adherence to drug regimes, loss of access to welfare support and free healthcare, the threat that their children could be taken into local authority care if the family was deemed to be destitute, and ultimately the loss of access to life-prolonging highly active antiretroviral therapy (HAART) through deportation to countries in the South with resource-limited healthcare systems (Doyal and Anderson, 2005; Conway, 2006b).

The mental stress surrounding immigration and asylum procedures compounds the traumatic experiences that many parents and children may have encountered when fleeing from persecution, violence and conflict in their country of origin and during their journey to the UK (see Yvonne's narrative in Box 4.9). Transnational families face the additional emotional burden of separation from close family members left behind in their country of origin or in neighbouring countries, and with whom they may have lost contact through displacement and migration. They may also experience pressure to send remittances to family members, particularly older children in their country of origin, in spite of their difficult socioeconomic circumstances in host countries in the global North.

Parents' narratives from Tanzania and the UK suggest that HIV illness can have a significant impact on the household economy and the wider socioeconomic well-being of family members. In the UK context this is exacerbated by immigration policies, racial discrimination and harassment that further marginalise African migrants living with HIV. Experiences of HIV-related stigma and discrimination within families and communities often compound the structural inequalities and exclusions that some people living with HIV face in both the global North and South. The following section discusses the different dimensions of stigma experienced by the mothers interviewed for our study.

Box 4.9: Dealing with trauma, immigration pressures and HIV: experiences of refugee and asylum seeking parents in the UK

Yvonne had to leave her country of origin in East Africa when her husband experienced political difficulties and disappeared. Her husband planned to follow with their daughters when he was released from prison, but Yvonne was informed that he had died in an accident. She related her depression and ill health at the time to the stress and emotional trauma she experienced:

> *I think that's some of the things that really made me so ill, because that time he disappeared, there were political issues, yeah, when they eventually told me where he was, then he'd passed away, when he just got out of prison.*

Yvonne's children joined her in the UK two years later. She commented on the extreme stress of living with insecure immigration status, waiting to hear if she and her daughters would be granted refugee status:

> *That was the most stressful thing, more even than my illness, because you think, well, if something happens to me and then maybe the girls are left hanging, they have no papers, they've got nothing, and they wouldn't know what to do really.*

The family were eventually granted indefinite leave to remain in the UK and her daughters had recently applied for British citizenship.

Lina and her husband (from Southern Africa) were seeking asylum in the UK with their three children. Their asylum claim had been rejected and although the family were still receiving welfare support from the NASS, Lina was worried that they would be deported and she would lose access to the life-prolonging HIV treatment she received in the UK:

> *I am sick, I am in this country, and I've got my family here. If they send me back home, where am I going to stay? Where am I going to live? Because if I go home, I'll die, and my kids they will have nowhere, they'll start going and being prostitutes, and they will die like me as well, so they have to consider. When I wrote that letter, they answered me, they said, 'Yours is a hard case, we are going to put this to Home Office for attention' or something like that, which I've never heard anything.*

Lina commented on people's assumptions about standards of living in the North and the pressure to support relatives in her country of origin, which made it even more difficult to return:

> *They don't understand that England life is tough, they're thinking when you're in England, you've got everything, you have got money, you are in your posh life, they don't know that you are struggling to live in this country.*

Stigma and discrimination within the family and community

As we discussed in Chapter 2, HIV is a highly stigmatised condition because of its association with promiscuous sexual behaviour, death and dying, and particularly marginalised 'at risk' groups such as gay men and prostitutes. It reflects all three types of stigma identified by Goffman (1963): 'abominations of the body', 'blemishes of character' and 'tribal stigma'. While Goffman's work helped to identify individual aspects of stigma, recent approaches have emphasised the social dimensions of stigma and discrimination (Ogden and Nyblade, 2005). Parker and Aggleton (with Attawell et al), for example, suggest that stigmatisation and discrimination are social processes that are 'used to create and maintain social control and to produce and reproduce social inequalities' (2002: 15). They suggest that stigmatisation is a process that involves 'identifying and using "difference" between groups of people to create and legitimize social hierarchies' (Parker and Aggleton, with Attawell et al, 2002: 15), transforming difference into social inequalities.

Studies conducted in many different countries suggest that there are many similarities in the key causes, the forms that HIV/AIDS-related stigma takes and the consequences of stigma across a wide range of sociocultural contexts (Ogden and Nyblade, 2005). The stigma and discrimination experienced by women with HIV participating in the study in Tanzania and the UK can be conceptualised in terms of both individual aspects and social processes that reproduce social inequalities. Their experiences relate to three main forms of stigma: enacted stigma (direct experiences of discrimination); perceived stigma (fear of stigmatisation) and self-stigma (internalised stigma).

Enacted stigma

Over half of the women in Tanzania and a third of those in the UK reported direct experiences of discrimination from family members, neighbours and others in the community. The enacted stigma they experienced can be seen as related to pre-existing sources of stigma and discrimination, particularly those linked to hierarchies of gender, sexuality and class (Parker and Aggleton, with Attawell et al, 2002).

Research in Africa, and other countries in the global South, such as India, suggests that women tend to be both more heavily stigmatised than men and blamed more often for bringing HIV into a family or marriage, which may result in the loss of children and home (Bharat and Aggleton, 1999; Parker and Aggleton, with Attawell et al, 2002; Ogden and Nyblade, 2005). In Tanzania, many women experienced discrimination from their husband's relatives following his death, including separation from their children, loss of assets and inheritance as well as social isolation, rejection and verbal abuse (see Box 4.10). This

---

Box 4.10: Enacted stigma within the family: women's experiences in Tanzania

Loss of property, assets and inheritance

Ester described how following her husband's death, his relatives took all their valuable assets, including her husband's pension, leaving her with very little to support her two children:

> Before he died, he was running a hairdresser's salon of his own. After he died his relatives tried to run it but they couldn't pay the rent and electricity bills. It closed down. They then took all the shaving equipment, three rotating chairs and two radios. They took away the TV and a fan from our house and they sold the farm. I was left with nothing. Then they started drawing his pension money. By the time I realised most of it was gone, I was left with very little.

Refusal to provide care and social support

Asha commented on her husband's relatives' refusal to help support her and her children after her husband's death:

> After his [my husband's] death I lived alone in town with the children. Then I became ill. My parents then came to collect me and brought me back home. While I was in town I had no help from my late husband's relatives, they shunned me. So I have been living here with my parents since then.

Abandonment

Farida and her youngest son were ostracised by her five adult children, who never came to visit or greet them even though they live in the same town:

> They have stayed put in their homes and don't come to visit me nor want anything to do with me.

Blame and shame

Mercy received insults and threats from her husband's relatives after his death:

> They used to tell me that I was an AIDS sufferer, that I would die, that they were going to throw me out of the house. Such things used to depress me and I despaired and got frustrated. I wondered why they didn't say this to their kin when he was alive.

---

discrimination can be related to existing gender inequalities in access to land, property and inheritance, such as customary laws that deny widows the right to inherit their deceased husband's land (UNICEF and UNAIDS, 1999). Similarly, African concepts of childhood mean that rights over children are vested in men by customary, religious and statutory law so that in the event of divorce, separation or the husband's death, the custody of the children remains with the father or his clan members (UNICEF, 1999; Evans, 2004).

The blame and shame women may experience may also result in the refusal of family members to provide care for women living with HIV or to respect customary obligations of care and social support within the family, as the examples in Box 4.10 show. As Ogden and Nyblade (2005) suggest, the refusal of family members to provide care within the household may be linked to fear of transmission, moral judgments, fear of stigma from others, combined with the impact of poverty and resource constraints, which affect the amount of support relatives are able or willing to provide to someone who is expected to die in the near future.

In the UK, only a small number of women reported direct experiences of discrimination from family members. Following her diagnosis, one White British woman experienced a loss of social networks both among her friends and within her family, which significantly affected her willingness to disclose her HIV status to others:

> *When I was diagnosed I lost all my friends, and then within sort of the following couple of years then the rest of my family, you know, sort of lost contact for [one] reason or another, or there was problems within the family, so it would cause arguments, so that's why I only have contact with my dad now. So, yeah, it's taken me quite a few years to get the confidence to be able to tell people again.*

Almost a third of the women in Tanzania and a few women in the UK had direct experiences of discrimination from neighbours and others in the community. Some women living in the UK experienced forms of physical stigma, such as marking out their 'differentness' through the separation of usually shared objects such as eating utensils (see Box 4.11). This expression of stigma has been reported within the home in many different countries and contexts (Ogden and Nyblade, 2005).

Some women in both countries experienced a combination of forms of enacted stigma within the community, including physical, social and verbal discrimination. One mother in Tanzania experienced physical and social isolation in her parents' village, linked to the gender-related

Box 4.11: Physical, social and verbal expressions of stigma: experiences from the UK and Tanzania

Physical isolation and separation

Laura expressed her frustrations with her mother's stigmatising treatment. Her mother made Laura feel different by separating her eating utensils and attempting to impose physical boundaries on her interactions with her daughter:

> *It's like you've got something really, really contagious that by eating, by talking to that person and by sharing something you'll give it, but I said to my – the doctors even said to her – 'You know you can't get it from sharing food.' [...] She said 'The food that we eat, if I share something [my daughter's] going to get contaminated.' That's what she said to [my daughter], 'She's going to get contaminated.'*

Laura felt that her mother was undermining her own role as a mother and was worried that her parents wanted to take custody of her daughter and raise her in their country of origin. While Laura's health had improved and she felt like she was living 'a normal life', she was reminded about her illness by her family's negative attitudes and assumptions about her capabilities:

> *I don't really think about it, only when my mum and my brother, it reminds me, you know. When I'm with them it's like they bombard me with things: 'Oh you can't do this because you're sick, you can't go out because you're sick, you can't go on holiday because you're sick', that's what they, my mum is always saying that. She's always putting me off when I want to do something you know. (UK)*

Verbal abuse and harassment

Julie experienced social isolation, verbal abuse and harassment from her neighbours and others in the community, which eventually forced her to move:

> *For a period of time, sort of, like, people find out and people were just making their own assumptions as to how I'd become infected and, you know, nobody, nobody would want to talk to you so eventually, you know, people started to drift away and I was just very isolated. And I was also, sort of, one of the odd ones out because not very many heterosexual women, you know, were positive and I was classified as a working woman and various, like, all sorts of slanderous comments were made and I had to move my flat and, you know, leave my flat and everything because of being pestered. (UK)*

In Tanzania, Eliza found that her neighbours physically and socially isolated her when she was forced to return to live at her parents' home:

> *It's very difficult here. If people know you are ill, they don't want to talk to you and don't even want to go past your house. It's not usual to return to your parent's place, but because I'm ill, I have to stay here. [...] If [a married woman] returns to the parental home, you are ostracised and just have to put up with it. You should be given your own place where you can build a house and live there.*

stigma associated with a married woman returning to her parental home (see example of Eliza, Box 4.11). Similarly, in the UK, Julie, a White British woman, experienced social isolation, verbal abuse and harassment when she was diagnosed in the early 1990s. Julie's neighbours and others in the community made moral judgements and assumptions about the way she had become infected, linked to sexual, gender and class-related stigma associated with promiscuity and prostitution, which eventually forced her to move (see Box 4.11).

Some women in both the UK and Tanzania had direct experiences of institutional discrimination from landlords and others they were reliant on for housing. When landlords, tenants and house owners discovered their HIV status, some women were evicted and were forced to rely on emergency informal support from neighbours or relatives in Tanzania, or in the UK, emergency housing provision from social services, such as bed and breakfast accommodation (see Box 4.12). Furthermore, women with HIV living in shared accommodation experienced difficulties concealing their medicines and ensuring that their HIV status remained confidential, confirming the findings of Anderson and Doyal's (2004) study with African women with HIV in London. Joyce's problems caused by having to use a shared refrigerator for her HIV medication (see Box 4.12) highlight the multiple impacts that a lack of privacy in shared accommodation can have for women with HIV.

As these experiences show, enacted stigma from neighbours and members of the community is often linked to the disclosure of a person's HIV status. Goffman draws a distinction between people who are 'discredited', that is those whose 'differentness' has been disclosed, and those who are 'discreditable', that is those whose 'differentness' has not been disclosed, who try to conceal their HIV status and may be able to 'pass' as 'normals' (Goffman, 1963; Cree et al, 2004). For example, Ester, a mother in Tanzania, found that people only started to gossip about her since she had shown physical symptoms of HIV-related illness: '*Now I'm ill, people gossip a lot about me. Some thought I wouldn't make it when I was hospitalised for ten days [...]. I was breathing with the aid of oxygen. Now they are stigmatising me.*' Previously, Ester had been able to 'pass' as 'normal' since her HIV status was not visible or disclosed,

Box 4.12: Institutional stigma: eviction and homelessness in the UK and Tanzania

When Lucy first came to the UK with her children, they lived with a neighbour from her home village in East Africa. Shortly after Lucy was diagnosed with HIV, the woman they were living with accidentally discovered her status and threw them out of the house. Lucy and her children became homeless and were forced to stay in temporary bed and breakfast accommodation provided by social services for one year before they were moved to more permanent social housing:

> – When I was diagnosed, I had put my letter on my bed, and the lady we are living with came and read that letter, and from that, I was still planning how to tell them, she was so horrid to me, she couldn't, she said, 'Oh you've been living here when you're ill with HIV, you and your son and you know I've got children' – she has four children. She said, 'You are going to contaminate our children,' so she said that I should remove my toothbrush from the bathroom, and she said I should leave her house, and go to hospital, so that the hospital can house me.

> – So what happened then?

> – I had to go back to the hospital, my HIV hospital, to declare [that I was] homeless and explain to her that I'd been sent away from home because the lady had read my letter. Then she got a letter to social services, that's how I've been getting support. So social services took us, I went to social services offices that day with the children and my bag. We waited in the office until 8 o'clock, then they gave us a bed and breakfast, where I went to sleep with my children.

The lack of privacy in shared rented accommodation made it very difficult for Joyce to keep her HIV status secret, because of the need to keep her antiretroviral medication in a communal refrigerator. Joyce had been forced to move house many times when other tenants in the private rented house discovered her HIV status. Joyce struggled with her current landlord to allow her to use her own refrigerator in her room:

> If you're living in a house with people, they already know you're HIV positive when they see your drugs in the fridge. [...] I had to move eight or nine times. So when I moved here I started to look for a one-bedroom. I went for about two months without a fridge. I had to just keep them in my room but after a while they started going off and when I would open them they smelt. And so when I took them I started to feel ill and I began thinking that these drugs I was taking weren't good. So I had to eventually get a fridge. But the landlord didn't like

> me having a fridge. Even this small one in my room [he didn't like] because it
> needs extra electricity. So I told him. I have to send Alice [her daughter] to get
> the drugs because I wasn't even able to carry them.
>
> Angelina, a parent in Tanzania, received a threat from her landlady to vacate the
> room if she became critically ill:
>
> Only the other day, the landlady, she lives in [nearby town], sent word saying,
> 'If that sick woman living in my house is in a very bad way, get her to vacate
> the house. I don't want her to die in there.' When the children heard that they
> were really upset.

but following a period of hospitalisation, she had become 'discredited' in people's perceptions.

Perceived stigma

A third of the women interviewed in the UK and some of those interviewed in Tanzania perceived that they and their children were vulnerable to stigma and discrimination if members of the community discovered their HIV status. Indeed, fear of stigma plays a significant role in women's decisions about whether to share their status with family members, friends, neighbours, professionals or others in the community. For example, a woman from the Horn of Africa living in the UK had many friends from her country of origin, but did not want any of them to know about her and her daughter's HIV status: '*They don't know nothing about us. They think we've got another illness, because of the stigma, they would run away from us.*' Another mother from East Africa living in the UK was fearful about anyone at her children's school finding out about HIV in their family: '*I've told them [her children] not to tell anybody at school because if you tell them about us they're going to be rejected, you'll not have any friends, they'll laugh at you....*' A few women in the UK also feared that if family members discovered their HIV status, they would lose their extended family support network and their children might experience 'stigma by association' through their association with their mother.

Despite a higher proportion of people being affected by HIV than in the UK, fear of stigma persists in Tanzania. Some women were worried about sharing their status with friends or others in community. One woman, for example, concealed her status from her friends and the people she worked with at the market: *'Whenever they ask me I tell them I am resting…. If they got to know your HIV status, they could turn against you.'* She also highlighted the ways that, as well as providing support, religious institutions and faith communities could reinforce stigma, because of gender-related discrimination that linked HIV with 'immoral' sexual behaviour:

> *At the mosque, once you declare your status, it spreads like wild fire. You hear them saying so and so is a prostitute, she has AIDS. I see that at the church they are more sympathetic and they help a lot in these situations. They accept that you were infected by accident.*

As will be shown in later chapters, the fear of stigma and desire to keep HIV secret within the family and community significantly affects children's and parents' ability to seek informal and formal support that they might otherwise be able to access.

Self-stigma / internalised stigma

According to Ogden and Nyblade (2005: 32), self-stigma or internalised stigma refers to the phenomenon when 'a person living with HIV imposes stigmatizing beliefs and actions on themselves'. This process of internalising dominant cultural values and norms about HIV/ AIDS found in wider society has been identified as a near universal phenomenon found in research findings across diverse contexts (Ogden and Nyblade, 2005). Only a few women's narratives illustrate the notion of self-stigma. One White British woman in the UK was diagnosed in the late 1980s before HIV treatment was available, when HIV was heavily stigmatised and there were common misconceptions about people who were HIV positive and how HIV was transmitted (Chapman, 2000). She did not receive any counselling following diagnosis and described feeling 'dirty', fearing that her HIV status was visible to people:

> *It's very difficult because you feel very dirty, you feel, at that time you did. I used to feel that everybody down the street would know and I started slinking like this you know walking around with my head down. Disinfectant baths, all sorts of things I was planning to do, it's ridiculous.*

The notion of the bodies of HIV-positive people as dirty and visibly contaminated has been found in a number of studies (Squire, 1997;

Chapman, 2000). While only a few women's narratives explicitly demonstrate the notion of self-stigma, as we saw earlier in the chapter, many women's narratives of living with a life-limiting illness point to a range of emotional impacts, such as a loss of hope and depression. Having explored the detrimental effects of HIV-related stigma and discrimination within the family and community on women living with HIV and their children, it is not surprising that HIV is often kept secret and disclosure to loved ones is a difficult and complex process. Indeed, people living with HIV are likely to engage in an ongoing process of managing their presentation of a 'discredited identity' to others in order to avoid stigmatisation in different contexts (Goffman, 1963). The final section explores mothers' and young people's accounts of the process of disclosure of parental HIV status within the family.

Deciding whom to tell: secrets and disclosure within the family

As we have noted above, fear of stigma prevented many parents from sharing their HIV status with family members, friends, neighbours and others in the community. The experiences of the women interviewed suggest that deciding whom and when to tell about their status is linked to a complex process of 'coming to terms' with their status over time, as well as their perceptions of the impact of their news on other members of the family. Several African women in Tanzania and the UK did not want to tell their elderly mothers about their illness, due to their fears about how they would cope with the news, particularly when they had already lost children to AIDS. This reflects Doyal and Anderson's (2005) and Doyal et al's (2005) study with HIV-positive African women and men in London. Although women with HIV were generally able to access more informal support from family members, friends and neighbours when they were open about their HIV status, their experiences of stigma discussed above suggest that disclosure can also lead to ill-treatment and a refusal to provide care and support. Indeed, because of the fear of stigma, many women sought informal support from neighbours and others in the community without disclosing their status (see Chapter 7 for discussion of the informal support that parents were able to access in the community).

As we discussed in Chapter 2, previous research has highlighted a reluctance among parents in many countries to tell their children about their HIV status (Lie and Biswalo, 1998; Thorne et al, 2000; Lewis, 2001; Chinouya, 2006; Wood et al, 2006). The majority of parents in our study had disclosed their status to at least one of their children, and the young people in our sample were all aware of their parent's illness. Many parents' narratives in both Tanzania and the UK suggest that their decisions about the 'right time' to share their status with their children were linked to their perceptions of the child's emotional maturity and competence to keep their status secret within the family, acknowledgement of the need for children to be aware of their parent's status and wanting to prevent children from discovering their status from someone outside the family. Most parents felt that sharing their status with their child would help them to understand why they were asked to take on a caring role when their parent was ill. For example, Christine shared her status with her daughter to help her understand why she was asked to care for her mother and younger siblings:

> *I did that [disclosed her HIV status] I suppose in a way to try and make her understand why she does the things she does, because she was beginning to be a teenager and she wasn't being – I think she had sometimes anger and I thought the longer I keep it the worst it will get.*

Some parents in Tanzania felt that telling children about their status was important in preparing them for their parent's illness and eventual death. For example, Angelina said: '*I told them [her sons] I have HIV so I may die at any time and I stressed that it's important for them to work hard and to mix with other people so that they don't have a tough time when I die.*'

Several parents in both countries chose to share their status first with the young person who had greatest caring responsibilities (often the eldest co-resident child) and kept their status secret from their younger children. When some parents eventually shared their status with their younger children, young people sometimes resented the fact that secrets about their parent's illness had not been shared with them. In a few instances, parents' decisions to tell their children about their status were motivated by a desire to avoid children discovering their status inadvertently from someone outside the family. For example, Yvonne, from East Africa who was waiting for a decision on her asylum application in the UK, received a threat from the immigration authorities that she would be dispersed to another part of the UK and her daughters would be sent to a detention centre, since they were over 18 and no longer considered her 'dependants'. Yvonne did not want her daughters to discover her status accidentally through an immigration official or lawyer and so decided to disclose her status:

> *It got me a bit worried because I knew that they would get involved in courts, things, together, and probably someone else would speak, a solicitor or whoever, bring it out in the open and then I didn't want them to be shocked. I didn't want them to hear it from someone else.*

Indeed, some children in the UK had discovered their parent's or their own HIV status accidentally through the family's contact with healthcare or other professionals, or when other members of the family assumed that they were aware of their parent's HIV status. In Tanzania, some parents decided to be open about their status with their children following children's negative experiences of bullying or gossip about their parent from their peers, neighbours or others in the community.

When parents shared their status with their children, many young people in both countries described feeling worried that their parent would die in the near future. In the UK, many young people described feelings of shock and numbness and some young people were also worried about their own health status. Several parents in the UK were surprised by the way their children reacted, expecting either a more or less emotional reaction to the news. For young people in Tanzania, their parent's disclosure often confirmed what they had suspected. Several children recognised the symptoms of HIV/AIDS that they had been taught at school and suspected that their mother's illness was HIV-related. For children who had already lost their father to AIDS, their parent's disclosure was often linked to memories of their father's illness and death. Some young people in Tanzania who recognised the symptoms were frustrated that their parent was not open with them about their illness. Neema for example felt hurt and confused about why her mother was not open with her:

> *At first she hid the truth about her test results from me. It took her three months to finally tell me the truth. But during all this time I could tell that she had HIV/AIDS. She had all the symptoms of people infected with HIV/AIDS we had been told about at school by our teacher. Our teacher had told us about how much they suffer and I knew how much my mother was suffering. I was really hurt and was debating within myself whether I should confront her and ask her to tell me the truth, when she finally told me the truth. She told me that [NGO] had told her she was infected with HIV/AIDS. (Neema, aged 18, Tanzania)*

Despite the process of disclosure being a difficult experience for parents and young people, parents felt that disclosure had helped children to understand why they needed to help care for their parent and led to more attentive and caring relationships within the family. Young people also felt that parental disclosure helped them to understand more about their parent's illness and how to care for them. After initial feelings of shock, fear and anxiety about their parent's illness, the children interviewed had accepted their parent's status and often became more caring and sensitive to their parent's needs. While many children continued to feel worried and afraid about their parent's eventual death, some found that caring for their parent helped them to feel valued and involved in their parent's care, as Magic's narrative suggests:

> *Well I still do get afraid that, you know, that sometimes, that something might, like really bad, will really, really happen to her; she might die. So there is, there is a, there is that, still that fear that she might die, but you know, you know, but you know, for it not to happen soon, so that then maybe she could live a bit longer. But I can help her and stuff and not let her get stressed and stuff. (Magic, aged 12, UK)*

Conclusion

This chapter has explored the ways that parents with HIV negotiate changing health identities and embodied experiences of living with a chronic, life-limiting illness within the family and community. As a 'ritual drama of illness' (James and Hockey, 2007), HIV illness is both an intensely personal as well as a social experience, embedded in normative notions of family and intimate relationships and social inequalities and hierarchies of gender, race, age, disability and religion. Mothers' changing health identities and embodied experiences of HIV intersected with structural inequalities and exclusions that compounded their experiences of ill health, including poverty, food insecurity, poor housing, inequalities in access to treatment and welfare support, unequal gender relations, stigma and discrimination within the family and community. As will be discussed further in Chapter 9, these structural and relational factors play an important role in influencing whether children and young people are drawn into caring roles. The following chapter examines the ways that young people care for their parents in the context of a lack of alternative support.

Notes

[1] The World Health Organization recommends that the criteria for the initiation of ART in adults in resource-limited settings is for ART to be considered when the CD4 cell count is between 200 and 350 and for those with CD4 counts of less than 200 to be treated irrespective of the clinical stage of HIV-associated disease, since this is associated with a significant increase in opportunistic infections and death (WHO, 2006).

[2] The level of cash support available to adult asylum seekers from NASS is 70% of the amount paid to people on income support, which was £42.16 per week in 2008 (see www.bia.homeoffice.gov.uk), well below subsistence levels. Housing is also provided by NASS.

FIVE

Children's and young people's care work in households affected by HIV and AIDS

This chapter discusses young people's everyday caring responsibilities within households affected by HIV/AIDS in both the global North and South. As discussed in Chapter 1, research in the UK and other high-income countries as well as in Sub-Saharan Africa has demonstrated that young carers' caring responsibilities do differ from other children's household responsibilities in both the North and the South in terms of the extent and nature of children's care work (Becker, 2007). The research in Tanzania and the UK further develops understandings of children's care work gained from research with children caring for parents with a range of mental and physical illness or impairments conducted predominantly in the North. Our findings provide an in-depth insight into the specific dimensions of children's care work in families affected by HIV/AIDS. In this chapter, we highlight similarities and differences between children's experiences within two divergent socioeconomic and welfare contexts. Drawing on young people's narratives, diaries, drawings and photographs[1] of their daily routines and caring responsibilities, we discuss the range of support that children provide for their parents/relatives and explore gendered and temporal aspects of children's care work.

Young people's everyday caring responsibilities

Becker (2007) has suggested that children's caring responsibilities can be located along a continuum of care, as discussed in Chapter 1. This ranges from most children who are engaged in 'routine' levels and types of caregiving, including household chores, regardless of the health status of their parent/relative, to children who are engaged in substantial, regular and significant caregiving *and* who provide considerable help with household chores. Research from the UK, Australia, the US and Sub-Saharan Africa suggests that it is the wider range of household and caring tasks, and particularly involvement in the personal care of their parent/relative, as well as the frequency and time spent on these tasks that distinguishes the work of young carers from the usual household chores that young people do in the North and South (Becker, 2007).

In a large survey of young carers in the UK, Dearden and Becker (2004) categorised children's caring tasks in terms of domestic tasks; general care; emotional support; intimate care; childcare; and other. Analysis of the data from families affected by HIV/AIDS revealed that these categories needed to be developed to recognise the importance of children's roles in providing home-based healthcare to parents/relatives with HIV/AIDS, as well as to take account of children's engagement in income-generation activities to support the household in the South. Children's care work in families affected by HIV and AIDS has thus been categorised here in terms of:

- *household chores* – including cooking, cleaning, washing dishes, laundry, shopping, (in Tanzania only) fetching water, tending livestock, cultivating crops and vegetables;
- *healthcare* – including reminding parent/relative to take their medication, giving and collecting medication, accompanying parent/relative to hospital and care while in hospital, assisting with mobility, preparing special nutritional food for parent/relative;
- *personal care* – including washing/bathing parent/relative, assisting to eat, dress and use the toilet;
- *childcare* – including getting siblings ready for school, bathing siblings, looking after/supervising them and accompanying them to/from school;
- *income-generation activities* – (in Tanzania only) begging, casual farm work, selling produce, domestic work, working in a shop;
- *emotional and practical support* – including talking and comforting parent/relative, helping to remember appointments and bills etc.

In Tanzania and the UK, all of the young people interviewed had significant, regular responsibilities for household chores and the majority were involved in providing healthcare for their sick parent/relative (see Table 5.1). Almost half of the young people in both countries provided some personal care for their parent/relative and many provided childcare for their siblings or other children in the household. The most noticeable difference in young people's caring responsibilities in the two countries relates to children's involvement in income-generation activities in Tanzania, where almost half of the young people were involved in casual work or begging. Overall, however, the range of support that young people provide for their

Table 5.1: Young people's different caring tasks in Tanzania and the UK

Caring tasks	Number of young people in Tanzania (n=22)	Number of young people in the UK (n=11)	Total (n=33)
Household chores	22 (100%)	11 (100%)	33 (100%)
Healthcare	18 (82%)	7 (64%)	25 (76%)
Personal care	10 (45%)	5 (45%)	15 (45%)
Childcare	10 (45%)	3 (27%)	13 (39%)
Income-generation activities	10 (45%)	1 (9%)	11 (33%)
Emotional & practical support	3 (14%)	5 (45%)	8 (24%)

parent/relative with HIV is broadly similar in Tanzania and the UK. The following sections explore each aspect of young people's care work.

Young people's household chores

Young people in Tanzania and the UK all reported significant and regular responsibilities for a number of household chores (see Table 5.1). Table 5.2 shows the range of chores they were engaged in, based on young people's narratives of their care work. The household chores performed by young people in both countries are broadly similar, with a majority in both countries engaged in cooking and preparing meals and cleaning/tidying the house, and roughly half of the young people had regular responsibilities for washing dishes. The majority of young people in Tanzania had regular responsibilities for washing clothes by hand, while laundry was not such a significant task for young people in the UK. Half of the young people in Tanzania fetched water, which was needed for several household activities, such as cooking, laundry, bathing, cleaning and washing dishes, and children living in rural areas were responsible for tending livestock and cultivating crops and vegetables for household consumption and sometimes for sale at the market. In contrast in the UK, going shopping, carrying and lifting heavy items for parents was a household task mentioned by some children.

Although the care tasks carried out by young people in both countries are broadly similar, children's care work differs considerably in the intensity and time taken to perform household chores because of disparities in living standards between the North and South. Household chores in Africa are considerably more time consuming

Table 5.2: Young people's responsibilities for household chores in Tanzania and the UK

Household chores	Number of young people in Tanzania (n=22)	Number of young people in UK (n=11)	Total number of young people (n=33)
Preparing meals and cooking	22	8	30
Cleaning and tidying	19	10	29
Laundry	15	3	18
Washing dishes	13	5	18
Making tea/drinks	12	2	14
Fetching water	11	0	11
Shopping/buying food	5	5	10
Tending livestock	9	0	9
Cultivating crops and vegetables	6	0	6
Heating water for baths	4	0	4
Carrying/lifting items	0	2	2
Fetching firewood	1	0	1

and labour intensive and often require physical strength and fitness. In Tanzania, young people's care work took longer and was more physically demanding than in the UK (see Figure 5.1). As Ogden et al comment,

> Caring for a person with HIV/AIDS requires considerable time and other resources, which is compounded in many developing countries by a lack of basic services such as clean water. About 24 buckets of clean water are required every day to care for a person living with HIV/AIDS, to wash the sick person, to clean soiled sheets, to wash dishes and to prepare food. (Ogden et al, 2006: 336)

Despite the gendered division of labour within households, young people's household chores in Tanzania[2] did not differ significantly according to gender. A slightly higher proportion of girls were involved in activities focused around the household, such as cleaning the house, preparing meals and heating water for baths, while slightly higher proportions of boys were involved in outdoor activities such as buying food at the market, tending livestock, cultivating crops and vegetables and washing clothes (see Figure 5.1). However, girls and boys were equally involved in some activities traditionally perceived as 'women's work', such as washing dishes, making tea and drinks and fetching water. Young people's daily routines in Box 5.1 illustrate the different kinds of household chores young people carry out in the North and South.

Figure 5.1: Drawing by Grace[3] (aged 19, Tanzania), who cared for her mother and four younger siblings, and photographs taken by Grace and a family member.

'This is me, carrying water. This is my pig and these chickens are mine. This is my home'

'Here I'm washing the dishes'

'My younger brother is digging'

Box 5.1: Household chores performed by young people in Tanzania and the UK

William (aged 16, Tanzania) lived with his grandmother, aunts and siblings in a village. His mother worked as a domestic worker and stayed at her employer's house. He had no contact with his father, who was separated from his mother and was an alcoholic. William was studying in the final year of primary school and did more household chores at the weekends, such as fetching water, washing clothes, washing the dishes and sweeping the compound. He described a typical week day:

> *On school days I wake up at 5 am and I milk the goat. At 6 am I make tea. At 6.30 am I put on my school uniform. I don't wash the dishes or cut grass [for the livestock] because I did that the previous evening. At 7 am I remind grandma to take her medicine and I go to school. At 4 pm when I come back I cut grass for the livestock and prepare the evening meal. [I study] when I've finished the work, maybe by 8 pm.*

Kerry (aged 18, UK) lived with her mother and was studying at college. Her household duties depended to some extent on her mother's health, but she felt that she had got into a regular routine of cooking and cleaning most days: '*I just kind of get on with it.*' She described a typical week day:

> *I wake up quite early about 6 usually to go to college, and I get there quite early usually, and we usually finish at 3.30 but sometimes we finish earlier, and I just get back. If she's not feeling well I usually do the cooking, and sometimes help her do the shopping or clean up for her, but sometimes she'll do it if she's feeling ok, but a lot of the time I'll do most of it, I usually do most of the cooking.*

Young people's healthcare responsibilities

According to their own accounts, most young people provided support with their parent/relative's healthcare in Tanzania and the UK, representing the second most significant care task after household chores. Support included administering medication, accompanying and providing care while their parent/relative was in hospital, assisting with mobility and preparing special nutritional food for parents/relatives (see Table 5.3).

Table 5.3: Young people's healthcare responsibilities in Tanzania and the UK

Young people's healthcare responsibilities	Number of young people in Tanzania (n=22)	Number of young people in UK (n=11)	Total number of young people (n=33)
Reminding/assisting to take medication	14	7	21
Seeking help to transport parent to hospital	5	1	6
Preparing special diet for parent	5	1	6
Accompanying parent to hospital/clinic	1	4	5
Overnight care for parent in hospital	3	1	4
Caring in emergencies	1	3	4
Assisting with mobility	1	2	3
Cooking food for parent in hospital	3	0	3
Washing sores and treating minor illnesses	2	0	2
Collecting medication	2	0	2

Almost two thirds of the young people in both countries played an important role in helping their parent/relative to remember to take their antiretroviral (ARV) medication at the right time. Many young people said the best thing about caring for their parent/relative was helping them to take their medication on time, as they felt that this would help to improve their health. As noted in Chapter 4, the majority of parents/relatives with HIV in Tanzania and the UK were taking ARV medication at the time of interview. Adherence to strict drug regimes is essential for the medication to be effective in controlling HIV and research suggests that anything lower than 95% adherence was associated with negative outcomes such as viral resistance to the medication (Beals et al, 2006). Children's roles in helping their parents/relatives to remember to take their medication at the right time may thus be important in helping parents/relatives to adhere to drug regimes, as shown in Figure 5.2 and Box 5.2.

Owing to the fluctuating nature of HIV illness, young people's responsibilities for household chores were interspersed with periods of more intensive care for their parent/relative during episodes of parental

Figure 5.2: Photograph of Sarah (aged 15, Tanzania), who cared for her mother and younger brother with HIV and three other siblings: *'Here, I'm giving my little brother his medicine.'*

ill health or hospitalisation. Over a third of the young people in both countries mentioned providing support with their parent's/relative's healthcare when they were ill, such as accompanying their parent/ relative to the hospital or doctor's, seeking help to transport them there, caring for them in emergencies and overnight in hospital, and, in Tanzania, preparing food to take to them in hospital (see Box 5.3). Some young people also provided assistance with mobility and helped to wash sores and treat minor illnesses, as well as the more regular task of cooking a special diet of nutritional food for their parent/relative and sometimes also for siblings with HIV (see Figure 5.3). There were some differences in the healthcare tasks that boys and girls carried out in Tanzania, with a focus for boys on reminding parents/relatives to take their medication and collecting it, while girls often performed more care-related tasks.

In the absence of adequate home-based care, nursing and palliative care programmes in the South, many young people may find themselves, like Good Luck and Maureen (see Box 5.3) in Tanzania, having to provide intensive nursing and personal care for parents/relatives with HIV at the end of their lives. Children in the UK were less likely to be directly involved in intensive nursing care, due to the universal healthcare system and provision of hospices and palliative care. However, some young people in the UK played important roles in responding to emergencies

Box 5.2: Young people's healthcare responsibilities in supporting their parent's/relative's adherence to ARV drug regimes in Tanzania and the UK

Young people's daily routines often included reminding their parent/relative to take their medication and preparing drinks and food for them to take with it. Juliette (aged 20, Tanzania) said:

> I wake up early in the morning ahead of mum. This is because she has to take medicines, so I make tea so that she can take her medication with the tea. After tea I do the cleaning, after that I cut grass for the goats, I feed the chickens. After that, I wash mum's clothes. Then I start preparing lunch and she has an afternoon rest. In the evening I prepare supper. At night I remind mum to take her medicines because she takes her medicines twice a day. After that we go to sleep.

When her father was seriously ill, Emily (aged 17, UK), who lived with her father and sister, used to wake up at 5 am to help wake her father and prepare something for him to eat before he took his medicine:

> He has to wake up really early to take his medication, so I would wake up at that time, and I wake him up and encourage him to go, help him maybe go to the bathroom. He'd wash up, and I'd have to prepare something for him to eat, because he would have to eat before taking the medication, or he would just, you know, would take his medication and if he wants to go back to bed, I'd help him back into bed, and then I would kind of just be there to check up on him and ask him if he was alright.

She thought that the worse aspect of caring for her father was her not knowing what to do when her father was ill and did not want to take his medicine because of nausea:

> At times when he's really, really ill and he's taking his medication and he doesn't really want to take it, he feels weak, and you just don't know what to do, you're thinking he can't take the medication because he'll feel sick, so you just, sometimes I just feel panicked into what to do. I'm thinking you have to take it to get better, and he doesn't want to eat. Times like that, those are the worse times.

Box 5.3: Young people's responsibilities for providing intensive nursing and personal care for parents in Tanzania

Good Luck (aged 18) cared for his mother until she died and, at the time of interview, lived with his grandparents in a village and cared for five younger siblings and cousins. He described his personal care and healthcare responsibilities when his mother was seriously ill:

> *Her health started deteriorating slowly. She would be poorly one day and would be better the next day and would resume doing her usual chores at home. She also ran a small business. Later she became very poorly and couldn't get out of bed. So that is when I started caring for her full time. [...] I used to bathe her, she didn't mind that I was a boy. When it was time to go to hospital I would take her there. When she was very poorly and couldn't walk, I used to carry her. Sometimes she wasn't able to eat on her own, so I would feed her. When she vomited, I used to wash the soiled clothing. Later when she disclosed her status to me, the doctors gave me gloves for washing soiled clothing and some for using when bathing her and tending her sores. So, that is how I cared for her until she died.*

Maureen (aged 19) used to live with her mother and step-father, who were both living with HIV and who experienced periods of serious illness at the same time. She cared for her step-father until he died and was caring for her mother at the time of interview. She described the high level of personal care and healthcare support she needed to provide for her parents over several months:

> *I had a very hard time of it, I had to wash the fungus on her [mum's] legs, and it smells very bad if you don't wash it properly. My dad was also ill in bed all the time; I had to care for him too, after finishing all that, I then went to school. [...] In March, mum was admitted to hospital, as she couldn't walk on her own. I had to take care of her in hospital. [...] After staying with my mum for two weeks in hospital, she was able to get up from bed and walk. Dad also had already had his hernia operation and went back home. Dad's hernia wound wouldn't heal, it ate deeper and deeper into the skin. So I had to take him to hospital every day for it to be dressed. At the same time I had to go to [another] hospital to visit mum who was still hospitalised there and take her food. [...] Meanwhile, dad's condition got worse. He was admitted to hospital, transferred to [another] hospital in September and died there on the 29th.*

Figure 5.3: Photograph of Maureen (aged 19, Tanzania), who cared for her step-father until his death and cared for her mother and younger sibling at the time of interview: *'I'm preparing vegetables for my mum.'*

and assisting parents with mobility and personal care following periods of hospitalisation and serious illness. For example, Gemma's mother had a number of fits when she collapsed and stopped breathing, which Gemma (aged 15) found 'scary'. On the last occasion, Gemma was the first person to call an ambulance and accompany her mother to hospital:

> *The last time I was in the house on my own and she collapsed and had a fit and I had to ring the hospital. I stayed there 'til about midnight and then her boyfriend came up. Then I went back about 6 in the morning and I ended up missing that day of school.*

Indeed, the importance of young people's healthcare responsibilities for parents/relatives with HIV is brought sharply into perspective by children's responses to the question, 'What do you think would happen if you didn't care for your parent/relative?' In Tanzania, most young people (13) felt that if they did not care for their parent/relative, their parent/relative with HIV would have died. While none of the young people in the UK mentioned this, over half (6) did think that their parent's health would get worse or their parent would have experienced a breakdown or mental health problems if they did not care for their parent/relative. These findings highlight the need for greater recognition of children's and young people's important roles in providing healthcare within the home as well as responding to emergencies and caring for parents/relatives with HIV during periods of serious ill health.

Young people's responsibilities for personal care

Previous research has shown that children's involvement in personal or 'intimate' care is one of the key aspects of their caregiving that most clearly distinguishes the work of young carers from that of other children (Robson et al, 2006; Becker, 2007). Almost half of the young people in Tanzania and the UK mentioned that they sometimes supported their parent/relative with personal care during periods of ill health. While bathing their parent/relative was the personal care task mentioned most frequently in Tanzania, young people in both countries saw their responsibility for encouraging and assisting their parent/relative to eat as an important priority (see Table 5.4 and Figures 5.4 and 5.5).

Table 5.4: Young people's personal care tasks in Tanzania and the UK

Personal care tasks	Number of young people in Tanzania (n=22)	Number of young people in the UK (n=11)	Total number of young people (n=33)
Encouraging and helping parent to eat	5	3	8
Washing/bathing parent	7	1	8
Assisting parent to use toilet/washing soiled laundry	3	1	4
Assisting with dressing	1	1	2
Tucking parent in bed	1	0	1

As discussed earlier, children have significant, regular responsibilities for cooking and preparing meals within the household. Many young people were aware of the positive health benefits of helping their parent/relative to eat a balanced, nutritional diet and overcome feelings of nausea and loss of appetite. For example, Good Luck in Tanzania said that the best aspect of caring for his mother was *'making sure she ate her food'* and used to encourage her to eat because he knew this would help her to live longer: *'She used to complain that the food made her vomit. So I would encourage her to eat because the food gave her strength and helped her to live longer'*.

The significance of young people's roles in encouraging their parent/ relative to eat is also apparent in the UK context, where Gemma commented on the difference in her mother's health if she was not available to ensure that she ate properly:

Figure 5.4: Drawings by Magdalena (aged 15, Tanzania), who cared for her mother until she died: *'These are pictures of me caring for my mum.'*

'This is me giving my mum porridge. I feel sad.'

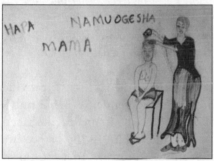

'Here I am giving mum a shower.'

Figure 5.5: Photograph of Isack (aged 12, Tanzania), who cared for his mother, taken by his brother: *'Here I'm giving my mum food.'*

> *I mean when I've been away for a week, you know, she just sort of,*
> *I've come back and she's asleep on the sofa, she doesn't eat, she loses*
> *a lot of weight quickly and like loses her appetite, that type of thing.*

Although overall there were few disparities between the care tasks boys and girls performed, there was some evidence of a preference for gender matching between the care recipient and caregiver when children provided personal care, confirming the findings of previous research (Robson et al, 2006; Becker, 2007). In Tanzania, a sister or female neighbour was often called on to bathe/shower a mother with HIV, despite a boy's involvement in every other aspect of his mother's care. For example, although Malcolm (aged 15) was responsible for performing a wide range of caring tasks for his mother, his sister was responsible for bathing her:

> *It is my sister who bathes my mum; I just take the water into the*
> *bathroom and the stool for mum to sit on. In the morning I help my*
> *mum brush her teeth. We share doing the rest of the work but I'm the*
> *one who goes shopping to the market and I also prepare the food.*

Similarly, in the UK, parents avoided asking their child to provide personal care if they did not share the same gender. When Emily's father was seriously ill and had mobility difficulties in the UK, he asked Emily (aged 17) to call a male friend to help him in the bathroom, rather than ask her to help, although she was prepared to assist him if required, as she commented: '*I wouldn't mind doing it if it was like to the point where I needed to do it, I wouldn't mind doing it. But it's just that he felt better with his friend helping him*'.

However, there was also evidence that gendered constructions of care were becoming more fluid when households were faced with a lack of alternatives. Almost as many boys (aged under 18) interviewed in Tanzania were providing care for their mothers/female relatives as the number of girls, contrasting with the UK sample. Some provided personal care for their mothers, despite the fact that this subverted dominant gender norms (see Chapter 9 for further discussion of gender norms regarding care and the influence of gender on whether children take on caring roles).

Young people's childcare responsibilities

Many young people in Tanzania and a quarter of those in the UK assisted their parent in providing childcare for younger children living in the household (usually their siblings and, in Tanzania, sometimes orphaned cousins), some of whom were also living with HIV. Their responsibilities included getting their siblings ready for school, accompanying them to and from school, supervising them, bathing young children, helping them with school work, preparing food for them, and in one instance caring for a younger sister during the night (see Table 5.5). Girls appear to be more likely to provide childcare than boys, although it is difficult to generalise from such a small number of respondents. The daily routines of Sarah and Janet in Box 5.4 show that some young people in both the UK and Tanzania spend considerable amounts of time caring for their siblings in addition to their household, personal care and healthcare responsibilities for their parent/relative.

Table 5.5: Young people's childcare responsibilities in Tanzania and the UK

Young people's childcare responsibilities	Number of young people in Tanzania (n=22)	Number of young people in the UK (n=11)	Total number of young people (n=33)
Getting siblings ready for school	6	2	8
Bathing siblings	5	I	6
Supervising siblings	I	3	4
Helping siblings with homework	3	0	3
Accompanying siblings to/from school	I	I	2
Preparing food for siblings	0	2	2
Caring for siblings during night	0	I	I

Young people's income-generation activities

Young people's involvement in income-generation activities in the global South represents the main difference in children's care tasks between the North and South. The loss of parents' income because of increasing ill health meant that almost half of the children in Tanzania regularly took on casual work and engaged in income-generation activities to meet the family's basic needs, in addition to their household reproductive tasks. Many children mentioned begging for food and

Box 5.4: Young people's daily routines in the UK and Tanzania: combining childcare with household chores, healthcare and personal care

Sarah (aged 16) lived in the UK with her mother and younger sisters, the youngest of whom had challenging behaviour. Three days a week she usually left early in the morning for her classes at college and had caring responsibilities in the evening and sometimes during the night. The days when she did not go to college, she had caring responsibilities during the day as well as the evening, as she describes below:

My little sister's awake most of the night. [...] So sometimes like I have to wake up and make her sleep with me or sometimes I go and make her something to drink or eat and then I have to stay up. I'll wake up again early in the morning and make sure that all my sisters are going to school and then they will go and make themselves some breakfast and I'll look after my little sister so she doesn't disturb my mum. And then my mum will wake up to take her medication at 8 o'clock and then I'll give my little sister some breakfast and then I would get her dressed and make sure she's ready for [nursery] school, help my mum help her get ready for school [...].

Then my mum would take her to school and then I would wash up the dishes, clean the house. My mum would come back, [I would] give my mum the bills, make sure she's paid her bills on time, check if she's got any appointments. Sometimes I help her fill up her medication box and then help her with the shopping in the afternoon, do some work, then I would help my mum cook before my sisters come back from school. And then when they're back from school usually she allows me to do my work and she'll look after my little sister because she's a bit of trouble [...] she's like very violent. And then I help my mum get my little sister ready to have a bath and when my mum is done with that I just rest until she goes to sleep.

Janet (aged 17) lived with her mother and five younger siblings in Tanzania. She described a typical day caring for her mother and siblings:

I wake up at 6.30 am and get my younger siblings ready for school. I feel sleepy. At 7.30 am I give my mum medicine and make tea for her, which she drinks. At 8 am I clean the house and wash mum's clothes. I feel fine. At 10 am I go to look for feed for the cow and feel fine. At 12.30 I prepare lunch and we eat. I am happy. At 1 pm I remind mum to take her afternoon dose of medicine. I feel happy. At 2.30 pm I bathe mum so that she can rest. I feel tired. My younger siblings come back from school at 4 pm. I give them food, wash their uniforms and bathe the little ones. I feel tired. At 6 pm I prepare the evening meal. I feel tired. At 8 pm we eat, I give mum her evening dose of medicine then we say our prayers and go to bed. I feel sleepy.

money or borrowing money from neighbours to meet the household's basic needs or to deal with particular crises, such as needing money to pay medical bills or for transport to take their parent to hospital. Several young people living in rural areas engaged in casual farm work when it was available, but this did not provide a regular income for their family and they rarely earned more than 500 Tanzanian shillings (TZS) per day (equivalent to 25 pence). Some young people ran errands or did domestic work for neighbours such as fetching water, cleaning and childcare, in return for small amounts of money, while others grew vegetables and sold produce at the market or sold water in their neighbourhood. Younger children fitted these income-generation activities around their school day or worked at the weekends, while young people who had completed primary school worked whenever they could to support the household (see Box 5.5).

As discussed in Chapter 4, many parents with HIV in the UK struggled to survive on the limited state benefits available and a few young people had part-time jobs. Sophia (aged 19) combined her studies and caring responsibilities with two part-time jobs, working as a cleaner in the evenings after college and as a shop assistant at the weekends. The money she earned was used to supplement the limited state benefits the family received and pay the household bills, as she commented: '*I pay for the bills for the internet, for the telephone and the TV licence, for transport, my mobile phone and, and do shopping sometimes, electricity. And at the end of the month I have nothing, it's all finished.*'

Some young people were keen to obtain part-time jobs, but acknowledged the difficulty of obtaining work before they reached the legal age requirement of 16 years. One parent said that her son worked part-time stacking shelves in a local shop to earn money to pay for his football activities, as she was not able to afford pocket money.

Emotional and practical support

As discussed in Chapter 4, parents may be reluctant to disclose their HIV status to their children because of fears about how children will react and the risk of disclosure outside the family (Lewis, 2001; Ely, 2006; Chinouya, 2006). Many children may thus have very little knowledge

Box 5.5: Children's and young people's income-generation activities in Tanzania

Younger children combining part-time income-generation activities with schooling

Happy (aged 12) grew vegetables and sold them at the market every weekend with her younger siblings. She usually earned about 1,000–1,500 TZS per day [equivalent to 50–75p].

John (aged 11) usually returned home from school at 2 pm and then worked until 6 pm, doing casual jobs for neighbours to earn money to buy vegetables for the family:

> *I wash people's clothes, dishes and I clean their houses. I earn about 1,500 TZS [equivalent to 70p] per day.*

Young people's responsibilities to provide for their family's basic needs

Neema (aged 18) had completed primary school and did casual work for neighbours to earn money for her mother with HIV and three younger siblings. However, she found that the money she earned was insufficient to meet their basic needs:

> *At the moment, I try to get work here and there so that we get food for the family, I got some work as a housegirl, selling water, looking after the neighbours' children while they're at work. I get a little money. I go to sift rice with the machine; the money I get is very little, not enough for our daily needs.*

Janet (aged 17) had also completed primary school and studied tailoring. She did casual agricultural work to earn money for her mother with HIV and five younger siblings but found that this did not provide a regular income and they did not have enough money for food:

> *If only I could get a sewing machine I would be able to help my mum more, it would be much better than helping her through casual work because sometimes I don't get any work at all, so we go to sleep hungry.*

of the illness of the person they are caring for (Robson et al, 2006). Our research found that, following disclosure of HIV status, young people were more likely to provide emotional support to their parent/ relative, as well as become more involved in performing healthcare and personal care tasks for their parent, because of greater understanding about their illness and greater willingness to care for them. According to young people's and parents' accounts, children provided emotional support by talking and comforting their parent/relative in dealing with the emotional impacts of living with HIV and related mental health problems, giving them hope and reassurance, offering advice, keeping them company and 'being there' for them when they needed support (see Figure 5.6).

Figure 5.6: Drawing by Grace (aged 19, Tanzania) who, along with her siblings, cared for her mother in bed over a period of several years: *'This is me sitting with my mum talking. I like being at home and having a nice time with my mum and younger brothers and sisters.'*

Although providing emotional support was only mentioned by a small number of girls in Tanzania and the UK, young people's and parents' accounts show that many children were sensitive to their parent's/relative's feelings and tried to provide encouragement and support to help their parent/relative to live positively with HIV. Many parents/relatives seemed to value highly the emotional support children provided and felt that their children kept them company and enhanced their emotional well-being (see Box 5.6).

Some children in the UK also provided practical support for their parents, such as helping parents who had experienced memory loss to remember appointments and bills, as Sarah (aged 16) commented: *'things like appointments I have to remind her. Things like bills, like if I remember a bill date that clicks in my mind I would ask her and if she's forgotten I have to tell her.'*

Box 5.6: Young people's involvement in providing emotional support to parents/relatives with HIV in Tanzania and the UK

Young people's perspectives:

I comfort my little brother [who is living with HIV] and give him courage, saying you will get well, and I tell him to pray to God to help him every day and I give him hope that he'll get better. (Saumu, aged 13, Tanzania)

I always talk to her, try and talk to her. Sometimes if she asks for advice I will, yeah, I will offer her advice. (Alice, aged 17, UK)

Parents' perspectives:

He loves listening to me and when he sees that I am very quiet, he always wants to know why; is it because I'm ill or something is wrong? Even when I put on a brave face, he knows when I am poorly and immediately hurries off to call the doctor. He really cares for me. (Elli, Tanzania)

She's the one who is helping me a lot, there is nobody else. She's like a friend, my mother, my friend, everything. She's like my everything. Sometimes I can rely on her, yes. So that's why I think that's she's really good for my life. (Lina, UK)

Conclusion

The research in Tanzania and the UK has demonstrated that children's and young people's caring responsibilities differ significantly from the usual household responsibilities of other children in the global North and South. The differences are focused on the extent and nature of their caregiving, the time involved, as well as the impacts on children and young people, which are discussed in the following chapters. Despite very different socioeconomic, cultural and policy contexts, the research suggests that the everyday caring responsibilities of children caring for parents with HIV in the global South and North are broadly similar. In Tanzania and the UK, all the young people interviewed had significant, regular responsibilities for household chores and healthcare and many provided childcare for their younger siblings. Because of the fluctuating nature of HIV illness, children's responsibilities for household chores were interspersed with periods of more intensive healthcare and personal care for their parent/relative during episodes of parental ill health or hospitalisation.

In the absence of sufficient home-based and palliative care programmes in Tanzania, some young people provided intensive nursing and personal care for parents with HIV at the end of their lives. Children in the UK were less likely to be directly involved in intensive nursing care, because of the universal healthcare system and provision of hospices and palliative care. However, some young people in the UK played important roles in responding to emergencies and assisting parents with mobility and personal care following periods of hospitalisation and serious illness.

The research found that young people were an important source of emotional support for their parent/relative with HIV, in addition to the practical care support they provided. Although overall there were few disparities between the care tasks boys and girls performed, more girls appeared to be involved in childcare for their younger siblings, and there was some evidence of a preference for gender matching between the care recipient and caregiver when children provided personal care.

Children's care work in the global North and South differs in the intensity and time taken to perform household chores because of disparities in living standards between low- and high-income countries. Our research found that children's care work in Tanzania took longer and was more physically demanding than in the UK. Many children in the South may also combine their reproductive work with income-generation activities to compensate to some extent for the loss of the parent's income-earning capacity. Having explored the specific dimensions of children's care work in families affected by HIV/AIDS, the following chapter explores the resilience of children and families and the impacts of children's care work on their personal development, health, emotional well-being and family relationships.

Notes
[1] Only young people from Tanzania drew pictures or took photographs specifically of their caring responsibilities and so we do not have any visual data about young people's caring responsibilities in the UK.

[2] The small number of boys interviewed in the UK makes it difficult to draw out any significant differences between girls' and boys' household chores.

[3] Young people chose pseudonyms for themselves to be used in written outputs and written consent was sought for the use of specific photographs.

SIX

Resilience and impacts of care work for individual young people and their families

The growing body of research on young carers in the North has suggested that many children experience a range of negative outcomes for their education, health, emotional well-being, social lives and transition to adulthood as a result of their care work, as we discussed in Chapter 1 (Aldridge and Becker, 1993; Dearden and Becker, 1995; Becker et al, 1998; Dearden and Becker, 1998; Frank et al, 1999; Thomas et al, 2003; Dearden and Becker, 2004). Research in the UK and Sub-Saharan Africa has also identified a range of positive outcomes for children who care for a family member, such as increased knowledge and understanding, a sense of responsibility, maturity and life skills, as well as closer relationships between children and parents (Gates and Lackey, 1998; Blackford, 1999; Dearden and Becker, 2000; Aldridge and Becker, 2003; Robson et al, 2006). Thus, there has been growing recognition that not all young carers experience negative outcomes (Dearden and Becker, 2004) and some researchers suggest that a resilience perspective may help to explain individual differences in coping with adversity (Rutter, 1990; Howard et al, 1999; Newman, 2002a; 2002b; Evans, 2005). In this chapter, we draw on the concept of resilience in examining the effects of children's care work for individual children and young people, focusing on their emotional well-being, health and welfare, personal development, aspirations and priorities for the future, as well as the effects on family relationships.

Resilience and impacts for children and young people at the individual level

Within the resilience literature, several protective factors have been identified that relate to attributes of individual children themselves, such as problem-solving skills, high aspirations, good social skills with peers and adults, feelings of empathy for others and self-efficacy (belief that one's efforts can make a difference) (Newman, 2002b; Schoon and Bynner, 2003). The following sections explore the impacts of caring responsibilities for individual children and young people.

Emotional well-being

Previous research suggests that children's caregiving can have a negative impact on their emotional well-being and psychosocial development (Elliott, 1992; Dearden and Becker, 1995; 1998; 2004). As discussed in Chapter 2, the literature on the impacts of HIV/AIDS also suggests that children's psychosocial well-being can be severely affected by parental HIV/AIDS, particularly when they have to deal with multiple losses of one or both parents and sometimes siblings and other relatives (Bauman with Germann, 2005). The death of a parent is considered one of the most significant risk factors for psychosocial problems in children (Bauman with Germann, 2005). Although it might be assumed that children in Africa and other low-income countries who are more often involved in caring for sick relatives may not experience as many psychosocial problems as their peers in the North, a comparative study in Zimbabwe and the US by Bauman and Germann (2005) found that on average more children in Mutare were significantly depressed than were children in New York.

Most young people interviewed in the UK and Tanzania were willing to care for their parent/relative and accepted their caring responsibilities because they felt that they were helping to make life easier for their parent/relative and helping them to stay in good health. However, several young people in both countries expressed their worry and anxiety about the life-limiting nature of their parent's illness. Many children were afraid about what would happen when their mother died and parents were concerned about the emotional impact of their illness on their children (see Box 6.1).

Many service providers also expressed their concerns that children may worry about their parent's illness while they are at school, making it difficult for them to concentrate, and that they often lack opportunities to talk about their feelings. Service providers suggested that children's fears may be exacerbated by a lack of communication between children and parents: *'The parents are afraid to tell them any more because they don't want to burden them, but yet the child is really worrying more than they need to, because of lack of information.'* Furthermore, the lack of communication within the family about the future may be particularly difficult to deal with for young carers who are living with HIV themselves.

Some young people experienced high levels of stress and anxiety in dealing with the uncertainty of their immigration status and whether their family would be able to remain in the country. As discussed in Chapter 4, for recently arrived African families, the threat of deportation was linked to a fear of losing access to the combination of drugs they were prescribed in the UK, which were unlikely to be available in Africa. In Tanzania, some young people felt sad and depressed about the poverty and difficult circumstances facing their family, as Sarah (aged 15) in Tanzania, said: *'Life in our family makes me very sad. I'm not happy like other children.'* Some felt overwhelmed by the responsibility of providing for their siblings following their parent's death (see Box 6.1). Others were distressed and hurt by experiences of stigma and ostracism within the family and community, as we discuss in more detail in Chapter 7 (see Box 7.11).

Despite these negative impacts on young people's emotional well-being, some commentators have suggested that caring for close family members can be seen as an expression of children's resilience

---

Box 6.1: Effects on young people's emotional well-being in Tanzania and the UK: anxiety and fears about their parent's life-limiting illness

Juliette (aged 20, Tanzania) sometimes felt overwhelmed by her responsibility to care for her mother and her future responsibility to look after her siblings after her mother's death:

> When [my mum] is very poorly I lose hope completely. That is when I think of my younger siblings, because they still depend on her. [...] I have a lot to deal with and I have nobody to help me.

Her mother also confirmed that Juliette's emotional well-being was affected by her caring responsibilities:

> She has a big burden on her young shoulders. I sometimes feel she is overwhelmed by worry. She thinks a lot about me and I think she dreads the day I will die because she will have to provide for her younger sisters.

Gemma (aged 15, UK) had witnessed her father's death and was afraid that her mother would die:

> My dad died of it before and I'm scared that, like, she'll do the same.

Her mother commented on the emotional impact on Gemma:

> It must be scary for her to think that I could die. I mean they all worry about whether their parent will die, but when they've already lost one....

---

and valued social roles in the household such as caregiving may have strong protective functions in families experiencing stress and adversity (Newman, 2002a; Woodhead et al, 2003; Evans, 2005). Furthermore, a study of children caring for a parent with severe mental illness found that caring can allay some of the fears, concerns and anxieties that children have about their parent's condition because it gives children some control and direct involvement in the provision of care work (Aldridge and Becker, 2003).

In Tanzania, many young people whose fathers had died wrote about their feelings of sadness, grief and loneliness. Only a few children who had been bereaved received any counselling or emotional support in dealing with their loss. However, some young people in Tanzania who had been bereaved expressed a sense of pride in taking on a caring role which was valued within the family. This sense of pride may help them to deal with their grief and fears about their parent's illness (see Figure 6.1 and Box 6.2). In the UK, some young people thought that their parent's illness and their caring responsibilities had helped them to become 'stronger' emotionally, as is illustrated in Box 6.2.

Physical health and welfare

The literature on the impacts of HIV/AIDS on children in Africa suggests that HIV/AIDS affects the health and welfare of children because of chronic poverty and a lack of access to healthcare and other basic needs. The reduction in family income caused by parental ill health and increasing need to cover the medical costs of HIV-related illnesses and treatments reduces the income available for general healthcare (Phiri and Tolfree, 2005). Previous research has suggested that young carers' health and welfare may be at risk through accidents in the home and the necessity of performing strenuous physical care tasks, such as lifting and assisting their parent with mobility (Aldridge and Becker, 1993; Coombes, 1997; Becker et al, 1998; SCARE, 2005). The findings of our research suggest that the health and welfare of some children caring for parents/relatives with HIV is affected by tiredness and fatigue, as well as poverty and reduced access to healthcare.

Over half of the young people in Tanzania described feeling tired or exhausted while they performed their caring tasks. For example, Saumu cared for her mother and younger brother. At the weekend, she did not have to attend school and had more time to rest but felt exhausted:

I wake up at 7 am. I help mum do some work around the house. I feel exhausted. I have tea with my mum and brother at 8 am. After that I take a rest because my body still feels tired. At noon, I go to the market to buy food, and come back home. I feel alright. At 1 pm, after we have had lunch, I wash the dishes, I feel tired. At 2 pm, I bathe my younger brother and he goes to sleep. I feel tired. At 6 pm I light the charcoal stove and prepare supper. I feel lonely. I serve supper at 8 pm. I clean the table and remove the dishes after supper. I feel sleepy. (Saumu, aged 13, Tanzania)

Figure 6.1: Drawing by Malcolm (aged 15, Tanzania): 'The most important thing that happened in my life was the death of my father, which filled me with grief. I am now left behind with my mum to bring me up, and for me to care for her until Almighty God separates us.'

As we discuss in more detail in Chapter 7, many children found it difficult to find time to do their school work after they had completed their caring responsibilities and had to study late at night or early in the morning, resulting in tiredness and concentration problems. Some young people in the UK also mentioned feelings of tiredness caused by their caring responsibilities, particularly if they had a lot of coursework or examinations to prepare for. Some young people sometimes needed to care for their parent or sibling during the night, which they found very tiring, as we saw in Chapter 5.

Some parents and service providers in Tanzania also raised concerns that some children had to perform a level of household chores and other care work that was physically demanding and considered inappropriate for their age. For example, one mother commented that since her son had started working after school to provide for the family, he had lost weight and her other children's health was also affected by the chronic poverty they experienced: *'He's lost weight and all of them generally don't look well.'* As one service provider commented: *'They are at an age when they are not strong enough to perform adult duties but they do them because they are forced to.'* A few young people mentioned difficulties getting to sleep or other physical symptoms that were caused by worry and anxiety about their situation. For example, Babu (aged 14) thought he had lost weight *'because I'm worrying about everything all the time.'* He also had fainting episodes at school.

Some young people and service providers in Tanzania commented on the effects of poverty and the lack of basic needs on children's health and welfare in households affected by HIV/AIDS. For example, when Isack (aged 12) was asked what he disliked about where he lived, he said he did not like going hungry, which usually happened every week, with him sometimes missing up to three meals a week. Similarly, June (aged 18) commented on the economic pressures the family faced, which reduced their access to healthcare when one of the children became ill: *'We have a very tough time. It is even worse when it comes to*

Box 6.2: Young people's resilience in dealing with fears about their parent's illness and bereavement in the UK and Tanzania

Alice (aged 17, UK) sometimes found it difficult caring for her mother, but she also thought that through her caring role, she had become stronger emotionally:

Helping my mum is sometimes tough, especially when she is really ill. I get scared and I just try and keep myself strong for her. But helping her has also given me strength to come to terms with her illness, yes.

Good Luck (aged 18, Tanzania) cared for his mother until she died. Taking on caring responsibilities for his grandparents and siblings after her death appeared to help him to deal with his loss and grief:

After my mum died I felt so much pain and grief but there was nothing I could do about it. So I decided to care for my younger siblings and my grandparents. That's what I am doing now.

---

someone falling sick and needing medicine.' A service provider explained that parents/relatives struggle to meet the costs of children's education and their basic needs as the person with HIV succumbs to ill health and money is needed to pay for medical expenses:

> *They lose their basic rights to food, clothing, schooling and shall I say shelter as well. Most of the money is spent on the person who is ill and there is none left to cater for the needs for these children.*

Some service providers highlighted the health risks of engaging in age-inappropriate behaviour. They suggested that because of poverty and vulnerability, girls and young women caring for a parent/relative with HIV may be at risk of engaging in early sexual activity and transactional sex in exchange for money or material support, which could result in unwanted pregnancies and sexually transmitted infections (STIs), including HIV. Boys and young men were also considered at risk of drug misuse and negative peer group influences.

Personal development

Research has suggested that young people's caring responsibilities can be associated with positive outcomes for individual children such as increased maturity and competencies, including life and social skills, greater knowledge and understanding and a sense of responsibility (Hetherington, 1989; Gates and Lackey, 1998; Blackford, 1999; Dearden and Becker, 2000; Robson et al, 2006). The findings from the UK and Tanzania suggest that many young people perceive the benefits of their care work predominantly in terms of their own personal development and life experience.

Greater maturity, independence and sense of responsibility

Over a third of young people in the UK felt that they had become more mature and independent as a result of their caring responsibilities, perceiving this as a positive benefit of their caregiving (see Box 6.3). Some parents and service providers in the UK also felt that children benefited from a more mature outlook which helped to prepare them for life and future responsibilities, as well as gaining useful experience and life skills in cooking, cleaning and looking after a family. In Tanzania, although this was rarely mentioned by young people, many parents and some service providers felt that children had become more mature and responsible and had learned important life skills which helped to prepare them for supporting and caring for their siblings and their own families in future (see Box 6.3).

> **Box 6.3:** Young people's increased maturity, independence and sense of responsibility in Tanzania and the UK
>
> *I feel like I've got more responsibilities, I feel like an adult now, more or less. So really kind of helped me gain my own independence, really, in a way. (Emily, aged 17, UK)*
>
> *They are learning how to do, how their family is run, how to take care if somebody is not well, to show love to that person. [...] They are more responsible now, they act responsibly, and feel for me more. They don't want me to do something when I'm not well. (Lucy, mother, from East Africa, UK)*
>
> *They are helping one another in their own life. They are getting used to being busy as you don't always have to depend on someone else for your livelihood. They have got to get used to the fact that one day they will be on their own and they will be able to survive. (Elli, mother, Tanzania)*
>
> *She's become more self-reliant, she's mature, she relates well to the other members in the group, she takes up the leading role. Yeah, she's got, you know, she's full of self-esteem, yeah, so I think all that is coming from her role as the carer, yeah. (Service provider, UK)*

While some parents and service providers viewed children's greater maturity as a positive outcome, several parents and the majority of service providers in the UK were concerned that younger children were having to 'grow up quicker' and take on 'adult' responsibilities before their time, which meant that they were missing out on their 'childhood'. As we discussed in Chapter 1, this reflects Western notions of childhood as a 'carefree' period when children should be free to play with their friends and go to school without having to think about responsibilities associated with 'adulthood'. In Tanzania, many parents viewed young people's greater maturity and life skills in a positive light. However, many service providers drew on the international discourse of children's rights to express their concerns that children were losing their 'rights to childhood' (see Box 6.4). As discussed earlier, the global notion of childhood set out in the UN Convention on the Rights of the Child conflicts with the lived experiences of most children in the majority world, as well as with African sociocultural constructions of the reciprocal responsibilities of children to their families and communities (Laird, 2005). The research thus highlights some of the tensions and contradictions in sociocultural constructions of childhood in the global North and South (discussed in more detail in Chapter 9).

Box 6.4: Having to grow up before their time: adult concerns about the 'loss of childhood' because of children's caring responsibilities in the UK and Tanzania

So he has changed because there's no time for him to be a child, to be a young man, you know experience things that other young men do or go out to play with the other boys. [...] He's always, he's always mature, he's always thinking faster. [...] I'd say, you know, the first ten years is quite important to a child and he didn't have that, he had to mature as fast as he can. (Rachel, mother, from Southern Africa, UK)

They don't have their childhood really, and it can be taken away from them in a way because they've got so much responsibility for them in the early years. (Service provider, UK)

They lose their right to be children because they are forced into adulthood. [...] So when their young minds are suddenly filled with adult thoughts, they end up being depressed. [...] You find they are preoccupied by things. (Service provider, Tanzania)

Increased ability to form caring and supportive relationships

As discussed in Chapter 1, the resilience literature suggests that good social skills, as well as the presence of strong supportive relationships, represent important protective factors that help to build children's resilience to adversity (Newman, 2002b; Schoon, 2006). When asked how they thought children had changed since they started caring for their parent/relative, some young people, parents and service providers in both the UK and Tanzania thought that young people had developed important social skills, becoming more caring, compassionate and supportive towards their parent. Many parents associated the change they had noticed in their children's attentiveness with the process of disclosing their HIV status to their child; following disclosure, parents felt that children had become more caring and responsive due to greater understanding about their parents' illness and the care and support that they needed. Furthermore, some service providers in the UK had witnessed strong supportive relationships develop through children's interactions with their peers at specialist youth groups. Box 6.5 illustrates some of the ways that caregiving appeared to increase young people's ability to form caring and supportive relationships with others.

Box 6.5: Young people's increased ability to form caring and supportive relationships in Tanzania and the UK

I listen to her more and when she tells me something, I understand her. (Tausi, aged 16, Tanzania)

I have learned how to be patient when caring for a sick person, you need a lot of patience. (Maureen, aged 19, Tanzania)

He has become a good kid. Before I explained the problem to him he did not understand. Whenever I asked him to do something, he was reluctant. Now he understands the situation, he is very close to me. (Patience, mother, Tanzania)

She is more compassionate, despite her young age. She has also matured and therefore understands things better. She knows how to take care of the little one when she is poorly, she knows how to control her temper in times of crisis. (Agnes, mother, Tanzania)

They are loving, caring, thoughtful young people who I have witnessed behaving in that way to other young people, which is obviously a very positive skill and gift they have and they are using that resource very positively. (Service provider, UK)

Greater knowledge and understanding about HIV/AIDS

Some young people, parents and service providers felt that young people had gained more knowledge and understanding about HIV/AIDS as a result of their caregiving. The knowledge young people gained helped them to protect themselves from HIV, through taking preventative measures while they were caring for their parent/relative, such as wearing gloves (in Tanzania), as well as helping them to understand the risks of unprotected sex and drug misuse. Furthermore, through caring for their parent, some young people felt that they had become more accepting and less judgemental about people living with HIV.

Magdalena, in Tanzania, for example, learned through caring for her mother until her death that it was important for relatives of people living with HIV to support and care for them, rather than stigmatise them. The importance of access to information about HIV and AIDS for young people is discussed in more detail in Chapter 8.

Aspirations and priorities for the future

High aspirations have been identified as an important protective factor for children experiencing adversity (Newman, 2002b; Schoon, 2006). Most young people in Tanzania and the UK said that continuing their education was their key priority for the future to enable them to have good employment prospects. Young people in both countries appeared to have high aspirations for future employment and careers; the majority expressed their aspirations to become professionals in the fields of education, healthcare, law, business and accountancy among others (see Figures 6.2 and 6.3). In Tanzania, the most frequently mentioned aspirations were to become a teacher, followed by a doctor or nurse, managing their own business, working in an office and becoming a lawyer. Only a few young people mentioned wanting to do semi-skilled or unskilled jobs, such as a tailoring, domestic work, or agricultural labour. In the UK, the most frequent responses from young people centred on their aspirations to become doctors or consultants, actors or singers, counsellors and psychiatrists and accountants. Other responses included a social worker and fashion designer.

Figure 6.2: Drawing by Casey (aged 9, UK): *'I want to be a fashion designer. This is one of my designs.'*

Figure 6.3: Drawing by Magdalena (aged 15, Tanzania): *'I would like to become a teacher.'*

Children's aspirations were influenced to some extent by their caring responsibilities, evidenced in a desire to help their family and pursue careers in health and caring professions, as illustrated in Box 6.6 and Figures 6.4 and 6.5. For example, young people in both countries who wanted to become a doctor or healthcare professional were motivated by their desire to help people with HIV/AIDS and treat TB and other AIDS-related illnesses. In the more immediate future, some young people saw continuing to care for their parent/relative and siblings as their most important priority. Several young people in both countries expressed their wish to obtain paid employment. In Tanzania, this was motivated by the need to earn a livelihood to support their parent/relative and siblings, while in the UK, young people wanted to do part-time work while they were studying to meet their own financial needs.

Box 6.6: Young people's aspirations to care for their families and for others in the future in the UK and Tanzania

I want to become a doctor surgeon and help people like my mum. (Kisha, aged 14, UK)

[I would like to be] someone well known, like on, on a global scale, like a famous actor or a famous singer, a good role model, someone that you know can help other people. (Magic, aged 12, UK)

[The most important thing for the future is] helping [my aunt] until she dies. (Happiness, aged 12, Tanzania)

I want to be a medical doctor specialising in the treatment of TB, dermatology and paediatrics. There are children suffering from TB and skin diseases. I want to be able to treat them until they recover fully, like God created them. (Malcolm, aged 15, Tanzania)

I would like to become an AIDS educator. I would like to teach people about proper behaviour, to live with their families and not to use things like razors, syringes carelessly. (Magdelena, aged 15, Tanzania)

Figure 6.4: Drawing by John (aged 16, Tanzania), who cared for his mother until she died: '*I would like to be a doctor because the illness is very bad. I saw when I was caring for my mum.*'

NINGEPENDA KUWA DAKTARI KWA SABABU
UGONJWA NI MBAYA SANA NILIONA WAKATI
NAMUUGUZA MAMA

Figure 6.5: Drawing by Happiness (aged 12, Tanzania), who cared for her aunt: '*I would like to be a nurse.*'

Previous studies in the global North have suggested that young carers may have significant difficulties in making a successful transition from childhood to adulthood (Aldridge and Becker, 1999; Dearden and Becker, 2000; Frank et al, 1999). Despite their high aspirations for their long-term future, some young people expressed a sense of uncertainty about their more immediate future, commenting on the constraints that poverty placed on achieving their goals (see Box 6.7). Some young people in Tanzania were not able to continue their studies due to their caring responsibilities and the need to earn a livelihood to support their family. In the UK, a few young people also expressed their worries and concerns about how their parent would manage on their own when they moved away from home to study at university. Indeed some service providers felt that young carers were at risk of social exclusion and poor outcomes in adulthood; in the UK, risks were perceived in terms of young motherhood and engagement in crime and antisocial behaviour; in Tanzania, the risks were seen as engaging in transactional sex and commercial sex work, domestic work and other forms of child labour and crime in order to meet their basic needs.

Box 6.7: Uncertain transitions to adulthood and barriers to young people's aspirations in Tanzania and the UK

Juliette (aged 20, Tanzania) was training to be a teacher and would qualify the following year. She wanted to obtain a teaching post near her mother's home so that she could continue to care for her. However, she would have preferred to have trained as a social worker and work with orphaned children and widows, but the pressure to support her mother and siblings had made this career path difficult for her:

I didn't want to become a teacher but I had to because I wanted to earn some money to be able to help mum. My ambition was to be a social worker.

Kerry (aged 18, UK) had applied to study medicine at university. As the youngest child to leave home, she was worried about how her mother would manage on her own if she went away to study:

If I wasn't here she'd have to do [everything] herself and she can't really always manage. It's a bit scary thinking I might be going away to uni and she'll be here on her own, so....

Resilience and impacts within the family

Recent literature on young carers has identified a positive effect of children's caregiving in terms of stronger emotional bonds and relationships between the child and their parent/relative (Aldridge and Becker, 2003; Robson et al, 2006). Within the resilience literature, there has been increasing recognition of the importance of children's family networks as a source of informal social support that helps to protect children from adversity and build their resilience (Gilligan, 1999). Previous research has identified a range of protective factors at the level of the family, including caring and supportive family relationships, a secure base and a sense of belonging (Gilligan, 2000; Newman, 2002b; Schoon and Bynner, 2003).

Love, reciprocity and supportive family relationships

Half of the young people in Tanzania and the UK commented on their close, loving relationships with their parent with HIV and many thought that their parent's illness and their caring responsibilities had helped to bring them closer together. Most young people did not identify themselves as a 'carer' but saw their care work as part of their reciprocal responsibilities, love and moral duty towards their family (discussed in more detail in Chapter 9). Furthermore, when young people were asked whom they could talk to if they had a problem or were worried or upset, the majority of young people in Tanzania and over a quarter of the young people in the UK said they would talk to their parent with HIV. This suggests that many children turned to their parent for emotional support, advice and guidance despite the parent's ill health.

For many young people and parents, closer relationships were linked to a sense of mortality and awareness that the time they could spend together was limited because of the life-limiting nature of HIV/AIDS (see Box 6.8). Many young people and parents in Tanzania felt that it was important for children to learn as much from their parents about community life and caring for their siblings while they still had the opportunity. As noted in Chapter 1, the informal teaching about the reciprocal rights and responsibilities of the child to their family and community represents an integral part of the socialisation process for children in Africa (UNICEF, 1999; Koda, 2000), and parents with HIV were keen for their children not to miss out on this part of their upbringing. Similarly, in the UK, some children and parents also felt it was important for children to benefit from their parent's advice and guidance while they were still alive (see Box 6.8). The findings suggest that despite their illness, parents with HIV maintain their parental roles in providing informal teaching, advice and moral guidance to their children.

Box 6.8: Reciprocal emotional support and advice in caring relationships in Tanzania and the UK

I chat to my mum about things in our neighbourhood. She gives me advice on how to get on with people, how to look after my younger brother and sister, how to live peacefully with them and how to stick together as a family. (Malcolm, aged 15, Tanzania)

Whatever happens to her she confides in me. [...] I like being with mum, seeing that she is still alive. I feel at peace and am comforted a lot seeing that she is still with us. (Juliette, aged 20, Tanzania)

She benefits from my advice. I give her adult advice like avoiding sex at all costs and not engaging in other worldly pleasures. I also tell her to educate herself as much as possible should she get such a chance. I explain everything to my child. (Annet, mother, Tanzania)

Before, I wasn't too close to my sister and my mum, but now I'm so close to them, they're my friends now. I talk to them about everything, they talk to me about everything. They're open and there's no secrets anymore, yes. (Sophia, aged 19, UK)

He's a lovely boy and I can talk to him. I can sit down with him and, you know, teach him a lot, because I told him that there will be times where I can't be here to talk to him, to do things and while I'm still alive it is good for me to talk to him now because if I'm dead there's no one who will be his mother out there. (Rachel, mother, UK)

Many children and parents in both Tanzania and the UK also commented on the closeness of young people's relationships with their siblings. Some felt that these relationships had become closer as a result of sharing their caring responsibilities and concerns about their parent's illness with one another. Relationships between children and other relatives in Tanzania were also characterised by a sense of reciprocity and shared caring responsibilities. Almost a third of children in Tanzania said that a sibling or close relative (such as aunts, uncles and grandparents) living nearby helped them to care for their parent/relative, offering material support and practical assistance with the care work (see Box 6.9). Several children mentioned asking an older sibling or relative living nearby for help when their parent/relative was ill, while some children also said that they turned to siblings or close relatives for emotional support and advice if they had a problem or were worried or upset.

In extended family households in Tanzania, caring responsibilities were often shared between female relatives and children. For example, Arafa lived with her three children, two adult sisters and their children. Although her eldest son had regular responsibilities for fetching water, cooking, cleaning, washing clothes, bathing his younger brother, going to the market and collecting medicines for his mother, Arafa's sister regularly helped with washing her clothes and cooking for her, as well as bathing her and buying medication and fruit for her when she was ill. Some parents also mentioned asking their older children or female relatives living nearby for help in caring for them, particularly when they were ill. Older children who had moved out of the household and relatives living nearby provided occasional material support, such as food or soap, as well as, emotional support for parents through visiting them at home, and sometimes practical assistance with care work (see Box 6.9). This suggests that supportive relationships within the extended family may represent important protective factors for children caring for parents with HIV in low-income countries with very limited formal welfare support.

In contrast, young people and parents in the UK often had more limited extended family support networks available in the locality or region. Indeed, over a third of the families had no other relatives living in the country since most had arrived in the UK as refugees. Some parents with HIV also found it difficult to seek support from extended family members because of stigma, discrimination and conflict within the extended family, and some chose not to disclose their status to family members. Only a few young people mentioned that their parent, their mother's partner, an adult relative in the immediate household or a sibling or relative living nearby provided practical support in caring for their parent with HIV. Some young people said that their aunts provided practical assistance in caring for their parent when they were ill, cooking for them and looking after their parent during the day when the young person was at school (see example of Sarah in Box 6.9). Within some African families, grandmothers sometimes came to the UK and helped children care for parents for temporary periods of up to a few months, particularly during periods of parental illness (see example of Rachel in Box 6.9). Only a few young people said that they asked a sibling, parent or other adult relative in the immediate household or a sibling or relative living nearby for help when their parent was ill. Few mentioned being able to talk to siblings or other relatives about their problems or concerns.

Box 6.9: Shared caring responsibilities: reciprocity and supportive relationships with siblings and other relatives in Tanzania and the UK

When I was caring for my mum, my little sister also grew older. When she was big enough we both started caring for her, the two of us. [...] If [my older brother] comes and finds I have gone to school and mum is left on her own and is ill, he gives her medicine and waits until I come back from school. (Christina, aged, 13, Tanzania)

[My sister] came from home to live here. She also has HIV. [...] There was a time when I was very ill. They phoned her and she came to take care of me. When I am really in a bad way she comes over and helps and tells the children not to touch my vomit. She washes my clothes, cooks and does other chores around the house. She is here now helping the children. (Angelina, mother, Tanzania)

Me and my sister cook in turn. If she cooks today I'll cook tomorrow, and do the washing up or whatever. [...] That kind of has got us together, we work as a team, because we know we want our dad to get better and so by us working together it helps him. (Emily, aged 17, UK)

My auntie always calls a lot so if she knows that my mum is not well she will come and she would look after my mum for the day while I've gone to school. (Sarah, aged 16, UK)

My mum came to see me because since I was diagnosed she's never seen me, so she flew from [Southern African country] and she'll be going back in two weeks' time. She's been here for three weeks now. [...] Today, for instance, [my son] didn't go to school, I was so weak, so sick, you know, he had to stay at home, kind of showing his grandmother what to do, what to give me, how to help me out. (Rachel, mother, UK)

Some parents in the UK said that relatives such as their siblings, parents or ex-partners provided practical assistance with childcare when they were ill and sometimes provided more regular assistance, such as helping with household chores or shopping. For example, when one mother with HIV was hospitalised, her children went to stay with her brother and his family in another city for three weeks. However, one mother, who was separated from her husband, highlighted the fact that providing childcare to give respite to parents when they are ill could have the unintended consequences of leaving parents even more isolated, without any support:

> *My ex-husband will support by taking the boys away from me, but then he doesn't realise by taking the boys away then it leaves me completely, you know, helpless because I don't have anybody then at all.*

Conflicts within the family, stigma and abuse

While the majority of parents in Tanzania and the UK felt that they got on well with their children, almost half of the parents in both countries expressed feelings of guilt and regret that they had to rely on their children to care for them. Some children and parents also felt that their relationships were sometimes more distant and communication was difficult when parents were very tired or ill. In the UK, some young people and parents expressed unease and tensions within the family because of changed roles and responsibilities (see Box 6.10). Several young people and parents thought that parents sometimes expected too much of their children, particularly with regard to their expectations about household chores, which resulted in arguments. Children were keen to avoid conflict with their parents and siblings, however, as they knew that this could cause them additional stress and make their illness worse. Some parents felt that their children no longer turned to them for support and advice as much as they used to, perhaps because of a fear of making their parent worried and stressed. Parents, in turn, sometimes tried to hide symptoms of illness from their children in order to minimise their worry and reduce their caring responsibilities. Some parents also commented on tensions between young people with caring responsibilities and their siblings, which were often related to their frustrations in looking after younger siblings, particularly those with challenging behaviour.

While loving and supportive family relationships could represent an important protective factor for young people in Tanzania, the research found that some parents, siblings and other relatives exploited unequal adult–child power relations and behaved in uncaring ways towards young people with caring responsibilities. Although the majority of children and parents/relatives with HIV commented on the love and closeness of their caring relationships, a few service providers in Tanzania suggested that children who care for parents with HIV may be at risk of neglect and verbal, physical or sexual abuse. One provider cited an instance where a father with HIV did not allow his son, who had cared for him for a long time, to wear protective gloves during his care work and threatened him with a powerful curse that caused the boy great anxiety and fear. The example of Maureen (in Box 6.11) also shows that some young people had to negotiate complex and antagonistic caring relationships with their parent/relative.

Box 6.10: Ambivalence and tensions in family relationships in the UK

Kerry (aged 18) felt that her mother sometimes expected too much of her, in terms of household chores:

> I think sometimes she expects too much because she's kind of obsessed with cleaning and that sort of thing, so she expects me to do it to her standards, and sometimes I can't be like her, so she'll expect me to do it her way and I can't do it.

Kerry liked being there for her mother, but also felt ambivalent about her caring responsibilities:

> Sometimes [I don't like] having responsibility and too much pressure on me to be a certain way.

Gemma (aged 15) felt that her relationship with her mother had become more distant since she had been caring for her, commenting on the difference she noticed from her friends' relationships with their parents:

> We used to be quite close and sort of drifted apart recently. [...] it's become like less close, like I'm, it's not like mother and daughter, it's more like helper and daughter more, helper and mum yes. [...] I'm quite used to it, but it's when I stay at friends and I see how they act with their parents that it's sort of different.

Several young people were stigmatised and ostracised by their relatives when they sought help from them, which they found very distressing. In particular, older siblings who had moved out of the household were sometimes unwilling to take on or help with caring responsibilities, leaving younger children in the household responsible for caring for the family. Furthermore, some young people's rights to condolence money and inheritance were denied following their parent's death (see Box 6.11). In many Sub–Saharan African countries, the stigma of HIV/AIDS coupled with poverty has been shown to result in children being denied access to schooling, healthcare, inheritance and property, particularly in the case of girls (Barnett and Blaikie, 1992; UNICEF/ UNAIDS, 1999; Evans, 2005).

Box 6.11: Difficult caring relationships and experiences of stigma and ostracism within extended families in Tanzania

Maureen (aged 19) used to care for her step-father, who died of AIDS, and was caring for her mother at the time of interview. She had found it particularly difficult to care for her step-father, as he had directed anger and criticism towards her:

> The time when mum was admitted to hospital, I would go visit her and when I got back he would be angry with me and deny me food saying I just go to care for my mum, leaving him to die of hunger at home. Sometimes when I was bathing mum, he would criticise me saying I just bathe mum and neglect him. I didn't mind, I would go and help him. I just accepted that his illness was bothering him.

A service provider commented that Maureen's step-father had left specific instructions in his will that, when her mother died, Maureen should not inherit the house that she and her mother lived in or any of their belongings, denying her inheritance rights.

Queenie (aged 24), who cared for her four younger siblings, found that following the death of her parents, their rights to the condolence money were denied by a relative of their father. He refused to offer them any support, which made her feel ostracised by her extended family:

> I went to someone, a close relative. I told him we had no food. He said I should go do casual work, get some money, then go to buy food. This is insulting. This is the same person who took all the condolence money we got. I expected him to give me some but he didn't. So the people I expected to help me shunned me. It was very hard to take.

Other pressures on family relationships

As noted in Chapter 4, many families in both Tanzania and the UK lived in overcrowded, poor-quality housing, resulting in a lack of privacy, which some parents and children in the UK felt caused conflict and arguments within the family. Sarah explained that she found it difficult to find space and time to herself away from her younger sisters at their home. Some parents in the UK commented on pressures caused by poverty and their frustrations at not being able to afford what they wanted for their children, including school uniforms, winter clothing, play and leisure opportunities. Other pressures on family relationships in the UK were related to parents' immigration status and separation from close family members, such as their children and partners, who were living in their country of origin in Africa and unable to join them in the UK at the time.

Conclusion

The research in Tanzania and the UK identified a number of negative effects of caregiving and HIV/AIDS for children and young people at the individual level, in terms of their emotional well-being, physical health and welfare, and transitions to adulthood. Many children in both countries expressed worry and anxiety about the life-limiting nature of their parent's illness, and only a few children who had been bereaved received any external emotional support in dealing with their loss. However, some young people expressed a sense of pride at taking on a socially valued role of caring for their parent/relative and siblings, suggesting that caregiving may have a protective effect for some young people, helping to mitigate the emotional impacts of parental HIV and bereavement. In terms of children's physical health and welfare, the study found that children caring for parents/relatives with HIV experienced tiredness and fatigue as a result of their care work. Poverty and reduced access to healthcare in HIV/AIDS-affected households also affected children's health and welfare. Service providers thought that young people might also be at risk of social exclusion and poor outcomes in adulthood, including the risk of engaging in transactional sex and commercial sex work, early pregnancy, child labour, drug misuse, crime and antisocial behaviour.

Despite these negative impacts, many young people perceived positive benefits of their care work in terms of their own personal development and life experience. Many thought they had become more mature and independent and had gained greater knowledge and understanding about HIV/AIDS as a result of their caring responsibilities. Some parents and service providers also thought young people had developed greater social skills and had an increased ability to form caring and supportive relationships with others, which has been identified as an important protective factor for children experiencing adversity. Most young people in both countries also had high aspirations and identified continuing their education as a key priority for the future to enable them to have good employment prospects. Despite their high aspirations, however, some young people experienced difficult transitions to adulthood. Some young people in Tanzania were not able to pursue their goals because of poverty and the need to earn a livelihood to support their family.

Within the domain of the family, most caring relationships were characterised by considerable reciprocity and interdependence, with fluid boundaries between the roles of caregiver and care-receiver. Most young people did not identify themselves as a 'carer' but saw their care work as part of their reciprocal responsibilities, love and moral duty towards their family. Loving, supportive family relationships between children, parents, siblings and other relatives appear to represent important protective factors that help to mitigate children's vulnerability. However, tensions in family relationships were also apparent, as children and parents adapted to changing roles and responsibilities.

Extended family relationships were an important source of social support for many families affected by HIV/AIDS in Tanzania, where formal welfare support was virtually non-existent. However, the resources of extended family members were limited and many relatives were unable, or sometimes unwilling, to meet the needs of children and parents in households affected by HIV/AIDS. Some young people in Tanzania were ostracised by older siblings or relatives and their inheritance rights denied following their parent's death. Evidence of discriminatory and sometimes abusive relationships with parents, siblings and relatives suggests that family relationships could also represent a potential risk that may increase young people's vulnerability to negative impacts of caregiving and the level of their involvement in care work.

In the UK, only a few children received practical support with their care work from extended family members: many families did not have access to extended family networks in the locality or region because of migration and geographical distance from their relatives. Some parents with HIV also found it difficult to seek informal family support because of stigma, discrimination and conflict within the extended family. Furthermore, poverty and overcrowded, poor-quality housing, as well as (in the UK) insecure immigration status and separation from other family members, placed additional pressures on families affected by HIV/AIDS. This reveals the difficulty of isolating the effects of young caregiving from other dimensions of social exclusion and marginalisation experienced by families affected by HIV/AIDS in both the global North and South. The following chapter investigates the impacts of young people's care work and their resilience within the domains of the school and wider community.

SEVEN

Resilience and impacts of young people's care work within the school and wider community

Previous research with young carers in the global North has suggested that young caregiving may have negative impacts on children's educational performance and school attendance as well as restricting children's opportunities for developing peer friendships and taking part in leisure and social activities in the wider community (Bilsborrow, 1992; Aldridge and Becker, 1993; Dearden and Becker, 1995; Marsden, 1995; Dearden and Becker, 1998; Crabtree and Warner, 1999; Thomas et al, 2003; Dearden and Becker, 2004). Following on from the previous chapter, this chapter discusses resilience and impacts of children's care work in families affected by HIV/AIDS within the domains of the school and wider community. We explore the ways that children and parents/relatives with HIV draw on social ties, networks and informal safety nets in the school environment and community in order to deal with household crisis and mitigate their vulnerability.

Resilience and impacts within the school environment

The literature on orphans and vulnerable children in the South has documented many negative impacts of the HIV/AIDS epidemic on children's educational performance and attendance (Kelly, 2005; Robson and Kanyanta, 2007b). Data from 20 Sub-Saharan African countries show that children aged 10-14 who have lost one or both parents are less likely to be in school than their non-orphaned peers (Rispel with Letlape and Metcalf, 2006). However, other studies have provided a less conclusive picture of the school attendance of orphans compared with non-orphans (Guest, 2001; Ainsworth and Filmer, 2002; Gould and Huber, 2003). Ainsworth and Filmer (2002) compared enrolment levels of orphans with other children in 28 countries and found that enrolment was related to income level and questioned whether orphan status should be used to target educational assistance (Kelly, 2005). Similarly, Gould and Huber's large study in Tanzania found that although HIV/AIDS affected children's school attendance, some children demonstrated considerable educational resilience:

> Just as many children from poor homes survive and do well in school, many children from HIV/AIDS affected households also survive and do well. Coming from an HIV/AIDS affected household is neither a necessary or a sufficient condition for irregular attendance, dropout or never being enrolled. (Gould and Huber, 2003: 35)

Research suggests that children, particularly girls, may be withdrawn from school to care for sick family members (Kelly, 2005). However, Gould and Huber's large-scale study of children's primary school attendance in Tanzania suggests that the majority of children combine their caring responsibilities with their schooling (Robson et al, 2006) and thus caregiving may have more significant effects on the regularity of children's school attendance rather than on school drop-out rates. Girls' attendance was more likely to be disrupted than boys' (Robson et al, 2006).

Previous research on young carers in the UK has highlighted a number of negative impacts of children's caring roles on their educational attendance and performance, including regularly missing school to care for a parent, poor concentration because of tiredness or worrying about their parent, as well as having limited time for homework (Marsden, 1995; Becker et al, 1998; Dearden and Becker, 1998; Crabtree and Warner, 1999; Dearden and Becker, 2004). Research with children affected by parental HIV in the UK has also suggested that children's educational performance and attendance were negatively affected by their caring roles (Lewis, 2001; Cree et al, 2006). Cree et al's (2006) study of children affected by parental HIV in Scotland suggested that children missed significant parts of their schooling, either through staying at home with a parent or through tiredness in class. However, claims about the impacts of children's caregiving on their educational performance have been refuted by some commentators, who suggest that poverty and socioeconomic class may represent the most significant variables associated with unexplained school absences rather than children's caregiving (Olsen, 1996; Newman, 2002a). Becker (2007) has also suggested that it is difficult to isolate caregiving from other variables that can impact on educational attainment. We examine the educational experiences of young people from Tanzania and the UK within this context.

Irregular school attendance

Most young people in Tanzania and the UK reported that they sometimes missed school because of their caring responsibilities, for periods of a few days to up to several months when their parent was seriously ill (see Box 7.1). A higher proportion of girls in Tanzania mentioned this in comparison with boys. As Robson et al (2006: 101) note, caring for a sick relative is 'likely to be an irregular demand on children's time', called on during 'times of severe need or temporary crisis' related to the parent/relative's ill health. Some young people mentioned that their caring duties made them late for school, which sometimes resulted in corporal punishment and having to miss further classes, as the example of Maureen in Box 7.1 shows.

Poor academic performance

Almost two thirds of the young people in Tanzania described a number of ways they thought that their parent's ill health and caring responsibilities had negatively affected their academic performance. A higher proportion of girls felt that their academic performance had been affected by their caring responsibilities than boys. Many young people cited difficulties concentrating on their school work both at home and at school because of tiredness or worry and anxiety about their parent's illness and their caring responsibilities. Some children and parents had noticed that children's class ranking had decreased since their parent's health deteriorated and, in a few instances, young people felt that stress, anxiety and tiredness led to their failure in national school leaving examinations. Some young people also felt that they had been prevented from continuing with secondary education because of their parent's high support needs and demand for their labour at home (see Box 7.2).

In the UK, over a third of the young people felt that their academic performance had been affected by their caring responsibilities, commenting on their difficulties concentrating at school and college because of worry and tiredness, as well as in a few instances missing exams because of their caring responsibilities. Kerry (aged 18) became very stressed and anxious about her mother's illness while she studied at a college located far from where they lived and eventually left to attend another college that was much closer to their home:

> *At my first college I got quite worried and I had to go and see the doctor because I felt like I just didn't know what to do, so that's*

probably one of the reasons which made me leave because I was just really stressed.

Box 7.1: Irregular school attendance caused by young people's caring responsibilities in Tanzania

Maureen (aged 19) used to arrive late for school because of her caring responsibilities for her mother and step-father with HIV. She was often punished by her teachers and had to miss further lessons because of her late arrival. She described her experiences:

> *I had to get up very early at 5 am. I had to plan what they were going to eat. I then boiled water to wash mum's legs. If need be, I bathed her. I also bathed my dad, got my younger brother ready for school. I was supposed to be at school by 7 am. I couldn't make it by then. [...] Every time you were absent or late they recorded the names. Then on the punishment day you got punished according to the number of times your name appeared in the book. It was either strokes or digging holes for rubbish or digging to plant flowers. So you wasted time doing the punishment during lessons.*

Maureen thought that teachers were 'not very attentive to pupils' problems' and would have liked her teachers to have been more supportive and sympathetic about her caring responsibilities for her parents, so that she wasn't always punished for being late and having to miss more classes.

Christina (aged 13) missed a few days of school every so often when her mother was ill, which she felt affected her academic progress:

> *Sometimes I don't go to school when mum is very ill. If that's the case, I have to stay with her at home. Often I fall behind in the lessons. If she became ill today, I wouldn't go to school until she gets better.*

Her mother confirmed that she relied on her daughter to care for her when she was ill:

> *No, she doesn't go. Who would care for me if she went to school? When I'm ill, she doesn't go. [It hasn't happened] very often. But there was a time she didn't go for two months because I was very ill.*

Box 7.2: Negative effects of worry and anxiety on young people's academic performance: young people's experiences in Tanzania

Grace (aged 19) felt that her progress at primary school suffered because of her concern about her mother's ill health, resulting in a lack of concentration on her school work and failure to qualify for secondary school:

> *I have not been to secondary school, but I would very much like to. When I was in primary school I was very clever but when mum became ill I was so worried about her and didn't think much about school.*

Even for young adults who have left home to study, worrying about their parent's illness and being called in an emergency can negatively affect their academic performance, as Juliette (aged 20, studying at teacher training college) said:

> *Sometimes I may be in the middle of an exam and I get a letter saying mum is seriously ill. Sometimes I fail the exam because of worrying about mum. I have to care for her and there are my younger sisters, I have to take care of them too. So I carry a very heavy burden.*

Temporal and spatial conflicts between school work and caring responsibilities

Half of the young people in Tanzania and the UK described how their caring responsibilities within the household conflicted with their time for private study and school work. In Tanzania, a higher proportion of boys mentioned this in comparison with girls. Many children in Tanzania found that they had to stay up late to do their homework after their caring tasks had been completed, resulting in tiredness and fatigue. Some young people found it difficult to negotiate time and space for themselves to study within a context of poverty and overcrowded living conditions. Maureen, for example, met resistance to her use of a kerosene lamp late at night when her sick step-father wanted to sleep (see Box 7.3).

In the UK, young people also experienced conflicts between their caring responsibilities and school work, which some parents were aware of and regretted (see Box 7.4). However, in both Tanzania and the UK, children can also be seen as negotiating spatialised boundaries and time for their studies within the context of the household and school, fitting their school work around their caring responsibilities

Box 7.3: Temporal and spatial conflicts between school work and caring responsibilities in Tanzania

Malcolm (aged 15) studied in Form One of secondary school in Tanzania. He sometimes struggled to find enough time to do his homework as well as fulfil his caring responsibilities and had to study late at night or early in the morning:

> My usual routine is that I go to bed at 10 o'clock but that is not always the case. Sometimes I go on working up to one in the morning. Sometimes, after saying my prayers at ten, I then go on to do my school work until I'm too sleepy. I finish off my school work in the morning while I'm waiting for the water to boil.

His mother also felt that his caring responsibilities were taking up valuable time that he ought to be devoting to his studies and was worried about how this would impact on his future:

> He doesn't gain from it at all because he wastes a lot of time caring for the family instead of spending it on his education.[…] I am very upset about it and I don't know how he is going to end up in future.

Maureen (aged 19) found negotiating time and space to do her school work very difficult when she was caring for her mother and step-father, who was unsympathetic to her needs to study:

> I used to leave [school] at 2.30 pm to come home. When I got home, I would prepare something for them to eat, wash mum's fungus, wash the soiled clothing because she used to relieve herself in bed. So I couldn't do any homework with all that going on. Then I had to prepare the evening meal, bathe dad while he criticised me. I tried to study at night but my dad would complain that the lamp was disturbing him so he couldn't sleep. So I had to put out the light and go to bed.

She felt that the conflict between her school work and caring responsibilities led to her failure in the school leaving examinations, which she was very upset about:

> That is what contributed to my failure in the national Form Four exams. I had no time at all for doing my homework and private study. Whenever I came back from school I had work to do around the house. I was tired all the time.

wherever possible. For example, both Malcolm and Magic in Boxes 7.3 and 7.4 did their homework early in the morning before school, when they found they had time to themselves. In a few instances, however, children and parents were worried that the conflict between school work and caring responsibilities would have detrimental effects on children's long-term educational outcomes.

Educational resilience and supportive school environments

Despite the negative impacts of HIV/AIDS and young people's caring responsibilities on their education described so far, over a third of the young people in both Tanzania and the UK did not think that their parent's illness and their caring responsibilities had any significant effects on their school attendance or academic performance. Furthermore, almost half of the parents in Tanzania and the majority of parents

---

Box 7.4: Temporal and spatial conflicts between school work and caring responsibilities in the UK

Emily (aged 17) sometimes found it tiring having to do household chores when she came home from a long day of lectures at college. She found her college coursework conflicted with her caring responsibilities for her father:

> Sometimes I get back and I'm tired. You just want to get home and just maybe have a rest, but no, you've got to come home and do something, cook, so sometimes it's really hard.[...] there's times when I feel like oh, do I really have to do some of the things I do, because, say like now with college, it's really intense. Sometimes I have to get my work done, sometimes I've got things that I need to do at home as well. Sometimes it is stressing.

Magic (aged 12) liked to get up early and sometimes do his homework on the computer at school before his classes, as he usually helped his mother collect his sisters after school:

> I wake up at, like, 5. My mum always tells me that I need to get more sleep but I always wake up at 5 o'clock in the morning so that I can just, like, get ready for school and, you know, because my school really opens at 7 o'clock, but school properly starts at 8.30. So sometimes I can go on the computer like to, you know, do some homework or stuff early in the morning and I can also do some after, going to do some homework after school as well. But I normally have to come and help my mum pick up my sisters every day.

in the UK felt that their child's academic progress was good despite their caring responsibilities. As one parent in Tanzania said about her daughters' educational progress: '*They are doing very well, so well that I am very pleased and very relieved. It makes my life worth living.*'

For the majority of young people in Tanzania and the UK, doing well at school and continuing their education was their main priority for the future, as education was seen by children and parents as key to improving their employment prospects and life chances. Indeed, several parents/ relatives emphasised their commitment to ensuring that their children did not miss school because of their illness and caring responsibilities. As one woman with HIV being cared for by her grandson in Tanzania said: '*I don't like children skipping classes because I only have Standard Four [four years of primary school] education. So I don't want them to be illiterate, I make sure they go to school even when I am seriously ill.*' Similarly, a mother with HIV in the UK commented on her commitment to ensuring her sons attended school despite her illness: '*I won't let them miss school or, you know. Very, very rarely have they missed school because of me, you know, so I do ensure that they go to school.*'

Positive school experiences and supportive school environments have been identified as potential protective factors for children experiencing stress and adversity at home (Newman, 2002b; Schoon, 2006). However, the research in the UK and Tanzania found that most children and parents did not want teachers to know about parent's illness or children's caring responsibilities because of fear of stigmatisation, confirming previous UK research (Lewis, 2001; Cree et al, 2006). Although almost half of the young people in Tanzania thought that teachers were aware of their caring responsibilities, very few thought that teachers knew about their parent/relative's illness. In the UK, very few young people said that teachers were aware of their parent's illness and none thought that their teachers knew about their caring responsibilities. The lack of awareness among school professionals of children's family situations prevents young people benefiting from potential support available within the school environment.

In a few instances in Tanzania when teachers were aware of a parent's illness or young people's caring responsibilities, young people and parents had found the teachers to be understanding, making allowances for individual children when they were needed to care for their parent at home (see examples in Box 7.5). Some mothers with HIV had explained to teachers that they were ill and were widows or lone mothers with very limited means so that children would not be sent home or punished for a lack of money for school contributions.

Indeed, in one instance, the school paid the necessary contribution on behalf of one widow and gave the family a food donation. However, some children reported that when they tried to explain to teachers about their parent's illness, they found teachers unsympathetic and children continued to be punished for lateness and concentration problems (see Box 7.5).

Box 7.5: Supportive school environments for children with caring responsibilities? Young people's experiences in Tanzania

Christina (aged 13) said that if her mother was ill, she told her teachers and they gave her permission to stay at home until her mother's health was better:

> When mum is sick, I tell my teacher and he tells me not to come to school until mum recovers.

Her school friends were also supportive; when she missed school, they usually brought her exercise books to her so that she could do private study.

Saumu's mother found teachers understanding when she explained about her daughter's caring responsibilities:

> I told them [about Saumu's caring responsibilities] so that they don't beat her. I told them I have problems and asked them to be tolerant with her because it's not her fault. They understood the situation. So when others get sent home for lack of fees or for lack of money for the other services we pay for at school, Saumu is excused.

Babu (aged 14) wished his teacher was more understanding of his difficulties:

> – Does your teacher know about your mum's illness?
> – I have explained to him but he doesn't seem to understand.
> – How would you like your teachers to help you more?
> – I would like them to stop telling me off. I am not doing this out of my own choice.

In only a few instances were teachers and school professionals in the UK aware of parents' HIV status and children's caring responsibilities. When parents had decided to tell teachers about their illness, they were motivated by a desire for teachers to be more understanding of any problems or stress their children might experience when they were ill, although young people did not necessarily think that this helped (see example of Gemma in Box 7.6). Although almost all of the young people said that tutors and pastoral care staff were available at school to talk to about any problems they experienced, they thought that the support they offered was focused mainly on difficulties with school work and they did not feel able to talk to them about family problems. Indeed, in one instance, a young person wanted her teachers to know about her caring responsibilities but felt uncertain of how teachers would react and did not feel able to approach her teachers about it (see example of Kerry in Box 7.6). Some parents found teachers unsupportive when children were bullied or had disruptive behaviour at school and did not feel that teachers took the time to listen to children and find out about their problems (see example of Magic in Box 7.6).

Thus, according to the experiences of young people and parents, young people's resilience, good school attendance and academic performance was related more to informal support from parents, peers and individual teachers, high aspirations, and the young person's individual interests and motivation to study, rather than supportive institutional environments or sensitivity and awareness of young caregiving among school professionals.

Other factors impacting on children's education

As discussed in Chapter 2, households affected by HIV/AIDS in the global South often experience chronic poverty. Despite the abolition of primary school fees in Tanzania in 2002 as part of government commitments to 'Education for All' and the Millennium Development Goal of achieving Universal Primary Education by 2015, parents still struggle to meet the costs of school uniforms and educational supplies, secondary school fees and other contributions. Thus, poverty, particularly in low-income countries is likely to have just as significant an impact on children's school attendance and performance as children's caring responsibilities.

Half of the young people and parents in Tanzania commented on not being able to afford exercise books, school uniforms, school meals, secondary school fees, examination fees and other contributions. This resulted in children regularly being sent home from school, suffering corporal punishment from teachers and sometimes missing several weeks of school until they received financial support from neighbours, relatives or community-based organisations, or in a few instances, were exempted from payments by teachers. Many of the young people

Box 7.6: Supportive school environments for children with caring responsibilities? Children's and parents' perspectives from the UK

Gemma's mother decided to tell teachers about her illness so that teachers would be more understanding if she became critically ill at short notice. She felt able to contact teachers if she was concerned that her illness might affect Gemma in school. However, Gemma was angry with her mother when she told her form teacher about her illness:

I got very angry with her when she did that, I didn't want anyone knowing. (Gemma, aged 15)

Furthermore, she did not feel that this had helped or made her teachers more supportive.

Kerry (aged 18) wished that her teachers knew about her caring responsibilities as she felt this would help them to be more understanding about fluctuations in her academic performance. However, she was worried about her teachers' reactions if she told them about her mother's illness and her caring responsibilities:

I don't know how to actually go and tell my teachers something like that. [...] I think I would probably be the one to have to tell them, but I don't know how they'd take it, or anything like that. I wouldn't even know how to approach the subject with my teachers, so I don't know.

Magic (aged 12) was often in trouble at school for challenging behaviour. His mother (from Southern Africa) described an incident when Magic had been bullied about his mother by another pupil, resulting in a temporary exclusion from school for violent behaviour:

So the boy basically was just calling me names and he got angry. He said he reported the boy to one teacher and the teacher ignored him and the boy carried on and then he just, he said 'Mum I just saw red.' He said 'To know how much you are ill and someone out there, you know, and I just saw red' and he punched the boy. So I went to school and I apologised and I asked the teacher have they spoken to the [other] boy at all. They said no the boy was sent home.

His mother felt frustrated with the teachers and thought that they did not give Magic *'a chance to have a say'*:

I don't know, it's like they already make up their mind and oh he's bad and he should carry everything that everybody does.

experienced difficulties attending secondary school because of not being able to afford the fees, even when they qualified to attend government secondary schools, which have substantially lower school fees than private schools. Magdalena, a 15-year-old girl who used to care for her mother and had lost both parents to AIDS, was selected to go to a government secondary school, but was unable to attend because of a lack of money for school fees. Her guardian commented on how upset Magdalena was when she could not continue at secondary school:

> *Her mum was illiterate, so [Magdalena] was very distressed when she couldn't continue with her Form One education. She used to cry a lot. She is bright, she used to do well in her class, she was normally first or second in the class.*

Other difficulties experienced by children at school in Tanzania included corporal punishment, missing classes when they were asked to run errands for their teachers and being bullied by their peers.

In the UK, some children and parents also highlighted issues related to poverty as impacting on children's education. Many of the families lived on low income in overcrowded social housing, which restricted the space available to young people for private study and homework. Several families did not have a computer or internet access at home (considered to be a necessity for families with secondary school age children in the UK: Bradshaw et al, 2008), which made it difficult for young people to do their coursework. This sometimes resulted in conflicts with parents when young people went to their friends' houses or to the library to study and returned home late.

Young people and parents also highlighted a number of difficulties children experienced at school related to immigration and racism, including language difficulties for newly arrived young people whose first language was not English, parents/siblings not being able to help them with their homework because of language and literacy difficulties, difficulties with bullying and peer group interactions and experiences of institutional racism in school and college. The problems that young people experienced at school reveal the difficulty of isolating the effects of caring from the broader socioeconomic impacts of HIV/ AIDS, poverty, migration and racism. These structural and relational aspects of social exclusion are likely to have just as significant impacts on children's educational outcomes and future life chances as their caring responsibilities.

Resilience and impacts within the wider community

Much of the previous research with young carers in the global North has identified negative impacts of children's caring responsibilities on their friendships, social lives and relationships in the wider community. This includes restricted opportunities for social networking and for developing peer friendships (Bilsborrow, 1992; Aldridge and Becker, 1993; Dearden and Becker, 1995; 1998; Thomas et al, 2003; Dearden and Becker, 2004) and limited opportunities for taking part in leisure and other activities (Aldridge and Becker, 1993). However, the resilience literature suggests that aspects of children's wider social environment, such as a supportive extended family, positive peer relationships, extracurricular activities, valued social roles and engagement in the community, membership of religious or faith communities, and the availability of external support or resources, represent important protective factors that can build children's resilience (Newman, 2002b; Schoon and Bynner, 2003). Gilligan (2004) suggests that a 'secure base' and supportive social networks in different domains, such as the home, extended family, school and social activities in the community can represent 'arenas of comfort' for children who experience adversity. Similarly, familiar routines, celebrations and rituals can be important in creating a sense of order, structure, collective identity and belonging for children exposed to risk and adversity (Gilligan, 2004). The different effects of young caregiving on young people's peer relationships and social lives within the context of the global North and South are discussed below.

Young people's friendships, supportive social networks and participation in the community

The majority of young people in Tanzania and the UK mentioned best friends and peers with whom they enjoyed spending time. When children were asked to take photographs of people and places that were important to them, many young people in the UK took photographs of themselves with their friends on the way to school, during class, dancing at an after-school dance club, with friends at a youth club and at a party for children affected by HIV. This reveals the importance young people attach to their peer friendships and their participation in social activities. Some young people in the UK had ambivalent emotional ties to 'home' and found it difficult to invite friends to their house. In contrast, many young people in both Tanzania and the UK valued school, college, church, youth clubs, leisure and extracurricular activities as places of respite or 'arenas of comfort' from the difficulties they were experiencing at home and as opportunities to socialise with their peers, as illustrated in Box 7.7.

While the opportunities for leisure and extracurricular activities were much more limited for young people in Tanzania, some young people described spending time with their peers as a *'relief'* and a way of *'taking your mind off things'*. Some young people took photographs of places they went to relax, such as chatting to friends outside particular places or watching TV at their house, or seeking out a secluded place where they had time to themselves to think or rest when they were tired. Many young people regularly attended church, sometimes on their own or with their siblings if their parent/relative was too ill to attend. Parents/relatives were keen to ensure that children participated in confirmation classes, religious celebrations and initiation ceremonies, despite their difficulty in affording new clothes for their children on these occasions.

Young people's peer relationships and engagement in their communities thus seem to play an important role in providing a break from difficult home situations and in reducing their social isolation. However, young people rarely perceived their peer relationships as sources of practical or emotional support with their caring responsibilities. In Tanzania and the UK, young people very rarely mentioned asking friends for help when their parent/relative was ill or for practical support in caring for their parent/relative. As discussed earlier, few children told their friends about their parent's HIV status because of a fear of stigma. Some young people did feel, however, that they could talk to a friend if they had a problem or were worried or upset, and a few young people felt able to talk to a trusted friend about their parent/relative's illness and their caring responsibilities. A few young people in Tanzania also valued their friendships in terms of providing emotional support and advice, as Good Luck (aged 18) commented: *'They give me advice and encourage me saying that I shouldn't lose hope, do my best and that it is all God's plan.'*

While young people's friendships and peer relationships offered limited emotional support, children and parents from households affected by HIV often relied on informal social networks with neighbours, family friends and members of their faith communities for material support and practical assistance with caregiving. The photographs taken by young people in Tanzania reveal the places they go to in their local neighbourhood and community to access both informal and formal support for their parent/relative and family as part of their everyday caring responsibilities. These included: markets and shops where they bought food for the family, places they went to fetch water and firewood, clinics and NGOs where they went to collect medicine for their parent/relative or to seek support to transport their parent to hospital (see Figure 7.1).

Box 7.7: Importance of positive peer relationships and social activities in the wider community: young people's experiences in the UK

Kerry (aged 18) described how she never invited her friends to her house because she associated 'home' with her caring responsibilities and did not feel she could relax there in the way that her friends could in their homes:

> *I never bring them round to my house. It's just an awkward place really for me, because it's just, home is kind of like work. I know that sounds really awkward, but it's, like, I have to do things at home, and it's not really like... at their homes their parents are usually maybe working or doing something, you know, and they're just sitting there watching TV or anything, but here it's not like that, so I never really....*

She valued college as a place where she could meet her friends and enjoy a sense of independence from her responsibilities at home:

> *It's just a place to get away, see your friends. It can be a bit stressful, but it's just nice to get out sometimes and have your own life.*

Kisha (aged 14) had found it difficult dealing with loss and separation within her family as well as her caring responsibilities. She valued her relationships with her friends and her dance and drama groups, as they helped her to forget about her family problems:

> *My friends are always there for me [...] mostly when I'm with my friends I don't think about stuff much, just have fun. And I like going to drama and dance because, like, it's something to do, you see friends too.*

Although she felt her friends were supportive and could be trusted, only one of her friends knew about her mother's illness and she was reluctant to talk to her other friends about this:

> *I have a lot of friends who support me, but I don't think I'll ever be able to tell them about my mum. There's a limit to what I can tell them, however I can trust them.*

Figure 7.1: Photograph taken by Malcolm (aged 15, Tanzania), who cared for his mother and younger siblings: *'This is where I go to get things I need at the market.'*

In Tanzania, most young people said that they asked their neighbours for material support when their parent was ill, and a few children said that neighbours helped them to care for their parent on a more regular basis. As discussed in Chapter 5, some children begged for food and money or borrowed money from neighbours to meet the household's basic needs or the costs of medication or transport to take their parent to hospital during times of crisis. Janet's account in Box 7.8 illustrates the importance of material support from neighbours. Some children experiencing extreme poverty and hunger also begged for food from the church or mosque. In some other cases members of faith communities helped families obtain food and clothing donations from the church when parents were seriously ill.

A few young people in Tanzania also said that neighbours sometimes offered practical assistance with their caring responsibilities when their parent/relative was ill, often according to conventional gender norms. For example, female neighbours sometimes helped with domestic and personal care tasks, while in one instance, a male neighbour helped William with the outdoor tasks of cutting grass for the goat and fetching water when his grandmother was ill. In the UK, neighbours were rarely asked for material support when parents were ill, but in a few instances neighbours and family friends provided practical assistance with childcare and children's caring responsibilities, as the example of Sarah in Box 7.8 shows.

Box 7.8: Young people's and parents' social support networks among neighbours and friends in Tanzania and the UK

Material support in Tanzania

Janet relied on financial support from her neighbours to pay her mother's medical bills:

> When mum's health got worse, life at home became even harder. Whenever she was hospitalised, we had no money to pay for her to be discharged so we had to beg from the neighbours to help us. (Janet, aged 17, Tanzania)

Practical assistance with children's caring responsibilities in the UK

Sarah talked about the close, supportive relationship the family had with their neighbour, who helped her to care for her siblings when her mum was in hospital:

> I have some help from my neighbour which we're very close to and she helps out but she can't help out that much because she's not really as strong as me. I am, so I try my best to do as much as I can. [...] If my mum's gone to the hospital she'll help cook, clean and she'll make sure that we're all eating, doing our homework, taking medication and then she'll go. She'll let us go to sleep and she'll go home and come and check on us in the morning, or she would stay. (Sarah, aged 16, UK)

Emotional support for parents with HIV

Mary, who was open about her HIV status, had developed a supportive social network of friends and neighbours in her neighbourhood in Tanzania:

> I have told a lot of people about my illness. So when I am ill, a lot of people come to see me, because they know about my problem. I go to see them and so they are close to me. If they hear that the children are ill, they come to help me.

Lucy (from East Africa) commented on the emotional support and advice she received from her friends living with HIV whom she had met at a support group in the UK:

> When I'm ill I have some HIV friends, my friends who are also the same. I call them and ask them this is this, what can I do, and they give me advice. [...] In our group here, we look out for each other, if you don't come this day, today is our day, if you don't come we shall call you and say, 'Oh what's happening, are you alright?'

Many young people and parents in Tanzania thought that neighbours did not know about their parent's HIV status and they did not want to disclose their status for fear of stigmatisation. However, some parents had told some of their close neighbours and friends about their illness and a few sought support from nurses or doctors living in their neighbourhood, who provided material support and informal medical advice about taking ARVs. Similarly, some parents, who were active members of support groups of people living with HIV and were open about their status, had developed supportive social networks among friends and neighbours in their local area (see Box 7.8).

Many parents with HIV in the UK had shared their HIV status with close friends and had developed supportive relationships with other people living with HIV through support groups in the community, to whom they felt able to turn for emotional, and sometimes practical, support with care tasks, particularly during the day when children were at school (see Box 7.8). Thus the social support networks that parents developed among their friends and neighbours provided highly valued emotional support for parents themselves, and also provided practical assistance that helped to alleviate children's caring responsibilities when parents were seriously ill.

Temporal and spatial conflicts between children's caring responsibilities and their social lives

Almost two thirds of the young people interviewed in the UK felt that their caring responsibilities in some way restricted their social lives and engagement in leisure and other activities, whereas just over a third of the young people in Tanzania reported this. A higher proportion of boys in Tanzania mentioned this in comparison with girls. Several young people in the UK felt that the negative aspects of their caregiving related to not having enough time and space to themselves, because their caring responsibilities conflicted with their own interests and activities. This appeared to be linked to age; as young people became teenagers they increasingly wanted to socialise with friends and engage in extracurricular activities independently from their family, but found their time to do so was limited because of their caring responsibilities. Furthermore, a few young people felt that their parent was sometimes overprotective and restricted the time they could spend with their friends or the leisure and extracurricular activities they could engage in, as the example of Gemma in Box 7.9 shows.

Box 7.9: Conflicts between young people's caring responsibilities and social lives in the UK

Gemma (aged 15) felt that her mother restricted her freedom to go out with her friends in the evening because of her caring responsibilities:

I mean it's just sort of being, like, quite controlled and not having, like, freedom, not being able to go out with my friends in the evening, like after school. All my friends are out at the park now. I'll have to stay in and, like, help and all stuff.

She mentioned a drama club she would have liked to attend in her neighbourhood, but commented on how difficult it was for her mother to collect her in the car on cold, dark winter evenings. Gemma felt that she had matured quite quickly and wanted to visit her sister abroad, but her mother did not want her to go because of her need for care:

I said, 'Well, can't I go on my own?' She said, no she doesn't want me to because, like, she can't manage on her own here.

Young people's narratives and the photographs that they took reveal that young people's caring tasks were focused predominantly in and around the household. As discussed earlier, some young people in the UK perceived 'home' as a place where they had considerable responsibilities and which they associated with worry and anxiety about their parent's illness, rather than a place where they could relax and enjoy spending time with their family or friends. Living on low income in overcrowded accommodation also impacted on young people's experiences of home, and a few young people in the UK described their difficulty or reluctance in inviting their friends to their home. A few parents in the UK were concerned that their children's spatial mobility and engagement with their peers in leisure and social activities was restricted to the household because of children's fear of leaving their parent alone (see Box 7.10). Indeed, a few children in the UK and Tanzania expressed a preference for staying at home, close to their parent, where they were able to respond to their parent's support needs when they were needed, rather than going out to play with their friends. Some parents in the UK also expressed their frustration and regret that they did not have more energy to take their children out and spend time doing leisure and social activities with their children because of their illness and physical impairments.

As we saw in Chapter 6, many service providers in the UK felt that a negative outcome of children's care work was often that they missed out on doing social activities with their peers, linking this, as parents did, to a sense of 'loss of childhood' (see Box 6.5). Some service providers also thought that children's spatial mobility was affected by their caring responsibilities, resulting in the risk of social exclusion.

Box 7.10: Fear of leaving their parent alone: children's reduced spatial mobility and engagement in leisure activities in the UK

Magic (aged 12) liked playing football, but said that he had not played with his friends for *'quite a few months'* and he preferred to stay at home with his mother rather than be taken out with his siblings by a family friend:

> If I'm getting taken out I don't really want to go. I want to stay with my mum most of the time. But I don't really go out and play that much.

His mother (from Southern Africa) was concerned that Magic was missing out on playing and socialising with his peers because of his anxiety about leaving her alone:

> He doesn't play much, he doesn't go out much and even if you do tell him to go out he'd say to me, 'No I'm not going', and I say 'Why?' He said, 'What about you?' I think he's got this fear that maybe if he leaves me alone I will die and I'll never wake up. I don't know, he has never said anything, but the way he is, it just worries me.

Very few young people or parents/relatives in Tanzania mentioned conflicts between young people's caring responsibilities and recreation, which is likely to be linked to much more limited play and leisure opportunities in comparison with the UK. It also appears to be linked to differing cultural expectations about children's free time and recreation. For example, when young people in Tanzania were asked what they liked doing in their free time, the majority said reading and private study, doing household chores or caring for their parent; play and leisure activities were rarely mentioned. This contrasts with the responses of young people in the UK, who cited a wide range of play and leisure activities they enjoyed doing, often in adult-supervised youth groups and clubs. Some service providers in Tanzania were concerned, however, that children may miss out on playing with their peers because of their caring responsibilities, as one project worker commented: *'They waste a lot of their childhood looking after their parents instead of playing and being happy with their friends'.*

Stigma and social isolation

Chapter 4 highlighted the different forms of stigma and discrimination that many mothers with HIV experienced from their relatives, friends, neighbours and members of the wider community in both the UK and Tanzania. Several young people caring for parents/relatives with HIV in Tanzania also had direct experiences of stigma and ostracism from their relatives, friends, neighbours and other community members (see Box 7.11; see also Box 6.12). Service providers in both countries felt that children caring for parents/relatives with HIV were vulnerable to 'stigma by association', as a result of their parents' illness. This confirms the findings of previous research with children affected by HIV/AIDS (Lewis, 2001; Cree et al, 2004; Evans, 2005; Foster et al, 2005; Ely, 2006) as well as research with young carers caring for parents with other stigmatised illnesses and impairments, such as mental health problems or alcoholism (Landells and Pritlove, 1994; Aldridge and Becker, 2003). However, the majority of service providers in Tanzania and the UK felt that children caring for parents/relatives with HIV experienced a much higher level of stigma and discrimination than other young carers, and it was this aspect that most clearly differentiated their experiences. As one service provider in Tanzania commented:

> *HIV is considered evil or unapproachable because of fear of infection from the sick person. In the case of HIV some people even change the route they walk for fear of passing near the house of a person with HIV/AIDS, such is the stigma attached to it.*

The stigma associated with HIV can lead to bullying and social isolation, which can be very distressing and affect young people's emotional well-being, as the examples in Box 7.11 show. In Tanzania, some service providers felt that the stigma experienced by young people could also affect their transitions to adulthood, such as the success of small business enterprises and marriage prospects.

Although direct experiences of discrimination and ostracism were not mentioned by young people in the UK, the secrecy surrounding HIV significantly affected their ability to talk about their parent's illness and their caring responsibilities and seek support from family, friends, neighbours, and professionals (see Box 7.12). Indeed, roughly half of the young people in both countries thought that none of their friends knew about their parent/relative's illness and very few said that their teachers knew. Most children did not feel able to talk to their friends, neighbours or teachers about their parent/relative's illness because of fear of stigmatisation or because they had been told by their parent/relative to keep it a family secret, as is illustrated in Box 7.12.

Box 7.11: Stigma by association: young people's experiences of social isolation and stigma within the family and in the wider community in Tanzania

Janet and her siblings were often bullied and stigmatised by other children because of their mother's HIV status when they went to fetch water, as she explained:

> Whenever you go to fetch tap water they tell you that you are infected with AIDS.[…] I feel very bad. I let them be if they stop me from getting water from their tap because they say you have AIDS, there is nothing you can do about it. We have to leave this place and go to a different place for water where we are not stigmatised. (Janet, aged 17)

June had also experienced discrimination and ostracism from her friends and neighbours, which had a major impact on her friendships, social networks and the support available to her:

> My friends don't like me anymore and have shunned me because of my mother's illness. I don't have any friends or neighbours who I can turn to for help. I am left with only one, a school friend, who sometimes comes to visit and help me here at home. (June, aged 18)

When she was asked who she could talk to about her mother's illness and her caring responsibilities, she felt she had no one to turn to:

> [There's] no one. It is useless because there is no one willing to listen. [Cries.]

Furthermore, when young people in the UK were asked more generally whom they could talk to if they had a problem or were worried or upset, over a quarter said that there was no one they could talk to. For some young people, the stigma and secrecy surrounding HIV also led to feelings of being different from their peers. For example, Kerry found it difficult to 'fit in' and was not able to talk to anyone about her problems:

> *It was quite difficult to fit in with people because no one has the same problems as I do. I mean they might do, but I don't know that, so I can't really speak to anyone. I find it difficult to integrate.*

Box 7.12: HIV stigma, secrecy and the effects on young people's ability to seek support in Tanzania and the UK

We can't tell our friends, because some friends you might be open with but it's not good to tell them. [...] People hassle us a lot. If you tell them something like that, people will hassle you. (Malcolm, aged 15, Tanzania)

Mum says I shouldn't talk about that at all to anyone. (Sarah, aged 15, Tanzania)

I mostly keep things to myself. I know I shouldn't, but I just find it difficult to speak to anyone really. (Kerry, aged 18, UK)

I don't really talk to no one. Probably my friends, but it's, if it's just like something deep I don't tell no one, I don't tell anyone. I like to keep it to myself. (Sarah, aged 16, UK)

Crystal (aged 15, UK) said that she did not talk to anyone at school about her mother's illness or if she was worried or had a problem. She said that no one else helped her and her brother care for their mother and she felt unable to ask anyone for help when her mother was ill:

—When your mum is ill, who do you ask for help?
— No one. We can't really, can we?

In Tanzania, when young people were asked whom they could talk to about their parent/relative's illness and their caring responsibilities, the most common response was that there was no one they could talk to. Similarly, when they were asked 'Who else helps you to care for your parent/relative?' the most common response was that no one else helped them. Half of the young people in Tanzania thought that their friends knew about their caring responsibilities, and a third knew other children who had caring responsibilities in their neighbourhood. Only a few young people, however, had the opportunity to meet other young people with caring responsibilities through youth groups and psychosocial support interventions targeted towards young people affected by HIV/AIDS.

In contrast, in the UK, half of the young people had got to know other young people with caring responsibilities through their engagement with youth groups targeted towards young people affected by HIV. However, attending a youth group for children from similar backgrounds did not necessarily mean that young people talked to their peers about their experiences or developed peer support. For example, Tolu (aged 13) attended three youth groups for young people who were aware of HIV within their family. He knew some other young people who cared for a parent with HIV, but did not know about their home situations and did not think they would want to talk about their parents' illness: *'I don't think they would like to talk about it as well because you know you keep everything to yourself like that, private stuff so.'* Some service providers suggested that young people had a strong sense of loyalty to their family, linked to African cultural values, which meant that they were reluctant to talk openly about their experiences until a high level of trust had been built up:

> *They're very good at keeping what is in the family to the family, and I think that's also another cultural thing. They're not willing to open up and speak to anybody very easily, and some of the things that you get from them may be fairly superficial until you build up a certain amount of trust.*

These findings suggest that, because of the stigma and secrecy surrounding HIV as well as young people's loyalty to their families, many young people caring for parents/relatives with HIV remain largely hidden and unsupported by friends, neighbours, teachers and other professionals. They often feel unable to seek informal support from their peers or other adults in the community in the context of both the global North and South. Some young people, particularly in communities severely affected by HIV and AIDS, have to deal with direct experiences of stigma and discrimination on an everyday basis, which can affect their emotional well-being and result in social isolation.

Effects of poverty on young people's friendships and social participation

As noted earlier, many families interviewed in the UK lived in poor, overcrowded housing, which resulted in a lack of privacy. Some parents and young people felt that the lack of space and privacy made it difficult for young people to invite their friends to their house. For example,

Alice and her mother rented a single room in a shared house with five other tenants. Alice found the lack of space and privacy the worst aspect of home. Her mother highlighted the difficulty in keeping her HIV status a secret within such crowded living conditions and the implications of the lack of privacy when Alice invited her friends to their place:

> *We just have one room. It's the same room that we live in, that we sleep in and it's the sitting room. Everything happens in that room. For example, I have my drugs in the fridge and perhaps her friends come around and they ask her whether the drugs are hers. So it's different for us.*

Some parents and service providers in the UK also commented on the difficulties parents experienced in being able to afford leisure and social activities for their children, such as dancing, swimming, football, horse-riding, climbing or going out as a family.

Conclusion

The research in Tanzania and the UK suggests that the school attendance of many children in households affected by HIV and AIDS is disrupted by their caring responsibilities. Many children in Tanzania and some in the UK also reported negative impacts of their caring responsibilities on their academic performance, finding it difficult to concentrate on their school work because of tiredness and/or anxiety about their parent's illness. Half of the children in both countries described how their caring responsibilities often conflicted with their time for private study.

Despite these negative impacts, over a third of children and most parents in both countries did not think that their parent's illness or their caring responsibilities had any significant effects on their school attendance or academic performance. Most children and parents did not want teachers to know about their parent's illness because of a fear of stigmatisation, as previous studies have found (Lewis, 2001; Cree et al, 2004). Children's resilience, good school attendance and academic performance was thus related more to informal support from parents, peers and individual teachers, high aspirations, and the young person's interests and motivation, rather than supportive institutional environments or sensitivity and awareness of young caregiving among school professionals.

Most young people mentioned best friends and peers with whom they enjoyed spending time, and many valued school, college, church, youth clubs, leisure and extracurricular activities as places of respite from the difficulties they were experiencing at home. Children and parents relied on social networks with neighbours, family friends and members of their faith communities for material support and practical assistance with caregiving. However, many young people in the UK felt that their caring responsibilities restricted their social lives because of conflicts between their caring responsibilities and their own activities. Some children preferred to stay at home, close to their parent, rather than play with their friends, and parents were concerned that children's spatial mobility and engagement with their peers was restricted. Some parents also expressed frustration that they did not have more energy to take their children out and do leisure and social activities with them.

Several young people in Tanzania experienced 'stigma by association', including bullying and ostracism from their peers and others in the community, which impacted on their emotional well-being and led to social isolation. Although direct experiences of discrimination were not mentioned by young people in the UK, the secrecy surrounding HIV significantly affected their ability to talk about their parents' illness and seek support from friends, neighbours, school teachers and other professionals. Poverty, overcrowded housing and problems related to immigration and racism also had significant effects on children's school experiences and opportunities for leisure and socialisation with their peers, revealing that families affected by HIV/AIDS face a complex array of problems that can result in the marginalisation and social exclusion of young people. The role of formal safety nets and external support in building the resilience of children and parents affected by HIV forms the focus of the next chapter.

EIGHT

The role of formal safety nets in building children's and families' resilience

This chapter focuses on the role of formal safety nets and external support from non-governmental community- and faith-based organisations and governmental/statutory providers in building the resilience of families affected by HIV/AIDS within the context of the North and South. In the previous chapters, we suggested that informal safety nets and supportive relationships within the family, neighbourhood, school and wider community play a crucial role in building children's and families' resilience and mitigating the negative impacts of young caregiving and HIV/AIDS on households. In severely affected communities in the South, however, these informal safety nets are being overstretched, and the capacity of families and communities to continue to support households affected by HIV/AIDS is being seriously diminished. Governmental/ statutory services and civil society organisations can thus help to reduce families' vulnerability, providing much-needed material and emotional resources and support for children and families affected by HIV/AIDS. In this chapter, we examine the different services and support that children and parents/relatives with HIV accessed in Tanzania and the UK. By drawing on service providers' and families' experiences, the chapter identifies practices and approaches that aim to build on children's and families' strengths, enhance resilience and promote protective factors within different domains, including the community, school, family and for individual children.

Services and support for families affected by HIV/AIDS

The ten non-governmental voluntary and community sector organisations (NGOs) involved in the study in the UK provided a range of services for children and families affected by HIV/AIDS, including: practical support for parents, peer support for parents, leisure and social activities for young people in similar situations, family support, emotional support for children and parents, practical support for young people, and HIV awareness-raising activities (see examples in Table 8.1).

Table 8.1: External support from non-governmental, community-based HIV/AIDS organisations in the UK

Service/ support provided	Examples of support	Number of NGOs (n=10)
Practical support for people living with HIV	• Advocacy and advice about immigration issues, housing, children's education, parenting issues, advice and support to access benefits and entitlements • Support to manage finances and debt • Financial support, grants for equipment and adaptations in the home, grants for family holidays • Crèche facilities • Signposting on to further sources of support	7
Peer support, leisure and social activities for young people in similar situations	• Youth club for children affected by HIV • Young carers club • Outings and social activities, including drama, dance, music workshops, health education sessions, playschemes and holiday activities • Peer mentoring programme • Homework club	6
Family support	• Short breaks for individual children/babies to provide respite to parents with HIV and fun activities for children • Assistance with family shopping • Childcare while parent attends hospital appointments • Supporting parent and child with issues of disclosure • Whole family counselling and emotional support sessions • Volunteer home visiting programme • Fun days out for families, parties and events	5
Emotional support for children	• Individual counselling and emotional support in school • Support with issues of disclosure of HIV status	5
Emotional support for people living with HIV	• Counselling and emotional support • Workshops and support with disclosure within the family • Spiritual support, quiet days for complementary therapies and relaxation activities	5

Table 8.1: External support from non-governmental, community-based HIV/AIDS organisations in the UK (continued)

Service/ support provided	Examples of support	Number of NGOs (n=10)
Peer support for people living with HIV	• Regular support group meetings • User involvement in organisation	4
Practical support for young people	• Small grants for leisure activities and equipment • Information and support to access mainstream leisure activities • Support with independent living • Liaison with teachers	3
HIV awareness-raising activities	• World AIDS day events • Workshops on HIV and the family and faith issues for professionals	3

In Tanzania, the seven NGOs involved in the study provided a range of services for families affected by HIV/AIDS, including: home-based care, support groups for people living with HIV, community education and awareness raising, material and emotional support for orphans and vulnerable children, opportunities for the development of young people's life skills, and voluntary testing and counselling facilities. Examples of the support offered are listed in Table 8.2.

As discussed in Chapter 3, the families interviewed for this study were recruited through local non-governmental voluntary and community sector organisations who were in contact with the family. Thus, families were likely to receive or have received some support from organisations either currently or in the past. In the UK, children and parents who were interviewed accessed services provided by eight of the ten organisations. In Tanzania, families interviewed received services from seven organisations. However, despite being recruited to participate in the study through community-based NGOs, a few parents and children in Tanzania had received no or very little support from the organisation that had referred them. The level of support accessed by families in this study should not be seen as representative of families affected by HIV. As we discuss in Chapter 9, few families affected by HIV/AIDS in Tanzania and other Sub-Saharan African countries receive external support, particularly if HIV remains undiagnosed. Similarly, in the UK, despite greater access to health, social care and social security benefits (as in many countries in the North), a significant number of people are diagnosed at a late stage in their illness (UK Collaborative Group for HIV and STI Surveillance, 2006), resulting in reduced take–up of services and support that families affected by HIV might otherwise be able to access.

Table 8.2: External support from non-governmental, community-based HIV/AIDS organisations in Tanzania

Service/ support provided	Examples of support	Number of NGOs (n=7)
Home-based care for people living with HIV and their families	• Food aid, nutritional food, clothing, medication and medical supplies • Counselling, emotional support, information and advice about HIV and AIDS • Financial support and transport to hospital	7
Peer support for people living with HIV	• Regular support group meetings • Seminars and advice about living positively with HIV • Small loans for income-generation activities	5
HIV education and awareness-raising activities in community	• Peer education in community to raise awareness about HIV and AIDS and reduce stigma • Seminars in schools • Young people's peer education clubs	5
Material support for orphans and vulnerable children	• Food, clothing, school uniform, school materials, secondary school fees • Financial support for families, housing support	5
Emotional support for orphans and vulnerable children	• Home visits, counselling, advice • Anticipatory grief processes residential camp and grieving groups • Memory club • Play and sports activities	5
Life skills for orphans and vulnerable young people and their families	• Training in vocational skills and livelihood strategies • Equipment and small loans to start small businesses • Health education seminars about HIV and AIDS	4
Voluntary counselling and testing for HIV	• Pre- and post-test counselling	4

Practices and approaches that promote resilience and protective factors for children and families

Drawing on service providers' perspectives and children's and parents' experiences, it is possible to identify practices and approaches that help to reduce negative impacts of young caring and build children's and families' resilience. The following sections discuss the ways that each approach helps to build children's and parents' resilience, based on service providers' perspectives and families' experiences.

Practical, material and emotional support for parents with HIV

In the UK, several service providers thought that providing practical and emotional support for parents with HIV helped to reduce the negative impacts of young caregiving and promote families' resilience. Indeed, seven of the ten voluntary organisations provided practical support and five provided emotional support for parents with HIV. Some organisations focused predominantly on supporting parents with HIV rather than directly supporting children, although they did organise some family outings and activities. Many organisations tried to ensure that parents, particularly those seeking asylum, accessed all the social welfare support they were entitled to. Another project worker commented on the need to respond to crises at short notice, such as assisting with housing problems related to HIV stigma or the dispersal of refugees and asylum seekers to other towns and cities. Many organisations played an important role in signposting parents with HIV on to further sources of support, and some provided advocacy support, such as accompanying parents to meetings with mainstream service providers.

Many parents valued highly the practical advice and advocacy support they had received from project workers in dealing with immigration issues, housing, managing finances and debt, transport, racial harassment, children's education and other parenting issues. Some project workers had helped parents to access benefits and hardship grants for equipment in the home and many signposted them on to further sources of information and support. Many parents also commented on the emotional support they received from project workers, particularly in dealing with issues of disclosure within the family and in living positively with HIV. They felt that the support they received had made a difference to their emotional well-being and acceptance of their HIV status, as the examples in Box 8.1 show.

Box 8.1: Practical and emotional support for parents with HIV: parents' experiences of voluntary sector services in the UK

Alice's mother came to the UK as a postgraduate student from East Africa. A school-based project worker supported Alice's mother with immigration issues, helping her to renew her visa, as Alice's mother explained:

> *It began when she first got to know Alice. She knew I was ill and that my visa had finished and that my lawyer had made a mistake. [...] I had become an 'overstayer' and the worst thing about it all was that they didn't tell me this. The lawyer stayed with the letter until [project worker] phoned me and went to sort it out. At this time I started being ill, I felt really bad. I was stressed and depressed and no one came to find us. I was just staying at home. [...] So it took five months to sort out my student visa.*

Alice summed up the difference that the project worker's support had made to them:

> *Getting visa is something that has changed me and my mum's life, especially my mum's as she was so depressed, confused, stressed, and I really felt helpless by the time we had refusal because I didn't know what to do to help and this really stressed me a lot.*

Sandra commented on the friendly atmosphere and emotional support she received from a project focused on adults with HIV:

> *Always very friendly there and if at any time.... Once I phoned them up, I was at my wit's end, I was in tears [...] they just took me straight up into a top room out the way and sat with me and let me cry my heart out. So they've been very supportive like that.*

Two thirds of parents in the UK reported some involvement with statutory professionals either currently or in the past. This was often linked to episodes of serious parental mental or physical ill health, particular crises linked to housing or immigration issues, or dealing with disclosure within the family. Some parents had received practical support from housing support workers and other statutory professionals in accessing benefits. Parents had also received statutory support with home adaptations, physiotherapy, massage, mental health services and residential respite care. A third of parents received some practical support from social services with childcare and domestic chores, such as taking their children to school, going shopping or other domestic tasks, during periods of serious illness or following hospitalisation. Parents valued highly the practical support that statutory home care and family support services provided, and some parents also felt that they gained emotional support from relationships with paid care workers, which helped to reduce their isolation as lone parents (see Box 8.2). Some parents felt satisfied that services had been withdrawn when they were no longer required and expressed their preference to manage independently once their support needs were no longer so acute. However, as we discuss in Chapter 10, several parents also had more negative experiences of accessing statutory home care support.

Box 8.2: Parents' experiences of statutory home care services in the UK

Laura was seriously ill in hospital for several months. When she was discharged, home care workers supported her in her home, taking her daughter to school and assisting her with shopping. While she was in hospital, her extended family did not think she would recover and cleared many of her possessions out of her flat. When she returned home, her social worker provided emotional support and she managed to retrieve some of her possessions, which a care worker helped to put back in her flat. The care worker also provided practical assistance with managing the debts that had accumulated while she was in hospital:

> For six months I had a lot of bills to pay and they – the carers – talked to the debt collectors and they managed to, you know, take off all my bills, all my debts, so I'm okay now.

Laura felt that she could manage independently, with the support of the carers to take her daughter to school:

> My social worker can see that I'm capable of doing things on my own now and I like to be independent.

She was satisfied with the support she received and felt able to contact her social worker if she needed further assistance.

Many service providers in Tanzania thought that providing material support and financial assistance to parents with HIV and their children helped to reduce the negative impacts of young caregiving and build families' resilience. Material support included food aid, nutritional food for people living with HIV, medicines, gloves and other medical supplies to protect carers from HIV infection, transport to hospital, financial support with housing, school uniform and educational materials, secondary school fees and vocational training. Indeed, half of the parents interviewed and several children saw the main benefits of services in terms of the material support they had received for their family, which helped to alleviate their poverty and hunger following the loss of parental income (see Box 8.3).

Box 8.3: Material and emotional support for parents with HIV and their families: young people's and parents' experiences in Tanzania

Annet felt that her health had improved and her children were able to continue with their education because of the support she received:

> *Personally, ever since I started going to [NGO] I have benefited as my health has improved and the children are doing well in their studies. Every year they are given uniforms and exercise books, I really don't know what we would have done without [NGO].*

Agnes (mother) thought that the best aspect of the services the NGO provided was the emotional support she received when they visited her at home every month:

> *They are very supportive, they make me feel more positive. I am very used to them now; they are like my own flesh and blood. [...] They are most loving. My happiest moments are when they visit me at home.*

Many service providers thought that providing training and capital for parents with HIV and other carers of orphaned children to start small businesses could help to protect children from the negative impacts of caregiving, enabling parents/relatives to engage in sustainable livelihood strategies that could meet the family's basic needs. One service provider felt that in addition to meeting families' basic needs, this also helped to improve the emotional well-being of people with HIV/AIDS and their families. A home-based care volunteer reported that supporting income-generation projects had been successful in his village, enabling people with HIV to meet their family's basic needs *'without having to rely on handouts'*. He highlighted the potential health benefits of rearing livestock for people living with HIV, as they gained access to protein-rich food such as goat milk or eggs. Many parents and children also highly valued the emotional support and advice that parents received from project workers through counselling, home visits and seminars (see Box 8.3).

Peer support for parents with HIV

Although not specifically identified by service providers as an approach that helped to build families' resilience, support groups of people living with HIV facilitated by NGOs were highly valued by many parents in both the UK and Tanzania. Five of the seven organisations in Tanzania facilitated support groups for adults living with HIV, while support groups were facilitated by four organisations in the UK. Many parents regularly attended support groups and felt that the opportunities to meet other women in similar situations improved their emotional well-being, helped them to live more positively with HIV and reduced their social isolation. For example, Lucy from East Africa highly valued a women's support group she attended twice a month. Members of the group had helped her financially by contributing towards her daughter's secondary school fees in her country of origin. She felt that the peer support helped to reduce her feelings of loneliness and isolation:

> *We have our own space to come every Wednesday and we spend time talking to each other, telling, advising each other, solving any kind of problems, have a cup of tea, sometimes we have a meal together, and then we go back when we are happy. [...] Sometimes you can be home too much alone. When you come here and talk to other ladies, you come back lifted. Even if you are sick you feel a bit better.*

Similarly, in Tanzania, Husna attended a monthly support group of people living with HIV, where they had recently started a poultry project in order to use the eggs to supplement their diet. She felt that meeting other women in similar situations helped to reduce her sense of isolation and loneliness:

> *Here at home I am lonely, there are no women of my age that I can talk to. When I go there, I am comforted. I mix with people who have similar problems to mine. We exchange ideas and learn about a lot of things.*

This suggests that peer support for parents with HIV may represent an important protective factor that may help to promote resilience at the level of the family and potentially alleviate the role of children in providing emotional support to their parents.

Holistic family support

Some service providers in the UK and Tanzania felt that holistic family support that was tailored to the individual needs of children and parents helped to reduce the negative impacts of young caregiving and promote family resilience. The majority of parents and several children in the UK said that projects provided opportunities for short breaks and leisure and social activities for children and/or for the whole family. Family support included individual children or siblings being taken out by a family support worker on a regular basis to provide short breaks for the parent and fun activities for the children. Family outings and social activities were also mentioned by many children and parents and some projects organised weekends away with other families in similar situations or helped individual parents access financial support for family holidays, which parents appreciated as a break that they would otherwise be unable to afford. Some service providers in the UK offered one-to-one support for the child and parent and facilitated whole-family therapeutic sessions to discuss issues of concern and improve communication within families. Project workers saw their role as facilitators and mediators, enabling all members of the family to express themselves and listen to young people's concerns and fears. Providers also highlighted the need to be flexible and tailor support to the individual needs and requirements of parents and children.

In Tanzania, service providers providing home-based care recognised the importance of engaging with children's family networks and encouraging them to share responsibility for supporting the person with HIV. One project worker commented on the need to engage with family members and combat relatives' assumptions that there was no need for them to help care for the person with HIV because their needs would be met by NGOs: *'When relatives see us helping their relative they have a tendency to stay away. But we advise them to get involved because they are important to the person with HIV.'* One project worker found that providing counselling and advice on issues of disclosure to children, parents, the extended family and community helped to reduce children's caring responsibilities and strengthen the family's social networks.

Most providers felt that it was important for children to be aware of the HIV status of the person they were caring for. Service providers identified practices and approaches that they had found effective in supporting families with disclosure (see Box 8.4). Most service providers emphasised the importance of building trust, supporting both the child and parent, working at their pace and respecting parents' decisions about when they felt ready to share their status with their children. However, some service providers in the UK suggested that, in their experience, many parents disclosed their status when they had been forced to or during a crisis, for example, an immigration official mentioning HIV in front of the children or health practitioners telling parents they have to disclose their child's status to the child: *'It's usually when there's a crisis that disclosure is told.'* Service providers suggested that statutory support from social workers, psychologists and community nurses was available to support parents and children with disclosure, but voluntary sector providers provided informal family support, counselling and advice, which parents might prefer to access because of the trust that they had developed with project workers.

In Tanzania, some service providers adopted holistic family approaches in supporting families with issues of disclosure through counselling, home-based care and memory work. Memory work is a child-centred, community-led approach that encourages families to communicate openly about HIV (Healthlink Worldwide, 2006; 2007). One of the

Box 8.4: Supporting children and parents on issues of disclosure within the family: practices and approaches from the UK and Tanzania

Service providers identified a number of practices and approaches that they found effective in supporting families on issues of disclosure:

- Disclosure should be seen as *'the start of a journey'*, an ongoing process that takes time.
- Preparatory workshops and seminars with parents may help to raise awareness and prepare them for disclosure.
- Encouragement, advice and support can be offered to parents, but it should be their decision to disclose to their children.
- Developing children's communication skills with their parent can help to empower children.
- Trust needs to be built with parents and children.
- Support should be at the child's and parent's pace and be flexible and responsive to individual needs.
- Support should be linked and coordinated with other relevant professionals or community leaders, where appropriate.

NGOs participating in the International Memory Project in Tanzania explained that memory work aimed to support both children and parents and facilitate communication within the family about issues of disclosure, loss and separation. Through the use of a memory book, children and parents were supported to write a family record and identify family members to whom children could turn for support after their parent's death. Maureen attended the memory project meetings and wrote a memory book with her mother. She found the process helpful in understanding more about her family, particularly about her father and his relatives, as her parents had separated when she was very young: *'Mum answered the questions and I wrote down the answers. I found I was getting to know about a lot of things that I wasn't very clear about at that time.'* She also felt that she had gained in terms of developing peer support and communication skills (see Box 8.5).

Opportunities for leisure, social activities and short breaks

The majority of NGOs participating in the study in the UK provided opportunities for leisure and extracurricular activities for children in similar situations, including drama, dance, music workshops, homework clubs, playschemes, outings and holiday activities. Service providers felt it was important for children to have time and space to have fun and *'just be children'* as a break from their caring responsibilities. One service provider was also concerned about children's physical fitness and felt that engaging young people in sports and leisure activities helped to tackle social exclusion and the reduced spatial mobility that they may experience as a result of their caring responsibilities. Service providers felt that providing activities for children during the school holidays was important to give children a break from their caring responsibilities and to help them not to feel isolated and unsupported in the absence of their school routine, as well as providing a break for parents.

Several young people valued opportunities to do new activities and learn new skills, such as swimming, rock climbing, abseiling and kayaking. One project also facilitated young people's access to mainstream leisure activities by offering practical support and information about opportunities as well as small grants to attend classes or buy sports equipment, such as a bicycle.

In some projects, family support workers or trained volunteers provided regular short breaks for individual children or siblings to provide respite for parents with HIV and to enable children to do fun activities that their parent might not otherwise have had the energy or financial means to organise. Service providers felt that these opportunities could provide a much-needed break for young people to have time for themselves away from other members of the family. Children and parents valued highly these opportunities for short breaks and said that parents would otherwise have struggled to afford these activities or did not feel well enough to accompany their children. For example, Magic (aged 12) thought that the best aspect of the activities he did with the youth group for children affected by HIV was that: *'They're fun, yes, get to enjoy myself. We just, you know, like go out [...] It's kind of like us having a break.'* As well as benefiting himself, Magic saw going to the youth group as an opportunity for his mother to have a break. His mother appreciated the opportunity for her children to go on holiday outings and do activities that she was not well enough to take them on herself:

> *That helps me as well because it's stress to the kids. I mean if your child is always locked up in the house they get frustrated, they need to go out and mix with people, talk to people. So, yeah, that helps me in terms of my kids going out because if I were to do on my own I don't think I can manage to do it.*

Many parents felt relieved that their child had opportunities to *'get out of the house'* and were confident that their children were in 'safe hands' while they were in the care of project workers.

In Tanzania, only a few projects provided play and leisure opportunities for children as a break from their caring responsibilities. A few organisations organised children's clubs at weekends, where orphans and vulnerable children could meet and play together and *'forget their problems'*. Organisations providing home-based care felt it was important to encourage children's school attendance and social participation, as this could help to promote a sense of belonging to the community and reduce feelings of isolation. A few children and parents mentioned occasional play and HIV awareness activities provided for younger children, but none of the young people interviewed had attended any of these activities, saying that they preferred to use their free time for private study. Some of their younger siblings had attended large group activities for orphans and vulnerable children, where they received educational materials and food on a few occasions each year.

Supportive safe places for children to express themselves and develop peer support

In the UK, many service providers felt that providing supportive safe places where children could express their feelings, ask questions and receive support and advice from project workers, either on a one-to-one basis or with their peers in a youth group setting, helped to reduce the negative impacts of caring and promote children's resilience. As noted earlier (see Table 8.1), six of the ten organisations participating in the study in the UK provided opportunities for peer support through youth groups and social activities with other children in similar situations and five organisations provided individual counselling and emotional support for children. Service providers felt that it was important that children had a place where they could talk about problems or fears about their parent's illness in confidence. For example, one project worker providing individual counselling and monthly group workshops aimed to offer a space where children could talk in confidence and receive non-judgemental advice. Another organisation provided one-to-one sessions in school, where project workers encouraged children to feel a sense of pride in their caring responsibilities and recognised their achievements in managing to combine their care work with school. The project worker helped to alleviate Alice's worry about her mother by negotiating with school staff for Alice to call her mother to check how she was during the school day.

Young people who received emotional support and counselling in one-to-one sessions valued the space to express their feelings in confidence and found it particularly useful in talking about tensions or difficulties in their relationship with their parent with HIV. Christine, for example, felt that her daughter benefited from being able to express her feelings at one-to-one counselling sessions:

> *She now has somewhere she can go and talk freely and that seems to help, you know. There was a time we got into an argument and she came back to me and said, 'Mum, make an appointment for me please.' So I think she was getting some help from that.*

A few young people also reported receiving counselling and emotional support from statutory professionals.

The majority of young people interviewed in the UK attended youth clubs for children affected by HIV, where they had opportunities to socialise and engage in social activities, such as workshops, performing arts, and 'chilling' with other young people in similar situations. Young people attending a youth club led by an African community organisation wrote articles and poems for a monthly newsletter distributed to a range of organisations and groups working with families across London. Over a third of the young people in the UK said they particularly valued the opportunities for peer support they experienced through meeting other young people in similar situations. However, only two young people interviewed attended mainstream young carers projects that provided leisure and social activities for children caring for parents/relatives with a range of long-term physical or mental illnesses or impairments. One project that facilitated a monthly youth group for young people who were aware of HIV within the family aimed to provide a safe place where young people could ask questions, build supportive relationships and enjoy spending time with their peers.

Project staff felt that providing opportunities for children with caring responsibilities to develop peer support with others in similar situations could play an important role in building children's resilience and reducing their isolation. One project had established a peer mentoring scheme that matched volunteers to young people from the same cultural, faith and linguistic background and, where possible, recruited peer mentors living with HIV as positive role models.

Several young people saw the main benefit of services in terms of socialising with other young people in similar situations, which helped to reduce their sense of isolation. Kisha (aged 14) said that the best aspect of the project was spending time with the other young people in the group: *'They're fun, and there's like a lot of people my age as well.'* She felt that she had benefited from meeting other young people in similar situations: *'I'm not so upset about my mum because I know there's other people like me.'* While some young people felt that they could talk to their peers about their problems or family situations, others just enjoyed spending time with their peers and did not feel the need to share their personal experiences or talk about family issues. For example, Crystal (aged 15) said that in specialist youth groups they rarely talked about their personal experiences or family situations, but she appreciated spending time with other young people in similar situations:

> Even though all the children that are there, even though we're all in the same situation going through the same things, we don't really talk about it. And it's really rare for us to talk about it. But it's just, the environment is just to be with people that we all know, who know, but we don't want to talk about it.

In Tanzania, many service providers felt that it was important to provide emotional (or 'psychosocial') support for children caring for parents/relatives with HIV to relieve their stress and reduce their sense of isolation. Five of the seven organisations participating in the study offered some emotional support to children. Home-based care volunteers recognised the need to offer emotional support to children with caring responsibilities during their home visits to reduce children's sense of isolation and help them to feel that their caring responsibilities were shared by others in the community.

Some children said that they had received emotional support, information and advice about HIV/AIDS and how to care for someone with HIV from project workers through home visits or seminars they had attended. Although only a small number of children mentioned receiving emotional support, some children felt that the advice and counselling they received about caring for their parent was the best aspect of the help they received from NGOs. Only a few children in Tanzania mentioned opportunities provided by projects to meet other young people in similar situations. One NGO organised an 'anticipatory grief processes' residential camp for children affected by HIV/AIDS that aimed to encourage the development of peer support. Neema and other young people who attended the camp highly valued the opportunity to share their experiences with other young people in similar situations and learn more about caring for their parent (see Box 8.5). Similarly, as mentioned earlier, the memory project organised by another NGO aimed to improve communication between children and parents and enable children to express their feelings through talking to their peers about their experiences of caring for their parent. Maureen, who attended the memory club, valued the opportunity to meet others in similar situations and develop useful life skills (see Box 8.5). Some service providers in Tanzania suggested that building young people's life skills through vocational training and providing capital to start small businesses could help to promote young people's resilience. Enabling young people to become 'economically empowered' and develop livelihood strategies was also seen as a way of reducing young people's, particularly young women's, vulnerability to HIV infection and unwanted pregnancies.

Box 8.5: Building resilience, peer support and life skills among young people affected by HIV/AIDS in Tanzania

'Anticipatory grief processes' residential camp

An NGO organised an anticipatory grief processes residential camp for three different groups of children: those who cared for a parent with HIV, children who were living with HIV themselves and children who had been orphaned by AIDS. The intervention aimed to encourage the development of peer support, life skills, greater knowledge about HIV and AIDS and improved communication between children and parents. Project workers supported children to get to know each other and build trust within the group, talk about their caring responsibilities, share their feelings with their peers, build life skills such as communicating with their parent, managing stress, talking about sexuality and making informed decisions, thinking about their present and future aspirations as well as relaxing and doing sport and leisure activities.

Neema (aged 18) highly valued the opportunity to attend the camp, where she found she could share her experiences with other young people in similar situations:

> I thank God for enabling me to attend the camp. I got to talk about how I felt inside there. [...] We discussed a lot of things about how to maintain a good relationship with other people in the community, caring for a sick person. We discovered that we had similar problems and it was a great relief and support for me.

A project worker felt that the camp helped to empower children to express themselves and facilitate communication about HIV within families:

> After we had done the session at [the camp] the children were empowered. They went to share with their parents and the parents came to [NGO] and thanked us for what we had done; they were now able to share their life experiences with their children.

Memory work with young people and parents

Another NGO ran a memory project that aimed to encourage communication between parents and children about their HIV status and to help prepare young people for the future. The project worked with groups of parents with HIV and young people to encourage the parent and young person to write a family record book with photographs of important family members who could help the young person after the parent's death. The project also facilitated memory clubs for young people to develop peer support.

> Maureen (aged 19) enjoyed meeting other young people in similar situations at the memory club and developed life skills, which she felt helped to reduce her isolation:
>
> *We go there and sit with our friends. We talk, we are taught, they help us feel free. [We have] lessons in openness and how not to feel lonely, how not to feel a failure and how to take care of our parents. We have learned about a lot of things [...] like keeping a diary, being open when you have a problem. We talked about how we care for our parents at home, about the problems we face, how to communicate, our rights, play games and sports.*

Access to information about HIV/AIDS

Some service providers in the UK felt that providing children with caring responsibilities with access to information about HIV/AIDS could help to reduce negative impacts of caregiving. Many project workers found that when parents disclosed their HIV status to their children, there was often little opportunity for children to ask questions and understand the full implications of their illness, because of the secrecy surrounding HIV, communication difficulties within the family and children's fear of upsetting their parent and exacerbating their illness. As one project worker commented:

> *They've been told and then left holding it, and they've felt that they couldn't ask any more questions, and then when they come to the group a lot of them don't even know the full implication of HIV or what it's about. It's just been blurted out by their parent.*

Project workers could thus play an important role in providing information, advice and support for young people to understand the full implications of their parent's HIV status. One project worker thought that children's lack of information and knowledge about HIV meant that they feared the worst about their parent's illness. Providing children with access to information and helping children and parents to communicate with each other about their fears and concerns could thus help to alleviate children's worry and stress.

Several service providers thought it was important to 'normalise' HIV and give information and support for children to overcome their fears and see that HIV was like any other long-term illness. One project worker felt that a session on sexual health at an HIV-specific youth group generated a helpful discussion in which young people were able to share their experiences of how they were told about HIV within the family. Indeed, some young people felt that their knowledge and understanding about HIV and how to care for someone with HIV had increased as a result of attending youth groups for young people who were aware of HIV within the family. Emily (aged 17) felt that since attending the youth group her understanding about HIV had increased and that it had helped to change her attitude towards people living with the virus:

> *I understand what it means to be ill and what it takes to kind of help out the person, so I wouldn't really underestimate if someone told me, yeah, I'm ill.[...] Yeah, I understand more about it, so if someone told me, I'm HIV positive, I wouldn't be, like, oh I'm scared to be around you, because now I know how it spreads.*

Several service providers in Tanzania thought it was important to educate children caring for parents about HIV/AIDS and the precautionary measures they should take in order to reduce the risk of transmission while they carried out their care tasks. Home-based care workers in particular saw educating people living with HIV and their carers about the use of gloves, detergent and boiling water when washing soiled clothing and so on, as a key part of their role. Some service providers also highlighted the importance of promoting messages about living positively with HIV and helping relatives to change their attitudes so that they love and care for the person with HIV rather than stigmatise them. Several children valued the advice they received and felt that this had helped to increase their knowledge and understanding about HIV. For example, Tausi (aged 16) felt that she had learned more about HIV and how to care for her mother since attending a seminar with her mother: *'We learned about taking care of the sick and that we shouldn't stigmatise them. We should love them. [I have changed] as they told me to love my parent because it is normal to do so.'*

However, in the absence of specialist youth groups or home-based care programmes, young people's experiences in Tanzania and the UK suggest that doctors and healthcare professionals can play an important role in providing information and advice to young people caring for parents/relatives with HIV. For example, the only information and advice one young person in the UK had received about HIV/AIDS and how to care for her mother and younger sister was from a health professional following her mother's and sister's diagnoses. A few children in Tanzania mentioned that they had received information and advice from doctors about how to care for their parent/relative with HIV and the preventative measures they should take to protect themselves from infection while caring for their parent/relative.

Confidentiality and building relationships of trust over time

In view of the stigma and secrecy surrounding HIV, confidentiality and non-judgemental, non-stigmatising approaches are paramount. Many service providers in the UK and Tanzania emphasised the importance of confidentiality and building relationships of trust with children and parents. One school-based project worker highlighted the importance of reassuring young people that she was independent from the school and that they could talk to her in confidence. Providers also highlighted the importance of flexible, informal approaches that responded to individual needs. One service provider in the UK offering support groups for young people as well as individual support commented on the importance of responding to children's support needs as and when they arise: *'It is a place where children feel that they can actually phone up, drop in, or ask for support when they need it. And I think that's what makes our service work very well.'* Another project established a mentoring scheme to enable young people to develop a trusting relationship with a mentor who listened to them and could offer ongoing informal support and advice when they needed it. Service providers acknowledged that it could take time to build trusting relationships with children and parents, but were also aware of the need to empower service users and ensure they did not become dependent on the support of individual project workers.

The time needed to develop relationships of trust between children and parents and service providers was confirmed by children's and parents' experiences. Sarah (aged 16) originally started attending the youth group two years previously, when she first discovered her mother's HIV status. However, she needed time to deal with the disclosure before she felt *'motivated'* to attend the youth group and develop trusting relationships with project workers and other young people in similar situations, as she explained:

> I wasn't really motivated in coming. I didn't want to come because I knew about everything. I didn't want to come. And then it was just this year when I started like getting to know everyone and I started to enjoy it and then I started coming more often.

Young people's experiences of services revealed the importance of informal approaches as a way of building relationships of trust with project workers. Sarah commented that project workers were 'very friendly', 'funny' and 'act like one of us sometimes'. She felt able to approach them about any problems or issues she wanted to talk about: *'They talk to us about anything, we can talk to them about anything.'*

Almost half of the children in Tanzania and the UK said that they got on well with project workers and felt they were understanding and listened to them, while some felt that they could talk to them about their parent's illness and their caring responsibilities. Parents whose children experienced behavioural difficulties at school in the UK also felt that project workers were approachable and were able to engage well with their children.

Most parents in both countries reported that they found project workers very supportive, treating them with respect and listening to their problems. Parents in the UK valued the non-judgemental support and advice that project workers offered. Similarly, in Tanzania, parents commented on their close relationships with project workers, whom they found approachable. Parents valued the emotional and practical support project workers provided when they were ill, offering advice on accessing treatment and sometimes providing transport to hospital. As Elli commented: *'They help me a lot when I get seriously ill. They are very attentive and full of compassion. If it hadn't been for them, I wouldn't be here today. [...] So I am just left with [NGO], they are like relatives to me.'* Parents felt that NGO workers were respectful and listened to their problems, even if they were not able to provide material support.

Despite the many relationships of trust that many children and parents reported, some children did not have such positive experiences of seeking support from project workers. Almost a third of children interviewed in Tanzania and a few in the UK said that project workers only talked to their parent or did not have much time to talk to them. Some children in Tanzania said that home-based care workers just talked to their parent when they conducted home visits or when children went to collect medicines for their parent, NGO workers were *'busy doing other things'*. This reflects previous studies with young carers that found that professionals tended to focus their support on the adult with a long-term illness or impairment and did not involve children or listen to their views as informal carers (Aldridge and Becker, 2003). Furthermore, some children and parents in Tanzania had negative experiences of seeking support from NGOs and did not find project workers sympathetic to their needs. For example, June, who cared for her mother and six younger siblings, commented: *'Even if I go there for help the workers there are not very helpful. There is really no one who I can turn to.'* In the UK, some young people did not perceive project workers as potential sources of support, despite young people's involvement in family activities organised by HIV organisations. In response to the question, 'Do you think you can talk to [project worker] about your mum's illness?', for example, Kerry said: *'No. I never imagined she was there for me to speak to really.'*

Cultural appropriateness and sensitivity to stigma

Service providers in the UK emphasised the importance of developing services that were culturally appropriate, sensitive to issues of HIV stigma and tailored to individual needs. One African community organisation found that matching the cultural and faith backgrounds of volunteers to that of families affected by HIV enabled them to do outreach work with Muslim communities and encourage the take-up of mainstream services. A project worker from an African community project providing counselling highlighted the importance of delivering individually tailored services with discretion. He also commented on the need to understand cultural values and intergenerational relations within families to support children affected by HIV.

Some parents also highlighted the importance of cultural appropriateness in the development and delivery of services. One lone mother from East Africa commented on how a mentoring scheme for young people filled a gap in the role usually played by the extended family within her culture. According to African cultural values, the role of educating children about sensitive issues, such as puberty and sexuality, was usually taken on by aunts, uncles or other relatives, rather than parents (Lie and Biswalo, 1998; Lewis, 2001). The mentoring scheme enabled her son with HIV to talk to an older male mentor about these sensitive issues, which she and her son would otherwise have felt uncomfortable discussing together:

> *Right now my son needs a man around him […] he can kind of talk to him about growing up, about many issues. And [he] asked my son to ask him, to feel free to ask him any questions, which he doesn't ask me because in our culture children don't feel free with their mum.*

Multi-agency collaboration

Some service providers felt that multi-agency collaboration and partnership working focused on the needs of children and parents helped to promote families' resilience. In the UK, one provider felt that regular contact with families and information sharing among the different statutory and voluntary organisations working with them helped to ensure that any concerns about children's well-being or, in extreme cases, child protection issues would be identified at an early stage and dealt with in collaboration with other agencies. Most service providers in the UK liaised with and made referrals to other HIV-specific organisations working with families, statutory health and social care services, social security, housing, immigration advice and schools. However, there was little evidence of collaboration between specialist HIV or African community organisations and dedicated young carers projects.

Some voluntary organisations found that hospital HIV clinics provided an important place where they could get to know parents with HIV and offer emotional support and advice, particularly around issues of disclosure, as well as providing play activities for children. One provider organised family outings and activities in association with another voluntary organisation for families they met in the clinic, which they found helped families to develop friendships and peer support, improving the atmosphere when they attended the clinic. A few young people said that project workers provided practical support to access other services and opportunities, such as facilitating access to mainstream leisure and social activities, helping them to access transport grants for college, providing homework support and liaising with teachers and school professionals.

In Tanzania, some service providers emphasised the importance of collaboration with other agencies providing welfare services to children and families affected by HIV and AIDS. In recognition of the fact that NGOs were not able to meet the needs of all the orphaned and vulnerable children identified in the districts and wards that they covered, some agencies felt that greater cooperation and collaboration with other NGOs would help to avoid duplication of services and maximise the number of families that NGOs could support.

Opportunities for participation

Opportunities for participation are commonly identified as important protective factors that may help to promote children's resilience (Howard et al, 1999; Newman, 2002b). Since the adoption of the UN Convention on the Rights of the Child in 1991, many voluntary and community organisations in the UK have embraced the principle of involving children in decision-making about all matters affecting them and sought to involve children and young people in the development of services and initiatives (Evans and Spicer, 2008). However, studies have shown that the participation of children and young people in the design, delivery and evaluation of services and programmes remains a challenge for policy makers and service providers and is often limited to consultation activities (Hill et al, 2004; Spicer and Evans, 2005). In the majority of projects in our UK research, children and young people were involved in informal consultation and planning of activities within service settings. Several voluntary organisations felt it was important to consult children and parents about the activities they wanted to do in their support groups and established mechanisms for them to give feedback and evaluate the services they received. One organisation, however, provided opportunities for young people to participate in strategic decision-making processes about the development of services in a youth forum, where they were involved in staff recruitment within the organisation, as well as giving their views on a range of issues affecting them. Providers felt that such opportunities for participation helped to raise young people's self-esteem and empower them:

> *We try and encourage as much as possible the service users to be part*
> *of the decision-making, you know, so I think that gives them a lot of*
> *self-esteem and raises their whole, well raises it to another level really,*
> *because I think some of them can feel that nobody's hearing me, and*
> *I'm like a very small voice or whatever, but we try and encourage them*
> *to come out and speak out for themselves.*

Despite widespread international commitment to the participation of people living with HIV in tackling the epidemic at all levels, evidenced in the 'Greater Involvement of People Living with or Affected by HIV/ AIDS' (GIPA) principle (declared at the 1994 Paris AIDS Summit), studies suggest that the level of involvement of people living with HIV has been tokenistic to date (Maxwell et al, 2008). In the UK research, some parents with HIV engaged in opportunities to participate in the management and development of services they accessed. One community-based organisation was led by a parent with HIV, and parents were involved in decision-making processes about the work of the organisation as members of the board of trustees. In Tanzania, some parents with HIV were involved in decision-making about the delivery of services through their participation in peer support groups. However, none of the parents or young people in Tanzania reported opportunities for more strategic level involvement in the design or evaluation of services and support.

Community awareness raising about HIV/AIDS and young caregiving

Service providers in the UK and Tanzania emphasised the importance of raising awareness in the community about HIV/AIDS and young caregiving to reduce stigma and increase understanding and support for children with caring responsibilities. In Tanzania, many service providers felt that dispelling people's fears about the risk of infection through caring for people with HIV would encourage community members to help children with their care work and enable them to attend school. One service provider suggested that each community leader from the grassroots level up to the district and regional levels should be trained about HIV/AIDS to enable community members to provide care and enable children to attend school. In the UK, a faith-based organisation felt that it was important to speak out about HIV within faith communities and among civil society organisations to try to reduce the stigma and secrecy surrounding the disease. As well as greater awareness about HIV/AIDS, some providers felt that there was a need to raise awareness about young caregiving within mainstream services. A young carers project worker felt it was important to raise awareness with children and teachers about the issue of young caring within primary and secondary schools, so that children with caring responsibilities could be identified early and supported during the transition period between primary and secondary school. She felt there was little information or awareness about the specific issues facing children caring for a family member with HIV.

Conclusion

In the context of limited informal support within family networks, schools and communities, NGOs, statutory services, social security benefits and other formal safety nets provide much-needed material and emotional resources and support for children and families affected by HIV/AIDS. The 17 NGOs involved in the study provided a range of services for children and families affected by HIV/AIDS, although their capacity to meet the specific needs of young people with caring responsibilities and parents with HIV was limited because of a lack of resources. The research suggests that key approaches that promote resilience for individual children and families include practical and emotional support for parents with HIV, holistic family approaches, opportunities for short breaks, development of life skills and knowledge about HIV, peer support and social activities with other young people in similar situations. However, parents' and children's fear of HIV stigma highlights the need for services to be delivered in culturally appropriate ways that ensure confidentiality, build trusting non-judgemental relationships with children and parents and remain sensitive to complex, diverse needs that may change over time.

NINE

Global and local processes influencing young people's caring roles in families affected by HIV and AIDS

Despite the growing body of research on young carers, only a few studies have theorised the factors influencing whether and why children become carers for family members with physical impairments, mental illness or chronic or life-limiting illnesses. However, since the 1990s, Becker's research with his colleagues on young carers in the UK and other European countries has shown that the reasons why a particular child becomes a carer within any family will be complex and will vary from household to household and from situation to situation. Building on the analyses of previous studies on young carers in both the North and South, this chapter explores the processes and factors that influence whether and why young people take on caring responsibilities in families affected by HIV/AIDS. We explore the perspectives of young people, parents/relatives and service providers on the factors and changes in family life that led to the commencement of young people's caring trajectories within families in Tanzania and the UK. Based on our analyses in previous chapters and the global literature on young caregiving and HIV/AIDS, we also analyse the wider structural and relational aspects that affect the socioeconomic, cultural and policy context of young caregiving at the global, national and local levels.

Individual, relational and structural processes shaping young people's involvement in care work

The experiences of children and parents in households affected by HIV/AIDS discussed in the previous chapters suggest that a complex range of structural, relational and individual processes shape the context in which young caregiving takes place. Becker et al's (1998) analytic framework of the factors that 'push' or 'pull' some children into unpaid caring roles in a household include the nature of the illness/disability, family structure, gender and co-residence, status and power, and the availability and nature of external support. Developing this framework, the different processes and factors influencing whether and why children take on caring roles in families affected by HIV/AIDS can be conceptualised as a nexus comprising the different levels of individual children, the family and household, community, sociocultural and national policy context and global processes and policy environment (see Figure 9.1).

The structural, relational and individual processes within the nexus represent both risk and protective factors for children living in households affected by HIV/AIDS. At each level, particular processes and factors may play an important role in protecting children from the negative impacts of young caring and limiting the extent of their caring roles; they may also represent potential risk factors, indicating a greater likelihood of children being drawn into caring roles, greater involvement in care work and greater vulnerability to negative impacts of caregiving. For example, extended family support may help to mitigate the impacts of young caregiving and reduce the level of children's involvement in caring for a parent with HIV. In contrast, the absence of such support, experiences of stigmatisation or conflict within the family may increase the likelihood that children take on caring responsibilities, increase the extent of their care work, as well as increase their vulnerability to negative impacts of young caregiving, especially social isolation.

As we discussed in Chapter 1, the literature on resilience has highlighted that risk and protective factors are context-specific and may vary cross-culturally (Schoon and Parsons, 2002). Much of the research to date on resilience has focused on children facing adversity in the North (Panter-Brick, 2002; 2004), although a growing number of studies and interventions for children orphaned and made vulnerable by HIV/AIDS in the South are drawing on the concept of resilience (see Healthlink Worldwide, 2006; 2007; Richter and Rama, 2006). In developing a nexus of risk and protective processes influencing children's involvement in care work in families affected by HIV, we are not seeking to identify a broad-based list of universal risk and protective factors or 'global composites' (Rutter, 1990: 182). Rather, our focus is on the dynamic interaction of individual, relational and structural processes that are involved in influencing children's caring trajectories in specific geographical contexts. Different processes will have more or less relevance or influence in particular contexts and places. For example, in the UK, the policy context of immigration policy and entitlements to welfare benefits is important in analysing the external support available to recently arrived African migrants and refugees living with HIV.

Figure 9.1: Nexus of risk and protective processes influencing whether children take on caring roles and the level of their involvement in care work in families affected by HIV and AIDS

National policies and infrastructure
• National legislative frameworks for children and families
• National health, social security and social care systems and infrastructure
• National HIV/AIDS policy
• Immigration policies and entitlements
• Education policies
• Capacity of non-governmental sector
• Multi-agency collaboration and coordination of services

Sociocultural beliefs and values
• Gender norms and sociocultural constructions of care
• Sociocultural constructions of childhood
• Stigma, knowledge and awareness of HIV/AIDS

Global processes and policy environment
• Global HIV/AIDS epidemic
• Transnational migration
• Economic restructuring and socioeconomic position of country in the global economy
• International development goals and commitments
• International donor aid, programmes and initiatives

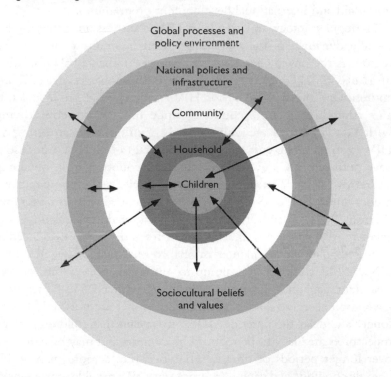

Children
• Gender, age and sibling birth order
• Quality of relationship with parent/family member with HIV
• Personal attributes
• Co-residence

Household
• Parent/relative's health
• Parent/relative's disclosure of HIV status to child
• Poverty and socioeconomic position of household
• Changes in family/ household structure

Community
• Availability of extended family support
• Informal safety nets and social networks among neighbours, friends and peers
• Information and access to external support from welfare institutions

Source: Adapted from Hill and Tisdall (1997: 4)

The following sections analyse the ways these individual, relational and structural processes interact and shape the experiences, needs and outcomes of children caring for parents with HIV in the context of the North and South, based on the perspectives of children, parents/ relatives and service providers from Tanzania and the UK.

Global processes and policy environment

A number of processes and policies intersect at the global level to structure the macro-environment in which young caregiving takes place. These include global forces such as the HIV/AIDS epidemic, economic liberalisation and migration, as well as policies and interventions such as the Millennium Development Goals, human rights commitments, donor aid and international development programmes.

The epidemiology and trends in HIV transmission influence the specific dynamics of the epidemic within particular countries and regions. As we saw in Chapter 2, the majority of the global population of adults and children with HIV live in Sub-Saharan Africa. While antiretroviral therapy (ART) for HIV has been available in the UK and other high-income countries since the 1990s, people living with HIV in Africa are only recently gaining access to effective HIV treatment. The cost and pricing policies of global corporations have until recently prevented low-income countries from obtaining antiretroviral medication, which partly explains the comparatively higher number of AIDS deaths in Africa compared with other regions (Perrons, 2004). Significant progress is being made towards widening access to ART in severely affected countries in the South, evidenced in increased political will and international commitments such as the 2006 UNGASS declaration to 'scale up to' universal access to prevention, treatment, care and support. People living with HIV in Africa who have good access to ART and a nutritious diet are now able to live longer and delay the onset of AIDS. This means that children's caring trajectories are likely to be reduced in intensity, but may be extended over longer periods of time, as HIV becomes a more manageable chronic condition and parents/relatives with HIV are able to live longer. The continued parenting roles of parents with HIV, providing love, support and guidance to their children, provide the most significant means of protecting and enhancing the well-being of children living in communities affected by HIV/AIDS.

Globalisation is widely recognised as accelerating changes in the mobility and movement of people across international borders and leading to more diverse forms of migration (Castles and Miller, 2003;

O'Connell Davidson and Farrow, 2006). Migration from the global South to the North is fuelled by widening disparities in people's life chances and employment opportunities, as well as conflict, insecurity and persecution (Borjas and Crisp, 2005). Within high-income countries in the North, declining birth rates and the ageing population has led to a growing demand for labour, particularly cheap and flexible labour (Standing, 1999; O'Connell Davidson and Farrow, 2006). As Sinka et al (2003) note, the international movement of people to and from the UK is influenced by strong links with Commonwealth countries, many of which are countries with high HIV prevalence rates in Sub-Saharan Africa. Since the 1990s, the UK, as well as some other countries in Western Europe, has seen high increases in new diagnoses of HIV acquired in high prevalence regions such as Sub-Saharan Africa (Sinka et al, 2003). As noted in Chapter 2, the global HIV/AIDS epidemic adversely affects recently arrived African migrants and refugee families in the UK.

Children's paid and unpaid work within the family and in the informal sector in the global South can be seen partly as a product of globalisation, structural adjustment, urbanisation and HIV/AIDS. The global HIV/AIDS epidemic has exacerbated global inequalities between low- and high-income countries and led to multiple reversals in human development, such as falling life expectancy, increased poverty, reduced food security and impacts on the health and education sectors (UNDP, 2005). Processes of globalisation have led to uneven economic development and widening disparities in people's life chances across the world (Scholte, 2000; Held and McGrew, 2003). The negative impacts of global economic restructuring on women and children in low-income households have been widely documented (Beneria and Feldman, 1992; Sparr, 1994). Structural adjustment programmes imposed by the International Monetary Fund and World Bank in many heavily indebted countries since the 1980s have resulted in higher prices for basic necessities, greater unemployment and job insecurity (Mohan et al, 2000; Sparr, 1994). Family livelihoods thus become increasingly dependent on casual income-generating opportunities in the informal sector (Evans, 2002). Structural adjustment policies imposed on many low-income countries since the 1980s have also undermined the redistributive mechanisms of the state and led to reductions in government expenditure on healthcare and education (Mohan et al, 2000). Cost-sharing measures in the education sector introduced as part of structural adjustment, for example, led to dramatic decreases in school enrolment and retention rates in low-income countries in the 1980s and 1990s, particularly for girls from poor households (De Vogli and Birbeck, 2005).

The deterioration in staffing, infrastructure and availability of drugs and equipment in basic healthcare as a result of reduced health spending in many low-income countries led to declines in child immunisation programmes, increased mortality rates for children under five, high maternal mortality rates and high numbers of AIDS deaths (Robson, 2004; McIntyre, 2007). In view of low pay and poor working conditions in many Sub-Saharan African countries, many doctors and nurses are seeking jobs in the global North, which combined with dramatic increases in death rates of health workers in the most highly affected countries, has created a health staffing crisis (UNICEF, 2005). Furthermore, the introduction of user fees for healthcare in many African countries in the 1980s as part of structural adjustment led to significant declines in the use of health services, reducing access for the poorest groups, particularly women and children (UNICEF, 2005; McIntyre, 2007). As a result of growing awareness of the potentially devastating effects of healthcare payments on poor households, combined with the recent policy emphasis on poverty reduction as part of debt relief initiatives, by 2007 several countries including South Africa, Uganda and Zambia removed some or all user fees at public health centres (McIntyre, 2007). Indeed, according to WHO (2008), conclusive evidence indicates that abolishing user fees at the point of service delivery leads to increased uptake of and adherence to ART.

The Millennium Development Goals, the United Nations Convention on the Rights of the Child, the International Labour Organization's campaign to eliminate the worst forms of child labour and other international development targets and commitments represent important attempts to improve the lives of children and reduce the gap between people's life chances in the global North and South. However, progress to date has been slow and difficult to implement in practice. The recent policy focus on Universal Primary Education as a key Millennium Development Goal has improved access to primary education for children in the South, evidenced in significant increases in primary school enrolments and attendance. For example, net primary school attendance ratios improved by 10% or more in 15 countries between 2000 and 2006 (UNICEF, 2007). However, many children continue to miss out on primary school. According to UNICEF (2007) the majority of primary school-age children not enrolled in school live in Sub-Saharan Africa (41 million) and South Asia (31.5 million). Secondary education remains inaccessible to many young people in low-income countries (only a quarter of children of secondary school age attend secondary school in Sub-Saharan Africa), with significant gender disparities continuing in male to female enrolment ratios in Africa and Asia (UNICEF, 2006). Secondary education for girls and young women, however, is perceived to have long-term benefits in terms of delaying the age at which young women first give birth, enhancing their bargaining power within households and increasing women's economic, social and political participation (UNICEF, 2006).

In the context of global processes of economic restructuring, the HIV/AIDS epidemic, widening disparities in life chances between the rich and poor and migration from the global South to the North, women and children in low-income households are increasingly likely to provide care for family members with HIV. Feminists have highlighted the ways that neoliberal economic policies fail to take account of the unpaid reproductive work, usually performed by women, that is required to sustain families and households and enable paid work to take place (Sparr, 1994; Afshar and Barrientos, 1999). Reductions in public health spending and cut backs in services, such as reducing the time that patients spend in hospital, increases households' reliance on private resources to sustain social reproduction and thereby implicitly increases women's and children's unpaid care work within the family (Sparr, 1994; Robson, 2004). Evidence from both the North and increasingly the South suggests that children who become carers usually live in low-income families, where parents are unable to access whatever care provision is available, are unable to afford private healthcare or pay for homecare services or domestic labour (Becker et al, 2001; Robson, 2004; Becker and Becker, 2008). Indeed, Robson (2004. 227) suggests that young people's caregiving is 'a largely hidden and unappreciated aspect of national economies, which is growing as an outcome of conservative macroeconomic policies and the HIV and AIDS explosion'.

National policy context and infrastructure

At the national level, legislative frameworks for children and families, policies and infrastructure for health, education, social security and social care systems and the capacity of the non-governmental sector all structure the macro-environment in which young caregiving takes place. This section highlights the ways that different national policy contexts affect the specific dynamics of young caregiving, using the UK and Tanzania as case study examples.

National policy context in the UK

Unlike Tanzania, young carers in the UK have become increasingly recognised in the last decade as a distinct 'social category' and now also have specific legal rights, both as 'children' and as 'carers'. Social policy for children in the UK has moved progressively during the last 20 years from a 'needs-based' approach to one more focused on 'rights' and entitlements, following to a large degree the 1989 UN Convention on the Rights of the Child. This move includes a greater policy emphasis on 'hearing the voices of children' and including them in consultations and decisions that relate directly to them. The Children Acts of 1989 and 2004 (for England and Wales; different legislation applies to Scotland and Northern Ireland) have been instrumental in placing (some) children at the centre of policy and legislative agendas.

The 'Every Child Matters' (ECM) agenda, introduced in England in 2004, combines both a needs-based and rights-based approach to identifying children's needs and promoting and safeguarding their well-being. Ridge (2008: 382) suggests that it represents a 'radical shift in the state's approach to children, bringing them, as subjects of social policy, in from the margins and right to the centre of government policies and services'. ECM sets out the government's five key aims for 'all' children, including young carers and those living in disadvantaged or difficult circumstances. The five 'outcomes' (as they are referred to) are: being healthy; staying safe; enjoying and achieving; making a positive contribution and economic well-being. The ECM agenda aims to provide strategic direction to all government departments and other agencies working with children or providing children's services, for example schools, general practice and hospitals, children's social care, police and third sector (voluntary and community) organisations.

The 2004 Children Act provides the legislative framework for the implementation of ECM outcomes. It established a Children's Commissioner for England (Wales, Scotland and Northern Ireland have had Commissioners for a number of years), and introduced Children's Trusts into the landscape of children's services – a new partnership between statutory, third sector and independent providers of children's services. The implementation of this agenda required a major reconfiguration of statutory social services (for example, Children's Social Care and Education departments were integrated into a new local authority department led by a Director of Children's Services). As a consequence, adult health and social care services are now provided separately to children's services within local authorities.

This has considerable implications for young carers and their families, who often need support from both children's and adult services.

Fox et al (2007) have shown how, for young carers at least, the rhetoric and promise of Every Child Matters is difficult to implement and sustain in practice. The separation of adult and children's services in particular has meant that the identification of need and the delivery of services are more fractured and problematic for young carers and their families, and support is more difficult to come by. Different service providers focus *either* on children (young carers) *or* ill or disabled parents, rather than on the 'whole family'. Given that much of the policy and practice development in young carers' services over the last five years has been to embrace a 'whole family' approach (Frank, 2002; Frank and McLarnon, 2008), this is now made more difficult by the separation of children's and adult services.

However, despite these difficulties, young carers in the UK do have specific legal rights and entitlements under a combination of children's and carers' legislation. The 1995 Carers (Recognition and Services) Act gives carers of *any* age – including young carers – the right to an assessment of their 'ability to provide and to continue to provide care'. Social services are required (if so requested by a carer) to carry out this assessment of the carer at the same time as assessing or reassessing the person for whom care is provided (the carers' assessment is therefore linked to the 'service user's' assessment). The Act applies to carers who 'provide a substantial amount of care on a regular basis'. The local authority guidelines (LAC (96, 7) state: 'it is for local authorities to form their own judgement about what amounts to "regular" and "substantial" care' (DH, 1996). Carers who do not provide substantial or regular care should also have their views and interests taken into account when an assessment is undertaken. 'Care' includes physical caring tasks as well as emotional care and 'general attendance to ensure the service user comes to no harm'.

Under the 1995 Act, local authorities are legally obliged to take into account the results of this assessment when making decisions about any services to be provided for the person with care needs. However, the Act did not carry with it any additional resources for local authorities in terms of implementation, for meeting carers' needs or for providing services directly to carers. The 2000 Carers and Disabled Children Act gives family carers *over the age of 16* (and caring for someone over the age of 18) specific rights:

• Carers may request an assessment of their own needs, even if the person receiving care does not wish to have an assessment.

- Local authorities may provide services for carers in their own right.
- Carers may receive vouchers for short-term breaks.
- Carers may receive direct payments in lieu of services for which they have been assessed.

The Practice Guidance to the Act (DH, 2001) provides guidelines on services and other provisions designed to sustain the caring relationship 'in a manner that is in the interests of all parties'. Support for carers (including young carers aged 16 and over) is considered essential both for carers' well-being as well as the well-being of the person they are caring for. The guidance suggests that carers should receive the support that they feel is most appropriate to their needs; for example, the guidance states that in some cases, a cash payment in lieu of services ('direct payments') may be more appropriate so that carers can make their own arrangements and pay someone of their own choosing. However, carers could be charged by local authorities for services provided directly to them, depending on a test of means. Young carers *under the age of 16*, however, are only able to access assessments and services through the 1995 Carers (Recognition and Services) Act or the 1989 Children Act (as 'children in need' under Section 17).

Recent changes to the legislation aim to ensure that carers are not placed at a disadvantage because of the care they provide. The 2004 Carers (Equal Opportunities) Act (which came into force on 1 April 2005) made three main changes to provide further support for carers. First, the Act requires local authorities to inform carers, in certain circumstances, that they may be entitled to an assessment under the 1995 and 2000 Acts. Second, when undertaking a carer's assessment, the local authority must consider whether the carer works, undertakes any form of education, training or leisure activity, or wishes to do any of those things. Third, the Act makes provision for cooperation between local authorities and other bodies in relation to the planning and delivery of services that are relevant to carers (HM Government, 2004, para 10). This applies to adult *and* young carers (Becker, 2008; see also Aldridge and Becker, 2003 for more discussion of the legislation and policies affecting young carers in the UK).

The legislative framework that supports young carers in England, Wales and other countries of the UK is made up of a combination of children's and adult carers legislation supported by a stream of policy guidance in particular spheres, such as Education circulars, National Service Frameworks in Mental Health and for Children, Guidance for Working Together to Safeguard Children (HM Government, 2006), two

National Carers Strategies (HM Government, 1999; 2008) and other policy documents. These provide a complex framework of policy, law and guidance, made even more difficult to *implement* because of the separation of adult and children's services described above. Evidence suggests that only around one in five of young carers have ever had an assessment of their needs under any piece of legislation (Dearden and Becker, 2004) and that the vast majority of young carers in the UK (over 80%) do not receive any targeted support in their own right (Becker, 2007).

Young carers that receive targeted services, estimated to be approximately 30,000 young people in the UK (Becker, 2007), rely most on interventions and support provided by a network of around 350 dedicated young carers projects. These projects, mostly run by third sector organisations, provide a range of activities and support for young carers, and some are increasingly focusing on 'whole family approaches' (Becker and Becker, 2008; see also Chapter 10). Projects also work with schools, colleges and other universal and targeted service providers to increase awareness of young carers and their families.

In theory, young carers *and* their families can also access other universal and targeted support and provision as part of the UK 'welfare state'. This includes free education provision at both primary and secondary level; access to free healthcare at the point of use; a social security system which combines contributory, non-contributory and income-based (mean-tested) benefits; and social care support (which may be subject to a charge). Within the UK's 'mixed economy of welfare' (Powell, 2007), private (for profit) providers and third sector (voluntary and community sector) providers work alongside and often in partnership with state provision and informal networks to provide services and support to 'people in need'. However, as we have already noted, most known young carers and their families in the UK live on low incomes, usually relying on social security benefits, and so private healthcare, social care, education and insurance-related income maintenance are beyond their reach. Thus, young carers and their families are heavily reliant on the (free or subsidised) support that they can access from the state and from third sector organisations working with specific groups or interests (for example, people with HIV/AIDS, young carers, people with mental health problems and so on). The third sector in the UK is a major provider of social welfare, not only 'filling the gaps' of state and informal provision, but leading developments in the recognition of population and individual need and the provision of services responsive to needs.

However, despite this pluralist welfare 'mix', many of the young people with caring responsibilities and their parents in our UK sample found it difficult to access services, support and interventions, for a number of interrelated reasons, such as the stigma associated with HIV/ AIDS, race, poverty, their immigration or asylum status and the rules governing those seeking to settle in the UK. Sales (2007) shows how UK asylum and immigration legislation during the last 15 years has become more punitive and has restricted access to welfare provision for those coming to the UK, often on race and ethnicity grounds, denying them work, income, benefits, services and support that are available to the general population. Asylum and Immigration Acts between 1993 and 2006 have introduced a series of measures, including setting the levels of any available social support to levels well below subsistence, and restricting access to basic welfare provision (including income and healthcare). These measures have served to separate, exclude and isolate families. Sales (2007: 152) concludes that the trajectory of policy:

> has been to treat asylum seekers with suspicion, as a risk to society rather than as people themselves at risk. Policy has therefore aimed at excluding them from developing connections with mainstream society in order to remove them as easily and speedily as possible.

While the UN Convention on the Rights of the Child guarantees the rights of children seeking refugee status to appropriate protection and humanitarian assistance in international law and policy, the UK government has a reservation to Article 22 of the UN Convention. The effect of this is that immigration law can take precedence over any child welfare legislation that prioritises the best interests of the child, and children who are subject to immigration control can be detained and excluded from the provisions of the UN Convention (Crawley and Lester, 2005; Conway, 2006b). The differential entitlements and unequal treatment of asylum seeking children in UK legislation and policy undermine the aims of the ECM agenda for joined-up policies between public bodies, the emphasis on ensuring good outcomes for *all* children and the recognition of the important protective effect of strong family relationships (Crawley and Lester, 2005; Conway, 2006b). The narratives of African refugee families interviewed for our UK research show the everyday lived experiences and outcomes of these exclusionary and restrictive policies.

These negative experiences are themselves exacerbated by health and social care policies for people living with HIV in the UK. A 2007

review of HIV social care, support and information services found that
HIV was not a political priority at national or local level and there
were no government targets against which NHS or local authority
performance with respect to HIV prevention, social care, support and
information for people with HIV is measured (Weatherburn et al, 2007).
Despite greater access to health, social care and social security benefits
in the UK and other countries in the North, a significant number of
people are diagnosed at a late stage in their illness and hence may not
benefit fully from therapy and have an increased risk of dying (UK
Collaborative Group for HIV and STI Surveillance, 2006). This results
in reduced take-up of services and support that families affected by
HIV might otherwise be able to access. In the UK, an estimated 32%
of adults (aged 16 and over) were diagnosed late and 11% had AIDS
at the time of diagnosis, with the highest rates among heterosexuals
(UK Collaborative Group for HIV and STI Surveillance, 2006). Some
studies suggest that African patients appear to present to services at
a more advanced stage of HIV illness compared with white patients
(Del Amo et al, 1998; Barry et al. 2002; Anderson and Doyal, 2004).
There is also evidence that African people face more difficulties in
gaining access to medical and social support interventions than other
groups in the UK, which may be related to HIV stigma in African
communities (Erwin and Peters, 1999; Anderson and Doyal, 2004; Ely,
2006; Weatherburn et al, 2007). Furthermore, as our research has shown,
immigration policy and discriminatory access to health, social care and
social security benefits affect the socioeconomic and emotional well-
being of Africans in the UK (Anderson and Doyal, 2004).

National policy context in Tanzania

The socioeconomic and political context within which children live has
a considerable impact on family life, in Tanzania as elsewhere. Poverty
in contemporary Tanzania strains the relationships between household
members (Evans, 2002). Levels of national poverty, combined with
inadequate health and social care provision, mean that progress towards
meeting the Millennium Development Goals has been very limited in
recent years. According to Household Budget Surveys, over a third of
the population (36%) lived below the poverty line in 2000, a reduction
of just 3% from 1991, with large disparities between urban and rural
areas (RAWG, 2005). Life expectancy at birth was 51 years in 2002,
with little change since 1988 (RAWG, 2005). Progress in combating
high maternal mortality rates (578 per 100,000 live births in 2004)
(RAWG, 2005) and high under five mortality rates (118 per 1,000 live

births) (UNICEF, 2007) has been slow in the period 2000 to 2006. In terms of household food security, while over half of all households report having at least three meals per day, a large minority have only two meals a day (43%) (TACAIDS et al, 2005). Furthermore, almost one in five households reports that it often or always has problems satisfying its food needs (TACAIDS et al, 2005).

The high debt burden and subsequent economic restructuring have been felt by both the agricultural and urban sectors, each of which is increasingly unable to provide a livelihood for most households (Koda 1995). Throughout the 1990s, children have increasingly engaged in income-generation activities in both rural and urban areas, especially in the informal sector, to meet the needs of their families and their educational costs (Koda, 2000; Evans, 2002). Cost-sharing measures in health and education, introduced in the 1980s as part of structural adjustment policies, have had a devastating effect on social services in Tanzania. The introduction of primary school fees resulted in sharply declining primary school enrolment rates, accompanied by high drop-out rates and very low performance, particularly of girls, because of the inability of parents and guardians to pay school expenses, combined with their need for children's labour at home (Bendera, 1999; Kuleana Center for Children's Rights, 1999; Evans, 2002). There has been considerable progress in primary school enrolment rates following the abolition of fees and the implementation of the Primary Education Development Plan in 2000 (RAWG, 2005). According to UNICEF (2007), the primary school net attendance ratio in Tanzania increased dramatically from 49% in 2000 to 73% in 2006. However, the cost of keeping a child in primary school can be considerable for poor families (RAWG, 2005). Factors limiting poor children's access to education include: parental contributions and community financing, distance to schools, poor-quality education and the need for children to engage in income-generation activities (RAWG, 2005). Only a minority of young people are able to access secondary education in Tanzania, with net secondary enrolment representing just 8% of the cohort of young people aged 14-17 in 2004 (RAWG, 2005).

Access to medical care is also now reduced through cost-sharing measures. Underfunding of the Tanzanian public health service has led to a deterioration in staffing, infrastructure and availability of drugs and equipment in basic healthcare, reflected in increased mortality rates for children under five, high maternal mortality rates and AIDS deaths (Koda, 1995; Bendera, 1999). Obstacles in accessing quality healthcare have been identified as: healthcare charges, 'unofficial costs', long distances, inadequate and unaffordable transport systems, poor quality of care, poor governance and accountability, and poorly implemented exemption and waiver schemes intended to protect the most vulnerable and poor people (RAWG, 2005). In the face of these difficulties, the *Tanzania Human Development Report* suggests that poor households with limited assets adopt short-term survival strategies to pay for healthcare, which further impoverish them (RAWG, 2005). Survival strategies include: using savings, engaging in petty trade, borrowing money, taking a loan, selling crucial assets, taking children out of school, reducing the number of meals per day (RAWG, 2005).

The HIV/AIDS epidemic is compounding many of the economic pressures facing Tanzania. As discussed in Chapter 2, throughout the 1990s, government funding of programmes to prevent the spread of the epidemic was very limited (Evans, 2005). The National Care and Treatment Plan (2003-08), adopted by the Tanzanian government in 2003, started to provide free ART in 2005 (Chipfakacha, 2006). Access to ART has increased dramatically, achieving between 31% and 50% coverage of those who require treatment in 2007 (WHO, 2008). However, because of stigma, limited resources and access to voluntary testing, counselling, treatment and care services, particularly in rural areas, many families affected by HIV in Tanzania and other Sub-Saharan African countries are unlikely to receive external support, particularly if HIV remains undiagnosed. According to the Tanzania HIV/AIDS Indicator Survey 2003-4, only 12%–16% of chronically ill adults[1] lived in households that received free medical support, emotional support, material or practical support from external sources (other than family or friends) (TACAIDS et al, 2005).

Governmental social care and welfare support for families affected by HIV/AIDS is very limited in Tanzania, despite growing recognition of the needs of the most vulnerable children, including those with sick parents. Of the total population 65% is under 25 years of age, with 47% under 15 years of age – a situation that places an enormous burden on the economically active working population, now being gradually diminished by illness and death due to AIDS (NBS/ORC Macro, 2005). The majority of orphans in Tanzania are being cared for by extended family members, although the resources of families and communities are overstretched (Evans, 2002). Over 1.1 million children were estimated to be 'most vulnerable' in 2007 (MHSW, 2006). However, only 4%-6% of orphans and vulnerable children[2] receive any external support, such as medical, emotional, material, practical support or support with schooling (TACAIDS et al, 2005). Despite a National Plan of Action on the Most Vulnerable Children agreed by the Tanzanian Government (MHSW, 2006), there is little recognition of the specific needs of young people with caring responsibilities within the broader category of the 'most vulnerable children' and very few governmental or non-governmental organisations provide specific services for children caring for a parent or relative with HIV/AIDS.

Having discussed global and national socioeconomic and political processes that influence young people's caring roles in families affected by HIV, the following sections examine sociocultural, relational and individual processes influencing children's level of involvement in caregiving, based on the narratives of young people, parents and service providers in Tanzania and the UK.

Sociocultural beliefs and values

At the national and regional levels, prevailing sociocultural beliefs and values influence the context in which young caregiving takes place. Most parents in Tanzania and the UK said that they expected their children to be supportive, to care for them when they were ill and help with household chores and other domestic duties. As discussed in Chapter 6, although many parents regretted having to rely on their children to help them, they saw children's involvement in household chores and care work as part of the socialisation process, providing an opportunity for children to learn useful life skills that helped to prepare them for the future.

In many societies in the global South, work is not seen only as an adult domain and children are expected to contribute to the productive and reproductive work of the household (Bass, 2004; Ansell, 2005; see also Chapter 1). Sociocultural concepts of childhood in Sub-Saharan Africa view children and communities as having reciprocal rights and responsibilities, based on a community values system (Omari and Mbilinyi, 1997). Van Blerk and Ansell (2007) suggest that the roles and responsibilities of family members in Africa can be conceptualised as an 'intergenerational contract' that is based on the moral obligation of families to transfer resources between generations, as a way of ensuring support in old age. Many children and parents interviewed in Tanzania perceived children's future roles predominantly in terms of the 'intergenerational contract'; children were expected to provide financial support for their parents and younger siblings when they were old enough to support them. However, because of parental ill health, the expectation for children to support their family increasingly became the responsibility of younger children who may not have received adequate informal education in livelihood strategies or formal education and training to secure employment.

Moreover, tensions were apparent between African concepts of the children's reciprocal responsibilities to their families and communities and more individualistic, global concepts of childhood that prioritised children's right to formal education. Several parents in Tanzania said that cultural values had changed over time and children's education was now perceived as the key priority for the future, as one parent commented: '*We do not follow our culture. What we value most is the children's education, so that they can make an independent life for themselves in the future.*' Some researchers suggest that the increasing importance placed on children's education in Africa can be seen as a modernisation of the intergenerational contract, which increases children's duty and capacity to provide for their parents in the future (Van Blerk and Ansell, 2007). However, others suggest that a contradiction is produced between the informal teaching of the family and community and the formal knowledge imparted at school, leading to a gap between the generations and a 'clash of world views' that can undermine parental authority (UNICEF, 1999: 53).

While parents in Tanzania and the UK emphasised the importance of children's education, many also perceived children's caring responsibilities as an integral part of the socialisation process. Some parents in the UK and service providers in both countries tended to draw on Western discourses of childhood that define 'play' as a key element in the global notion of childhood, as enshrined in the UN Convention on the Rights of the Child (1989: Article 31). According to this concept, childhood is perceived as a protected phase of 'innocence' when children should be free from work and adult responsibilities and instead spend their time predominantly in full-time education and recreation.

In the absence of alternative support, parents' expectations of children's responsibilities to their family, including supporting parents during periods of ill health, may conflict with this global concept of childhood. The findings discussed in earlier chapters suggest that during periods of household crisis and ill health, children's responsibilities towards their families may take precedence over Western notions of children's rights to education and recreation. Indeed, formal education and training may delay young people's engagement in livelihood strategies needed to support the family. Withdrawal from school or the discontinuation of young people's schooling can thus be seen as a short-term survival strategy adopted by households affected by HIV/AIDS. One mother in Tanzania, for example, explained that parents' main priority was for their children to attend school: '*There are no bad customs, they expect them all, and insist that they go to school.*' This conflicted with her own expectations of her children to help care for her when she was ill: *'I expect them to help me as I am poorly, for Neema to care for me, and when I can't get out of bed I can send them on errands.'* As discussed later in the chapter, when her eldest daughter, Neema completed primary school, she was called to the city to care for her mother. Neema was unable to continue her studies at secondary school because of her caring responsibilities and the need to earn a livelihood to support the family.

Indeed, Van Blerk and Ansell (2007: 872) suggest that in the context of children caring for a parent with HIV-related illness, the moral obligation of children to provide for their parent in later life is being 'cashed in' much earlier than usual and care is based on immediate reciprocal relationships rather than 'the long term "moral economy" of the generational contract'. Furthermore, because of their caring responsibilities, children's chances to achieve their full potential in adulthood may be reduced through missing out on schooling and investments in their education (Van Blerk and Ansell, 2007). As seen in Chapter 7, several young people, particularly young women, in Tanzania were unable to continue their secondary school education because of their caring responsibilities and the extreme poverty the household experienced.

As we have discussed in earlier chapters, children's roles in caring for parents/relatives with HIV conflict with hegemonic Western notions of childhood as a protected phase when children should be free to play with their friends and go to school without having to think about responsibilities associated with 'adulthood'. In the UK, African parents with HIV highlighted tensions between African and Western constructions of childhood, as their children negotiated their way through conflicting cultural values and expectations. Parents tried to ensure that children were brought up according to African cultural values, such as respecting their elders and recognising their responsibilities towards their family, but acknowledged that this sometimes conflicted with dominant constructions of childhood in the UK. For example, one mother explained that if they still lived in Southern Africa, her son would view his involvement in household chores as a normal part of the socialisation process that helped to prepare him for later life. In the UK, however, her son found that his friends were not expected to help with household chores, which made him feel different from his peers and more reluctant to help his mother. White British parents in the UK also perceived a change in the cultural values and expectations of children over time, revealing the historically contingent nature of the concept of childhood. They felt that in contemporary society, children's roles were seen primarily in terms of the pursuit of education and recreation, rather than in terms of helping the family with household chores. This suggests that Western notions of childhood may have become more individualistic than in previous generations.

Gender is a significant factor that influences cultural expectations of girls' and boys' roles within the household in both the North and South. As we discussed in Chapters 1 and 2, dominant gender norms in many societies construct women's roles as 'natural' nurturers and carers of the sick and girls are often socialised into caring and domestic roles. In Tanzania (as in many other countries) the literature suggests that girls and boys are assigned different roles and tasks from an early age at the household level, based on the traditional division of labour (Koda, 2000: 250). Furthermore, girls often have a heavier workload at home than boys, restricting the amount of time available for recreation and study, which has a proven adverse effect on girls' educational performance (Bendera, 1999; Kuleana Center for Children's Rights, 1999). The evidence from Tanzania discussed in Chapter 5 suggests, however, that the roles and tasks assigned to boys and girls caring for parents/relatives with HIV do not differ as much as might be expected. The main differences related to girls' greater involvement in activities focused around the household, such as cooking and cleaning, childcare and providing personal care, while a slightly greater proportion of boys were involved in the outdoor activities of buying food at the market, collecting medicines, cultivating crops and tending livestock.

Several parents and service providers in Tanzania and some parents and providers in the UK suggested that girls were expected to do more domestic work than boys and were socialised into caring roles within the household, while boys were expected to spend more time looking after the farm and doing outdoor activities (see Box 9.1). In Tanzania, mothers said that traditionally girls were expected to marry and leave the household and hence their education was not prioritised, while boys were expected to go to school and would inherit the family's farm and property. However, several mothers in both Tanzania and the UK felt that such cultural expectations were 'old fashioned' and that in recent years, there were few gender disparities in girls' and boys' roles, responsibilities and rights to education and inheritance. Indeed, while the majority of young carers interviewed in both Tanzania and the UK were girls, there was also significant evidence of boys' involvement in caring for their mothers in Tanzania, which subverts traditional gender norms (discussed in greater detail in the section that considers factors at the level of individual children).

Box 9.1: Gendered constructions of household responsibilities and care work

In my country [in East Africa] girls would start doing the housework when we're about 12, so from that age you would know what you need to do, like washing up, and you'd know. Elders sometimes ask you to do things and you have to do it. So that kind of prepares you for later on. (Emily, aged 17, UK)

The girls are expected to do domestic work like cooking, washing dishes, washing clothes and cleaning in and outside the house. Boys are not expected to do any work at all. Even if you ask a boy to fetch water, he doesn't like doing it. [Laughs.] Very often it's just the girls. (Agnes, mother, Tanzania)

Most of the time, it is the girls who are more likely to look after their parents. This is more to do with culture; women are more likely to take care of sick people than men; so the girls copy from their mothers and the boys copy from their fathers. (Project worker, Tanzania)

Some parents and service providers in Tanzania and the UK suggested that according to African cultural values, there is a preference for sick family members to be cared for within the family. They suggested that the emotional bond between care-receiver and care-recipient – in this instance between the parent and child – was an important element of caring relationships, reflecting the findings of previous studies (Aldridge and Becker, 2003; Robson et al, 2006; Becker, 2008; Becker and Becker, 2008). Close, loving relationships between children and parents and cultural expectations about providing care within the family influence children's sense of moral obligation to care for their parents and reluctance to seek outside support (see Box 9.2; see also the section that considers the quality of relationships with the parent with HIV later in this chapter). Service providers also suggested that in the UK context African cultural constructions of care may conflict with Western notions and expectations about the role and involvement of external welfare institutions in supporting families in need, which may result in a reluctance to seek outside support from professionals. This highlights the need for cultural awareness and sensitivity in the development and delivery of services for families affected by HIV, as identified in Chapter 8.

The level of stigma, knowledge and awareness of HIV/AIDS in the community, as we saw in Chapters 6 and 7, is also a significant factor influencing whether young people take on caring roles in families affected by HIV. The fear of stigma and secrecy surrounding HIV prevents children and parents from seeking support from neighbours, friends, community members and professionals and makes it difficult for young people to talk about their parent's illness (see Box 7.12).

Box 9.2: Preference for sick family members to be cared for within the family: perspectives of parents and service providers in Tanzania and the UK

A mother in Tanzania felt that her daughter's support was more dependable than the support offered by someone outside the family:

> *You know, a neighbour's help is not the same as that of your own child. A neighbour cannot help you every day. As she is my own child, I am at peace, I feel very happy.*

Service providers in the UK suggested that African cultural norms of care may lead to a reluctance to seek external support among African families:

> *They're coming from an African background, they feel it has to be contained in the family, you know. The care has to be contained in the family first before any outside care is sought. (Family support worker).*

> *Culturally Africans believe that you have to look out for your own, so when the children are growing up they know that they will have to look after their parents [...] it is culturally embedded that the child needs to look after their parents, so they cannot run away from you or otherwise, they cannot rebel. That's why they need support from someone who understands their culture. (Service provider)*

Factors influencing whether young people take on caring responsibilities at the level of the community

A number of risk and protective factors influencing children's caring responsibilities can be identified at the level of the community. These include the availability of extended family support, informal safety nets and social networks among neighbours, friends and peers, and information and access to external support from welfare institutions.

Availability of extended family support

The extended family, clan and kinship systems are widely recognised as representing the main source of assistance when family members experience illness or death in Sub-Saharan Africa (Robson et al, 2006). Several commentators suggest that African extended family relationships are based on complex patterns of reciprocal support, childcare responsibilities and decision-making processes that differ considerably from Western notions of the nuclear family (Foster et al, 1997; Lewis, 2001; Van Blerk and Ansell, 2007). As discussed in Chapter 6, supportive relationships within the extended family and community may represent important protective factors for young people caring for parents with HIV in low-income countries with very limited formal welfare support.

However, while some parents and children in Tanzania received material support and some practical assistance with care work from members of the extended family, several families experienced stigma and ostracism from their relatives, which was a significant factor influencing children's involvement in care work. For example, Malcolm's mother found that she was forced to rely on her children to care for her because her relatives were unwilling to help: '*I have many [relatives] but they are of no help because everyone minds their own business. If I didn't have my children, it would be very difficult for me.*' Malcolm described their efforts to seek support from his grandmother: '*There is no one to help us. Our grandmother left us and went to live in [town]. We sent someone to tell her to come back but she doesn't care and hasn't come back.*'

Service providers highlighted the fact that some relatives stigmatised the surviving parent and children following the death of a family member, while others stigmatised lone mothers, blaming them for becoming infected with HIV through prostitution and bar work. Some service providers also suggested that ostracism was related to an assumption that people with HIV would die soon and hence helping to care for a sick relative was perceived as a 'waste' of time and effort. For example, one home-based care worker said:

> *The relatives are too busy with their own lives and feel that the person with HIV is a lost cause. So they are better off looking after their farms and livestock instead of wasting time on her. But the children are determined to stay with their mother and see her through to the end.*

Some service providers linked national levels of poverty in low-income countries such as Tanzania to a weakening of social ties and extended family support. The experiences of children and parents/relatives discussed in Chapters 6 and 7 showed that in severely affected communities informal safety nets of the extended family and community are being overstretched, leaving sick parents and children vulnerable to impoverishment and social isolation. Thus, national levels of poverty combined with stigma and discrimination reduce the availability of informal family support that families affected by HIV are able to access, and parents are forced to rely on children to care for them.

When extended support was available to families in the UK, the evidence from young people and parents discussed in Chapter 6 demonstrated that supportive family networks represented an important protective factor that helped to mitigate the negative impacts of young caregiving and support young people in their caring roles.

However, many children and parents with HIV in the UK had limited extended family networks and a third of families had no other relatives living in the country. This reflects the findings of other studies with migrant families affected by HIV in the UK, for whom traditional support structures may be missing (Chinouya-Mudari and O'Brien, 1999; Lewis, 2001). Service providers felt that extended family networks were limited because of the geographical distance between relatives living in different parts of the country, separation from extended family members resulting from international migration, as well as stigmatisation and isolation from other family members.

Informal safety nets and social networks among neighbours, friends and peers

The narratives of young people and parents suggest that informal support and social networks among neighbours, friends and peers can represent important protective factors that help to alleviate children's caring responsibilities in families affected by HIV/AIDS in both the North and South. Children and parents often relied on informal social networks with neighbours, family friends and members of their faith communities for material support and practical assistance with caregiving. As discussed in Chapter 7, in Tanzania, most young people said that they asked their neighbours for occasional material support when their parent was ill, and a few children said that neighbours helped them to care for their parent on a more regular basis. As we saw in Chapter 5, some children begged for food and money or borrowed money from neighbours to meet the household's basic needs or the costs of medication or transport to take their parent to hospital during times of household crisis. In the UK, neighbours were rarely asked for material support when parents were ill, but in a few instances, neighbours and family friends provided practical assistance with childcare and caring for the parent with HIV. The practical support that neighbours and friends provided was highly valued by children and parents and helped to alleviate young people's caring responsibilities.

However, the narratives of children and parents also suggest that because of the stigma and secrecy many young people caring for parents/relatives with HIV remain largely hidden and unsupported by friends, neighbours, teachers and other professionals. They often feel unable to seek informal support from their peers or other adults in the community, in the context of both the global North and South. While children's friendships and peer relationships offered some limited emotional support in Tanzania and the UK, some young people commented on difficulties in interacting with their peers, which could increase their isolation and vulnerability to negative impacts of caregiving. Furthermore, several young people caring for parents/relatives with HIV in Tanzania directly experienced stigma and ostracism from their relatives, friends, neighbours and other community members (see Box 7.11). Thus, as well as representing a potential source of support, relationships with others in the community could also represent a potential source of stigma and discrimination that exacerbates young people's vulnerability, impacting on their emotional well-being and sense of isolation.

Information and access to external support from welfare institutions

In the context of limited informal support, schools, NGOs, statutory services, social security benefits and other formal safety nets provide much needed material and emotional resources and support for children and families affected by HIV/AIDS. As we saw in Chapter 8, the 17 NGOs involved in the study provided a range of services for families affected by HIV that were highly valued by children and parents. However, in both Tanzania and the UK, the capacity of NGOs to meet the specific needs of young people with caring responsibilities and parents with HIV was very limited.

While social security and social care provision was virtually non-existent in Tanzania, children and parents had mixed experiences of statutory services in the UK. Service providers in the UK felt that because of the success of ART, it was increasingly difficult for people with HIV to access statutory social care services unless they have high support needs, because HIV was perceived as a chronic rather than a life-limiting condition. Several parents expressed their frustrations with trying to access statutory social care support, commenting on the bureaucratic, time-consuming process of assessment and the strict criteria to qualify for support (see Chapter 10).

Even when they were entitled to support, families with HIV in the UK could still find it difficult to access their entitlements. Service providers highlighted the importance of providing adequate information and awareness about available support services for particularly marginalised groups, such as African refugee and asylum-seeking families. As is discussed in Chapter 10, providers suggested that refugee and asylum-seeking families affected by HIV may be fearful of engaging with mainstream agencies because of uncertainty about their immigration status, and that they often prefer to access services provided by the voluntary sector. As discussed in Chapters 2 and 4 and in the earlier section on the UK policy context in this chapter, access to health and social care support in the UK was linked to parents' immigration status, which had direct implications for some of the families interviewed. The lack of formal safety nets for parents with HIV who have insecure immigration status places families under enormous pressure, as they face the threat of deportation and loss of access to HIV treatment and social support, which reinforces poverty and social exclusion.

Thus, formal safety nets can represent both a source of protection for children caring for parents with HIV, as well as potentially increasing the vulnerability and social isolation of particularly marginalised groups whose entitlements to external support are restricted. Moreover, in some families, there can also be anxiety (and fear) about becoming 'known' to formal service providers, particularly those from the statutory sector, whose 'powers' (as agents of the state) can be used in punitive as well as benign ways, including bringing children into public care (Aldridge and Becker, 1993).

Factors influencing whether young people take on caring responsibilities at the level of the household

At the micro-level of the household, several risk and protective processes can be identified as influencing whether young people take on caregiving roles within families affected by HIV/AIDS and the level of their involvement. These include parental ill health, disclosure of HIV status to children within the family, the socioeconomic position of the household and changes in the household or family structure over time.

Parental ill health

The majority of children and parents in Tanzania, and some families in the UK, cited the ill health of the parent/relative as the major trigger for children to take on caring responsibilities within the household. As noted in Chapters 4 and 5, the unpredictable nature of HIV-related illness means that the level and intensity of care support that young people provide varies considerably, depending on the health of the parent/relative. For some parents with HIV, the onset of ill health was a gradual process and young people started to 'help out' more with household chores and caring for siblings before they took on more significant care-related activities. For some parents, however, an episode of serious ill health, reduced mobility or illness following childbirth propelled young people into more intensive caring roles. For example, Isack (Tanzania) said that he started caring for his mother when she became seriously ill. He cared for her in bed for two months until she was 'a bit better' and was able to walk again. Following this period of serious illness, he continued to perform household chores and health and personal care tasks, such as assisting his mother to eat and take her medicine.

Research with young carers in the UK and Australia suggests that children's caregiving tasks can start at a very early age and continue for many years (Dearden and Becker, 2004; Morrow, 2005). In contrast, a study on children's caregiving in the context of HIV/AIDS in Zimbabwe and Lesotho (Robson and Ansell, 2000; Robson et al, 2006) found that most young people's caring responsibilities were temporary, as they provided care at the end of their parent/relative's life: 'They were carers for a matter of weeks, or months, and more often than not the death of their care recipient, sooner or later, brought freedom and relief from caregiving, but also deep sadness...' (Robson et al, 2006: 105). The evidence from Tanzania and the UK confirms the findings of research with young carers in the North and suggests that caring is a long-term commitment for most young people caring for a family member with HIV in the context of both the North and the South. The majority of young people and parents in both countries reported that children had been caring for three years or more (ranging from less than a year to seven years). As discussed earlier, the majority of parents in Tanzania and the parents interviewed in the UK were accessing ART, which helped to prolong their lives. While this may extend the duration of children's caregiving responsibilities, more significantly it enables children to benefit from the love, moral guidance and support of their parent/relative over a longer period of time, which has a strong protective effect (see section on quality of relationship between child and parent/relative later in this chapter).

Parental disclosure of HIV status to children

Over half of the young people and some of the parents interviewed in the UK associated the commencement of young people's caring responsibilities with the parent's disclosure of their HIV status. Some children in Tanzania also mentioned this as a factor influencing when they started caring for their parent/relative. For example, Tausi (aged 16, Tanzania) said: '*She became ill and then decided to be open about her situation with me. I reassured her that it was alright. We kept on helping each other from then on.*' A service provider in the UK pointed out that in a context of stigma, fear of disclosure outside of the immediate family and isolation from alternative sources of support, parents' disclosure to their children could be a significant factor influencing whether children take on caring responsibilities: '*In the case where people aren't disclosing their status to other family members, that child might feel they have no other choice but to help.*'

The experiences of children and parents suggest several benefits of disclosure in terms of greater understanding and the development of more caring, supportive relationships within families. Many young people and parents said that disclosure helped children to understand more about their parent's illness and made them more willing to help with household chores and support their parent. Magic (aged 12, UK) said that since finding out about his mother's illness, he felt more able to understand why he needed to support her and this had changed his attitude towards his caring responsibilities:

> *Before I found out my mum, you know, was sick I just, you know, used to moan and 'Oh why do I have to do this and that', but now I understand why, I can, you know, I don't really mind. Sometimes I even enjoy it.*

Poverty and socioeconomic position of the household

Research in low-income countries has consistently demonstrated the links, at the household level, between HIV/AIDS-related illness and death and financial crisis and deepening poverty (Yamano and Jayne, 2004; Evans, 2005; Hosegood et al, 2007). As we discussed in Chapter 4, low-income, female-headed households are particularly vulnerable to chronic poverty, as women's ability to perform their usual productive and reproductive tasks is gradually reduced through ill health and children are increasingly relied on to engage in income-generation activities and reproductive tasks. Many parents/relatives in Tanzania associated their ill health and poverty with the start of children's caring trajectories. As the health of parents/relatives deteriorated, they found it increasingly difficult to work and earn a livelihood. This propelled some children into caring roles, as they engaged in casual work, income-generation activities and begging to help meet their family's basic needs (see also Chapter 5). John (aged 11, Tanzania) cited his mother's ill health as his motivation for seeking casual work to earn money for food: '*She was very sick so I told her I was going to work for people so that we could have something to eat.*' Some parents and service providers also highlighted the fact that because of poverty many parents/relatives were unable to afford to employ a domestic worker, who might otherwise perform many of the household chores that form a substantial part of young people's caring responsibilities in the South. For example, Agnes commented that if she had more financial resources, she would employ a domestic worker to perform the household chores and alleviate her daughter's responsibilities: '*It is also due to my poverty [that my daughter has caring responsibilities], if I was better off I would hire a helper to take care of the housework.*'

Changes in family/household structure

Some children, parents and service providers identified a number of changes in the family/household structure that led to children taking on caring responsibilities. As noted in Chapter 3, over half of the children interviewed in Tanzania and over two thirds of those in the UK lived in one-parent households, usually co-residing with their mother with HIV. Many service providers in the UK suggested that, in their experience, most children caring for a parent with HIV lived in one-parent households. Some parents in the UK and Tanzania linked the start of children's caring trajectories to the period when they became lone parents and had a greater need for care, since no other adults were available to help within the household. Previous research has shown that in some families where there is illness or disability, two-parent families may change to become lone-parent households if one parent (usually a 'well' man) declines to take on caregiving responsibilities for his wife, partner, child or other family member (Aldridge and Becker, 1993; 2003).

Parents in the UK and Tanzania appeared to have higher expectations of the support and help with household chores that their children were providing since they had become lone parents because of the financial and time pressures they were under, struggling to earn enough money to support their children (see Box 9.3). This confirms the findings of Ridge's research in the UK that children living in low-income, lone-mother households make considerable contributions to their families, helping to 'sustain family cohesion around issues of work and care' (Ridge, 2006: 215). Some children and parents in the UK and Tanzania said that children started to take on caring responsibilities when their older siblings, who used to care for their parent, moved out of the household and no one else was available to help. Within the majority of the families interviewed in both countries, the oldest co-resident child had more caring responsibilities than their younger siblings (see Box 9.3). Thus, sibling birth order and children's co-residence with their parent with HIV appear to be important factors determining which sibling within families assumes caring responsibilities (see also the following section).

Some parents who had migrated to the UK from Africa felt that the lack of affordable domestic help in the UK represented a factor that contributed to children taking on caring roles. In many African countries, young women (and sometimes young men) often perform domestic work in the homes of wealthier families in return for board, lodging and a small wage (UNICEF, 1999; Koda, 2000). Researchers report that in Tanzania, for example, a typical domestic servant is a young girl of between 9 and 18 years of age, who may have been brought to her employer by a relative, friend, or village-mate, or who has migrated to the urban area on her own (Koda, 2000). One mother from Southern Africa highlighted the fact that this system of domestic labour prevented children in wealthier families, particularly boys, being drawn into caring roles. However, this domestic help was not available to African immigrant families in the UK:

> In our culture we don't allow boys to do housework, like cooking, washing plates, but here we don't have a choice. They have to do it because we don't have the help like we used to back home, because back home we can have helpers to help us.

Box 9.3: The influence of changes in family/household structure on children's caring responsibilities: perspectives of young people and parents in the UK and Tanzania

Lone parenthood

Julie commented on the way she felt lone parenthood changed the dynamics of family life and children's caring responsibilities:

> *It would be a different situation, I suppose, if me and their father, you know, we lived together. It might be slightly different because of the setup and the pressure within the family would be different. But because it is only the three of us I think the expectations and demands are slightly different.*

She expected her children to be supportive, since she was working hard to ensure she earned enough money to be able to afford a good standard of living for her children:

> *I do expect them to be helpful and I think that it's only, it's only fair in a sense because I'm going out to work, even though I struggle some days to go out to work to ensure that they're getting the nice things. [...] So in return I expect them to then be supportive, you know, for me. (UK)*

Sibling birth order and co-residence

Kerry commented on how she used to share the caring responsibilities with her older sisters, but since they had moved out of the home to study at university, caring for her mother and doing the household chores had become her responsibility:

> *I suppose at the time my sisters were here, and they kind of got me into a routine as well to help out, so when they left it was sort of natural to just carry on doing it. [...] I have more responsibility now. Even when they come back I'm usually doing most things because I'm used to it now. (Kerry, aged 18, UK)*

Husna said that since her eldest daughter had moved away, Juliette (aged 20) had most caring responsibilities since she was the eldest co-resident daughter who was available to care for the family:

> *She has more responsibilities because she is the oldest one around. The elder sister is in a convent so she isn't around here to help. So she has to do all the work because her younger sisters are still at school. (Tanzania)*

Loss of a co-resident domestic worker

Joyce said that her daughter Alice had started to take on caring responsibilities in East Africa during the period when several domestic workers left the household in rapid succession on discovery of Joyce's HIV status:

> My neighbours back home came and told the young woman working in my house that I had AIDS and so she left and life became much harder. During one year I had ten different young women working for me who all left. It was at this point that I really had to rely a lot on Alice. There were just the two of us left and Alice was still little. [...] They didn't know about AIDS and so they thought it was true and left. They were scared of getting infected. [...] So then it was just me and my daughter left. So my child had to take the weight of the responsibility. (UK)

Migration and separation from family members

Emily (aged 17) and her sister had joined their father in the UK for educational purposes, but missed their mother and other siblings in East Africa. When they migrated to the UK, they found they needed to do most of the household chores and care for their father when he was ill, since their mother and siblings were absent:

> Now I kind of have to help out more because mum's not around, so we have to do most of the housework, all of that.

As noted earlier, poverty also prevented many parents/relatives in Tanzania from employing a paid domestic worker who lived in the household. However, the experiences of Joyce, who had migrated to the UK from East Africa, revealed that stigma also impacted on the availability of domestic help, as she found it very difficult to retain domestic workers who discovered her HIV status in her country of origin (see Box 9.3). She linked losing the help of a co-resident domestic worker to the start of her daughter's involvement in caring tasks.

Some children and parents in the UK also highlighted changes in the family structure brought about by migration and separation from family members that contributed to a need for children to take on caring responsibilities. A fifth of the families were separated from close family members who remained in their country of origin or lived in neighbouring countries (to where they had fled as refugees), and thus can be considered transnational families. For some young people who joined their parent in the UK migration was associated with the commencement of their caring responsibilities, as they found that in the absence of other family members, they were the only ones available to care for their parent with HIV (see Box 9.3).

Factors influencing whether young people take on caring responsibilities at the level of individual children

At the level of individual children, a number of factors intersect with those at other levels of the nexus to influence whether young people take on caring responsibilities and the level of their involvement within households affected by HIV. These include gender, age and sibling birth order, love, compassion and moral duty, personal attributes and co-residence.

Gender, age and sibling birth order

Many young people and parents in Tanzania saw children's position as the eldest child in the family or as the eldest co-resident child (when older siblings no longer lived in the household) as one of the main reasons they had more caring responsibilities than their younger siblings. For example, Christina was the eldest child available to care for her mother and younger sister, since her step-father had died and her older brother and sister lived elsewhere: '*Mum was all by herself. My little sister was too young then. She had no one to help her, so I was the one who helped her.*'

The research suggests that sibling birth order was often interlinked with gendered notions of care and the socialisation of girls into caring roles, particularly in one-parent families. One service provider in Tanzania commented on the characteristics of some of the young people with caring responsibilities interviewed:

> They all have a single parent – the mum. They are the eldest and they are females, so for them it was automatic. As the mum is poorly so the eldest female child is the one that takes care of her. She will then have to cook for mum, cook for her younger siblings.

Some service providers felt that according to cultural norms there was a preference for gender matching in caring relationships between children and parents with HIV; it was considered more culturally appropriate for a girl to care for her mother and a boy to care for his father, particularly when children were providing personal care. However, some service providers in Tanzania suggested that older boys, who might be the eldest sibling, often left the household when they became adolescents and thus were not available to care for their fathers. Girls, on the other hand, were expected to stay at home and perform domestic work and care for the sick, including their father or other male relatives (see Box 9.4). This suggests that gendered constructions of care and the socialisation of girls into caring roles may represent a more salient factor influencing which child takes on caring roles within the family than sibling birth order.

Butler's concept (1990) of 'gender performativity' is useful in analysing the process through which gender identities are constantly reproduced and 'naturalised' through everyday practices. Gender is conceived as a set of acts that are reiterated to produce the appearance of a stable identity category in the regulation of hegemonic gender norms (Butler, 1990). Butler suggests that it is a 'compulsory performance', since society punishes individuals who do not conform to hegemonic gender norms, but through the constant repetition of gender performances in difference contexts, hegemonic gender norms can be destabilised and subverted (Butler, 1993).

As we suggested in Chapter 5, there was evidence that gendered constructions of care were becoming more fluid when households were faced with a lack of alternatives. Almost as many boys (aged under 18) interviewed in Tanzania were providing care for their mothers/female relatives as the number of girls, in contrast to the UK sample. Boys who take on caring roles, particularly those providing personal care for their mothers, can be seen as subverting dominant cultural norms and expectations of gender roles within the family. For example, Good Luck used to bathe his mother and clean soiled bedsheets and clothing, despite the fact that this was not considered an appropriate care task for a boy to do for his mother.

The examples in Box 9.4 show that some boys felt uncomfortable about having to perform care tasks that were considered culturally inappropriate and were marginalised by society because of their caring roles. However, faced with a lack of alternative support, they accepted their responsibility to care for their mother. This can be seen to some extent as destabilising conventional gendered notions of care and the meanings associated with masculinity, all be it at an individual rather than societal level. Indeed, boys who take on caring roles that are considered to transgress culturally accepted gender boundaries may face significant social consequences, such as bullying and ostracism. This confirms the findings of Becker and Becker's (2008) study in the UK, which revealed that some boys and young men who take on caring roles for mothers

Box 9.4: Subverting gender norms within the household?
Boys caring for their mothers in Tanzania

*— I used to bathe her, she didn't mind that I was a boy [...] According to our
culture it is not good [for a boy to bathe his mother], but I had to do it. I used to
do everything for her, I couldn't leave her like that when everything was soiled.
— So according to your culture, a girl is supposed to look after her mum, is that
right?
— Yes, it is a girl who cares for her mum and a boy cares for his dad. (Good
Luck, aged 18)*

Malcolm felt different to his friends, because they did not understand why he
had caring responsibilities:

*— They are surprised when they see me doing the things I do. They say they
can't understand why I do what I do. But I have to do these things to help my
family. (Malcolm, aged 15)*

A home-based care volunteer suggested that older boys and young men often
move out of the household and so may not be available to care for their
fathers:

*— In your culture, is it more usual for a girl to care for her mum than a boy?
— Yes. But a girl can also care for her dad because a large percentage of boys
don't stay at home once they become adolescents. So when the girl remains at
home, it is then her duty to care for her dad.*

may experience bullying or ridicule at school, including acts of hostility
and extreme violence.

As discussed earlier, the research sample only included two instances
of young people (both young women) caring for their fathers with HIV.
Providers in Tanzania suggested that the lack of visibility of children
caring for fathers with HIV could be linked to a lack of openness
about men's HIV status, as well as the fact that many men with HIV
became seriously ill and often died before their wives, who were their
main carers rather than their children. This is supported by evidence
on the higher prevalence of paternal orphans (estimated to be 4%–8%
of children under 15) than maternal orphans (2.5%–4.5%) in many
countries in Sub-Saharan Africa (Bicego et al, 2003). Furthermore,
the experiences of women with HIV presented in Chapter 4 suggest
that when women discover their HIV status they may be blamed for

infecting their male partner, resulting in separation or abandonment; hence fathers with HIV may no longer live in the household.

Valentine (1999) suggests that age can also be conceived as a performative identity, as children demonstrate their competencies and actively negotiate the meanings attached to their biological age in their relations with parents and siblings. Within families affected by HIV in the UK and Tanzania, young people and parents were involved in complex negotiations over the boundaries of children's care work depending on their performance of age and gender. Most of the children interviewed started caring for their parent/relative when they were 10 years old or older (ages ranged from 6 to 16 years), with a mean age (based on children's accounts) of 12 and 11 years old in Tanzania and the UK, respectively. Many young people felt that their parents' expectations of them and their caring responsibilities had increased as they became older and were considered more competent to perform particular caring tasks, confirmed by Becker and Becker's (2008) study of young adult carers in the UK. Similarly, some parents commented on the way that children's capabilities to perform caring tasks increased as they grew older.

Age and stage of education appeared to be important factors determining which child within the family took on caring responsibilities in Tanzania, confirming the findings of Robson's (2004) study on young carers in Zimbabwe. For example, some young women who had completed primary school education were specifically selected to become carers when their mother became ill rather than other children who were still studying at school, as Neema's story shows (see Box 9.5). Neema's story also reveals that children's caregiving can involve migration; sending a child to care for sick relatives represents a possible strategy employed by some families to meet the needs of households affected by AIDS-related illness, confirming the findings of Young and Ansell's (2003) research in Southern Africa.

As discussed in Chapter 4, many parents in both the UK and Tanzania chose to disclose their HIV status to the eldest child in the family and to keep it secret from younger siblings. Parents decided to tell their children when they considered that their child was competent and emotionally mature enough to deal with the disclosure and keep their status secret. Thus, social age and parental perceptions of young people's emotional maturity and competence were important factors in parents' decisions to share their HIV status and, as discussed earlier, for some children this marked the beginning of their caring trajectories. Several young people in the UK felt that they had more responsibilities than their younger siblings because their mother had shared her HIV status

Box 9.5: Age, sibling birth order and education as factors influencing young people's caring roles in Tanzania

Neema (aged 18) used to live with her grandmother and younger sister in the south of Tanzania. Following her husband's death, Neema's mother migrated to Dar es Salaam in search of business opportunities and Neema stayed with her grandmother to complete primary school. When her mother became sick, she asked her eldest child, Neema, to move to Dar es Salaam to care for her and her younger siblings:

> *My mum's business started to do badly when a consignment got burnt in storage. When that happened her younger sister advised her to move from Mbeya to Dar es Salaam as business prospects were much better than in Mbeya. So my mum moved to Dar es Salaam; I had just completed Standard Seven [final year of primary school] then. I continued living with my grandmother in Mbeya. Later, word was sent to me saying that my mum wasn't well. So I was brought to Dar es Salaam and started looking after her. [...]*

> *I'm the main person to care for our family. I couldn't go on to Secondary School because of my mother's illness. She had no close relatives to care for her because her younger sisters are all married. I was the only close relative that could help her; so it was my responsibility. I have been helping her from the onset of her illness until recently when her health got better.*

Neema thought that she had greater responsibilities than her younger siblings because of her position as the eldest girl in the family:

> *Because they look up to me, their elder sister; they look to see what their elder sister is doing.*

with them and they understood more about her illness and how to support her.

Quality of relationship with parent with HIV

Children's emotional attachments and loving, supportive relationships between a child and parent or other significant adult have been recognised as important protective factors for children experiencing adversity (Newman, 2002b; Schoon and Bynner, 2003). Recent research with young carers and young adult carers has suggested that caregiving can lead to the development of stronger emotional bonds and relationships between the child and their parent (Aldridge and Becker, 2003; Robson et al, 2006; Becker and Becker, 2008). The evidence from Tanzania and the UK suggests that most caring relationships within families were characterised by love, reciprocity and interdependence (see Chapter 6 and also Chapter 1). Despite their illness, parents with HIV maintain their parental roles in providing love, informal teaching, moral guidance and support to their children. Loving, supportive family relationships between children, parents, siblings and other relatives appear to represent important protective factors that help to mitigate children's vulnerability.

Many young people in Tanzania expressed their love for their parent and a sense of moral duty to look after their parent as the main reasons they had taken on caring responsibilities. They felt that they had reciprocal responsibilities towards their mother, since she had brought them up and it was now their moral duty to help her when she was sick. For example, June (aged 18) said: *'I feel quite normal because this is my mother. I can't abandon her. I thank God for everything and pray that God gives me the strength to persevere until the end. I can't walk away from my responsibility, because she's my mother.'* This was linked to African sociocultural concepts of childhood and the reciprocal responsibilities of children towards their families and communities, in terms of caring and providing for parents and relatives in sickness and old age as part of an 'intergenerational contract' (as discussed earlier). Some young people who had migrated to the UK from Africa also saw their caring responsibilities in terms of the love and moral duty they felt towards their family.

Some parents and service providers felt that young people's sense of moral duty to care for their parents was also related to the child's compassion and empathy for their parent since disclosure of their HIV status. As one service provider in Tanzania commented: *'They were told by the parents themselves that they were sick, so I think they realised the need to look after their parents. It is due to feelings of compassion and a sense of moral responsibility.'* Similarly, a service provider in the UK perceived African cultural values and children's sense of moral duty and loyalty to their family as the main reasons young people took on caring responsibilities in families affected by HIV.

While loving and supportive family relationships represent an important protective factor for young people, the research found that some parents, siblings and other relatives exploited unequal adult–child power relations and behaved in uncaring ways towards young people with caring responsibilities (see Chapter 6). While the majority of children and parents/relatives with HIV commented on the love and closeness of their caring relationships, a few service providers in Tanzania suggested that children who care for parents with HIV may be at risk of neglect and verbal, physical or sexual abuse. Evidence of discriminatory and sometimes abusive relationships with parents, siblings and relatives suggests that family relationships could also represent a potential risk that may increase young people's vulnerability to negative impacts of young caregiving and the level of their involvement in care work. In the UK, policy guidance has recognised that some children with caring responsibilities can be at risk of harm, neglect or abuse, particularly in families where parental capacity has been impaired through, for example, the misuse of alcohol or drugs or severe and enduring mental ill health. Guidelines exist to promote interprofessional working to safeguard and protect children in these circumstances (HM Government, 2006).

Personal attributes

Some parents/relatives in Tanzania thought that children's personal attributes meant that they had a greater aptitude for caring than their siblings or other children within the household and that this had influenced why they took on caring responsibilities. Personal attributes that parents in Tanzania valued in terms of enabling children to perform their caring tasks more effectively were intelligence, attentiveness, being calm, mature and close to their family. One parent commented on the qualities of her daughter: *'She is quick to understand, knows how to keep secrets and is generally more intelligent than the rest.'* Similarly, another parent, who lived with her two sons and whose eldest son no longer lived at home, felt that Isack, her youngest son, had more responsibilities than his older brothers because: *'He is more attentive than the others.'*

A few parents and service providers in the UK also commented on the personal characteristics of particular children that they felt partly explained why children took on greater caring responsibilities within families. Attributes valued by parents included: intelligence, maturity, sense of responsibility and a caring and loving nature. One parent related her son's caring responsibilities to his personal attributes: *'I think it's because I know that he is responsible, and he is very, very caring, but he's very intelligent, he's a very intelligent child and I think it's all down to trust and belief as well. [...] he likes to have responsibility.'*

Some young people in both countries also mentioned personal qualities they felt helped them to perform their caring responsibilities. These included being calm and patient, *'having hope'*, being *'strong'* and living peacefully with others. For example, Sophia (aged 19), who was caring for her mother and sister in the UK, thought that young people with caring responsibilities needed: *'to be strong, calm, caring and be tolerant. That's the main thing that I do and it helps me a lot.'*

Co-residence

Previous studies have identified the co-residence of children within the household of a sick or disabled parent/relative as a key factor in determining why young people take on caring responsibilities (Becker et al, 1998; Aldridge and Becker, 2003). Several young people and parents in both Tanzania and the UK commented on the fact that the young person was the only child living in the household who was available to care for their parent/relative with HIV. Indeed, as noted in Chapter 3, the majority of young people interviewed in both countries were children (aged 9-17) who were caring for their mother with HIV in one-parent households where no other adult was available to care for their mother. Previous studies confirm that children and young people living in one-parent households affected by parental illness are more likely to take on caring roles than in families where there is a second adult who can provide informal care and support (Dearden and Becker, 2000; Aldridge and Becker, 2003). In a large survey of over 6,000 young carers in the UK (Dearden and Becker, 2004) 56% of all children were living in one-parent families, and in these families 70% of people receiving care and assistance were mothers. Thus, co-residence intersects with issues of poverty and gender, as most one-parent families in the UK and Tanzania are headed by women (usually mothers), invariably living on low incomes (extreme poverty in Tanzania), and, in the absence of another adult or external support, mothers have to rely on their children to provide care and support.

Some service providers in Tanzania suggested that increasing trends towards urbanisation and the formation of nuclear families meant that extended family support might not be as readily available as in the past; thus, the co-residence and proximity of children to the person with HIV were significant factors in children taking on caring responsibilities. For example, one service provider commented: *'In African cultures, we are moving away from that to the nuclear family. So as a result people are not bothered to look after their relatives these days, let alone living with them.'* Several service providers also highlighted the benefits of children's co-residence for parents/relatives with HIV in terms of being able to provide care and support as and when they needed it, while maintaining their privacy and dignity. For example, one service provider in Tanzania commented: *'It may be that the person with HIV doesn't want people to come and see him/her in such a state, so he/she only wants his/her children to care for him/her.'*

Conclusion

This chapter has explored a range of structural, relational and individual processes influencing whether young people take on caring roles and the level of their involvement in care work in families affected by HIV/AIDS, using Tanzania and the UK as case studies. Global forces such as the HIV/AIDS epidemic, economic restructuring and transnational migration, as well as global and national policies, infrastructure and interventions structure the macro-environment in which young caregiving takes place. At the community level, the availability of formal and informal safety nets represents a significant influence on whether young people take on caring roles and can potentially either alleviate or exacerbate the level of young people's involvement in care work within the family. Micro-level factors such as the parent/relative's health, disclosure of their status, poverty and changes in household structures, as well as individual differences for children and young people, such as cultural norms and performances of gender, age and sibling birth order, the quality of their relationship with the parent/relative they are caring for, personal attributes and co-residence may all have significant influences on young people's caring roles within families affected by HIV/AIDS.

While the framework of risk and protective factors we have developed gives insight into the complex interplay of structural, relational and individual processes at work within particular households affected by HIV/AIDS, we do not wish to present this as an all-encompassing static model that determines children's level of vulnerability or resilience. Children and young people are social actors who are actively engaged in constructing and determining their own social lives and environments (James et al, 1998). Thus, children and young people negotiate their caring trajectories within both the constraints and the possibilities of structural, relational and individual factors. They embrace, resist and contest the identity of carer and the responsibilities and expectations placed on them in different ways in specific temporal and spatial contexts. Thus the meanings attached to young people's caregiving within families affected by HIV/AIDS are constantly changing, varying according to different cultural, socio-economic, political, historical and geographical contexts.

Notes

[1] Chronically ill adults are defined as women and men aged 18–59 who were very ill for 3 or more months during the 12 months preceding the survey (TACAIDS et al, 2005).

[2] Orphans and vulnerable children are defined by TACAIDS et al (2005) as children aged under 18 whose mother or father has died or whose mother or father has been very sick for at least 3 months during the 12 months preceding the survey.

TEN

Responding to the support needs of children and young people caring for parents with HIV

In our final chapter, we focus on the support needs of children and young people who care for parents with HIV and discuss local and global strategies and responses. The previous chapters have highlighted positive and negative outcomes of young caring for children, young people and parents and have analysed the structural, relational and individual factors that influence young people's caring roles in the context of HIV/AIDS. In this chapter, we discuss the implications of these experiences for the needs and requirements for support of families affected by HIV/AIDS. First, we examine the perspectives of young people, parents and service providers on their support needs in Tanzania and the UK. We discuss providers' views of the development of services and support for this hidden group of young people and their suggested improvements to existing service provision. We explore debates about targeting support for children caring for parents/relatives with HIV, issues of disclosure of HIV status for accessing services, and providers' views on whether efforts should be focused on preventing children being drawn into caring roles or on responding to children's support needs once they have taken on caring responsibilities. We also examine some of the limitations of service provision and the barriers to the development of services and support, based on the perspectives of young people, parents/relatives and service providers. The final section raises pertinent issues and concerns that have emerged from our findings in Tanzania and the UK in relation to policy responses to young caregiving in the context of HIV/AIDS and suggests future directions for policy and practice at the local and global levels.

Needs and requirements for support

In the context of experiences of extreme poverty among the majority of interviewees, most children and parents in Tanzania saw their practical needs predominantly in terms of financial and material support for the family, as Table 10.1 shows. Children's access to education and vocational training was identified as a key priority by most young people and parents. As Judith, one mother, commented: '*I just wish my children could get as much education as possible. Equipped with a good education they will be able to lead good lives.*' Similarly, Neema emphasised the importance of education for young people's future employment prospects: '*They should receive education. This is very important because when someone gets an education, they can manage their life.*'

Table 10.1: Views of young people and parents/relatives in Tanzania on their support needs

Identified need	Young people (n=22)	Mothers/ relatives with HIV (n=21)	Total (n=43)
Access to education and training for children	19	15	34
Financial support for family	12	11	23
Material support to meet basic needs	12	10	22
Capital for small business activities	5	11	16
Better quality housing	5	10	15
Medical care and treatment	6	7	13
Emotional support	7	3	10
Nutritional food and balanced diet for those with HIV	3	5	8
Paid work to support family	3	4	7
Assistance with domestic and care work	5	0	5
Improved health of parent	2	3	5
Support from relatives	3	0	3
Information and training about caring for someone with HIV	2	0	2
Other	0	2	2

Many parents also expressed a need for capital to start small business activities so that they would be able to support their families, rather than rely on handouts from NGOs, as Mary commented: '*I think they should give us loans to empower us economically. When you feel better, you can run your own business, selling something. That would free us from the shame of having to beg from services.*' Several parents mentioned a need for financial support for better quality housing for their family. This would help to reduce the stress caused by the constant threat of eviction if parents failed to pay their rent for those living in urban areas and/or enable parents to renovate homes that were in a poor state of repair. As Rose commented:

> *If I carry on living in poverty like the way I am doing there will come a time when I won't be able to pay the rent without help from somewhere. If I will get to that point then I will be evicted from the house and I will then be destitute. I would like a place of my own where I can live with my family [...] so I wouldn't have to worry about paying the rent.*

Faced with their own mortality, some mothers also saw building a house for their children as important for their children's inheritance and security in the future, as Angelina commented: *'If I could get a good business, I would be able to build them a small house and open bank accounts for them, you know, to provide for their future when I'm gone.'* A third of parents also mentioned a need for medical care and treatment, while some identified a need for nutritional food and paid work to support their family. As Flomina, one mother, commented: *'If I could get help with the rent, food, school fees and materials, that would really help to reduce the stress I have now.'*

In addition to financial support to meet the costs of education and vocational training emphasised by almost all the young people, some identified other aspects of practical and material support that would help to alleviate their caring responsibilities and improve their family's situation. These included assistance with their household chores and care work, better quality housing, medical treatment, financial support for emergencies and transport to hospital, capital to start a small business, nutritional food for their parent and paid work with a regular income to support their family. Young people in the 18-24 age group who were relied on to provide an income for the family emphasised the need for paid employment or capital to start a small business; as Queenie (aged 24), caring for her four younger siblings in a youth-headed household, explained: *'If I could get capital to start a business, that would make a big difference because I would then have a regular income. This would enable me to meet a lot of our daily needs.'*

Although parents did not identify a need for practical assistance with domestic and care work within the household, some young people saw this as important. William (aged 16), caring for his grandmother and younger siblings, commented: *'If I could be given a worker who could help to do some of the work at home, it would help me a lot, because it's me who cooks and fetches water.'* Similarly, Magdalena (aged 15), who cared for her mother in the last two months of her life, identified young people's need for practical support, particularly in providing personal care for people who are sick, as well as meeting the family's basic needs: *'They need to be given food, money. Friends and relatives should help them by cooking for [the person who is ill], washing their clothes and giving them baths.'* A small number of children and parents identified the improved health of the parent and greater support from relatives as helping to alleviate children's caring responsibilities. Babu (aged 14), for example, who, as we saw in Chapter 6, had been ostracised by his older siblings, thought that greater support from his relatives would relieve his caring responsibilities: *'I wish my relatives would come to help me. That would be a good thing. I would then be able to attend school on a regular basis and improve my ranking in the class.'*

Despite greater access to welfare and the formal safety net of health and social care, education and social security, several parents and children in the UK also mentioned a need for financial support, struggling to survive on the limited state benefits available for families on low income and the minimal support available to families seeking asylum. As we saw in Chapters 4 and 8, families with insecure immigration status are particularly vulnerable to destitution because of inequalities in entitlements for welfare support and employment opportunities. Some mothers with insecure immigration status highlighted the need for the government to reduce disparities in access to welfare support and employment opportunities for those with insecure immigration status. They emphasised their desire to work full time so that they could support their children without having to rely on state benefits. As Joyce, whose temporary visa meant that she and her daughter had 'no recourse to public funds', commented:

> *These other people are HIV positive just like I am. They're ill, I'm ill, we're all the same — we're all humans [...]. But they get help and I don't. So if the government could give me assistance as well, that would be great. They could help me even just in a small way. For example, if I was allowed to work full time that would just be great. I would be able to work and I would be able to support myself instead of having to rely on the government to give me things.*

Many young people and parents saw opportunities for young people to meet their peers and engage in social and leisure activities as the most important priority, as Table 10.2 shows. Gemma (aged 15) thought it was important for young people with caring responsibilities to meet others in similar situations in informal youth group settings:

> *They should set up, like, a group of people like my age that you can talk to, who actually know about it and not just, like, go, 'Yeah, I know how you feel.' It's like, 'No, you don't.' [...] places like relaxed, things like the youth club where you can just go and relax but with*

people, like young people, yeah, and then just places to go where you can just sort of forget about it and just have fun without having to worry about coming back and, like, helping.

Table 10.2: Views of young people and parents in the UK on their support needs

Identified need	Number of young people (n=11)	Number of mothers with HIV (n=12)	Total (n=23)
Opportunities for young people's social and leisure activities with peers	6	5	11
Assistance with domestic and care work	6	4	10
Financial support for family	4	5	9
Emotional support for children	5	4	9
Improved health of parent	3	4	7
Better quality housing	2	2	4
Respite opportunities for parent and child	2	2	4
Support with school work	3	1	4
Cure for HIV	1	3	4
Support from relatives	1	2	3
Information and support about caring for someone with HIV	2	1	3
Information, advice and support about accessing services	0	3	3
Medical care and treatment	0	1	1
Paid work to support family	0	1	1

As in Tanzania, several young people and some parents in the UK also identified a need for practical assistance with household chores and children's care work. Lucy, a mother from East Africa, commented: *'If somebody could be there to help when I'm sick, because I can't do the house chores, and support for somebody to be there if I'm not well, to cope with the children, to do the shopping, take them to hospital [...]'.* Young people whose first language was not English highlighted their need for greater support with their school work.

Young people and parents living in overcrowded social housing saw better quality housing that provided greater privacy for young people as an important priority which would help to alleviate tensions in caring relationships. Alice (aged 17), for example, felt that life would be easier for her:

> *If I had my own room without having to share with my mum because we quarrel a lot on that. And if, if I pass my school exams and everything and, yeah, if I had someone to help me look after my mum as well.*

While a few identified a need for a cure for HIV, several children and parents saw the improved health of the parent as important in alleviating children's caring responsibilities. A few children and parents thought that more support from relatives and information about support services, both for parents with HIV and for those caring for people with HIV, would improve their situation.

Children and young people in both Tanzania and the UK identified a need for emotional support and opportunities to share their feelings and talk to 'professional friends' (Pinnock and Evans, 2008) and others in similar situations about caring for their parent with a chronic, life-limiting illness. They thought that having 'someone to talk to' would help them continue to care for their parent. As Kerry (aged 18) commented: *'It would be nice to get, like, regular check ups, not really checking up, just seeing how you're coping and things like that. Because it can get quite hard and you just don't know who to speak to or anything.'* As we saw in Chapter 8, the trusting relationships that young people and parents developed with project workers could help to promote their resilience.

Many also highlighted the importance of opportunities to meet other young people in similar situations to themselves and develop peer support, which they thought would help to reduce their isolation. For example, Neema (aged 18) in Tanzania said that young people with caring responsibilities need: *'advice and support, to spend time with other people in our situation so that they realise that they are not alone and so are comforted. Then they would see there are lots of people with problems like this.'* Similarly, Alice in the UK said that young people with caring responsibilities *'need to, like, form, like, a youth club or something, like, with people who care for people, so people can see there's not only themselves that do that'*. A few young people in both countries also thought that more information, training and support about caring for someone with HIV would help to make their caring responsibilities easier.

Service providers' perspectives on the support needs of children and parents broadly reflected the views of children and parents themselves, as Table 10.3 shows. Many providers in Tanzania perceived a need for greater recognition, awareness and support for children with caring responsibilities within the community. Several also mentioned the need to meet children's basic needs, provide material support and access to high-quality healthcare for parents with HIV, information and advice for children about caring for a person with HIV, basic medical supplies and emotional support for children. Others mentioned the need for measures to ensure that children with caring responsibilities continue to attend school regularly, income-generation initiatives for families to tackle poverty, and greater awareness about HIV/AIDS at all levels of the community. Other needs identified included skills training in income-generation activities, small business development for young people, and support for parents in making a will and ensuring children's inheritance rights were protected.

Table 10.3: Views of service providers in Tanzania and the UK on children's and parents' support needs

Identified need	Number of service providers Tanzania (n=13)	Number of service providers UK (n=14)	Total (n=27)
Emotional support for children	3	8	11
Material and practical support for parents with HIV	7	3	10
Greater recognition and support for young people with caring responsibilities within community	8	0	8
Access to information and support about HIV and caring for someone with HIV for children	4	3	7
Greater awareness about HIV within schools and the wider community	2	4	6
Family and school-based support for children	2	4	6
Leisure and social activities for young people	0	6	6
Peer support	0	4	4
Building capacity of professionals and teachers	2	2	4
Advocacy and signposting to entitlements and further sources of support	1	3	4
Other	2	0	2

In the UK, most service providers identified emotional support and a supportive safe place where children could express their feelings as key priorities. Many providers also saw short breaks and opportunities for young people to engage in leisure and extracurricular activities with their peers in similar situations as a priority, corresponding to children's and parents' perspectives. In common with Tanzanian service providers, several saw a need for greater awareness about HIV within the community, suggesting that good practice guidelines in supporting children affected by HIV should be disseminated in schools, among HIV organisations and mainstream children and youth services. Some providers thought that children needed improved access to information about HIV and the effects on their parent's health, and parents needed practical support and advocacy to access their entitlements to health and social care, social security benefits and housing, and immigration advice, particularly for African migrants and refugee families, as well as signposting to further sources of support. Other needs identified by service providers included: greater availability of family and school-based support, greater coordination of services, increased staff capacity and more qualified professionals with specialist knowledge in supporting children caring for parents with HIV.

Having discussed the support needs of children and parents in families affected by HIV/AIDS, the following sections focus on possible strategies and approaches that could address these identified needs. First, we discuss service providers' perspectives on the development of services and support for this group of young people and identify suggested improvements to existing provision.

Developing services and support for young people caring for parents with HIV

While service providers' perspectives differed considerably between Tanzania and the UK because of very different service provision and welfare contexts, some common themes emerged about the way that services and support for this group of children should be developed, as can be seen in Table 10.4.

Table 10.4: Views of service providers in Tanzania and the UK on the development of services and support for children caring for parents with HIV

Suggested strategies to improve services for children caring for parents with HIV	Number of service providers Tanzania (n=13)	Number of service providers UK (n=14)	Total (n=27)
Funding to develop services for this group	4	7	11
Education, awareness raising and advocacy about HIV and young caregiving in mainstream services and the community	7	3	10
Development of peer support, respite opportunities, play and leisure activities and youth groups for young people	3	6	9
Greater provision of material support to meet basic needs of families affected by HIV	8	0	8
Make services more accessible and culturally appropriate for particular groups	0	8	8
Capacity building of professionals in supporting this group	1	7	8
Development and implementation of inclusive AIDS policy and guidelines regarding identification and support needs of this group	7	0	7
Development of home-based care services	6	0	6
Greater availability of preventative family support services	1	5	6
Development of specific organisations, services and youth groups for this group	2	3	5
Individually tailored support and specialist counselling for children affected by HIV	3	2	5
Greater coordination of services	2	2	4

Service providers in both countries felt that more funding was needed to develop services and support for this previously hidden group of children, who, as our research has shown, are largely unsupported in their caring roles in both Tanzania and the UK. They also suggested a need for greater awareness about HIV more generally and greater recognition of the specific experiences and support needs of children caring for a parent with HIV among mainstream and specialist service providers, including schools, mainstream young carers services (in the UK), the HIV sector, faith-based and community organisations and community leaders. In Tanzania, providers thought that the development and implementation of a more inclusive AIDS policy, with guidelines on the identification and requirements for support of children with caring responsibilities, from the grassroots to strategic levels, would help to ensure that children's roles as caregivers were recognised and alleviated. Providers also highlighted the importance of available funding and support being channelled to the most vulnerable families.

Providers in Tanzania and the UK identified a number of approaches to supporting this group of young people, with a particular focus on providing opportunities for children to have a break from their caring responsibilities through leisure and play activities and socialising with their peers in youth groups. Although there is little existing play and leisure provision for children in Tanzania, community groups felt it was important to provide more child-focused activities and opportunities for young people to socialise with their peers as a break from their caring responsibilities, as well as providing training and advice to children about how to care for a parent with HIV. Service providers also saw the need to support the whole family as a key priority, suggesting the development of more preventative family support services (in the UK) and home-based care (in Tanzania). One project worker working with women with HIV in the UK felt that there was a gap in preventative family support services for people with HIV and services were usually only able to respond to crises. She thought that supporting parents with HIV and their children over a longer period of time would help to intervene earlier and address more complex family issues such as disclosure, caregiving and the emotional support needs of families: *'I'd love to be able to sort of say, right, we'll do an assessment and then maybe spend ten weeks seeing somebody and trying to really get to grips with the bigger issues.'*

In Tanzania, suggestions for improving family support were focused on expanding the remit of home-based care for people with HIV/AIDS. Providers thought that home-based care should include counselling and emotional support for people with HIV; provision of basic medical kits, education, training and guidance for children with caring responsibilities on how to care for someone with HIV and how to minimise the risk of infection; and home-based care workers should make regular home visits and spend more time with the family to understand their situation. One home-based care volunteer suggested that home-based nursing and palliative care should be provided by paid nurses to alleviate the burden of care on family members, particularly children:

> *When people with HIV/AIDS live far away from treatment at a dispensary or hospital, nurses should be there [at their home] all the time. This will relieve the children, so that it is the nurses who shave their hair, apply ointment to their bodies, dress sores and boils and bathe them, generally. I think this will be a great relief and reduce the burden for the children so that they can get on with their own lives.*

However, Ogden et al (2006) note that initial efforts in Southern Africa to provide nursing care to people with AIDS in the community through hospital-based outreach (whereby hospital staff travelled directly to patients' homes) were found to be time consuming and expensive.

Specific targeted support for this group of children was also identified by a few service providers in both countries in terms of emotional support and counselling and the development of specific youth groups for children caring for a family member with HIV. However, there was concern in the UK about establishing separate services for this group and labelling children as 'young carers', as this could potentially further stigmatise a group already experiencing discrimination and fear of stigma because of their parent's HIV status (discussed in more detail in the following section).

Capacity building of professionals was also seen as a priority in the UK, where providers suggested that schools, mainstream young carers services and HIV organisations required specific information and awareness-raising activities about the particular dynamics of young caregiving in the context of HIV/AIDS, including supporting parents with immigration issues, sensitivity to confidentiality and the stigma surrounding HIV, and approaches that encouraged pride in young people's caring responsibilities. Ensuring that services were accessible to particular groups and sensitive to diverse faith and cultural needs was also an important priority for providers in the UK.

Children and parents also identified a number of suggested improvements to services. In Tanzania, young people highlighted the importance of improving access to life-prolonging ART for people living with HIV. Several children wanted home-based care workers to spend time talking to them as well as their parents during home visits, and Malcolm thought that a system for confidential sharing of information between staff should be established instead of having to keep telling different workers about his mother's and his situation. Similarly, Pascali (aged 16) identified the need for more home-based care support for young people caring for parents with HIV and sensitivity to confidentiality about people's HIV status: '*I would like you to visit us who are caring for the sick more often and not to break the confidentiality of people who are ill.*'

In the UK, a few children suggested improvements to youth clubs that they attended, including doing more social activities and outings, more activities for older teenagers and more flexible opening times, to enable young people to use computers and access homework support during weekends. Some parents also suggested ways that existing services they accessed could be improved, including greater recognition and support for family carers of people with HIV, more specialist counselling for children affected by HIV, more creative and performing arts activities for children, and dating opportunities provided by HIV organisations for lone parents to meet potential partners also living with HIV.

Targeting of support for children and young people caring for parents with HIV

Our research has shown that service providers clearly felt that policy, services and support for children caring for parents with HIV needed to be developed and improved to better address their needs and requirements for support. In Chapter 8, we discussed key practices and approaches that appeared to promote children's and families' resilience. Several important issues and debates emerged from service providers' accounts about the targeting of services and support to this hidden group of young people, which we discuss in this section.

Preventing young caregiving or providing support once children have become carers?

When service providers were asked about their professional approach to the issue of young caregiving, the majority in both countries said that they responded to children's support needs once they had taken on caring roles, rather than aiming to prevent children being drawn into caring roles in the first instance. Most service providers felt that it was important to respect parenting roles and support the whole family, rather than focus support only on the young person with caring responsibilities. This reflects recent 'whole family' (Frank, 2002; Frank and McLarnon, 2008) approaches to young caregiving adopted by many young carers services in the UK. Many service providers in the UK felt that it was difficult to prevent children from taking on caring roles within families and were concerned that approaches that aim to prevent young caregiving could undermine the close relationships that develop between children and parents. Some service providers in the UK also felt that the professional approach they took depended on the child's age, extent of their care work and the impacts on the child, which should be monitored regularly and, if appropriate, referrals made to social services or to family support workers.

Some service providers in Tanzania said that they aimed to both support young people in their caring roles and prevent children being drawn into caring roles, and a few said that the main focus of their work was on preventing young caregiving through home-based care, education and awareness-raising about HIV/AIDS in the community. However, some stakeholders were concerned that the scale of young caregiving in the context of HIV/AIDS in Tanzania and other African countries meant that the priority should be clearly focused on supporting young people in their caring roles, rather than diverting attention away from this group by attempting to prevent young caregiving. One provider saw education about HIV/AIDS as key to involving community members in caring for people with HIV and helping to alleviate children's caring responsibilities:

> *The community around the person with HIV/AIDS should be involved in helping to lessen the children's burden. [...] When they are equipped with this education, the adult members of ten-cell system[1] would take turns to care for the person with HIV/AIDS. This would be a great relief to the child who would feel comforted and cared for instead of being stigmatised.*

Providing support through specialist or mainstream services?

The perspectives of service providers and parents in the UK highlighted tensions around the targeting of services and whether specialist HIV or mainstream services were most appropriate to meet the needs of families affected by HIV. Service providers suggested that some people with HIV were reluctant to access specialist HIV services because of the risk of disclosure and fear of stigma. The success of combination therapy in managing HIV and increasing life expectancy in the UK and other high-income countries has led to a shift in perceptions of HIV from a terminal to a chronic illness and hence growing pressure to move away from specialist support services. Service providers acknowledged that, ideally, people with HIV and their families should be able to access non-stigmatised mainstream services, but were concerned that at present professionals within these services might not have adequate knowledge and awareness of the complex issues surrounding HIV.

Service providers were also concerned that mainstream services may not be responsive to the diverse needs of African refugee families and other minority groups affected by HIV. Providers suggested that many refugee and asylum-seeking families affected by HIV may be particularly marginalised and fearful of engaging with mainstream agencies, preferring to access services provided by the voluntary sector: *'Why voluntary? Because most of those affected are refugees and asylum seekers, with language needs, cultural needs, faith needs, of which they do not trust the mainstream services.'* Another project worker who advised families with HIV about statutory benefits and welfare support highlighted the need for outreach work to ensure that families accessed the social support they were entitled to: *'You see, it's about having people go out into the community to embrace these families, rather than sitting in agencies waiting for them to access their rights, because they're not accessing their rights.'*

Some parents and service providers were concerned about whether mainstream young carers groups would be appropriate for children caring for a parent with HIV, because of the risk of disclosure of the parent's HIV status and stigma within the group, as well as the level of professionals' knowledge and expertise in supporting families affected by HIV. One White British mother, for example, found out about opportunities for her daughter to join a young carers group, but was concerned that her daughter would face stigma within the group:

> *Not everybody would be HIV, so I think that was the thing then, because of the stigma, whether she would cope with that and that held me back a bit […] I've got mixed feelings because I don't want it to be, if you separate something off it becomes a bit more that you could stick a label on it. If it's just general carers it would be more out in the open and talked about it, but whether she would find that better or not I don't know.*

Another mother with HIV, Christine (from East Africa), felt that mainstream young carers services were inappropriate for children caring for parents with HIV because of the stigma and thought that they needed to have separate, dedicated services:

When I've asked social services they've directed me to, there's a group, but I know for sure that my daughter wouldn't fit in [...] A young carers group for children affected by HIV has to be separate because those children can't go and say, 'Oh my mum is ill.' 'What's she suffering from?' 'Oh my mum has diabetes.' This child is not going to stand up and say my mum has HIV because that's more difficult.

A project worker from an African community-based organisation hoping to develop more support for children caring for parents with HIV suggested that it was important to target services towards a wider group of children from similar backgrounds and then tailor support to the individual needs of children with caring responsibilities in order to avoid labelling children as 'carers of people with HIV' and minimise the risk of stigmatisation.

In the Sub-Saharan African context, debates about the targeting of services have been focused around the use of the category 'Orphans and Vulnerable Children' and the acknowledgement that targeting interventions only at orphans is inappropriate, as is acknowledged in the UNAIDS et al (2004) report *Children on the Brink* (Meintjes and Giese, 2006). Interventions and support that target orphans generally focus on alleviating the poverty they experience (Meintjes and Giese, 2006). However, in communities affected by HIV/AIDS in Sub-Saharan African, many millions of children experience poverty and can all be seen as 'vulnerable' (Mcintjes and Giese, 2006). Meintjes and Giese argue that targeting poverty-reduction strategies and support only towards orphans, while ignoring the majority of other vulnerable children, is 'locally inappropriate' and can even place orphans at increased risk in poor neighbourhoods (2006: 420).

While the language of international agencies and government initiatives appears to have shifted in recent years towards the more inclusive language of 'Children living in communities affected by HIV/AIDS' or 'Orphans and Vulnerable Children', some commentators argue that responses to the epidemic remain 'orphan-centred' and do not adequately address the multiple ways that children are made vulnerable by the HIV/AIDS pandemic (Bray, 2003; Meintjes and Giese, 2006). As Foster (2006: 701) argues, 'Guaranteeing the rights of all children who live in communities affected by AIDS is more beneficial than singling out specific groups, such as so-called "AIDS orphans"'. In Tanzania, governmental support for children affected by HIV/AIDS has been formulated using the term 'Most Vulnerable Children', based on local understandings of vulnerability. This category includes not only children whose mother or father has died or whose mother or father is very sick, but also children who are vulnerable because of chronic poverty and because of other social problems, including living on the streets, those engaged in child labour, those who have been abused and exploited (MHSW, 2006).

Some young people and parents interviewed in Tanzania highlighted the fact that orphans were seen as the main priority for donor support and that there was a need for greater recognition of the needs of children and young people made vulnerable by the epidemic in other ways, such as by caring for sick parents and relatives, siblings and elderly grandparents in households experiencing extreme poverty. For example, June, who was caring for her mother and six siblings and orphaned cousins, called for greater recognition of young people's caring responsibilities among organisations supporting people with HIV: *'They should also pay attention to those who are caring for parents with HIV/AIDS, they should think about us and increase the support to help us with our problems.'* In view of the focus on orphaned children, several service providers thought that children with caring responsibilities needed to be identified at local level, in collaboration with NGOs, and for support to be specifically targeted towards this group.

Disclosure and access to services for children affected by HIV

Targeting specialist support to children affected by HIV raises questions about disclosure and whether children's awareness of HIV should be used as a criterion to access specialist services. In the UK, three of the seven organisations providing youth group activities for young people affected by HIV offered specialist groups for young people who were aware either of their own or a family member's HIV status, as well as providing open access groups for younger children affected by HIV. Although project workers checked that young people accessing the specialist groups were aware of HIV before they joined, there was a risk that children could inadvertently learn of their parent's HIV status through accessing the group. Indeed, Emily had been unaware of her father's HIV status until she attended a specialist youth group. After a project worker's telephone call to her father, he told Emily about his HIV status. Project workers needed to remind members of the group about confidentiality and that the group was closed to young people who were not aware of HIV.

Some service providers in the UK felt that it was important to provide open access services for children affected by HIV, whether they were aware or not of HIV in the family, as otherwise children who did not 'know' would be excluded from accessing services. Some providers felt that open access services helped to 'normalise' HIV, while others felt that this prevented young people who 'know' being able to talk openly about HIV with their peers. In open access groups, project workers tried to prepare parents for the possibility of HIV being raised within the group. Project workers said that in practice they found it rare for the issue to arise, but when it happened they telephoned the parent and supported them with the disclosure.

Service providers in the UK commented on the difficulty of providing inclusive family services without mentioning HIV. A tension was apparent between wanting to encourage openness about HIV to reduce stigma, while respecting the wishes of service users to keep HIV secret from members of their family or community and offering discreet services, which they felt was 'colluding' with the stigma and secrecy. Providers in Tanzania also highlighted the need for discretion in providing services for families affected by HIV, both in NGO centres or through home visiting programmes. They recognised that fear of stigma was one of the major barriers to the take-up of services.

Parents in the UK expressed their concerns about their children discovering their HIV status through accessing services or by accompanying them to HIV organisations where posters and leaflets about HIV were on display. Sandra, of White British ethnicity, used to take her children to an HIV organisation when they were younger, but was worried that they would discover her status before she felt ready to tell them and stopped attending until she had disclosed to her children:

> *In those days they didn't know. I was always anxious that it would come out because it was always spoken about openly there. And I didn't go for a while because I didn't want them to know. They were getting to an age where they'd have found out about me, and then I started going back again once they did know.*

In contrast, a mother from Southern Africa was less concerned about her children seeing posters about HIV at an African community organisation or asking awkward questions, because she thought that her children were unlikely to ask her directly about culturally taboo topics such as sexuality or death (as discussed in Chapter 2).

Some service providers felt that although their parent may not have openly 'disclosed' their status to their children, many children have some level of awareness of their parent's illness and know more than their parents think: '*I honestly think that they do talk among themselves, and they know a lot more than what the parents actually think they know.*'

This confirms the findings of Lewis's (2001) and Wood et al's (2006) studies with young people affected by HIV in the UK and Zimbabwe, respectively. Indeed, project workers at a specialist youth group for children who are aware of HIV in the family found that they had to turn away young people who had been brought along by their peers, because their parents thought that the young people were not aware of their HIV status.

Barriers to the development of services and support

Despite service providers' suggested improvements and views about the strategies and approaches that would help to develop services and support for the hidden group of children caring for parents with HIV, a number of limitations and barriers to the development of services and support were identified in the accounts of children, parents and service providers. The following sections discuss the ways that these barriers impact on the development of services and support for families affected by HIV/AIDS at local and national levels.

Restricted access to statutory/governmental support

As we discussed in Chapter 9, HIV was not seen as a political priority for social care, support or information services at national or local level in the UK (Weatherburn et al, 2007). Service providers interviewed in the UK felt that it was increasingly difficult for people with HIV to access statutory social care services unless they have high support needs, because HIV was perceived as a chronic rather than a life-limiting condition because of the success of combination therapy:

> *People can still access support through kind of social care assessments if they need the high, of the high level, but if your needs aren't considered, if you don't fulfil that criteria, then social services won't, don't have an input.'*

Providers suggested that there was a lack of recognition of the social care needs of families affected by HIV and that statutory interventions were focused on crisis management rather than prevention, as one provider commented:

> *So as long as that child does not show any signs of being at risk, this will be just assessment, and maybe access to things like uniforms and being given a house and paid for rent, but apart from that there's nothing more that the mainstream does for these families.*

Access to health and social care support in the UK was linked to parents' immigration status, which had direct implications for some of the families interviewed. As we saw in Chapter 4, people with HIV who come to the UK on temporary visas have no recourse to public funds and are not entitled to the statutory benefits available to other low-income families affected by HIV, as the experiences of Joyce in Box 10.1 illustrate. The lack of formal safety nets for parents with HIV who have insecure immigration status places families under enormous pressure, as they face the threat of deportation and loss of access to HIV treatment and social support; this reinforces poverty and social exclusion.

Service providers felt that the limited statutory social support available to families with HIV placed voluntary organisations under increasing pressure to deal with immediate practical issues facing parents, in terms of medication and entitlements to benefits, housing and immigration support, rather than being able to develop preventative work with families. Providers highlighted the difficulty for the statutory sector of providing flexible services that were responsive to the changing needs of parents living with HIV. They identified childcare and family support as a particular gap in provision for lone parents, particularly when they need to attend hospital appointments. Several parents expressed their frustrations with trying to access statutory social care support in the UK, commenting on the bureaucratic, time-consuming process of assessment and the strict criteria to qualify for support (see Box 10.1).

As discussed earlier, governmental health and social care support was very limited in Tanzania, despite growing policy recognition of the needs of the most vulnerable children, including those with sick parents. A service provider suggested that exemptions from paying the costs of school fees and medical care for orphans were possible, but expressed frustrations about the bureaucratic process that NGOs had to go through to obtain exemptions for individual children:

> *The services available have to be fought for. The government hasn't [yet] declared that orphans should have free education, free medical care and that they shouldn't contribute money for services like school meals, security etc. Whenever they don't pay such contributions they are barred from going to school until payment is made. The government should take a clear stand about this and declare such services free for these children. At present you have to go through a lot of bureaucratic red-tape to get an exemption for a child to access such services free of charge. It is sometimes impossible to get this exemption. It is only NGOs that have been helping them in these situations.*

Box 10.1: Restricted access to statutory services in the UK: parents' perspectives

Joyce came from East Africa to the UK as a postgraduate student and found that because of her immigration status she had 'no recourse to public funds'. This meant that when she was ill and unable to work to support herself and her daughter, she was not entitled to any welfare benefits and could be charged for hospital treatment. She had been advised that if she tried to change her immigration status, however, she was likely to be deported and would lose access to the combination therapy that she received:

> Once I was really ill and I was admitted to hospital, but the doctor said he wouldn't be able to help me again because of my 'no recourse'. They close their eyes and block their ears. He wrote a letter to social services. I went there for an interview and to find out about the passport and the 'no recourse to public funds' but they couldn't help me at all. They said 'perhaps if you change your status'. But if you go to these organisations that deal with AIDS and so on, they tell you not to change anything. Because then you'll get sent back and your drugs will be stopped.

Despite negative experiences of trying to access support from social services when she was previously unwell, Julie (of White British ethnicity) tried to access home care support following a period of critical illness in hospital: '*I did try and get support when I was unwell this year but the social worker failed profoundly.*' She found the support offered '*absolutely atrocious [...] the level of support was very, very poor*' and commented: '*the dealings that I have had with them have always been failures rather than positives. You know, I don't feel very confident in service provision and things so I've sort of dealt with things myself and coped on my own.*'

Christine, a mother from East Africa wanted to access carers support for her daughter and husband, but because of her previous experiences of social care assessments, she was reluctant to go through a bureaucratic, time-consuming process that was unlikely to result in any support:

> I was asking about support for my daughter and my husband and I was given a number to call and you have to go through the process, duty desk or something like that and then you have to go and tell the story and then you have to go through somebody and I just didn't do it because I'd done it before and it didn't work because they will do it and people come to your house and they will ask questions and then in the end they will say no you actually don't qualify for help so....

Limited capacity of NGOs to meet needs of families affected by HIV/AIDS

The majority of service providers in Tanzania and the UK identified a lack of resources and limited capacity of NGOs to meet the support needs of families affected by HIV/AIDS as a barrier to the development of services. Service providers in the UK reported that statutory funding to support HIV organisations remained the same or was being reduced, despite increases in HIV prevalence and growing demand for services. Voluntary sector providers commented on the difficulty of having to constantly chase short-term funding streams, which were often only available for activities lasting one year, and the implications of this for building staff capacity and sustainability of service provision (see Box 10.2).

Several providers in the UK suggested that services for people with HIV from migrant communities were regarded as a low political priority for funding and felt that voluntary organisations working with people living with HIV were being increasingly 'sidelined'. They found it particularly difficult to secure funding for refugee families affected by HIV, who were doubly marginalised on account of their immigration and HIV status (see Box 10.2). Some organisations providing youth groups for children affected by HIV commented that although the young people would like to meet more often, the group could only meet once a month due to limited funding. Some organisations expressed frustrations about having to turn away service users and refer them on to other services that they knew would be unable to offer support. Some children and parents also reported more limited availability of services and financial support than in the past due to funding constraints and greater demand for services (see Box 10.3).

Service providers in Tanzania also felt that services for families affected by HIV and AIDS were regarded as a low priority for government, despite the scale of the epidemic and the large numbers of people in need of support. Providers commented on the limited resources of NGOs to meet the high levels of need of families affected by HIV/AIDS in their localities and identified sufficient food, medicine, clothing, housing and children's educational expenses as key priorities that the government should be providing (see Box 10.2). Many organisations found it difficult to visit all the families in need of support as part of home-based care programmes, because of limited resources, staff capacity and lack of transport.

The experiences of many young people and parents in Tanzania suggest that while the material support that they received from NGOs was highly valued, it was insufficient to meet their needs (see Box 10.3). In many instances, the food, medicine, financial support and children's educational materials that families received from NGOs was the only external support they were able to access, apart from free antiretroviral therapy (ART) provided by government. Young people and parents recognised that the capacity of NGOs to meet the needs of large numbers of families affected by HIV/AIDS was limited, and a few parents expressed disappointment that so little financial support or food aid was available.

Box 10.2: Limited capacity of NGOs to meet needs of families affected by HIV/AIDS in the UK and Tanzania: service providers' perspectives

We run on a very small budget and every year I'm looking for different things, different community projects that I can use that I don't have to pay for, but it gets more and more difficult. (UK)

The mixture of people, being immigrants and people being HIV positive, it just doesn't switch, it doesn't push any buttons. And, you know, so politically I suppose it's a hot potato.(UK)

These days our home-visiting service is not adequate because of the large numbers of children needing this service. We used to visit almost all of them because they were few. Not now. The resources now are stretched thin, so we cannot afford to help them as much as we would like to. (Tanzania)

At present the government isn't concerned by what the people living with HIV/ AIDS eat. [...] They bring antiretrovirals (ARVs) but they must make sure they bring food too. You can't give a person with HIV/AIDS ARVs without a proper meal. The government hasn't put enough resources into the provision of food, clothing and shelter. It leaves these matters to us, the NGOs, but we can't manage because we only have limited resources. (Tanzania)

Limited knowledge and expertise among professionals

Service providers in the UK suggested that limited knowledge and expertise in supporting families affected by HIV and young carers among mainstream professionals was a barrier to the development of support for children caring for parents with HIV. Several providers commented on the lack of awareness of HIV-related issues and limited understanding of the needs of people affected by HIV in mainstream services. Some providers felt that the lack of specialist HIV counselling services for children partly explained parents' reluctance to disclose their status to their children. Project workers also expressed their frustrations with the school system and felt that there was a lack of recognition of children's individual needs and little understanding of HIV-related or young caregiving issues. One school-based young carers worker felt that teachers did not recognise and understand the difficulties that individual children are experiencing at home that impact on their school work, because of the time pressures and heavy workloads. Similarly, a project worker working with young people living with or affected by HIV felt that there was a need for greater awareness and understanding about HIV issues among school staff to enable them to identify and provide emotional support to young people with complex needs.

Box 10.3: Formal safety nets failing to meet the needs of families affected by HIV/AIDS: young people's and parents' perspectives from the UK and Tanzania

Parents' perspectives

We do get [complementary] therapy, but now it's not much, it's become less and less often, used to be every fortnight, for different therapies, but now you can take like three or four months without having any, which I think is a shame really. (UK)

I get medicine from [NGO] and food too. Our finances are very bad at the moment. The food I get from [NGO] is not enough for us and I have to pay for extra things like buying charcoal, cooking oil and other things to prepare the food. All this is a big burden on my finances as I don't have enough money, so I am forced to beg from here and there. (Tanzania)

Young people's perspectives

We're living off benefit but it's not enough, it's not enough. It's just stressing [my mum] and she tries to go to these youth clubs to get some money but they're not doing it and she's stressed and she's – everything is just wrong. (Crystal, aged 15, UK)

They haven't helped me with my schooling because when went I there to request for help after I had passed to go to Form One, they said they don't deal with secondary school students. They said they only deal with primary school pupils. (Magdalena, aged 15, Tanzania)

In Tanzania, service providers highlighted a more general lack of education and awareness about HIV/AIDS in the community as a barrier to the development of services and support for young carers. Because of the stigma surrounding HIV, some faith-based organisations and communities actively resisted prevention and awareness-raising activities about HIV, as one provider commented: *'Some religious denominations are not willing to talk about HIV/AIDS and some are against the use of condoms.'* Providers also felt that the presence of NGOs providing services for families affected by HIV, combined with stigma and discrimination, resulted in a lack of community engagement in, and responsibility for, caring for people with HIV. In the context of overstretched material and emotional resources within severely affected communities, it is unsurprising that family members and others in the community are reluctant to provide care and support if they perceive that people living with HIV or orphaned children have secured targeted support and assistance from non-governmental, community- or faith-based organisations. Home-based care providers also identified a lack of awareness and recognition of the needs of young people with caring responsibilities within schools as a barrier for developing services for this group of children. One service provider commented on the dilemma faced by young people who were selected to attend government secondary schools far from their homes, which meant that they were unable to combine their education with their caring responsibilities.

Corruption and diversion of material support from the most vulnerable children

A few young people, parents and service providers in Tanzania felt that corruption was a barrier to the development of services for children caring for parents/relatives with HIV. In their view, donor or governmental aid allocated for families affected by HIV/AIDS was sometimes diverted and failed to reach those most in need of support (see Box 10.4).

Box 10.4: Corruption and diversion of material support from the most vulnerable children: young people's, parents' and service providers' perspectives in Tanzania

There are NGOs that have been coming here telling us to register with them. So we registered with them. Whenever help comes we go there only to find that someone else has signed and taken our share. When we complain we are told that we have already taken our share. But we don't know who does that. (Queenie, aged 24, caring for her four younger siblings since the death of her parents)

They should stop taking bribes. Funds come in for children's education, but they channel it to their own children's education. So the project is going backwards instead of making progress. (Ester, mother)

You see sometimes the government releases funds but they end up in people's pockets or are diverted for other uses. So when you check the government expenditure, you might find that funds were allocated for people affected by HIV/AIDS in a certain area but unfortunately it goes to the people the officials favour. (Home-based care volunteer)

Global and local strategies and responses

In this final section we draw together a number of themes and issues from the research evidence presented in this book, to offer a range of possibilities and approaches for working with young people caring for parents/relatives with HIV and their families at the local (national) and global levels. Our concern here is not to offer a series of recommendations, but rather to highlight some of the key issues and challenges to be addressed if policy, services and interventions for children and families affected by HIV/AIDS are to become more responsive to the needs of 'whole families', to reflect an ethic of care approach, and to incorporate perspectives that are sensitive to poverty and gender and age-based inequalities.

Identifying and labelling 'young carers'

First, we wish to discuss the issue of language and the use of categories and labels. The evidence we have presented from young people, parents with HIV and service providers in Tanzania and the UK suggests that young caregiving in the context of HIV/AIDS is a highly complex and contested global phenomenon. Parents' embodied experiences of

HIV-related illness intersect with HIV stigma and discrimination that compound experiences of poverty, social exclusion and inequalities based on gender, race, disability, sexuality and religion, among others. Furthermore, children's and young people's experiences are closely related to those of their parent, and consequently stigma and fear of stigma significantly affects their ability to seek support from both informal and formal safety nets.

Our research suggests that the use of the term 'young carer' in the context of HIV/AIDS appears to be particularly complex and contentious. As we discussed in Chapters 1 and 9, the term 'young carer' has become an accepted policy and legal term in the UK with accompanying rights and entitlements (see Chapter 9 and Frank and McLarnon, 2008, for more details about these rights and the policy framework). However, a range of issues mean that the use of the term 'young carer' is contested in relation to the hidden young people caring for parents with HIV that have formed the focus of our research. These include: the fact that HIV is a highly stigmatised, unseen disability, especially when parents are living 'well' on ART. Parents may therefore be reluctant for their children to be identified as 'young carers' and to access targeted support, as this could result in exposure to HIV-related stigma, fears about confidentiality and wider disclosure of a parent's HIV status within the community. Furthermore, as we discussed above, African migrant and refugee families may be reluctant to engage with mainstream services because of a fear of deportation, stigma and a perceived lack of culturally appropriate services that are sensitive to diverse cultural and religious needs and familial expectations and responsibilities for care.

In the context of Sub-Saharan Africa, the term 'Orphans and Vulnerable Children' dominates policy discourses and interventions for children affected by HIV/AIDS. As discussed earlier, despite the potentially 'inclusive' nature of this term, most policy interventions have remained 'orphan-centred' (Meintjes and Giese, 2006) and paid little attention to other children who have been made just as vulnerable by the HIV/AIDS epidemic, such as those experiencing extreme poverty or those caring for a chronically ill parent with HIV. The term 'young carer' is not widely recognised in international or national social policy discourses in the global South. While our research has highlighted the need for greater recognition of young people's caring responsibilities in families affected by HIV/AIDS globally, lessons from research and targeted interventions with marginalised young people in both the global North and South suggest the dangers of labelling young people with fixed identity categories (Glauser, 1997;

Panter-Brick, 2000; Williams, 2004; Evans, 2005; 2006; Meintjes and Giese, 2006; Evans and Pinnock, 2007). Many childhood researchers have highlighted the fact that the lived realities and circumstances of children perceived as especially 'vulnerable' or 'at risk' rarely fit neatly into one or other of the fixed categories of vulnerable children that have emerged in international discourses (such as 'AIDS orphans', 'street children', 'child soldiers', 'trafficked children', and so on) (Glauser, 1997; Panter-Brick, 2000; Meintjes and Giese, 2006). Such fixed categories are often based on stereotypical assumptions about children's lives and do not take account of the diversity of young people's lived and shared experiences.

Our research has shown that young people with caring responsibilities, like all children and youth, are a highly differentiated group of people, with differences of age, gender, race, ethnicity, class, disability and other characteristics affecting their experiences and responsibilities within the family (Hill and Tisdall, 1997). Furthermore, identifying particular groups of children and singling them out for development assistance can lead to stigmatisation and resentment within local communities by excluding the many other children experiencing chronic poverty who are just as vulnerable (Evans, 2005; Meintjes and Giese, 2006). The continuing stigma and discrimination surrounding HIV/AIDS means that labelling children and young people as 'young carers' could potentially lead to further stigmatisation, both for themselves and their parent/relative living with HIV. We propose instead that the specific ways that young people's caring responsibilities may impact on their vulnerability (and resilience) are recognised and emphasised under the broader, more inclusive term of 'children living in communities affected by HIV/AIDS' (Richter and Rama, 2006) rather than necessarily labelling children as 'young carers'.

However, these issues need to be balanced with the potential advantages for some children of being identified and labelled as 'young carers', particularly in the UK social policy environment, in terms of their access to legal rights, targeted interventions and opportunities for peer support with others in similar situations. Indeed, specialist and peer support were seen as priorities by both young people and parents. While we recognise the value for some children and young people of being referred to and labelled as 'young carers' (especially in the UK), particularly where children themselves acknowledge and value the label, we are sensitive to the fact that in the context of the global South, the terms 'children living in communities affected by HIV/AIDS' or 'most vulnerable children' may be more helpful in conceptualising these children and young people in policy and interventions aimed at supporting them. These terms may offer greater possibilities for developing more inclusive, widespread and sensitive responses and services for both children with caring responsibilities and other young people affected by HIV/AIDS.

Recognising, valuing and supporting informal caregiving within an ethic of care

Our second point is concerned with gendered constructions of care and the lack of recognition and low status afforded to 'caregivers' (of any age, but particularly to children). While there is considerable recognition of carers of all ages in UK social policy and legislation, including a wide range of services and interventions specifically targeted towards them, there is far less recognition of the roles and contribution of carers in other countries, both in the North and especially in the South. Globally, therefore, there is little specific recognition or value placed on the unpaid contribution of family caregivers, who, as we have shown, are often women and girls, or their place within a 'care economy' (Ogden et al, 2006), even though there are some national estimates of the economic 'costs' associated with this unpaid care work (Access Economics Limited, 2005; Arno, 2006; Buckner and Yeandle, 2007). Additionally, research on adult and young carers in the UK shows consistently that their contribution is often not recognised or identified by health and social welfare professionals, despite carers' legal entitlements and policy guidance on the need for, and how to conduct, carers' assessments. In the global South, particularly Sub-Saharan Africa, expectations of family roles and responsibilities (see Chapter 1) mean that women's and girls' care work is most often constructed as part of the familial intergenerational contract and gendered division of labour within the household and community, rendering 'carers' almost invisible.

Research evidence on both young and adult carers in the UK and on young carers in other high-income countries (Becker, 2007) shows that not all informal carers can cope with the extra demands placed on them and their families with the onset or continuation of illness or disability, including HIV/AIDS. There can be severe consequences for carers' own physical and mental health, well-being, development and social and labour market participation. Timely interventions and services can either prevent caregiving from having to take place or can alleviate pressures on family caregivers. In the UK, a formal assessment of the carer's needs and their ability to continue to provide care is an important gateway to services and support from the state and from other welfare sectors and providers (Becker, 2008). This is not the case in Tanzania or other Sub-Saharan countries, or indeed in many other high-income countries where there is little recognition, policy or services for adult or young carers.

Our research has therefore highlighted the need for greater national *and* global recognition of the particular gendered and age-related roles, responsibilities, contributions and value of informal caregiving, in its diverse forms, among adults and children, whilst acknowledging the interdependence and reciprocity that characterises many caring relationships. While alliances of carers and organisations concerned with adult and young carers have emerged in recent years in high-income countries and at the international level (Becker, 2007), most carers globally are still unrecognised and unsupported. Given that care continues to be constructed as the 'private' responsibility of women and girls at the household level in many countries,

> making this unpaid work (and the unpaid workers) visible is of value to governments and policy makers in order to be able to capture the benefits of these activities, but also to be able to enumerate their costs – so that the unpaid contributions of women to the productive economy can be acknowledged and compensated. (Ogden et al, 2006: 334).

Moreover, '[m]aking the carer visible, and bringing her into the focus of national and international HIV/AIDS policies, will enable these policies to provide a truly holistic continuum of care for those living with HIV and AIDS, their families and communities' (Ogden et al, 2006: 334).

Furthermore, our research highlights the importance of an ethic of care for the development of policies and interventions to support people living with HIV and their families. The ethic of care offers an approach to social justice that recognises the interdependence and interconnectedness of human relations, responsibilities and practices of care. The ethic of care values caring as a daily practice in everyone's lives:

> A democratic ethic of care starts from the idea that everybody needs care and is (in principle at least) capable of care giving, and that a democratic society should enable its members to give both these activities a meaningful place in their lives if they so want. (Sevenhuijsen, 2000: 15)

From an ethic of care perspective, recognition of the interdependence and interconnectedness among people and of the values of care should represent the starting point for the development of social policies and interventions in all sectors and social institutions, including healthcare, education, employment, community development, family practices and social care, among others (Sevenhuijsen, 2000; Barnes, 2006).

Holistic family support

Our third point, which relates closely to the second, is the need for a holistic approach towards supporting caring relationships. Rather than targeting support and interventions solely towards young people with caring responsibilities, our research has revealed the crucial importance of holistic family approaches to support children and parents affected by HIV/AIDS within the context of both the global North and South. The evidence from Tanzania and the UK has highlighted the fact that caring relationships within households are often characterised by reciprocity and interdependence and young people saw their caring responsibilities as 'normal' and part of their everyday responsibilities towards their family. Furthermore, parents with HIV, even those with physical impairments who had to be cared for in bed for months or, in some cases, years, continued to perform their parenting role, providing love, care, support and guidance to their children, which was of paramount importance in protecting young people from the negative impacts of HIV/AIDS on the family. This suggests that there is no fixed distinction between the identities of 'caregiver' and 'care-receiver' and care is embedded in social relations between children, parents, relatives and members of the wider community.

As we discussed in Chapter 1, it is possible to conceptualise young caregiving along a continuum (Becker, 2007), with some young people involved in low levels of caring and others in high levels of caring, with differential outcomes partly dependent on the extent and nature of the caregiving as well as being related to structural and other factors. This caregiving continuum, however, is not static and children's caring roles shift and change over time and vary, as we have shown, in different places. In the context of families living with HIV/AIDS, a more dynamic and fluid understanding of children's positioning on the continuum *over time and space* is required as children's and young people's levels of caring responsibilities change, depending on fluctuations in a parent's health as well as a parent's requirement for assistance and their access to informal and formal safety nets in particular cultural, geographical and welfare contexts that can alleviate children's caring responsibilities. The unpredictable nature of HIV-related chronic illness and parents' changing requirements for assistance over time mean that children's caring responsibilities are likely to be constantly shifting and moving along the continuum from the lower levels to the higher levels and, significantly, towards lower levels of caring during periods of recovery and when more informal or formal support from others is available. The ethic of care perspective also highlights the need for the response of the person receiving care to be recognised as an integral part of the caring process, which Becker's (2007) continuum of young caregiving does not address.

The earliest forms of services and support to young carers in the UK (during the 1990s) focused on supporting children with caring responsibilities with little attention being paid to the ill or disabled parent or any other person requiring care and support. Most young carers projects focused on working with young people to offer them breaks from caring and opportunities to meet with other young people in similar situations, as well as one-to-one therapeutic work (Becker and Becker, 2008). However, as we discussed in Chapter 1, proponents of the social model of disability have argued forcefully against the development of services and support specifically for young carers without reference to the requirements for support of parents (Keith and Morris, 1995; Olsen, 1996; Olsen and Parker, 1997; Newman, 2002a; Wates, 2002). Many of these authors have suggested that the best way to support children who take on caring roles is to improve the services and support offered to ill or disabled parents themselves. Parker, Morris and others have argued that the best way to prevent 'inappropriate' caring by children *and* to support them is for their ill or disabled parents to receive services and support as disabled people and as disabled *parents* (Keith and Morris, 1995; Olsen and Parker, 1997; Wates, 2002).

In recognition of these critiques, researchers and policy makers working from a 'young carers perspective', and government, have increasingly supported a shift to a 'whole family' approach (for example, Becker et al, 1998; Dearden and Becker, 2000; DH, 2000; Frank, 2002; Aldridge and Becker, 2003; Cabinet Office, 2008; Frank and McLarnon, 2008). This 'turn' away from a policy focus solely on young carers *or* ill parents recognises the interdependence between parents, children and external sources of care. In the context of HIV/AIDS, and in recognition of the importance of informal family- and community-based care and support in sustaining many African communities, a whole family approach would require at least two interwoven elements:

1 a recognition and assessment of the (interrelated) needs of the person living with HIV, children and young people with caring responsibilities and other family members;
2 services and interventions planned and directed towards family members living in the immediate household, as well as an engagement with extended family members and the family's wider social networks within the community.

In a UK context, Frank and McLarnon (2008: 50) outline a set of six principles and standards for working with young carers and their families, the second of which is concerned with a whole family approach: 'The key to change is the development of a whole family approach and for all agencies to work together, including children's and adults' services, to offer co-ordinated assessments and services to the child and the whole family'. They suggest that '[a]ssessments should not only identify regular individual personal care needs, but also consider the range of parenting, caring and family tasks that are needed when professional carers are not present and that may result in the child assuming responsibility'; and '[t]he development of cross-agency whole-family assessments should provide an opportunity for service providers to be proactive rather than reactive. It also provides for effective partnership working inter-departmentally, across agencies and helps to bridge the gap between children's and adults' services' (Frank and McLarnon, 2008: 50).

In terms of support services for families living with HIV, these may take many forms depending on the specific context, but should include a focus on supporting both children and young people *and* parents/relatives. Support services should involve a range of agencies within the statutory (government) and third (civil society) sectors, and the private sector where relevant. Children and young people may need support that relates to their position as children, their roles as carers, or both, such as financial and material support to meet basic needs, educational support, opportunities for short breaks, leisure and social activities, emotional and peer support, access to information about HIV/AIDS, opportunities to develop life skills, livelihood strategies and support in making transitions to adulthood. Parents living with HIV/AIDS require practical assistance (financial support, housing, home-based health and social care, domestic help, basic medical supplies, equipment and home adaptations, information and support to access entitlements and services, immigration advice where appropriate), emotional and peer support, and support in their parenting role (flexible childcare and short breaks, family support to help children attend school, financial support and opportunities for children's leisure and social activities, financial support for family breaks and holidays, and so on). Children and parents may also require services that relate to children's caring roles (respite care, young carers projects, support services to prevent or alleviate young caring), or support may be family oriented (family therapy or counselling, family group conferences, family activities, and so on).

Community home-based care

Our fourth point concerns the role of home-based care in supporting families affected by HIV/AIDS. It is clear that as governments in the South have come under intense pressure to restructure both their economies and welfare systems, they have increasingly had to transfer the so-called 'burden', responsibility and cost of caring for those living with HIV/AIDS to individual families and local communities. This is evidenced across Sub-Saharan Africa but also in high-income countries where 'community care' or 'home-based care' has become a policy solution to a 'retreating' state sector or as a consequence of the realignment of health and social care under conservative, liberal *and* third way social policies. Most people with HIV in the North and South are cared for within their own home by family carers, including, as we have shown, children and young people. Supporting carers in these roles promotes their own health and well-being and improves the overall quality of care within the family.

Good-quality and reliable home-based care and emotional support, as part of the infrastructure of primary healthcare and the continuum of care provided by a range of actors, is a critical intervention and service for people living with HIV/AIDS *and* for those caring for them. It is also compatible with an ethic of care approach, which recognises the interdependence of all family members. In the UK, home-based care is increasingly being provided by private agencies, although the voluntary and state sectors continue to play a strong role. Government takes the lead in defining policy in this field and the standards of care that must be reached. However, as we have seen, HIV/AIDS has not been regarded as a key priority over recent years in the UK, and several families we interviewed had very unsatisfactory and difficult experiences of accessing statutory services and qualifying for support.

Good-quality home-based care can support and enable people to live positively with HIV, address the material and emotional needs of household members and help to reduce the pressures on family carers, mostly women and girls. It is a policy that may help to address the gender and health inequalities dominant in poorer households in both the global South and North. Home-based care needs to be delivered as part of a 'continuum of care' aimed at supporting people living with HIV/AIDS *and* those who care for them. This requires an infrastructure of services, interventions and support networks that are also capable of recognising and responding to the diverse and interrelated needs of family members. Specific services for children with caring responsibilities exist in the UK, where it has been suggested that the policy response to young carers can be termed 'advanced' (Becker, 2007). However, in most high-income countries and in Sub-Saharan Africa the identification and response to children with caring responsibilities is far less developed. While we have already discussed the contested issue of 'labels', it seems clear that globally there is a need for greater identification and specific support of children and young people with caring responsibilities within and alongside community home-based care.

Engaging and joining up multisectoral responses

The fifth point we wish to make concerns the need for a greater engagement with children and families affected by HIV/AIDS and a 'joined up' policy response from state, voluntary, private and informal service providers, requiring the closer integration of their efforts and services. This 'mixed economy of welfare' (see Powell, 2007), provides considerable opportunities to provide a 'continuum of care' (Ogden et al, 2006) for families affected by HIV/AIDS and to satisfy the conditions for the 'Care Continuum' model advocated by the WHO (2002). This model places the person with HIV/AIDS at the centre of a range of actors and services, including primary and secondary healthcare provisions, community care, home care and tertiary care. In the UK there are long-established responsibilities of the state in all of these fields, and a flourishing 'market' in private (for profit) providers as well as a highly developed third (voluntary) sector. However, despite this 'mixed economy' we have shown how, for many of the UK families affected by HIV in our study, there is little support available to them, not least because of punitive immigration controls and policies which restrict access to state provisions, and the stigma associated with HIV. In Tanzania, and Sub-Saharan Africa generally, structural adjustment programmes and the interventions of the International Monetary Fund and World Bank, among others, have forced reductions in public expenditure and state provision in health, social welfare, education and social security protection; have reduced the redistributive mechanisms and regulatory powers of states to ensure access to basic services and to protect citizens and communities; and have introduced greater 'privatisation' of health and community care services. In low-income countries across Sub-Saharan Africa most primary and home-based healthcare is provided by NGOs, community groups and private organisations. Effectively, this has meant that families affected by HIV/AIDS, particularly the poorest households, must rely on themselves, their communities and NGOs for assistance, all of which are overstretched and unable to cope with the growing demands for care.

This has resulted in the grave injustice that those who require the most help in both high- and low-income countries are those least likely to be able to afford or access any support other than that which can be provided from within families or communities themselves, or from overstretched NGOs with limited means. A key challenge is how government, NGO, community and private interventions and support should be coordinated and more effectively integrated in order to link more closely with the stated needs of families, particularly children with caring responsibilities and other marginalised children in communities affected by HIV/AIDS. In addition, attention needs to be paid to the ways that the efforts of different sectors, including independent (private) providers and the 'informal' community care sector, can be supported to address national health and other priorities commensurate with social justice and other progressive principles, including reducing health and gender inequalities in the context of HIV/AIDS. Governments need to take the lead in helping to coordinate and integrate, where possible, the diverse sectors working in this field to produce high-quality care and support that results in positive outcomes for families and carers, and to reduce gender and health inequalities exacerbated by poverty. There is also a need for more resources to be directed towards NGOs, community- and faith-based organisations working in the HIV/AIDS sector in the North and South to provide more sustainable responses.

Universal or targeted services?

Our sixth point concerns the balance between targeted and universal services. Our discussions earlier about the need to avoid labelling young people and focusing solely on targeted interventions for young carers point to the crucial role of formal safety nets and universal or mainstream services in meeting the needs of families affected by HIV/AIDS. Our research highlights the need to increase the capacity of universal or mainstream services to provide culturally appropriate support for children, young people and parents affected by HIV/AIDS that is sensitive to stigma and the need for confidentiality. Service providers in the UK and Tanzania suggested that professionals in mainstream services have limited understanding and expertise in supporting families with HIV-related issues. They also revealed the need for greater engagement between mainstream providers and welfare institutions and specialist HIV organisations and community groups that are currently supporting these families. This would help to improve the accessibility and cultural appropriateness of universal services, building the capacity of professionals to deal with the complexity of issues surrounding HIV within the family, in addition to young caregiving.

Cree et al (2004) identify two significant implications of the stigma of parental HIV for mainstream social work professionals. First, in many cases, social workers will not know that a family member is living with HIV. The authors note, 'The onus is therefore on practitioners to seek to work in an open and non-judgemental way with children and families so that they feel able to trust us with such a difficult family secret' (Cree et al, 2004: 16). The second implication is that: '[o]nce the secret has been shared, we must work with the child and family to ascertain who needs to know about parental HIV and what supports should be put in place for individual family members' (Cree et al, 2004: 16). However, 'practitioners should not automatically assume that everyone in a child's network needs to know about parental HIV. It is essential to remember that HIV is the parent's illness, suggesting that it should be their decision to share what is confidential, medical information with others' (Cree et al, 2004: 16).

Our research suggests, however, that because of the specific nature of HIV-related stigma, there is still a need for specialised support for parents *and* children caring for them to be provided by family-focused HIV organisations, young carers services (in the UK) and community organisations, especially when supporting families on particular issues such as disclosure and caring relationships. Specialist services for young people affected by HIV were highly valued by the young people interviewed in the UK and Tanzania for providing opportunities for social activities and emotional and peer support with others in similar situations. While targeted approaches may create safe spaces for children from marginalised groups to develop peer support and a positive sense of identity, open access or universal approaches can potentially encourage greater interaction between marginalised groups and the wider community and challenge discriminatory attitudes (Evans et al, 2006). Thus, young people may wish to access targeted support (either for young people affected by HIV or for young people with caring responsibilities) initially, but when they have developed a positive sense of identity and feel supported in their caring roles, they may move on to more universal services over time (Evans et al, 2006).

Most of the young people we interviewed in the UK regularly attended at least one specialist youth group targeted towards young people affected by HIV or African young people (and in addition, in two instances, young carers groups). However, the majority of these projects were concentrated in London and specialist support was unevenly developed outside the capital. Furthermore, as we have discussed earlier, there was considerable apprehension among parents and service providers about the accessibility of young carers projects for young people caring for parents with HIV, because of concerns about stigma, confidentiality and cultural appropriateness of services, particularly for African refugee families. This suggests that, where specialist family-focused HIV services do not exist, there is a need for more inclusive young carers projects and other mainstream services that are sensitive to the culturally diverse support needs of young people and parents living with HIV.

Although specialist youth-focused support for young people affected by HIV was not widely available in Tanzania, the few young people interviewed who had been able to attend memory clubs or other therapeutic opportunities (see Chapter 8) highly valued the opportunity to learn more about HIV/AIDS, develop life skills and share their feelings with other young people in similar situations. Child- and youth-focused activities that provide opportunities for emotional and peer support, access to information about HIV/AIDS and the development of life skills and livelihood strategies thus appear to provide considerable scope to address some of the support needs identified by young people caring for a parent/relative with HIV at the community level in Sub-Saharan Africa.

Furthermore, research has shown that many targeted initiatives and preventative programmes designed to promote resilience and prevent the risk of social exclusion for children and families (largely based in the global North) have tended to focus on outcomes for individual children rather than on outcomes for families and communities (Peters et al, 2003; France and Crow, 2005; National Evaluation of Sure Start, 2005; Evans et al, 2006; Evans and Pinnock, 2007). While approaches focusing on individual children may be important in developing their resilience to deal with adversity in the short term, such approaches have limited potential to address the complex interplay of structural and attitudinal dimensions of poverty, social exclusion and marginalisation facing families and communities affected by HIV/AIDS in the global

North and South. In addition to providing opportunities for specialist support for young people with caring responsibilities, policies and interventions designed to promote the resilience of children *and* families need to provide financial, material, practical and emotional support for parents with HIV, engage with children's family networks, as well as facilitate the collaboration of specialist HIV organisations, community groups, schools, social welfare institutions and other mainstream agencies to develop more supportive social environments and service systems. This will help to reduce HIV stigma and address some of the wider structural and relational dimensions of social exclusion and marginalisation experienced by children and families affected by HIV/AIDS, and thereby help to alleviate children's caring roles.

Conclusion

The experiences of service providers, young people and parents have raised a number of important debates and challenges for developing and delivering services for this hidden group of young carers and their families, including concerns about stigma and labelling children as 'young carers'; whether approaches should aim to prevent children being drawn into caring roles or respond to children's support needs once they have become carers; whether specialist HIV or mainstream services are most appropriate to meet the needs of young people with caring responsibilities and their families; the need for greater global recognition of the role of carers within an ethic of care; the need for a shift to a whole family approach; the centrality of home-based care within a continuum of care; the importance of 'joining up' services and support from diverse sectors; and the need for governments to take a lead in driving these agendas forward. Service providers, children and parents also identified a number of limitations and barriers to the development of services for young carers, which included: limited access to governmental/statutory support; limited capacity of NGOs to meet the needs of families affected by HIV/AIDS; limited knowledge and expertise among professionals; and, in Tanzania, concerns about corruption and diversion of aid from the most vulnerable families.

Using evidence from the UK and Tanzania, our research has highlighted the experience of HIV/AIDS from multiple perspectives (parents, young people, service providers), in very different economic, political, social and cultural contexts. It has revealed the stigma and discrimination that confronts parents and children in both the global North and South; the fluctuating nature of HIV-related illness; the reciprocal and interdependent nature of caring relationships; the diversity and fluidity of household structures, particularly in Sub-Saharan Africa; the changing nature of children's and young people's caring responsibilities over time and place; the limitations of existing services and strategies for supporting families and children living with HIV/AIDS; and the challenges for future local and global responses. Policies, services and interventions that take as their starting point the recognition of diverse and changing gendered and age-related caring roles and responsibilities within poor households affected by HIV/AIDS, and that offer children, parents, relatives and communities support in these roles, will help to promote the welfare, well-being, resilience and caring capacity of families and communities in both the global North and South.

Notes

[1] Ten-cell leaders are village elders responsible for ten households at the local political level in Tanzania.

Bibliography

ABS (Australian Bureau of Statistics) (2003) *Disability, Ageing and Carers, Australia: Caring in the Community*, Canberra: ABS.

Access Economics Limited, for Carers Australia (2005) *The Economic Value of Informal Care*, Deakin ACT: Carers Australia.

Action for Young Carers (2005) *Young Carers: The Next Step Forward*, The Carers Federation (unpublished).

Afshar, H. and Barrientos, S. (1999) 'Introduction: women, globalization and fragmentation', in *Women, Globalization and Fragmentation in the Developing World*, London: Macmillan Press, pp 1-17.

Ainsworth, M. and Filmer, D. (2002) 'Poverty, AIDS and children's schooling: a targeting dilemma', *World Bank Policy Research Working Paper 2885*, Operations Evaluation Department and Development Research Group, World Bank (www.worldbank.org).

Akeroyd, A. (2004) 'Coercion, constraints and "cultural entrapments": a further look at gendered and occupational factors pertinent to the transmission of HIV in Africa', in E. Kalipeni, S. Craddock, J. Oppong and J. Ghosh (eds) *HIV and AIDS in Africa: Beyond Epidemiology*, Oxford: Blackwell Publishing, pp 89-103.

Alderson, P. (2000) 'Children as researchers – the effects of participation rights on research methodology', in P. Christensen and A. James, *Research with Children: Perspectives and Practices*, London: Falmer Press, pp 241-57.

Aldridge, J. and Becker, S. (1993) *Children Who Care: Inside the World of Young Carers*, Loughborough: Young Carers Research Group.

Aldridge, J. and Becker, S. (1994) *My Child, My Carer: The Parents' Perspective*, Loughborough: Young Carers Research Group.

Aldridge, J. and Becker, S. (1999) 'Children as carers: the impact of parental illness and disability on children's caring roles', *Journal of Family Therapy*, vol 21, no 3, pp 303-20.

Aldridge, J. and Becker, S. (2003) *Children Caring for Parents with Mental Illness: Perspectives of Young Carers, Parents and Professionals*, Bristol: The Policy Press.

Alldred, P. (1998) 'Dilemmas in representing the voices of children: ethnography and discourse analysis', in J. Ribbens and R. Edwards (eds) *Feminist Dilemmas in Qualitative Research: Public Knowledge, Private Lives*, London: Sage Publications, pp 147-70.

Alsop, R., Fitzsimons, A. and Lennon, K. (2002) *Theorizing Gender*, Cambridge: Polity Press.

Anderson, J. and Doyal, L. (2004) 'Women from Africa living with HIV in London: a descriptive study', *AIDS Care*, vol 16, no 1, pp 95-105.

Ansell, N. (2005) *Children, Youth and Development*, Abingdon: Routledge.

Ansell, N. and Van Blerk, L. (2004) 'Children's migration as a household/ family strategy: coping with AIDS in southern Africa', *Journal of Southern African Studies*, vol 30, no 3, pp 673-90.

Arno, P. (2006) 'The economic value of informal caregiving', paper presented at the Veterans Association Conference on Care Coordination, Bethesda, MD, 25 January.

Arno, P., Levine, C. and Memmott, M. (1999) 'The economic value of informal caregiving', *Health Affairs*, vol 8, no 2, pp 182-88.

Atkin, K. and Rollings, J. (1992) 'Informal care in Asian and Afro/ Caribbean communities: a literature review', *British Journal of Social Work*, vol 22, no 4, pp 405-18.

Barnardo's (2007) *Flintshire Young Adult Carers Research Project 2006–7* (unpublished).

Barnes, C. (1991) *Disabled People in Britain and Discrimination*, London: Hurst and Company.

Barnes, C. and Mercer, G. (1996) *Exploring the Divide: Illness and Disability*, Leeds: The Disability Press.

Barnes, M. (2006) *Caring and Social Justice*, Basingstoke: Palgrave Macmillan.

Barnett, T. (1998) 'The epidemic in rural communities: the relevance of the African experience for India', in P. Godwin (ed) *The Looming Epidemic: The Impact of HIV and AIDS in India*, London: Hurst and Company, pp 150-70.

Barnett T. and Blaikie, P. (1992) *AIDS in Africa: Its Present and Future Impact*, London: Belhaven.

Barnett, T., Whiteside, A. and Desmond, C. (2001) 'The social and economic impact of HIV/AIDS in poor countries: a review of studies and lessons', *Progress in Development Studies*, vol 1, no 2, pp 151-70.

Barry, S., Lloyd-Owen, S, Madge, S., Cozzi-Lepri, A., Evans, A., Phillips, A. and Johnson, M. (2002) 'The changing demographics of new HIV diagnoses at a London centre from 1994-2000', *HIV Medicine*, vol 3, no 2, pp 129-34.

Bass, L. (2004) *Child Labor in Sub-Saharan Africa*, Boulder, CO: Lynne Rienner Publishers.

Bauman, L. with Germann, S. (2005) 'Psychosocial impacts of the HIV/ AIDS epidemic on children and youth', in G. Foster, C. Levine and J. Williamson (eds) *A Generation at Risk: The Global Impact of HIV/AIDS on Orphans and Vulnerable Children*, Cambridge: Cambridge University Press, pp 93–133.

Bauman, L., Foster, G., Johnson Silver, E., Gamble, I. and Muchaneta, L. (2006) 'Children caring for their ill parents with HIV/AIDS', *Vulnerable Children and Youth Studies*, vol 1, no 1, pp 1–14.

Bauman, L., Johnson Silver, E., Berman, R. and Gamble, I. (2009) 'Children as caregivers to their ill parents with AIDS', in K. Shifren (ed) *How Caregiving Affects Development: Psychological Implications for Child, Adolescent and Adult Caregivers*, Washington, DC: American Psychological Association, pp 37–63.

Baylies, C. (2000) 'Perspectives on gender and AIDS in Africa', in C. Baylies, and J. Bujra (eds) *AIDS, Sexuality and Gender in Africa: Collective Strategies and Struggles in Tanzania and Zambia*, London: Routledge, pp 1–24.

Baylies, C. (2002) 'The impact of AIDS on rural households in Africa: a shock like any other?', *Development and Change*, vol 33, no 4, pp 611–32.

Beals, K., Wight, G., Aneshensel, S., Murphy, D. and Miller-Martinez, D. (2006) 'The role of family caregivers in HIV medication adherence', *AIDS Care*, vol 18, no 6, pp 589–96.

Becker, F. and Becker, S. (2008) *Young Adult Carers in the UK: Experiences, Needs and Services for Carers aged 16-24*, London: Princess Royal Trust for Carers.

Becker, S. (2000a) 'Young carers', in M. Davies (ed) *The Blackwell Encyclopedia of Social Work*, Oxford: Blackwell, p 378.

Becker, S. (2000b) 'Carers and indicators of vulnerability to social exclusion', *Benefits*, vol 28, April/May, pp 1–4.

Becker, S. (2005) 'Children's hidden care work within the family: a labour of love or a matter of necessity?', paper presented at 'Cash and Care: Understanding the Evidence Base for Policy and Practice' – A Conference in Memory of Sally Baldwin, University of York, 12 April.

Becker, S. (2007) 'Global perspectives on children's unpaid caregiving in the family: research and policy on "young carers" in the UK, Australia, the USA and Sub-Saharan Africa', *Global Social Policy*, vol 7, no 1, pp 23–50.

Becker, S. (2008) 'Informal family carers', in K. Wilson, G. Ruch, M. Lymbery and A. Cooper (eds) *Social Work: An Introduction to Contemporary Practice*, London: Pearson Longman, pp 431–60.

Becker, S. and Bryman, A. (eds) (2004) *Understanding Research for Social Policy and Practice: Themes, Methods and Approaches*, Bristol: The Policy Press.

Becker, S. and Silburn, R. (1999) *We're in This Together: Conversations with Families in Caring Relationships*, London: Carers National Association.

Becker, S., Aldridge, J. and Dearden, C. (1998) *Young Carers and Their Families*, Oxford: Blackwell Science.

Becker, S., Dearden, C. and Aldridge, J. (2001) 'Children's labour of love? Young carers and care work', in P. Mizen, C. Pole and A. Bolton (eds) *Hidden Hands: International Perspectives on Children's Work and Labour*, Abingdon: Routledge Falmer, pp 70-87.

Bendera, S. (1999) 'Promoting education for girls in Tanzania', in C. Heward and S. Bunwaree (eds) *Gender, Education and Development: Beyond Access to Empowerment*, London: Zed Books, pp 117-32.

Beneria, L. and Feldman, S. (eds) (1992) *Unequal Burden: Economic Crises, Persistent Poverty and Women's Work*, Colorado and Oxford: Westview Press.

Bharat, S. and Aggleton, P. (1999) 'Facing the challenge: household responses to AIDS in India', *AIDS Care*, vol 11, no 1, pp 31-44.

Bicego, G., Rutstein, S. and Johnson, K. (2003) 'Dimensions of the emerging orphan crisis in sub-Saharan Africa', *Social Science and Medicine*, vol 56, no 6, pp 1235-47.

Bilsborrow, S. (1992) *'You Grow up Fast as Well...' Young Carers on Merseyside*, Liverpool: Carers National Association, Personal Services Society and Barnardo's.

Blackford, K. (1999) 'A child growing up with a parent who has multiple sclerosis: theories and experiences', *Disability and Society*, vol 14, no 5, pp 673-85.

Bloch, A. and Schuster, L. (2005) 'At the extremes of exclusion: deportation, detention and dispersal', *Ethnic and Racial Studies*, vol 28, no 3, pp 491-512.

Bor, R., Miller, R. and Goldman, E. (1993) 'HIV/AIDS and the family: a review of research in the first decade', *Journal of Family Therapy*, vol 15, no 2, pp 187-204.

Borjas, G. J. and Crisp, J. (2005) *Poverty, International Migration and Asylum*, Basingstoke: Palgrave Macmillan,

Bowlby, S., Gregory, S. and McKie, L. (1997) '"Doing home": patriarchy, caring and space', *Women's Studies International Forum*, vol 20, no 3, pp 342-50.

Boyden, J. (1997) 'Childhood and the policy makers: a comparative perspective on the globalization of childhood', in A. James and A. Prout (eds), *Constructing and Reconstructing Childhood*, London: Falmer Press, pp 190–229.

Bradley, C. (1993) 'Women's power, children's labor', *Cross-Cultural Research*, vol 27, no 1–2, pp 70–96.

Bradshaw, J., Middleton, S., Davis, A., Oldfield, N., Smith, N., Cusworth, L. and Williams, J. (2008) *A Minimum Income Standard for Britain: What People Think*, York: Joseph Rowntree Foundation.

Bray, R. (2003) 'Predicting the social consequences of orphanhood in South Africa', Centre for Social Science Research Working Paper No. 29, Capetown: University of Cape Town (available at www.uct. ac.za/depts/cssr/pubs.html).

Brown, M. and Stetz, K. (1999) 'The labor of caregiving: a theoretical model of caregiving during potentially fatal illness', *Qualitative Health Research*, vol 9, no 2, pp 182–97.

Brydon, L. and Chant, S. (1989) *Women in the Third World: Gender Issues in Rural and Urban Areas*, Aldershot: Edward Elgar Publishing.

Buckner, L. and Yeandle, S. (2007) *Valuing Carers – Calculating the Value of Unpaid Care*, London: Carers UK.

Butler, J. (1990) *Gender Trouble: Feminism and the Subversion of Identity*, New York and London: Routledge.

Butler, J. (1993) 'Imitation and gender insubordination', in *Lesbian and Gay Studies Reader*, London: Routledge, pp 307–20.

Cabinet Office (2008) *Think Family: Improving the Life Chances of Families at Risk*, London: Cabinet Office.

Campbell, C., Nair, Y., Maimane, S. and Sibiya, Z. (2008) 'Supporting people with AIDS and their carers in rural South Africa: possibilities and challenges', *Health and Place*, vol 14, no 3, pp 507–18.

Cancian, F. and Oliker, S. (2000) *Gender and Caring*, Walnut Creek, Canada: AltaMira Press.

Carers Australia (2001) *Young Carers Research Project: Background Papers*, Canberra: Commonwealth Department of Family and Community Services.

Carers UK (2007) *Real Change, Not Short Change: Time to Deliver for Carers*, London: Carers UK.

Castles, S. and Miller, M. (2003) *The Age of Migration: International Population Movements in the Modern World* (3rd edn), Basingstoke: Palgrave Macmillan.

Chambers, R. (1998) 'Foreword', in J. Holland with J. Blackburn (eds), *Whose Voice? Participatory Research and Policy Change*, London: Intermediate Technology Publications.

Chapman, E. (2000) 'Conceptualisation of the body for people living with HIV: issues of touch and contamination', *Sociology of Health and Illness*, vol 22, no 6, pp 840-57.

Child Protection Society (2004) *How Can we Help? Approaches to Community Based Care: A Guide for Groups and Organisations Wishing to Assist Orphans and Other Children in Distress*, Harare, Zimbabwe: Zimbabwe Child Protection Publication.

Chimwaza, A. and Watkins, S. (2004) 'Giving care to people with symptoms of AIDS in rural sub-Saharan Africa', *AIDS Care*, vol 16, no 7, pp 795-807.

Chinouya, M. (2006) 'Telling children about HIV in transnational African families: tensions about rights', *Diversity in Health and Social Care*, vol 3, no 1, pp 7-17.

Chinouya-Mudari, M. and O'Brien, M. (1999) 'African refugee children and HIV/AIDS in London', in P Aggleton, G. Hart and P. Davies (eds) *Families and Communities Responding to AIDS*, London and New York: Routledge, pp 21-33.

Chipfakacha, V. (2006) *The Belgian Government Supported Home-based Care Project in Tanzania – Report of the Evaluation Mission*, Dar es Salaam: UNAIDS.

Christensen, P. and James, A. (2000) *Research with Children: Perspectives and Practices*, London: Falmer Press.

Christiansen, C., Utas, M. and Vigh, H. (2006) *Navigating Youth, Generating Adulthood: Social Becoming in an African Context*, Uppsala, Sweden: The Nordic Africa Institute.

Ciambrone, D. (2001) 'Illness and other assaults on self: the relative impact of HIV/AIDS on women's lives', *Sociology of Health and Illness*, vol 23, no 4, pp 517-40.

Cluver, L. and Operario, D. (2008) 'Young carers for AIDS-unwell parents: mental health, physical health and education outcomes', Centre for Evidence-based Intervention, Department of Social Policy and Social Work, Oxford University (unpublished research information sheet).

Cluver, L., Gardner, F. and Operario, D. (2007) 'Psychological distress among AIDS-orphaned children in urban South Africa', *Journal of Child Psychology and Psychiatry*, vol 48, no 8, pp 755-63.

Conway, M. (2006a) *Developing Support Services for Children, Young People and Families Living with HIV: A Handbook for Service Providers*, London: National Children's Bureau.

Conway, M. (2006b) *Children, HIV, Asylum and Immigration: An Overview of the Current Situation for Children Living with HIV and Insecure Immigration Status*, London: National Children's Bureau.

Cooke, B. and Kothari, U. (2001) 'The case for participation as tyranny', in B. Cooke and U. Kothari (eds) *Participation: the new tyranny?*, London: Zed Books, pp 1-15.

Coombes, R. (1997) 'On the shoulders of children', *Nursing Times*, vol 97, no 28, pp 10-11.

Crabtree, H. and Warner, L. (1999) *Too Much To Take On: A Report on Young Carers and Bullying*, London: The Princess Royal Trust for Carers.

Crawley, H. and Lester, T. (2005) *No Place for a Child. Children in UK Immigration Detention: Impacts, Alternatives and Safeguards*, London: Save the Children (www.savethechildren.org.uk).

Cree, V., Kay, H. and Tisdall, K. (2002) 'Research with children: sharing the dilemmas', *Child and Family Social Work*, vol 7, no 1, pp 47-56.

Cree, V., Kay, H., Tisdall, K. and Wallace, J. (2004) 'Stigma and parental HIV', *Qualitative Social Work*, vol 3, no 1, pp 3-21.

Cree V., Kay, H., Tisdall, K. and Wallace, J. (2006) 'Listening to children and young people affected by parental HIV: findings from a Scottish study', *AIDS Care*, vol 18, no 1, pp 73-6.

Creighton, C. and Omari, C. (eds) (1995) *Gender, Family and Household in Tanzania*, Aldershot: Avebury.

Dearden, C. and Becker, S. (1995) *Young Carers: The Facts*, Sutton: Reed Business Publishing.

Dearden, C. and Becker, S. (1998) *Young Carers in the United Kingdom: A Profile*, London: Carers National Association.

Dearden, C. and Becker, S. (2000) *Growing Up Caring: Vulnerability and Transition to Adulthood – Young Carers' Experiences*, Leicester: Youth Work Press for the Joseph Rowntree Foundation.

Dearden, C. and Becker, S. (2004) *Young Carers in the UK: The 2004 Report*, London: Carers UK.

De Vogli, R. and Birbeck, G. (2005) 'Potential impact of adjustment policies on vulnerability of women and children to HIV/AIDS in Sub-Saharan Africa', *Journal of Health, Population and Nutrition*, vol 23, no 2, pp 105-20.

Del Amo, J., Petruckevitch, A., Phillips, A., Johnson, A., Stephenson, J., Desmond, N., Handsheid, T., Low, N., Newell, A., Obasi, A., Paine, K, Pym, A., Theodore, C. and De Cock, K (1998) 'Disease progression and survival in HIV infected Africans in London', *AIDS*, vol 12, no 10, pp 1203-9.

DH (Department of Health) (1996) *Carers (Recognition and Services) Act 1995: Policy Guidance and Practice Guide* (LAC (96) 7), London: DH.

DH (2000) *A Jigsaw of Services: Inspection of Services to Support Disabled Adults in their Parenting Role. Key Messages for Practitioners and First-line Managers,* London: DH.

DH (2001) *A Practitioner's Guide to Carers' Assessments under the Carers and Disabled Children Act 2000,* London: DH.

DH (2005) 'Caring about Carers: government information for carers', available online at www.carers.gov.uk/ (accessed 14 November 2005).

Dhemba, J., Gumbo, P. and Nyamusara, J. (2002) 'Social security in Zimbabwe', *Journal of Social Development in Africa,* vol 17, no 2, pp 111-56.

Disability Rights Commission (2005) *A Guide to the Disability Discrimination Act for People with HIV, Cancer and MS,* December 2005, DRC (www.drc-gb.org).

Donahue, J. (2005) 'Strengthening households and communities: the key to reducing the economic impacts of HIV/AIDS on children and families', in G. Foster, C. Levine and J. Williamson (eds) *A Generation at Risk: The Global Impact of HIV/AIDS on Orphans and Vulnerable Children,* New York: Cambridge University Press, pp 37-65.

Doyal, L. and Anderson, J. (2005) '"My fear is to fall in love again ….": how HIV-positive African women survive in London', *Social Science and Medicine,* vol 60, no 8, pp 1729-38.

Doyal, L., Anderson, J. and Apenteng, P. (2005) *'I want to survive, I want to win, I want tomorrow': An exploratory study of African men living with HIV in London,* London: Homerton University Hospital and Terrence Higgins Trust.

Dwyer, D. and Bruce, J. (eds) (1988) *A Home Divided: Women and Income in the Third World,* Palo Alto, California: Stanford University Press.

Dyck, I. (1995) 'Hidden geographies: the changing lifeworlds of women with multiple sclerosis', *Social Science and Medicine,* vol 40, no 3, pp 307-20.

Edwards, M. (1996) 'New approaches to children and development: introduction and overview', *Journal of International Development,* vol 8, no 6, pp 813-27.

Elliott, A. (1992) *Hidden Children: A Study of Ex-Young Carers of Parents with Mental Health Problems in Leeds,* Leeds: City Council Mental Health Development Section.

Ellis, C., Kiesinger, C. and Tillman-Healy, L. (1997) 'Interactive interviewing: talking about emotional experience', in R. Hertz (ed), *Reflexivity and Voice,* London: Sage Publications, pp 119-49.

Ely, A. (2006) *Children and Young People Living with HIV/AIDS,* Highlight No 228, London: National Children's Bureau.

Erwin, J. and Peters, B. (1999) 'Treatment issues for HIV – Africans in London', *Social Science and Medicine*, vol 49, no 11, pp 1519-28.

Evans, C. and Evans, R. (2004) 'What users have to say about their own organisations: a local user-controlled study', *Journal of Integrated Care*, vol 12, no 3, pp 38-46.

Evans, R. (2002) 'Poverty, HIV and barriers to education: street children's experiences in Tanzania', *Gender and Development*, vol 10, no 3, pp 51-62.

Evans, R. (2004) 'Tanzanian childhoods: street children's narratives of "home"', *Journal of Contemporary African Studies*, vol 22, no 1, pp 69-92.

Evans, R. (2005) 'Social networks, migration and care in Tanzania: caregivers' and children's resilience to coping with HIV/AIDS', *Children and Poverty*, vol 11, no 2, pp 111-29.

Evans, R. (2006) 'Negotiating social identities: the influence of gender, age and ethnicity on young people's "street careers" in Tanzania', *Children's Geographies*, vol 4, no 1, pp 109-28.

Evans, R. and Becker, S. (2007) *Hidden Young Carers: The Experiences, Needs and Resilience of Children Caring for Parents and Relatives with HIV/AIDS in Tanzania and the UK: Stakeholder Report*, Nottingham: School of Sociology and Social Policy, University of Nottingham.

Evans, R. and Pinnock, K. (2007) 'Promoting resilience and protective factors in the Children's Fund: supporting children and young people's pathways towards social inclusion?', *Journal of Children and Poverty*, vol 13, no 1, pp 21-36.

Evans, R. and Spicer, N. (2008) 'Is participation prevention? A blurring of discourses in children's preventative initiatives in the UK', *Childhood*, vol 15, no 1, pp 50-73.

Evans, R., Pinnock, K., Beirens, H. and Edwards, A. (2006) *Developing Preventative Practices: The Experiences of Children, Young People and Their Families in the Children's Fund*, London: Department for Education and Skills.

Fielding, N. (1993) 'Ethnography', in N. Gilbert (ed) *Researching Social Life*, London: Sage, pp 154-71.

Foster, G. (2004) 'Safety nets for children affected by HIV/AIDS in Southern Africa', in R. Pharoah (ed) *A Generation at Risk? HIV/AIDS, Vulnerable Children and Security in Southern Africa* (monograph 109), Pretoria, Cape Town: Institute of Security Studies, pp 65-92.

Foster, G. (2006) 'Children who live in communities affected by AIDS', *The Lancet*, vol 367, no 9511, pp 700-1.

Foster, G. and Williamson, J. (2000) 'A review of current literature of the impact of HIV/AIDS on children in sub-Saharan Africa', *AIDS*, vol 14, no 3, pp S275-S284.

Foster, G., Levine, C. and Williamson, J. (eds) (2005) *A Generation At Risk: The Global Impact of HIV/AIDS on Orphans and Vulnerable Children*, New York: Cambridge University Press.

Foster, G., Makufa, C., Drew, R. and Kralovec, E. (1997) 'Factors leading to the establishment of child-headed households: the case of Zimbabwe', *Health Transition Review*, Supplement 2, no 7, pp 155-68.

Fox, A., Becker, F. and Becker, S. (2007) 'Does every young carer matter? What does Every Child Matters mean for young carers?', *Childright*, vol 235, pp 16-19.

France, A. and Crow, I. (2005) 'Using the "Risk Factor Paradigm" in prevention: lessons from the evaluation of Communities That Care', *Children and Society*, vol 19, no 2, pp 172-84.

Frank, J. (2002) *Making It Work: Good Practice with Young Cares and Their Families*, London: The Children's Society and The Princess Royal Trust for Carers.

Frank, J. and McLarnon, J. (2008) *Young Carers, Parents and their Families: Key Principles of Practice*, London: The Children's Society.

Frank, J., Tatum, C. and Tucker, S. (1999) *On Small Shoulders: Learning from the Experiences of Former Young Carers*, London: The Children's Society.

Fulton, R. and Gottesman, D.J. (1980) 'Anticipatory grief: a psychosocial concept reconsidered', *British Journal of Psychiatry*, vol 137, pp 45-54.

Gates, M. and Lackey, N. (1998) 'Youngsters caring for adults with cancer', *Image: Journal of Nursing Scholarship*, vol 30, no 1, pp 11-15.

Gays, M. (2000) 'Getting it right for young carers in the ACT', paper delivered at the 7th Australian Institute of Family Studies Conference, 'Family futures: issues in research and policy', Sydney, 23-26 July.

Gershuny, J. (2000) *Changing Times: Work and Leisure in Post-Industrial Society*, Oxford: Oxford University Press.

Gilligan, R. (1999) 'Working with social networks: key resources in helping children at risk', in M. Hill (ed) *Effective Ways of Working with Children and their Families*, London: Jessica Kingsley, pp 70-91.

Gilligan, R. (2000) 'Adversity, resilience and young people: the protective value of positive school and spare time experiences', *Children and Society*, vol 14, no 1, pp 37-47.

Gilligan, R. (2004) 'Promoting resilience in child and family social work: issues for social work practice, education and policy', *Social Work Education*, vol 23, no 1, pp 93-104.

Glauser, B. (1997) 'Street children: deconstructing a construct', in A. James and A. Prout (eds) *Constructing and Reconstructing Childhood*, London: Falmer Press, pp 145-64.

Godwin, P. (1998) 'Another social development crisis?', in P. Godwin (ed) *The Looming Epidemic: The Impact of HIV and AIDS in India*, London: Hurst and Company, pp 1-9.

Goffman, E. (1963) *Stigma: Notes on the Management of Spoiled Identity*, London: Penguin Books.

Gould, W.T. S. and Huber, U. (2003) *Estimating School Enrolment Demand in HIV/AIDS Affected Populations*, Summary Research Report, DFID Research Project ED2000/38, Liverpool: The University of Liverpool, Department of Geography.

Graham, H. (1983) 'Caring: a labour of love', in J. Finch and D. Groves (eds) *A Labour of Love: Women, Work and Caring*, London: Routledge and Kegan Paul, pp 13-30.

Grainger, C., Webb, D. and Elliott, L. (2001) *Children affected by HIV/AIDS: Rights and Responses in the Developing World*, London: Save the Children.

Green, G. and Smith, R. (2004) 'The psychosocial and health care needs of HIV-positive people in the United Kingdom: a review', *HIV Medicine*, vol 5, supplement 1, pp 5-46.

Guest, E. (2001) *Children of AIDS: Africa's Orphan Crisis*, London: Pluto Press.

Hall, E. (2000) '"Blood, brain and bones": taking the body seriously in the geography of health and impairment', *Area*, vol 32, no 1, pp 21-9.

Hargreaves, J. and Boler, T. (2006) *Girl Power: The Impact of Girls' Education on HIV and Sexual Behaviour*, Johannesburg: ActionAid International.

Harrison, K. and O'Rooke, D. (2003) *'I Grew Out Of The Service But Not The Support': A Report Into The Needs Of Young Adult Carers* (unpublished).

Healthlink Worldwide (2006) *Building Children's Resilience in a Supportive Environment: Reflecting on Opportunities for Memory Work in HIV Responses*, Policy Brief, London: Healthlink Worldwide.

Healthlink Worldwide (2007) *Changing Children's Lives: Experiences from Memory Work in Africa*, London: Healthlink Worldwide.

Held, D. and McGrew, A. (2003) *The Global Transformations Reader: an Introduction to the Globalization Debate* (2nd edn), Cambridge: Polity Press.

Hertz, R. (ed) (1997) *Reflexivity and Voice*, London: Sage Publications

Hetherington, E. (1989) 'Coping with family transitions: winners, losers and survivors', *Child Development*, vol 60, pp.1-14.

Hill, M. (1997) 'Research review: participatory research with children', *Child and Family Social Work*, vol 2, no 3, pp 171-83.

Hill, M. and Tisdall, K. (1997) *Children and Society*, Harlow: Addison Wesley Longman.

Hill, M., Davis, J., Prout, A. and Tisdall, K. (2004) 'Moving the participation agenda forward', *Children and Society*, vol 18, no 2, pp 77-96.

HM Government (1999) *Caring about Carers: A National Strategy for Carers*, London: The Stationery Office.

HM Government (2004) *Explanatory Notes to Carers (Equal Opportunities) Act 2004*, London: The Stationery Office.

HM Government (2006) *Working Together to Safeguard Children*, London: The Stationery Office.

HM Government (2008) *Carers at the Heart of 21st-century Families and Communities: 'A Caring System on Your Side, a Life of Your Own'*, London: Department of Health.

Holmes, R. (1998) *Fieldwork with Children*, London: Sage Publications.

Honwana, A. and De Boeck, F. (2005) *Makers and Breakers: Children and Youth in Postcolonial Africa*, Oxford: James Currey.

Hosegood, V., Preston-Whyte, E., Busza, J., Moitse, S. and Timaeus, I. (2007) 'Revealing the full extent of households' experiences of HIV and AIDS in rural South Africa', *Social Science and Medicine*, vol 65, no 6, pp 1249-59.

Howard, B.H., Philips, C.V., Matinhure, N., Goodman, K.J., McCurdy, S.A. and Johnson, C.A (2006) 'Barriers and incentives to orphan care in a time of AIDS and economic crisis: a cross-sectional survey of caregivers in rural Zimbabwe', *BMC Public Health*, vol 6, no 27, pp 1-11.

Howard, S. and Johnson, B. (2000) 'What makes the difference? Children and teachers talk about resilient outcomes for children "at risk"', *Educational Studies*, vol 26, no 3, pp 321-37.

Howard, S., Dryden, J. and Johnson, B. (1999) 'Childhood resilience: review and critique of the literature', *Oxford Review of Education*, vol 25, no 3, pp 307-23.

ILO (International Labour Organization) (2006) *The End of Child Labour:Within Reach*, International Labour Conference, 95th Session 2006, Report I (B), Geneva: ILO.

Imrie, J. and Coombes, Y. (1995) *No Time to Waste: The Scale and Dimensions of the Problem of Children Affected by HIV/AIDS in the United Kingdom*, Ilford: Barnardo's.

IOM (International Organization for Migration) (2005) *HIV/AIDS, Population Mobility and Migration in Southern Africa: Defining a Research and Policy Agenda*, Geneva: IOM (www.iom.int).

James, A. and Hockey, J. (2007) *Embodying Health Identities*, Houndmills, Basingstoke: Palgrave Macmillan.

James, A. and Prout, A. (eds) (1997) *Constructing and Reconstructing Childhood: Contemporary Issues in the Sociological Study of Childhood*, London: The Falmer Press.

James, A., Jenks, C. and Prout, A. (1998) *Theorizing Childhood*, Cambridge: Polity Press.

Jani-Le Bris, H. (1993) *Family Care of Dependent Older People in the European Community*, Dublin: European Foundation for the Improvement of Living and Working Conditions.

Jeffrey, C. and McDowell, L. (2004) 'Youth in comparative perspective: global change, local lives', *Youth and Society*, vol 36, no 2, pp 131-42.

Jones, A., Jeyasingham, D. and Rajasooriya, S. (2002) *Invisible Families: The Strengths and Needs of Black Families in which Young People have Caring Responsibilities*, Bristol: The Policy Press.

Kandiyoti, D. (1998) 'Gender power and contestation: rethinking bargaining with patriarchy', in C. Jackson and R. Pearson (eds) *Feminist Visions of Development: Gender, Analysis and Policy*, London: Routledge, pp 135-52.

Kaseke, E. (2003) 'Social exclusion and social security: the case of Zimbabwe', *Journal of Social Development in Africa*, vol 19, no 1, pp 33-48.

Katz, C. (1993) 'Growing circles/closing circles: limits on the spaces of knowing in rural Sudan and US cities', in C. Katz and J. Monk (eds) *Full Circles: Geographies of Women over the Life Course*, London: Routledge, pp 88-106.

Katz, C. (2004) *Growing up Global: Economic Restructuring and Children's Everyday Lives*, Minneapolis, MN: University of Minnesota Press.

Keith, L. and Morris, J. (1995) 'Easy targets: a disability rights perspective on the "children as carers" debate', *Critical Social Policy*, vol 15, no 44-45, pp 36-57.

Kelly, M. (2005) 'The response of the educational system to the needs of orphans and children affected by HIV/AIDS', in G. Foster, C. Levine and J. Williamson (eds) *A Generation at Risk: The Global Impact of HIV/AIDS on Orphans and Vulnerable Children*, New York: Cambridge University Press, pp 66-92.

Kielland, A. and Tovo, M. (2006) *Children at Work: Child Labor Practices in Africa*, Boulder, CO: Lynne Rienner Publishers.

Koda, B. (1995) 'The economic organisation of the household in contemporary Tanzania', in C. Creighton and C.K. Omari (eds) *Gender, Family and Household in Tanzania*, Aldershot: Avebury, pp 139-55.

Koda, B. (2000) 'Democratisation of social relations at the household level: the participation of children and youth in Tanzania', in C. Creighton and C.K. Omari (eds) *Gender, Family and Work in Tanzania*, Aldershot: Ashgate, pp 237-65.

Kuleana Center for Children's Rights (1999) *The State of Education in Tanzania – Crisis and Opportunity*, Mwanza: Kuleana Center.

Landells, S. and Pritlove, J. (1994) *Young Carers of a Parent with Schizophrenia: A Leeds Survey*, Leeds: Leeds City Council, Department of Social Services.

Laird, S. (2005) 'International child welfare: deconstructing UNICEF's country programmes', *Social Policy and Society*, vol 4, no 4, pp 457-66.

Leask, C., Elford, J., Bor, R., Miller, R. and Johnson, M. (1997) 'Selective disclosure: a pilot investigation into changes in family relationships since HIV diagnosis', *Journal of Family Therapy*, vol 19, no 1, pp 59-69.

Lee, M. and Rotheram-Borus, M. (2002) 'Parents' disclosure of HIV to their children', *AIDS*, vol 16, pp 2201-7.

Levine, C., Gibson Hunt, G., Halper, D., Hart, A.Y., Lautz, J. and Gould, D. (2005) 'Young adult caregivers: a first look at an unstudied population', *American Journal of Public Health*, vol 95, no 11, pp 2071-5.

Lewis, E. (2001) *Afraid To Say: The Needs and Views of Young People Living With HIV/AIDS*, London: National Children's Bureau.

Lewis, J. (2006) 'Care and gender: have the arguments for recognising care work now been won?', in C. Glendinning and P. Kemp (eds) *Cash and Care: Policy Challenges in the Welfare State*, Bristol: The Policy Press, pp 11-20.

Lewis, J. and Meredith, B. (1988) *Daughters who Care: Daughters Caring for Mothers at Home*, London: Routledge.

Liddell, C., Barrett, L. and Bydawell, M. (2005) 'Indigenous representations of illness and AIDS in Sub-Saharan Africa', *Social Science and Medicine*, vol 60, no 4, pp 691-700.

Lie, G. and Biswalo, P. (1998) 'HIV-positive patient's choice of a significant other to be informed about the HIV-test result: findings from an HIV/AIDS counselling programme in the regional hospitals of Arusha and Kilimanjaro, Tanzania', in R. Bor and J. Elford (eds) *The Family and HIV Today: Recent Research and Practice*, London and New York: Cassell, pp 14-27.

Longhurst, R. (1997) '(Dis)embodied geographies', *Progress in Human Geography*, vol 21, no 4, pp 486-501.

Longhurst, R. (2001) *Bodies: Exploring Fluid Boundaries*, London: Routledge.

Luthar, S. and Cicchetti, D. (2000) 'The construct of resilience: implications for interventions and social policies', *Development and Psychopathology*, vol 12, no 4, pp 857-85.

Mackay, R. (2003) 'Family resilience and good child outcomes: an overview of the research literature', *Social Policy Journal of New Zealand*, vol 20, no 3, pp 98-118.

Madziva, R. (2008) *Who Cares for Children Caring for Parents and Relatives with HIV/AIDS in Rural Zimbabwe?* (unpublished essay, School of Sociology and Social Policy, University of Nottingham).

Marsden, R. (1995) *Young Carers and Education*, London: Borough of Enfield Education Department.

Maxwell, C., Aggleton, P. and Warwick, I. (2008) 'Involving HIV-positive people in policy and service development: recent experiences in England', *AIDS Care*, vol 20, no 1, pp 72-9.

McIntyre, D. (2007) *Learning from Experience: Health Care Financing in Low- and Middle-Income Countries*, Geneva: Global Forum for Health Research (www.globalforumhealth.org).

McLeish, J. (2002) *Mothers in Exile. Maternity Experience of Asylum Seekers in England*, London: The Maternity Alliance.

Meintjes, H. and Giese, S. (2006) 'Spinning the epidemic: the making of mythologies of orphanhood in the context of AIDS', *Childhood*, vol 13, no 3, pp 407-30.

MHSW (Ministry of Health and Social Welfare) (2006) *The Costed MVC Action Plan 2006–2010*, Dar es Salaam: Ministry of Health and Social Welfare, Government of Tanzania, Family Health International and USAID.

Millar, J. and Warman, A. (1996) *Family Obligations in Europe*, London: Family Policy Studies Centre.

Miller, P. (2005) 'Useful and priceless children in contemporary welfare states', *Social Politics*, vol 12, no 1, pp 1-39.

Miller, R. and Murray, D. (1999) 'The impact of HIV illness on parents and children, with particular reference to African families', *Journal of Family Therapy*, vol 21, no 3, pp 284-302.

Milligan, C. (2000) '"Bearing the burden": towards a restructured geography of caring', *Area*, vol 32, no 1, pp 49-58.

Mohan, G., Brown, E., Milward, B. and Zack-Williams, A. (2000) *Structural Adjustment: Theory, Practice and Impacts*, London and New York: Routledge.

Mok, J. and Cooper, S. (1997) 'The needs of children whose mothers have HIV infection', *Archives of Disease in Childhood*, vol 77, no 6, pp 483-7.

Momsen, J. (1991) *Women and Development in the Third World*, London: Routledge.

Moore, T. (2005a) *Stop to Listen: Findings from the ACT Young Carers Research Project*. Lyneham: Youth Coalition of the ACT.

Moore, T. (2005b) *Reading Between the Lines: Listening to Children and Young People about Their Experiences of Young Caring in the ACT*, Lyneham: Youth Coalition of the ACT.

Morgan, J. (2008) 'Memory work', *AIDS Bulletin*, available at www.10mmp.org (accessed 13 July 2008).

Morris, J. (1991) *Pride Against Prejudice: Transforming Attitudes to Disability*, Philadelphia: New Society Publishers.

Morris, J. (1993) *Independent Lives*, Basingstoke: Macmillan.

Morrow, R. (2005) *A Profile of Known Young Carers and Identification and Snapshot of the Ones Who are Hidden*, Perth: Curtin University of Technology.

Morrow, V. (1996) 'Rethinking childhood dependency: children's contributions to the domestic economy', *Sociological Review*, vol 44, no 1, pp 58-77.

Moser, C. (1989) 'Gender planning in the Third World: meeting practical and strategic needs', *World Development*, vol 17, no 11, pp 1799-825.

Moss, P. and Dyck, I. (1999) 'Journeying through M.E.: identity, the body and women with chronic illness', in E. Teather (ed) *Embodied Geographies: Spaces, Bodies and Rites of Passage*, London: Routledge, pp 157-74.

Mutangadura, G. (2001) 'Women and AIDS in Southern Africa: the case of Zimbabwe and its policy implications', *Jenda: A Journal of Culture and African Women Studies*, vol 1, no 2, pp 1-8.

National AIDS Trust (2006) *Dispersal of Asylum Seekers Living with HIV*, London: National AIDS Trust (available at www.nat.org.uk/document/113), (accessed 9 July 2008).

National Alliance for Caregiving in collaboration with the United Hospital Fund (2005) *Young Caregivers in the U.S.: Report of Findings September 2005*, Bethesda, MD: NAC (available at www.caregiving.org and www.uhfnyc.org).

National Children's Bureau (1993) *Guidelines for Research*, London: National Children's Bureau.

National Evaluation of Sure Start (2005) *Implementing Sure Start Local Programmes: An In-depth Study*, London: Department for Education and Skills.

NBS/ORC Macro (National Bureau of Statistics and ORC Macro) (2005) *Tanzania Demographic and Health Survey 2004-05*, Dar es Salaam: NBS and ORC Macro.

Ndaba-Mbata, R. and Seloilwe, E. (2000) 'Home-based care of the terminally ill in Botswana: knowledge and perceptions', *International Nursing Review*, vol 47, no 4, pp 218-223.

Nelson, L. (1999) 'Bodies (and spaces) do matter: the limits of performativity', *Gender, Place and Culture*, vol 6, no 4, pp 331-53.

Newman, T. (2002a) '"Young carers" and disabled parents: time for a change of direction?', *Disability and Society*, vol 17, no 6, pp 613-25.

Newman, T. (2002b) *Promoting Resilience: A Review of Effective Strategies for Child Care Services*, Exeter: Centre for Evidence-based Social Services, University of Exeter and Barnardo's.

Nsutebu, E., Walley, J., Mataka, E. and Simon, C. (2001) 'Scaling-up HIV/AIDS and TB home-based care: lessons from Zambia', *Health Policy and Planning*, vol 16, no 3, pp 240-7.

Nyambedha, E., Wandibba, S. and Aagaard-Hanen, J. (2003) 'Changing patterns of orphan care due to the HIV epidemic in Western Kenya', *Social Science and Medicine*, vol 57, no 2, pp 301-11.

O'Connell Davidson, J. and Farrow, C. (2007) *Child Migration and the Construction of Vulnerability*, Stockholm: Save the Children Sweden.

Ogden, J. and Nyblade, L. (2005) *Common at its Core: HIV-related Stigma Across Contexts*, Washington, DC: International Center for Research on Women (ICRW).

Ogden, J., Esim, S. and Grown, C. (2004) 'Expanding the care continuum for HIV/ AIDS: bringing carers into focus', *Horizons Report*, Washington, DC: Population Council and International Center for Research on Women.

Ogden, J., Esim, S. and Grown, C. (2006) 'Expanding the care continuum for HIV/AIDS: bringing carers into focus', *Health Policy and Planning*, vol 21, no 5, pp 333-42.

Oliver, M. (1990) *The Politics of Disablement*, Basingstoke: Macmillan and St Martin's Press.

Olsen, R. (1996) 'Young carers: challenging the facts and politics of research into children and caring', *Disability and Society*, vol 11, no 1, pp 41-54.

Olsen, R. and Parker, G. (1997) 'A response to Aldridge and Becker – "Disability rights and the denial of young carers: the dangers of zero-sum arguments"', *Critical Social Policy*, vol 17, no 50, pp 125-33.

Omari, C.K. (1995) 'Decision-making and the household: case studies from Tanzania', in C. Creighton and C.K. Omari (eds), *Gender, Family and Household in Tanzania*, Aldershot: Avebury, pp 203-20.

Omari, C.K. and Mbilinyi, S. (1997) *African Values and Child Rights: Some Cases from Tanzania*, Dar es Salaam: Dar es Salaam University Press.

Opiyo, P., Yamano, T. and Jayne, T. (2008) 'HIV/AIDS and home-based health care', *International Journal for Equity in Health*, vol 7, p 8 (available at www.equityhealthj.com/content/7/1/8).

Oreb, M. (2001) *Children As Carers Report: An Overview of Literature and Projects on Children as Carers,* Adelaide: Carers Association of SA Inc.

Ostergaard, L. (ed) (1992) *Gender and Development: A Practical Guide*, London: Routledge.

Pakenham, K., Dadds, M. and Terry, D. (1998) 'Carers' burden and adjustment to HIV', in R. Bor and J. Elford (eds) *The Family and HIV Today: Recent Research and Practice*, London and New York: Cassell, pp 74-91.

Panter-Brick, C. (2000) 'Nobody's children? A reconsideration of child abandonment', in C. Panter-Brick and M. Smith (eds) *Abandoned Children*, Cambridge: Cambridge University Press, pp 1-26.

Panter-Brick, C. (2002) 'Street children, human rights and public health: a critique and future directions', *Annual Review Anthropology*, vol 31 (October), pp 147-71.

Panter-Brick, C. (2004) 'Homelessness, poverty, and risks to health: beyond at risk categorizations of street children', *Children's Geographies*, vol 2, no 1, pp 83-94.

Parker, G. and Olsen, R. (1995) 'A sideways glance at young carers', in *Young Carers Something to Think About*, London: Department of Health, pp 63-74.

Parker, R. and Aggleton, P. with Attawell, K., Pulerwitz, J. and Brown, L. (2002) *HIV/AIDS-related Stigma and Discrimination: A Conceptual Framework and Agenda for Action*, New York: The Populations Council.

Parr, H. and Butler, R. (1999) 'New geographies of illness, impairment and disability', in R. Butler and H. Parr (eds) *Mind and Body Space: Geographies of Illness, Impairment and Disability*, London and New York: Routledge, pp 1–24.

Perrons, D. (2004) *Globalization and Social Change: People and Places in a Divided World*, London and New York: Routledge.

Peters, R., Petrunka, K. and Arnold, R. (2003) 'The Better Beginnings, Better Futures Project: a universal, comprehensive, community-based prevention approach for primary school children and their families', *Journal of Clinical Child and Adolescent Psychology*, vol 32, no 2, pp 215–27.

Phiri, S. and Tolfree, D. (2005) 'Family- and community-based care for children affected by HIV/AIDS: strengthening the front line response', in G. Foster, C. Levine and J. Williamson. (eds) *A Generation at Risk: The Global Impact of HIV/AIDS on Orphans and Vulnerable Children*, New York: Cambridge University Press, pp 11–36.

Pierret, J. (2000) 'Everyday life with AIDS/HIV: surveys in the social sciences', *Social Science and Medicine*, vol 50, no 11, pp 1589–98.

Pink, S. (2001) *Doing Visual Ethnography*, London: Sage.

Pinnock, K. and Evans, R. (2008) 'Developing responsive preventative practices: key messages from children's and families' experiences of the Children's Fund', *Children and Society*, vol 22, no 2, pp 86–98.

Powell, M. (ed) (2007) *Understanding the Mixed Economy of Welfare*, Bristol: The Policy Press.

Price, K. (1996) *How do I Get them to Come? Interim Report*, New South Wales: Interchange Respite Care (NSW) Incorporated.

Prost, A. (2005) *A Review of Research among Black African Communities Affected by HIV in the UK and Europe*. Occasional Paper No 15, Medical Research Council, Glasgow: University of Glasgow.

Punch, S. (2001) 'Household division of labour: generation, gender, age, birth order and sibling composition', *Work, Employment and Society*, vol 15, no 4, pp 803–23.

Punch, S. (2002) 'Youth transitions and interdependent adult–child relations in rural Bolivia', *Journal of Rural Studies*, vol 18, no 2, pp 123–33.

RAWG (Research and Analysis Working Group) (2005) *Poverty and Human Development Report 2005*, Dar es Salaam: RAWG of the Poverty Monitoring System, Government of Tanzania.

Reinharz, S. (1992) *Feminist Methods in Social Research*, New York: Oxford University Press.

Reyland, S., Higgins-D'Alessandro, A. and McMahon, T. (2002) 'Tell them you love them because you never know when things could change: voices of adolescents living with HIV-positive mothers', *AIDS Care*, vol 14, no 2, pp 285-94.

Ribbens McCarthy, J. with Jessop, J. (2005) *Young People, Bereavement and Loss: Disruptive Transitions?*, London: National Children's Bureau and Joseph Rowntree Foundation.

Rich, A. (1980) *On Lies, Secrets and Silence*, London: Virago.

Richter, L. and Rama, S. (2006) *Building Resilience: A Rights-based Approach to Children and HIV/AIDS in Africa*, Stockholm: Save the Children Sweden.

Ridge, D., Williams, A., Anderson, J. and Elford, J. (2008) 'Like a prayer: the role of spirituality and religion for people living with HIV in the UK', *Sociology of Health and Illness*, vol 30, no 3, pp 413-28.

Ridge, T. (2006) 'Helping out at home: children's contributions to sustaining work and care in lone-mother families', in C. Glendinning and P. Kemp (eds) *Cash and Care: Policy Challenges in the Welfare State*, Bristol: The Policy Press, pp 203-16.

Ridge, T. (2008) 'Children', in P. Alcock, M. May and K. Rowlingson (eds) *The Student's Companion to Social Policy* (3rd edn), Oxford: Blackwell Publishing, pp 378-85.

Rispel, L. with Letlape, L. and Metcalf, C. (2006) *Education Sector Responses to HIV and AIDS: Learning from Good Practices in Africa*, London: Commonwealth Secretariat.

Robson, E. (2000) 'Invisible carers: young people in Zimbabwe's home-based healthcare', *Area*, vol 32, no 1, pp 59-69.

Robson, E. (2001) 'Interviews worth the tears? Exploring dilemmas of research with young carers in Zimbabwe', *Ethics, Place and Environment*, vol 4, no 2, pp 135-42.

Robson, E. (2004) 'Hidden child workers: young carers in Zimbabwe', *Antipode*, vol 36, no 2, pp 227-48.

Robson, E. and Ansell, N. (2000) 'Young carers in Southern Africa: exploring stories from Zimbabwean secondary school students', in S. Holloway and G. Valentine (eds) *Children's Geographies*, London and New York: Routledge, pp 174-93.

Robson, E., Ansell, N., Huber, U.S., Gould, W.T.S. and van Blerk, L. (2006) 'Young caregivers in the context of the HIV/AIDS pandemic in sub-Saharan Africa', *Population, Space and Place*, vol 12, no 2, pp 93-111.

Robson S. and Kanyanta, B. (2007a) 'Orphaned and vulnerable children in Zambia: the impact of the HIV/AIDS epidemic on basic education for children at risk', *Educational Research*, vol 49, no 3, pp 259-72.

Robson, S. and Kanyanta, B. (2007b) 'Moving towards inclusive education policies and practices? Basic education for AIDS orphans and other vulnerable children in Zambia', *International Journal of Inclusive Education*, vol 11, no 4, pp 417-30.

Rutter, M. (1990) 'Psychosocial resilience and protective mechanisms', in J. Rolf, A. Masten, D. Cicchetti, K. Nuechterlein and S. Weintraub (eds) *Risk and Protective Factors in the Development of Psychopathology*, Cambridge: Cambridge University Press, pp 181-214.

Sales, R. (2007) *Understanding Immigration and Refugee Policy: Contradictions and Continuities*, Bristol: The Policy Press.

Salway, S., Platt, L., Chowbey, P., Harriss, K. and Bayliss, E. (2007) *Long-term Ill Health, Poverty and Ethnicity*, Bristol: The Policy Press.

SCARE (2005) 'The health and well-being of young carers', eLSC, available at www.elsc.org.uk/briefings

Scheyvens, R. and Leslie, H. (2000) 'Gender, ethics and empowerment: dilemmas of development fieldwork', *Women's Studies International Forum*, no 23, pp 119-30.

Scholte, A. (2000) *Globalization: A Critical Introduction,* Hampshire and New York: Palgrave.

Schoon, I. (2006) *Risk and Resilience: Adaptations in Changing Times*, Cambridge: Cambridge University Press.

Schoon, I. and Bynner, J. (2003) 'Risk and resilience in the life course: implications for interventions and social policies', *Journal of Youth Studies*, vol 6, no 1, pp 21-31.

Schoon, I. and Parsons, S. (2002) 'Competence in the face of adversity: the influence of early family environment and long term consequences', *Children and Society*, vol 16, no 4, pp 260-72.

Seaman, P., Turner, K., Hill, M., Stafford, A. and Walker, M. (2005) *Parenting and Children's Resilience in Disadvantaged Communities*, London: National Children's Bureau and Joseph Rowntree Foundation.

Seeley, J., Kajura, E., Bachengana, C., Okongo, M., Wagner, U. and Mulder, D. (1993) 'The extended family and support for people with AIDS in a rural population in south west Uganda: a safety net with holes?', *AIDS Care*, vol 5, no 1, pp 117-22.

Sen, A. (1995) 'Gender inequality and theories of justice', in M. Nussbaum and J. Glover (eds) *Women, Culture and Development: A Study of Human Capabilities*, Oxford: Oxford University Press, pp 259-73.

Sen, A. (1999) *Development as Freedom*, Oxford: Oxford University Press.

Sevenhuijsen, S. (1998) *Citizenship and the Ethics of Care. Feminist Considerations on Justice, Morality and Politics*, London and New York: Routledge.

Sevenhuijsen, S. (2000) 'Caring in the third way: the relation between obligation, responsibility and care in *Third Way* discourse', *Critical Social Policy*, vol 20, no 1, pp 5-37.

Shakespeare, T. (1993) 'Disabled people's self-organisation: a new social movement?', *Disability, Handicap and Society*, vol 8, no 3, pp 249-64.

Shifren, K. (ed) (2009) *How Caregiving Affects Development: Psychological Implications for Child, Adolescent and Adult Caregivers*, Washington, DC: American Psychological Association.

Siegel, K. and Gorey, E. (1998) 'Childhood bereavement due to parental death from Acquired Immunodeficiency Syndrome', in R. Bor and J. Elford (eds) *The Family and HIV Today: Recent Research and Practice*, London and New York: Cassell, pp 262-72.

Silburn, R. and Becker, S. (2009) 'Life beyond work? Safety nets and security for those who cannot work', in J. Millar (ed) *Understanding Social Security* (2nd edn), Bristol: The Policy Press, pp 55-73.

Sinka, K., Mortimer, J., Evans, B. and Morgan, D. (2003) 'Impact of the HIV epidemic in Sub-Saharan Africa on the pattern of HIV in the UK', *AIDS*, vol 17, pp 1683-90.

Social Exclusion Unit (2006) *Transitions: Young Adults with Complex Lives – A Social Exclusion Unit Final Report*, London: Office of the Deputy Prime Minister.

Solberg, A. (1997) 'Negotiating childhood: changing constructions of age for Norwegian children', in A. James and A. Prout (eds) *Constructing and Reconstructing Childhood: Contemporary Issues in the Sociological Study of Childhood*, London: The Falmer Press, pp 126-44.

Sparr, P. (1994) *Mortgaging Women's Lives: Feminist Critiques of Structural Adjustment*, London: Zed Books.

Spicer, N. and Evans, R. (2005) 'Developing children and young people's participation in strategic processes: the experience of the Children's Fund Initiative', *Social Policy & Society*, vol 5, no 2, pp 177–88.

Squire, C. (1997) 'AIDS panic', in J. M. Ussher (ed) *Body Talk: the Material and Discursive Regulation of Sexuality, Madness and Reproduction*, London: Routledge.

Stables, J. and Smith, F. (1999) '"Caught in the Cinderella trap": narratives of disabled parents and young carers', in R. Butler and H. Parr (eds) *Mind and Body Spaces*, London: Routledge, pp 256-68.

Standing, G. (1999) 'Global feminization through flexible labor', *World Development*, vol 27, no 3, pp 583-602.

Steinberg, M., Johnson, S., Schierhout, G., Ndegwa, D., Hall, K., Russell, B. and Morgan, J. (2002) *Hitting Home: How Households Cope with the Impact of the HIV/AIDS Epidemic – A Survey of Households Affected by HIV/AIDS in South Africa*, Washington DC: Henry J Kaiser Family Foundation.

Stephens, S. (1995) 'Children and the politics of culture in "Late Capitalism"', in S. Stephens (ed) *Children and the Politics of Culture*, Princeton, NJ: Princeton University Press, pp 3–50.

Such, E. and Walker, R. (2004) 'Being responsible and responsible beings: children's understanding of responsibility', *Children and Society*, vol 18, no 3, pp 231–42.

Such, E. and Walker, R. (2005) 'Young citizens or policy objects? Children in the "rights and responsibilities" debate', *Journal of Social Policy*, vol 34, no 1, pp 39–57.

TACAIDS (Tanzania Commission for AIDS), NBS (National Bureau of Statistics) and ORC Macro (2005) *Tanzania HIV/AIDS Indicator Survey 2003–04*, Calverton, MD: TACAIDS/NBS/ORC Macro.

Teather, E. (1999) 'Introduction: geographies of personal discovery', in E. Teather (ed) *Embodied Geographies: Spaces, Bodies and Rites of Passage*, London: Routledge, pp 1–26.

Terrence Higgins Trust (2001) *Social Exclusion and HIV: A Report*, London: Policy Campaigns and Research Division, Terence Higgins Trust.

Terrence Higgins Trust (2003) *Meeting the Rising Challenge: The Growing HIV Epidemic and its Implications for Primary Care Trusts*, London: Terence Higgins Trust.

Thomas, F. (2006) 'Stigma, fatigue and social breakdown: exploring the impacts of HIV/AIDS on patient and carer wellbeing in the Caprivi region, Namibia', *Social Science and Medicine*, vol 63, no 12, pp 3174–87.

Thomas, N., Stainton, T., Jackson, S., Cheung, W.Y., Doubtfire, S. and Webb, A. (2003) '"Your friends don't understand": invisibility and unmet need in the lives of "young carers"', *Child and Family Social Work*, vol 8, no 1, pp 35–46.

Thorne, C., Newell, M. and Peckham, C. (2000) 'Disclosure of diagnosis and planning for the future in HIV-affected families in Europe, *Child: Care, Health and Development*, vol 26, no 1, pp 29–40.

Tisdall, K., Kay, H., Cree, V. and Wallace, J. (2004) 'Children in need? Listening to children whose parent or carer is HIV positive', *British Journal of Social Work*, vol 34, no 8, pp 1097–113.

Tronto, J. (1993) *Moral Boundaries: A Political Argument for an Ethic of Care*, New York and London: Routledge.

UK Collaborative Group for HIV and STI Surveillance (2006) *A Complex Picture. HIV and other Sexually Transmitted Infections in the United Kingdom: 2006*, London: Health Protection Agency, Centre for Infections.

UN (2008) *UN Millennium Development Goals*, available at www.un.org/millenniumgoals (accessed 10 July 2008).

UN (2007) *World Youth Report 2007 Young People's Transitions to Adulthood: Progress and Challenges*, New York: United Nations.

UNAIDS (Joint United Nations Programme on HIV/AIDS) (2000) *Caring for Carers: Managing Stress in Those Who Care for People with HIV and AIDS. UNAIDS Case Study*, Best Practice Collection, May, UNAIDS.

UNAIDS (2006) *Report on the Global HIV/AIDS Epidemic*, UNAIDS: Geneva.

UNAIDS and WHO (2007) *AIDS Epidemic Update*, December 2007, Geneva: UNAIDS/WHO.

UNAIDS, UNFPA (United Nations Population Fund) and UNIFEM (United Nations Development Fund for Women) (2004) *Women and HIV/AIDS: Confronting the Crisis*, Geneva: UNAIDS, and New York: UNFPA/UNIFEM.

UNAIDS, UNICEF and USAID (2004) *Children on the Brink 2004: A Joint Report of New Orphan Estimates and A Framework for Action*, New York: UNAIDS/UNICEF/USAID.

UNDP (United Nations Development Programme) (2005) *Human Development Report 2005*, New York: UNDP.

Ungar, M. (2004) 'A constructionist discourse on resilience: multiple contexts, multiple realities among at-risk children and youth', *Youth and Society*, vol 35, no 3, pp 341–65.

Ungerson, C. (1983) 'Why do women care?', in J. Finch and D. Groves (eds) *A Labour of Love: Women, Work and Caring*, London: Routledge and Kegan Paul, pp 31–49.

UNICEF (1999) *Children in Need of Special Protection Measures: A Tanzanian Case Study*, Dar es Salaam: UNICEF.

UNICEF (2005) *Children: The Missing Face of AIDS. A Call to Action*, New York: UNICEF.

UNICEF (2006) *The State of the World's Children 2007. Women and Children: The Double Dividend of Gender Equality*, New York: UNICEF (www.unicef.org).

UNICEF (2007) *Progress for Children: A World Fit for Children Statistical Review* Number 6, New York: UNICEF.

UNICEF/UNAIDS (1999) *Children Orphaned by AIDS: Frontline Responses from Eastern and Southern Africa*, New York: UNICEF.

Urassa, M., Boerma, J., Ng'weshemi, J., Isingo, R., Schapink, D. and Kumogola, Y. (1997) 'Orphanhood, child fostering and the AIDS epidemic in rural Tanzania', *Health Transition Review*, supplement 2, no 7, pp 141-53.

Valentine, G. (1999) '"Oh please, mum, Oh please, dad": negotiating children's spatial boundaries', in L. McKie, S. Bowlby and S. Gregory (eds) *Gender, Power and the Household*, London: Macmillan, pp 137-54.

Valentine, G. (2003) 'Boundary crossings: transitions from childhood to adulthood', *Children's Geographies*, vol 1, no 1, pp 37-52.

Van Blerk, L. and Ansell, N. (2007) 'Alternative strategies for care giving in the context of AIDS in Southern Africa: complex strategies for care', *Journal of International Development*, vol 19, pp 865-84.

Van Blerk, L., Ansell, N., Robson, E., Hadju, F. and Chipeta, L. (2008) 'Youth, AIDS and rural livelihoods in Southern Africa', *Geography Compass*, vol 2, no 3, pp 709-27.

Wanless, D. (2006) *Securing Good Care for Older People: Taking a Long-Term View*, London: King's Fund.

Ward, L. (1997) *Seen and Heard: Involving Disabled Children and Young People in Research and Development Projects*, York: Joseph Rowntree Foundation.

Warren, J. (2005) 'Carers', *Research Matters*, April-October issue, pp 5-10.

Warren, J. (2007) 'Young carers: conventional or exaggerated levels of involvement in domestic and caring tasks?', *Children and Society*, vol 21, no 2, pp 136-46.

Wates, M. (2002) *Supporting Disabled Adults in their Parenting Role*, York: York Publishing Services.

Weatherburn, P., Keogh, P., Dodds, C., Hickson, F. and Henderson, L. (2007) *The Growing Challenge: A Strategic Review of HIV Social Care, Support and Information Services Across the UK*, Sigma Research (available at www.sigmaresearch.org.uk/downloads/report07b.pdf).

Weedon, C. (1999) *Feminism, Theory and the Politics of Difference*, Oxford: Blackwell.

Wendell, S. (2001) 'Unhealthy disabled: treating chronic illnesses as disabilities', *Hypatia*, vol 16, no 4, pp 17-33.

WFP (United Nations World Food Programme) (2007) *World Hunger Series 2007 – Hunger and Health*, London: Earthscan with UNWFP.

WHO (2000) *Community Home-Based Care in Resource-Limited Settings: a Framework for Action*, Geneva: World Health Organization (www.who.org).

WHO (2002) *Developing and Validating a Methodology to Examine the Impact of HIV/AIDS on Older Caregivers*, Geneva: World Health Organization.

WHO (2006) *Antiretroviral Therapy for HIV Infection in Adults and Adolescents: Recommendations for a Public Health Approach 2006 Revision*, Geneva: World Health Organization.

WHO (2008) *Towards Universal Access: Scaling Up Priority HIV/AIDS Interventions in the Health Sector*, Progress Report 2008, Geneva: World Health Organization.

Widdowfield, R. (2000) 'The place of emotions in academic research', *Area*, vol 32, no 2, pp 199-208.

Williams, F. (2004) 'What matters is who works: why every child matters to New Labour. Commentary on the Department for Education & Skills' Green Paper Every Child Matters', *Critical Social Policy*, vol 24, no 3, pp 406-27.

Wilson, S. (2007) '"When you have children, you're obliged to live": motherhood, chronic illness and biographical disruption', *Sociology of Health and Illness*, vol 29, no 4, pp 610-29.

Wilton, R. (1999) 'Qualitative health research: negotiating life with HIV/AIDS', *Professional Geographer*, vol 51, no 2, pp 254-64.

Wolkow, K. and Ferguson, B. (2001) 'Community factors in the development of resiliency: considerations and future directions', *Community Mental Health Journal*, vol 37, no 6, pp 489-98.

Wood, K., Chase, E. and Aggleton, P. (2006) '"Telling the truth is the best thing": teenage orphans' experiences of parental AIDS-related illness and bereavement in Zimbabwe', *Social Science and Medicine*, vol 63, no 7, pp 1923-33.

Woodhead, M., Burr, R. and Montgomery, H. (2003) 'Adversities and resilience', in H. Montgomery, R. Burr and M. Woodhead (eds) *Changing Childhoods: Local and Global*, Milton Keynes: The Open University and Chichester: John Wiley and Sons, pp 1-44.

Wrubel, J. and Folkman, S. (1997) 'What informal caregivers actually do: the caregiving skills of partners of men with AIDS', *AIDS Care*, vol 9, no 6, pp 601-706.

Yamano, T. and Jayne, T. (2004) 'Measuring the impact of working-age adult mortality on small-scale farm households in Kenya', *World Development*, vol 32, no 1, pp 91-119.

Yeandle, S. and Buckner, L. (2007) *Carers, Employment and Services: Time for a New Social Contract?*, Report No 6, London: University of Leeds and Carers UK.

Yeandle, S., Bennett, C., Buckner, L., Fry, G. and Price, C. (2007) *Diversity in Caring: Towards Equality for Carers*, Report No 3, London: University of Leeds and Carers UK.

Young, L. and Ansell, N. (2003) 'Fluid households, complex families: the impacts of children's migration as a response to HIV/AIDS in Southern Africa', *The Professional Geographer*, vol 55, no 4, pp 464–76.

Index